Rightsizing Inventory

Series on Resource Management

Rightsizing Inventory

Joseph L. Aiello

CFPIM, CIRM, CSCP

 Auerbach Publications
Taylor & Francis Group
Boca Raton   New York

Auerbach Publications is an imprint of the
Taylor & Francis Group, an **informa** business

Auerbach Publications
Taylor & Francis Group
6000 Broken Sound Parkway NW, Suite 300
Boca Raton, FL 33487-2742

10 9 8 7 6 5 4 3 2 1

International Standard Book Number-10: 0-8493-8515-6 (Hardcover)
International Standard Book Number-13: 978-0-8493-8515-5 (Hardcover)

Library of Congress Cataloging-in-Publication Data

Aiello, Joseph L.
  Rightsizing inventory / Joseph L. Aiello.
    p. cm. -- (Series on resource management)
  Includes bibliographical references and index.
  ISBN 978-0-8493-8515-5
  1. Inventories. 2. Inventory control. I. Title.

HD40.A45 2008
658.7'87--dc22   2007011237

Visit the Taylor & Francis Web site at
http://www.taylorandfrancis.com

and the Auerbach Web site at
http://www.auerbach-publications.com

Dedication

This work is dedicated to my wife, Pat, the love of my life.

Table of Contents

Preface

One of the best early inventory models was George Plossl's bathtub model. The water level in the tub represented the inventory level. Anyone could see there were only two ways to reduce the water level, i.e., to "rightsize" the inventory. The faucet could be shut off, stopping additional water from filling the tub; this was analogous to shutting off purchasing. The drain opening could be widened, allowing water to flow out of the tub more quickly; this was analogous to marketing, generating more sales. Although modeled on a bathtub, Plossl's model was elegant because it exposed the basics of a complex subject.

In *Rightsizing Inventory* Joe Aiello exposes deeper basics about the same complex subject, using what could be called an "ice cube tray" analogy. Everyone can understand that when an ice cube tray is filled with water, the total amount of water depends on the number of cubes in the tray and the relative wall heights for each cube. Rightsizing the total amount of water in the tray (inventory) depends on filling each of the ice cubes (the segmentation of inventory in the supply chain) to the desired cube height as allowed by the tray walls (the silo views of each functional area that impact inventory). Effective inventory management takes the end-to-end supply chain network into account. Joe does this by detailing the real-world conflicts between functional areas that often prevent sound inventory decisions. Joe describes the segmentation of inventory both by product line and by fast turn, slow turn, and no turn inventory components. The different inventory segments require different control strategies. Joe explains all this from his unique inventory perspective, learned through decades of practitioner and consulting experiences.

Left unattended, many an inventory investment will spiral out of control; Joe Aiello's book is the complete antidote on how to wrestle inventory back into control. I could have benefited greatly from Joe's inventory insights during those times in my own career when as a materials manager, I was under intense pressure to rightsize the inventory! Joe writes in first person functional roles from a cast of characters that is right on target. I would have responded to my peers differently had I better understood then their functional priorities. This book presents dozens of inventory management tips and summarizes them in management e-mails. My team would have made better inventory decisions had we had access then to Joe's tips. Joe presents a consistent inventory accounting format throughout the book to educate the reader about the basics of inventory dynamics. The measurement of my inventory should have begun much earlier had the definition and interpretation of the right inventory metrics been made available. The power of the business results achievable by overcoming functional role bias and by leveraging inventory segmentation cannot be overstated.

William T. Walker, CFPIM, CIRM, CSCP
Resource Management series editor and supply chain architect
November 24, 2006
Summit, New Jersey

Acknowledgments

A person is fortunate in life to have a mentor who gives them the guidance and direction to build a solid business foundation. I was fortunate to have two, Ed Linden and Pat Hourihan. They not only taught me the basics of supply-chain management but instilled the confidence in me to go forward with my career. I learned so much from you guys — thank you.

I wish to acknowledge my brother, Mike Aiello, for his insight, support, and encouragement. Mike, you will recognize many of the charts shown in this book; thank you, Mike. To my friends and colleagues, John Taggart and Dave Rumsey, thank you for giving up so many of your lunch hours to give me guidance and direction in the early stages of writing this book.

To my many APICS friends, from whom I learned so much over the years: thank you all, especially Jim Clark, Marty Edelman, Howard Forman, Don Frank, John Hegranes, Jack Symon, Rick Titone, Charlie Vigorita, and Blair Williams. To Stephanie Imperato, who corrected my grammar, punctuation, and run-on sentences; you made me look good — thank you.

A special thank you to my friend, Joe Shedlawski, 2007 APICS president, for canceling an APICS class you were scheduled to teach. I filled in for Joe and met a student named Pat, who became my wife. Thanks, Joe, for the teaching opportunity and my wife.

To my son, Michael Aiello, who while in college gave me a blank bound book with my name on the spine as the author along with a note, "Here's that book you've been meaning to write." I've kept that note and blank book all these years. Well, here it is … thanks, kid.

To Bill Walker, friend, author, and my series editor at Taylor & Francis; simply stated, there would be no book without your support, confidence, and guidance. You kept me on course for the 15 months it took me to write this. To say thank you doesn't seem to be enough.

Last, but certainly not least, I wish to thank my wife, Pat, who tolerated my frustrations and the many long hours and weekends it took to write this book. Without her patient temperament and support, I couldn't have written this book. You've had a profound effect, not only on this book but my life as well.

About This Book

This book is about a mid-sized manufacturing company facing the daunting task of managing inventory effectively and efficiently. Woodstock Lighting Group is a composite case study from my practitioner and consulting experience working with many companies in a variety of industries. I have developed a scenario about facing the day-to-day challenges of running a business and at the same time dealing with the company culture and politics. The problems and issues facing Woodstock Lighting Group will be quite familiar to the reader and are commonplace in many industries today.

The reader will recognize and hopefully appreciate the problems Woodstock is facing. Perhaps you have experienced some of the same issues. This book is divided into 12 chapters with different characters from the supply chain presenting to a team that is leading the Woodstock inventory "rightsizing" effort. Each speaker represents a different link in the supply chain and discusses his or her role and responsibility in managing inventory. They also speak about their issues and problems and how they interact with other links in the supply chain.

Each chapter also includes tips on how to rightsize inventory. There are 150 tips given in this book. Each tip is repeated twice in the same chapter. The first time is when the presenter gives the tip to the team, called the "Harmony Team." It is highlighted in the text. The second time the tip appears is at the end of the chapter where the author explains how to apply and use the tip in your company.

The objective of each chapter (and this book) is for the reader to gain an understanding of what each link is responsible for and how each link in the supply chain manages inventory. The reader will learn how decisions made in one link impact the upstream and downstream decisions of the other links in the supply chain. All major links in the supply chain are discussed, even the unsung heroes of inventory management: human resources, maintenance, field service, and facilities management.

How This Book Is Organized

Each chapter is presented as one or more meetings of the Harmony Team and the date of the meeting. This is followed by the financial value of the inventory on the date of the meeting (or the closest month end value).

The presenters then introduce themselves, followed by a "stream of consciousness" musing about what they are thinking before they go to the meeting. They then present their case giving examples and formulas to support their presentation. Periodically during their presentation they will offer a tip on rightsizing inventory. Almost as if the thought just popped into their head as they were speaking.

This is followed by an e-mail sent to all supply-chain managers at the end of each meeting (each chapter), which highlights and summarizes the key points made in the chapter. Immediately following the e-mail is an inventory rightsizing model that the Harmony Team adds to at the end of each chapter. The last activity in the model leads the reader to "go to the next chapter" to continue building the model. After the latest version of the inventory "rightsizing" model, the author takes over and in textbook format discusses how to apply the tips, tools, and philosophies to your company. This is the "how to" part of this story.

Each chapter ends with the latest "dashboard" of vital company statistics such as year-to-date actual sales to forecast, production and inventory position by category, raw materials, work-in-progress, and finished goods. By year end the complete model is built.

This format is used for the first ten chapters but changes in the last two. In Chapter 11, Jack, the supply-chain manager, warns the team about the ten most common mistakes companies make when trying to rightsize their inventory. He goes on to explain how Woodstock can avoid making those same mistakes.

Chapter 12 is where the company president presents the final inventory rightsizing model to the Harmony Team, which will be used as a checklist for the future. The book concludes with Adriana addressing all company employees using a video conference as the media. At the conference she discusses the highlights of the year just concluded and plans for the coming year, and thanks all employees for their contributions to the inventory rightsizing effort. The following summarizes each chapter:

Chapter 1: Inventory as a Strategic Advantage

Joe, vice president of operations, and Arnie, plant manager, are presenters.

This chapter sets the tone for the rest of the book. Woodstock is losing money and inventory is out of control. Adriana, the president, forces Joe to take action. A supply chain team is formed and given the name "Harmony Team." Arnie is the Harmony Team leader. Inventory issues are discussed, and the team starts by developing a plan and discussing how inventory can be used as a strategic advantage to the company.

Chapter 2: Is the Customer Always Right?

Maria, customer service manager, is the presenter.

Maria discusses inventory life cycles and customer service levels. Customer and Woodstock inventory attributes are presented. Customer relationship management as a tool is discussed. Maria talks about aligning inventory to the product life cycles and why inventory exists in the company.

Chapter 3: Having Inventory Costs the Company Money

Pat, director of finance, is the presenter.

She discusses monitoring cash inflow and outflows. A discussion on whether inventory is an asset or liability follows. Inventory carrying costs, days of supply, and inventory turns are covered. Inventory accuracy, evaluation, and costing are talked about and examples given. Performance metrics are shown and discussed.

Chapter 4: Not Having Inventory Costs the Company Money

Rudy, vice president of sales and marketing, is the presenter.

Rudy discusses sales and operations planning in detail using mathematical examples. Demand planning and forecasting techniques are reviewed. He reviews the relationship between the inventory and production plans and discusses how to validate the sales and operations plan and then execute the plan.

Chapter 5: How Much Inventory Should We Make or Buy?

Cyndie, materials manager, is the presenter.

Cyndie discusses the reasons for plan changes and the importance of reacting quickly to change. She goes into a detailed explanation of master production scheduling and material requirements planning. She highlights the differences and significance of dependent demand and independent demand, and talks about planning time fences and zones. Purchasing topics include supplier relationship management, strategic sourcing, and vendor-managed inventory.

Chapter 6: How Can We Improve the Product and Process Design to Minimize Inventory Levels?

Michael, packaging engineer, is the presenter.

Michael discusses parts numbering methods and the use of substitutions. He talks about combining and eliminating parts and parts standardization. Workcell and facility layout are covered and examples shown. Value stream mapping and the use of takt time are reviewed. Reduction in work-in-progress is discussed.

Chapter 7: How Much Inventory Should We Make?

Orlando, assistant plant manager, is the presenter.

Orlando discusses capacity management and the impact on inventory. Plant utilization and efficiency measurements are talked about and examples given. Lean manufacturing is covered as well as using pull systems in the plant. Storeroom management and procedures are reviewed.

Chapter 8: How Much Inventory Should We Stock?

Carlos, director of distribution and logistics, is the presenter.

Carlos discusses the significance of transportation costs and just-in-time delivery. The use of cycle counting to improve inventory accuracy is presented. The use of various automation tools is reviewed. Third-party logistics and reverse logistics are topics of discussion. Material handling and warehouse inventory management are reviewed.

Chapter 9: What Information About Inventory Do We Need?

Dinish, vice president of information technology, is the presenter.

Dinish discusses the importance of timely and accurate data. He discusses turning data into meaningful information. He reviews enterprise resource planning and supply-chain management philosophies. He talks about data warehousing and important tools and techniques available in the marketplace.

Chapter 10: The Unsung Heroes of Inventory Management

Presenters are James, field service manager; Aimee, manager of human resources; Anthony, maintenance manager, and Jon, facilities manager.

All four discuss how their team can help the company with the inventory rightsizing effort. Examples are shown and discussed.

Chapter 11: Rightsizing Inventory: A New Way of Life for the Supply Chain

Jack, supply chain manager, is the presenter.

Jack discusses the ten most common mistakes companies make when they try to rightsize their inventory. He goes on to discuss how you can avoid making those same mistakes. Jack talks about the change in company culture required so that the effort can be sustained over time.

Chapter 12: Silos Can Be Turned into a Collaborative Supply-Chain Network

Adriana, president, is the presenter.

Adriana reviews the inventory rightsizing model developed by the Harmony Team that will be used as a checklist in the years to come. She addresses all employees through a video conference in which she discusses the year end results of the inventory rightsizing effort.

Appendix A:

Additional influential book titles

Appendix B:

TIPS on "rightsizing" inventory

Index

About the Author

Joseph L. Aiello, CFPIM, CIRM, CSCP, is an inventory management professional and an accomplished practitioner, consultant, and educator. Joe has over 45 years experience in supply-chain management. He started his manufacturing career as a shipping clerk, advancing to machine operator and then department foreman. In 1962 he became plant manager of Einiger-Feuer Textiles, a position he held until 1968. In 1968 he joined Beaunit Corporation, advancing to director of materials management, Tricot Division. In 1978 Joe joined Sperry Univac as a staff consultant, providing consulting services to clients around the world. He later became director of consulting services and application development for Sperry Univac (now Unisys).

In 1991 Joe founded Woodstock Group, a company providing customized education and consulting services to manufacturing and distribution industries. His expertise in inventory management has led to consulting and education engagements with many Fortune 500 companies as well as regional and local manufacturing and distribution companies. Joe's client base spans various industry segments, from process industries to discrete product manufacturers and distributors.

Joe is an active member of APICS, the Association for Operations Management. He served many years on the chapter board of directors in various positions and also served on the Region 2 board of directors. In 1994, he received the "Lifetime Achievement Award" from the Northern New Jersey Chapter of APICS. He has also achieved APICS certifications as a Certified Fellow in Production and Inventory Management (CFPIM) and Certified Integrated Resource Management (CIRM), and most recently achieved certification as a Certified Supply Chain Professional (CSCP). Joe has spoken at over a dozen APICS international conferences, spanning four decades, starting in 1979.

Today Joe is a nationally recognized lecturer, consultant, and educator on inventory management topics. He continues to work with manufacturing and distribution companies across the United States. Academically, Joe is a graduate of the New York Fashion Institute of Technology, as well as Fairleigh Dickinson University where he received a degree in business management.

How to Get the Most from This Book

Each chapter is presented by people represent the various links found in most supply chains. The story line centers on Woodstock Lighting Group, which has many typical inventory problems found in many companies. Many companies that are world-class today went through the trials and pains Woodstock is experiencing. You will find many problems and challenges similar to a typical manufacturing company. While all this is going on, the employees have to deal with the company culture and politics. As the story progresses, you will see the fluctuations in inventory. Some months it goes up and other times it goes down. Overall the trend is downward and can be attributed to the things learned by the Harmony Team.

This is a story about a company that managed inventory from a silo perspective until it fully understood the role it plays in managing inventory. The discussions, along with the figures, tables, formulas, and tips will help the reader understand how a supply chain can work, given the understanding, knowledge, management support, and tools as discussed in this book. By the end of this book you and your team will be able to apply the tips, tools, and technologies to rightsize your own inventory. You, too, can turn your inventory silos into a collaborative supply-chain network. Good luck!

Joe Aiello, CFPIM, CIRM, CSCP
Mahwah, New Jersey

Woodstock Lighting Group Characters in Order of Appearance

Joe, Vice President of Operations:
Worked 15 years at Woodstock and responsible for rightsizing inventory. He has a bad attitude and is self-centered. If it isn't his idea, it's a bad idea. Uses his position to force people to do things his way. Half way through the book he leaves the company.

Arnie, Plant Manager:
A long-time employee, well liked and respected by other employees, suppliers, and customers. Knows the operation really well and is chosen by Joe and Adriana to head up the team leading the inventory rightsizing effort. Gets promoted about halfway through the book.

Maria, Customer Service Manager:
Has been with Woodstock ten years and dislikes Joe. She came out of the sales department and understands the needs of the customers very well. Doesn't like managing people and is thinking of returning to sales.

Pat, Director of Finance:
Looking for a new job and is going out on interviews. Comes from a small family-run business and has a difficult time adapting to the way Woodstock does business. Hates going to work and is starting to bring the problems home with her at night.

Rudy, Vice President of Sales and Marketing:
Finds the politics and pressure at Woodstock to be the worst he has experienced in his career. He is tired of making up excuses to customers about the reasons for late orders. He doesn't trust Joe and thinks planning doesn't know what it is doing.

Cyndie, Materials Manager:
Works ten hours a day trying to keep everyone happy. Not career-oriented and expects to be moving out of state soon. Likes the fact that Joe lets her leave work early when she has family business to attend to. She believes the inventory rightsizing effort is just another project.

Michael, Packaging Engineer:
Likes his job and is a team player. Wants to stay at Woodstock for a long time. He is excited about the inventory rightsizing effort and wishes people would stop complaining and work together to fix the problems.

Orlando, Assistant Plant Manager:
Long-time employee, started out as a machine operator and knows the plant very well. Excited about being asked for his opinions and ideas and wants the effort to be successful. He is working 12–15 hours a day and realizes he can't keep it up.

Carlos, Director of Distribution and Logistics:
Respects Arnie and Orlando, but doesn't like Joe. A team player and eager to help. With Woodstock three years and likes the company. Recognizes the importance of managing inventory effectively and will do all he can to help rightsize the inventory.

Dinesh, Vice President of Information Technology:
He is an ally of Joe and has a bad attitude. Fights with the end-users all the time and blames them for the systems not working correctly. Frustrated with the rapid advancements in technology and the lack of time to understand and use them effectively.

James, Field Service Manager:
Likes his job and enjoys visiting the customers but doesn't like the fact that no one asks his opinion about the products his department services. Thinks field service should have been involved in the inventory rightsizing effort from the very beginning.

Aimee, Manager of Human Resources:
With the company for five years and likes the employees a lot. When Joe left, she was glad. She had a lot of complaints from employees because of him. Doesn't understand why she was asked to help with the inventory rightsizing effort.

Anthony, Maintenance Manager:
Doesn't believe the company appreciates how much his group does to keep the plant running. He is surprised but pleased that the team is asking for his input. Had a difficult time with Joe but happy that he now works for Arnie.

Jon, Facilities Manager:
New to the company, only with Woodstock for six months. Doesn't know all the players on the team, but does know that inventory is out of control and must be dealt with. Wants to reduce inventory for selfish reasons: He has no space to store it.

Jack, Supply-Chain Manager:
New to the company, started work on January 2 of this year. He is an experienced supply-chain professional with a successful background in supply-chain management. He offers guidance and direction to the team. A team player who gains respect as time goes by.

Adriana, President:
Had difficulties in managing Joe but recognized the importance of managing inventory correctly. She is the catalyst that leads the effort. She is committed and involved in the effort and sees this not as a project but a new way of life for the company.

Chapter 1

Inventory as a Strategic Advantage

January 2, First Work Day of the New Year

Woodstock Inventory: $40 Million

My name is Joe, I'm vice president of operations at Woodstock Lighting Group.

I couldn't sleep last night. Today is going to be a bad one. With any luck, I'll get fired, go home, and sleep for the rest of the winter. Yeah, right; with a stiff mortgage, a wife, two little ones, a car payment (soon to be two, with 175,000 miles on "Jerry," my car), food, and other bills, getting fired is the last thing I need in my life right now. I earn a decent living. I'll just have to tough it out until something better comes along. Let's see if I can get them — before they get me.

In my job, I am responsible for most supply-chain activities. Old traditions die hard here, and the only thing that changes is the calendar. I have tried to get them to switch my title to a more contemporary one: vice president of supply chain or vice president of logistics, but they won't do it. To quote my boss, "We have had a vice president of operations position ever since the company was founded in 1942, and we are not about to change it now just to make you happy." So be it. The reason I've stayed here for 15 years is that the salary and benefits are great. I'm 48 years old now, too old to start over and have to prove myself somewhere else. That is, if I could find a job somewhere else.

1

Woodstock Lighting Group manufactures and distributes three distinctly different product lines: flashlights, spotlights, and beacon lights. My job is to buy materials, make the products, and ship the products to customers. Well, it's actually much more complicated than that, but let's keep it simple for now. Woodstock has lost money and market share for two years in a row, and unless we turn things around quickly, I may get my wish to catch up on my sleep. What my job is really about is managing inventory. I buy inventory, I make inventory, and I ship inventory.

*The reason I'm not sleeping well is because I'm worried about inventory: our inventory, our suppliers' inventory, and our customers' inventory. How much inventory is enough? Just when I think I have the answer, something happens in **my** supply chain that causes **my** inventory to grow or shrink to undesirable levels, and **I** have to bring it back into balance again. **I** could do it if all the other links in our supply chain cooperated and did what **I** said. Most of the people here are only interested in **their** own problems and whether or not **they** are meeting **their** own performance measurements for the year. Then **they** can get a raise, bonus, promotion — or all three.*

Just before I went off on holiday, I received an inter-office e-mail from Adriana, our company president, expressing her displeasure about the amount of inventory in our supply chain. Here is what she said:

Inter-Office E-mail

To: Joe, Vice President, Operations   December 31
From: Adriana, President
Subject: High Inventory

Joe, I just received the results of the physical inventory we took last week. I am concerned and disappointed. Inventory is up $5 million from last year's physical inventory. This is far too high and unacceptable. Based on our COGS (cost of goods sold) and average inventory throughout the year, we only turned our inventory 1.7 times. This cannot continue. I expect you and your team to implement a plan to reduce inventory dramatically ASAP. I expect a plan of action on my desk by the end of January. Call me if you have any questions. Adriana

---

I knew this was coming. Well, it's a new year, and I'm determined to change things, or get fired for trying. In December, knowing inventory

was going to be a hot topic this year, I committed a significant portion of my meager budget and hired a supply-chain professional. His name is Jack, and I've given him the title of supply-chain manager. They won't change my title, but they can't stop me from calling my new manager what I want. Jack comes from a large company recognized as a leader in supply-chain innovations. Jack is smart, ambitious, experienced, and has what I believe to be a most outstanding attribute: He is a team player. Professionally, Jack recently achieved the prestigious CSCP (Certified Supply-Chain Professional) certification from APICS, The Association for Operations Management.

Jack has one broad but important task this coming year. I can state it in one sentence. His job is turning inventory silos into a collaborative supply-chain network, with the objective of "rightsizing" inventory in each link of our supply chain. By rightsizing, I mean having the right quantity inventory at the right location in our supply chain. The reason I said today is going to be a bad one is that today is my weekly production meeting with planning, manufacturing, and purchasing to review inventory levels. It won't be a pleasant meeting. Today is Jack's first day of work. I invited him to attend the meeting and instructed him to listen to the dialog and report back to me after the meeting to discuss his observations. Jack e-mailed me his report:

Inter-Office E-mail

To: Joe, VP Operations   January 2
From: Jack, Supply Chain Manager
Subject: Weekly Production Meeting — Observations

1. No formal agenda was published and distributed in advance.
2. The end time of the meeting was not preset (9:00–??).
3. The word "I" was used over 100 times (I stopped counting at 105), mostly by you.
4. The word "we" was used twice.
5. The term "production meeting" was too narrow because you all talked about many topics not related to production.
6. The Materials Manager (Cyndie) and the Purchasing VP (Eddie) talked a lot, mostly defending their positions relative to the current inventory levels. The plant manager (Arnie) said very little and seemed anxious to get the meeting over with.

7. All groups that impact production were not present at the meeting. I understand that no minutes of the meeting are published for distribution, not even to attendees.
8. Because action items were not clearly defined, responsibility and accountability was unclear. It seemed that if someone felt like taking on an action item, they might do so if they felt inclined.
9. No goals for the week were discussed and planned for.
10. No weekly, monthly, or annual performance measurements were set or, worse yet, even discussed.
11. The meeting was held in your office with you sitting behind a desk and the others in chairs with no place to put their "stuff" on.
12. No visual aids were used for all to see.
13. There were no handouts.

In summary, Joe, the meeting was poorly run and didn't accomplish much. Goals need to be set, responsibilities need to be assigned, and other links in the supply chain must get involved in these discussions. You cannot have a collaborative supply-chain network unless all of the links in the supply chain understand the issues and concerns of the other links. This can only be done through communication and interaction between all the links in the supply chain. This company culture of operating independently has to change, and change must start at the very top levels of the company.

Respectfully submitted, Jack

I read Jack's report, and my first reaction was to get mad. Gee, tell me how you really feel, Jack! However, being a mature adult and remembering my New Year's resolution to change things, I calmed down and met with Jack to discuss how to proceed. We recognized that two significant issues needed to be addressed immediately: inventory levels and supply-chain communication. Our first action was to make a list of all the links in our supply chain. We came up with the list represented in Table 1.1.

These are the major links in our supply chain. Each of the major links has many sublinks. We listed some of the inventory-related activities as a point of reference only; it is not intended to be all inclusive. For example, quality products and services is an important aspect of our business and

Table 1.1 Supply-Chain Role and Inventory Function

Supply-Chain Function	*Inventory-Related Activities*
External Customers	Buy inventory
Suppliers, 3PL and 4PL	Supply inventory and services
Finance and Accounting	Track cash inflow and outflow
Sales and Marketing	Create demand and sell inventory
Planning and Purchasing	Buy inventory and plan production
Product and Process Design	Design, enhance products and processes
Manufacturing	Production and quality of inventory
Warehousing, Distribution, and Transportation	Store, pick, pack, and ship inventory
Facilities and Maintenance	Keep environment safe and operational
Human Resources	See to the care and well being of all employees
Information Technology	Provide data and information related to inventory
Field Service	Provide services and inventory to customers

is everyone's responsibility. The quality group reports to manufacturing and is not considered a separate link in our supply chain. Jack and I took our list and met with Adriana, our company president. Adriana has been president for two years and has been with the company for fifteen years, most recently as vice president of finance. Her experience and education are in finance and accounting. We explained to her that we wanted to survey people in each of our internal and external links. Our goal was to discover the inventory problems they were facing on a daily basis and what we could do collectively to improve things. We asked her to e-mail or meet with all the key players and explain what we were doing and why we were doing it.

We decided that every time someone made a point worth communicating to all our supply-chain links, we would highlight and communicate it by denoting it as a **TEAM IMPORTANT POINT (TIP)**. For example, **TIP** number one is:

> **TIP #1: *Communicate, communicate, communicate ... with everyone.***

Adriana said she would tell everyone, stay involved, and help in any way she could. On a personal level she said she was delighted that I was taking a leadership position in this effort, and she looked forward to our working together (like I had a choice after receiving her e-mail).

TIP #2: *Someone in the company must recognize that change is needed, become the champion, and take a leadership role to make it happen.*

TIP #3: *Executive management must be committed and involved for change to take place.*

Jack and I conducted our survey in person, one on one. Because we identified 19 links in our supply chain, the survey took several weeks. Our approach was simple. There was no formal document to read or fill out. When we set up the meetings, we only said we wanted to discuss how we could help make their job easier in managing inventory levels, so that their group could operate more efficiently. We asked the same three questions to all 19 people:

1. What is the single biggest obstacle your group faces in managing inventory?
2. What would you do to change things?
3. How would you go about it?

We just let them talk and listened carefully to what they had to say. Some people talked for hours (the longest interview took three hours and the shortest one took 30 minutes). With some, it was like pulling teeth, and we had to provide examples of things that were thought to be wrong. In the end, we weren't surprised by the results. Once we got people talking, we couldn't stop them. Boy, did they let us have it — with both barrels! The list was long, and there was a lot of repetition. We determined (I'm using the word "we" already) that there was one problem common to all the links in our supply chain. It was the perceived lack of understanding by the other links regarding their role and responsibility in managing inventory in our supply chain. The second, more tangible, problem they all faced was managing inventory into and out of their link in the supply chain.

TIP #4: *If you want to learn anything, ask questions — lots of questions.*

Our findings showed that some links had too much inventory, and others didn't have enough. It is interesting that the links with too much inventory, in general, mentioned having fewer problems than those that said they didn't have enough. Gee, what a surprise! The result of this imbalance was high inventories, stockouts, late customer orders, inefficient manufacturing, and unhappy suppliers, customers, and employees. Inter-

Table 1.2 Year-End Inventory

Division	Raw Material ($)	Work-in-Process ($)	Finished Goods ($)	Totals ($)
Flashlights	10,000,000	5,000,000	13,000,000	28,000,000
Spotlights	6,000,000	1,500,000	500,000	8,000,000
Beacon lights	1,000,000	1,000,000	2,000,000	4,000,000
Totals	17,000,000	7,500,000	15,500,000	40,000,000

estingly enough, each link blamed the other links for their inventory problems; it was never their fault. There was a lot of "us" and "them" in the dialog. This was very interesting. We documented the facts related to inventory to benchmark our current position. Table 1.2 represents the baseline numbers from which we would measure our success (or failure) from this point on.

> **TIP #5:** *When starting out on an inventory rightsizing effort, you must first benchmark where you are in terms of current inventory levels by category and location in the supply chain.*

As you can see, we have $40 million worth of inventory for a company with $90 million in sales. Our cost of goods sold (COGS) last year was $60 million. COGS is made up of three elements: material used in our product (direct material), labor to make the product (direct labor), and overhead costs associated with making the product.

Here at Woodstock, our overhead calculation includes many of our salaried operations employees, such as planning, purchasing, engineering, and plant supervision. The breakdown of COGS is material 55 percent, labor 15 percent, and overheads, 30 percent. At Woodstock, we define *direct material* as material that goes into our product. On the other hand, indirect material is used to make our product. For example, in our Flashlight Division, a direct material would be the springs used in the base of the flashlight. An indirect material would be the sandpaper used on our deburring machines to get rid of the rough edges. The sandpaper would be categorized as an expense item.

Direct labor occurs when someone touches the product and adds value to the product. Indirect labor occurs when someone touches the product but doesn't add value to it. For example, the machine operator on the injection molding machine would be considered direct labor because he or she is adding value to the product. On the other hand, the forklift driver would be considered indirect labor because he or she touches the product but doesn't add value to it. This might be considered part of overhead. Our average inventory last year was about $35 million a month, with a high of $40 million at the end of the year. Adriana mentioned in her e-mail that our inventory turns last year were 1.7. *Inventory turns* is defined as the number of times inventory cycles out of the company during the year. Her comment was based on the following data:

Formula for Inventory Turns:

Inventory turns = Cost of goods sold/average inventory

Woodstock inventory turns = $60,000,000/$35,000,000 = 1.7

Although the year-end inventory was $40,000,000, the average throughout the year was $35,000,000. This is terrible! For a company of our size to turn inventory less than two times a year is criminal. I happen to know that our competition is turning its inventory 3.5 times a year. That isn't great either, but it is a lot better than what we are doing.

Jack and I met with Adriana to discuss our findings. We concluded the following would be the objectives in our inventory rightsizing effort:

- The company has to change from a "them versus us" culture to a "we" culture.
- All links in our supply chain need to understand the roles, responsibilities, and the issues of all the other links in our supply chain in managing inventory efficiently.
- The focus of this understanding would be to rightsize the inventory in our entire supply chain; that is, have the right item, in the right quantity, of the right quality, and at the right time to satisfy all downstream customer requirements. Not just external customers, but internal customers as well.
- We need to develop quantitative performance metrics that make sense and are achievable.

The next thing we did was to have Adriana call a meeting (teleconference) with all senior managers representing each link in our supply chain to explain what we were going to do. She told them they would all participate on an as-needed basis and meet formally once a month to review the status of this effort. She made it clear that everyone had to cooperate and participate in this effort, and rightsizing inventory would be a significant part of their shared performance evaluation for the year. Point well made.

TIP #6: *Rightsizing inventory is the responsibility of everyone in the supply chain, and performance metrics should be shared by all links in the supply chain.*

Now that the president's commitment and involvement had been communicated to the senior members in our supply chain, we needed a plan of action. Jack and I didn't think we should dictate a plan of action to these managers. If we did, it would be our plan, and buy-in would become difficult. What we needed was a panel of supply-chain experts within our company who could take the lead in coordinating this culture change. Because it was not reasonable to have all 19 supply-chain managers on this panel (nothing would get done), we sought to find 6 employees, in our company of 300 people, who could best succeed in this. The common characteristics of the employees we sought were

1. Well respected by their peers
2. Excellent communication skills
3. Broad-based knowledge on how the company currently operated

What we didn't want:

1. People with abrasive personalities.
2. Senior managers, just because they had position, title, or longevity with the company.
3. Knowledge experts in one particular supply-chain link. We would call on the experts later.

We knew we couldn't make everyone happy. What is that old saying, "you can please some of the people some of the time, but you can't … "? So Adriana, Jack, and I picked the team. Because I was already on the Steering Committee (Adriana had already made this decision for me), we thought it best that I not be on the team. Besides, I was still getting used to the "we" word and had a long way to go. At this point, we decided to give the team a name. We had to call it something besides "the team." We didn't want something long-winded or a fancy acronym that nobody would understand. We didn't want to waste a lot of time trying to be original or clever. We just wanted to give the team a name that everyone in the company would recognize. We decided to call it the **"Harmony Team."** By definition, the word *harmony* implies a state of agreement in feeling, action, ideas, and interest. The following people were chosen for the Harmony Team:

Harmony Team facilitator: Arnie, Plant Manager

We thought about making Jack the Harmony Team leader but decided against it. Jack was too new to the company, and it might be difficult for him to be accepted by many of the longtime employees. Besides, although he brought an outside perspective of how successful supply chains functioned, he didn't know our supply chain that well. We decided that Jack would be on the Harmony Team but not lead it. We believed Arnie would be an excellent choice. His position as plant manager put him at the very heart of our supply chain. Arnie runs our only manufacturing facility. He has been with the company 25 years and worked his way up through the ranks. He started out as an order picker in the distribution center and held many different positions in the company before becoming plant manager five years ago. He is well respected in the company and has kept up with the latest techniques, technologies, and methodologies used in manufacturing today.

On top of all that, he is on a first-name basis with our major suppliers and some of our major customers. Perfect! Adriana and I met with Arnie and explained the position to him. We told him we recognized that this would increase his workload short-term, and he would have to shift much of his daily work to Orlando to his capable assistant plant manager. We also indicated that rewards, deliverables, and performance measures would be forthcoming and would be team-based rather than individual-based. Arnie accepted the terms and took on the role as Harmony Team leader. He also got to pick the rest of the team along with Adriana, Jack, and myself. Here is the rest of the team:

> **Harmony Team Members:**
> **Eddie:** Senior vice president of purchasing, 40 years' service, retiring at the end of the year. Well liked and knowledgeable in how the company operates in all areas of materials management (planning and purchasing).
> **Pat:** Director of finance, five years' service, spent eight years as controller of her family's wholesale business before it was sold to a large conglomerate.
> **Maria:** Customer service manager, ten years' service, first job out of college, eight years as a sales representative before moving into the customer service position.
> **Michael:** Packaging engineer, two years' service with Woodstock, six years' experience overall. Came up through our apprentice program; he spent six months in Product Design, six months in Cost Accounting, and six months in Process Design before his latest position as packaging engineer.

Jack: Supply-chain manager. You already met Jack; he reports to me.

TIP #7: *Pick a team, establish goals and objectives, benchmark where you are, and identify shared performance measurements. Communicate this to everyone.*

All right, it looks like we are ready to start. Did we forget anything? Oops, we almost forgot two of the most important links in our supply chain: our suppliers and our external customers. We'll let the Harmony Team work with the supply-chain managers to decide who should be asked to join the team. Where was I? Oh yeah, we are organized, have set up communications, and selected the Harmony Team. We have top management commitment and involvement, and we have a goal to right-size inventory in all our supply-chain links.

What we don't have is a vision of what the new supply chain will look like, quantitative goals of where we want to be, or a plan on how to get there, once we decide! One thing we have plenty of is questions such as: How can we position inventory so it can be used as a strategic advantage against our competition? Should we view inventory as an asset or a liability? What constitutes a "perfect order" from our customers' perspective? What constitutes a perfect order from our company perspective? Is the customer always right? Questions, lots of questions — it's time we started to get some answers. Only when we understand the answers to these questions (and others) can we begin to turn inventory silos into a collaborative supply-chain network.

TIP #8: *Delegate authority, accountability, and responsibility to those who can best accomplish the task of right-sizing inventory in the supply chain.*

I called the first meeting of the Harmony Team for February 2. After the meeting, Adriana and I are going on a road trip to visit some of our key suppliers and customers to ask them what they think about our relationship with them.

February 2, First Meeting of the Harmony Team
Woodstock Inventory: $41 Million

My name is Arnie. I'm plant manager for Woodstock and the Harmony Team leader.

Our inventory is out of control. In the past month, inventory has increased by $1 million. Part of this increase in inventory can be attributed to the typical "noise level" of inventory fluctuation. We have also identified that about $200,000 of the increase is due to incoming raw materials for the new lantern product line, which has not gone into production yet. In addition, our actual sales for January were off by $1.4 million, so this also contributed to the inventory increase. To top it all off, we had asked our suppliers to hold off shipping to us in December, but few of them did. We got hit with over $4 million in incoming raw material.

We can't complete customer orders because of part shortages, and our warehouses and distribution centers are loaded with "stuff." It's gotten so bad that we will run out of warehouse space by the end of April. Even as I speak, we have two trailers sitting in the yard that we can't unload, and we are paying daily demurrage fees to the trucking company.

Sales is screaming because we are late on a big order for one of our largest customers. Finance is all over us because inventories are at record levels. We've lost money for two years in a row and, as you know, we have had a hiring and wage freeze since the first of the year. Morale is the worst I have ever seen it in the 25 years I have been with the company. Things have to change for the better and change quickly. Each of our supply-chain links operates in an independent fashion, working as silos or islands unto themselves. If we are going to survive, we must become a collaborative network, delivering products and services to our customers in a timely fashion and at a profitable level for our stakeholders.

We no longer compete against other companies; we compete against other supply chains, as depicted in Figure 1.1. We are only as good as the weakest link in our chain. Today, we begin to change things.

You have been chosen for the Harmony Team because you possess three common attributes: you are well respected by your peers, you have excellent communication skills, and you have a solid understanding of how our supply chain operates today.

You are not expected to be the knowledge experts in each of our links. We will call on the knowledge experts as we get into the details of each link in our supply chain. The objective of the Harmony Team is to rightsize inventory by turning inventory silos into a collaborative supply-chain network. This is not "just another project" with a start date and an end date. This will become a new way of life for our company.

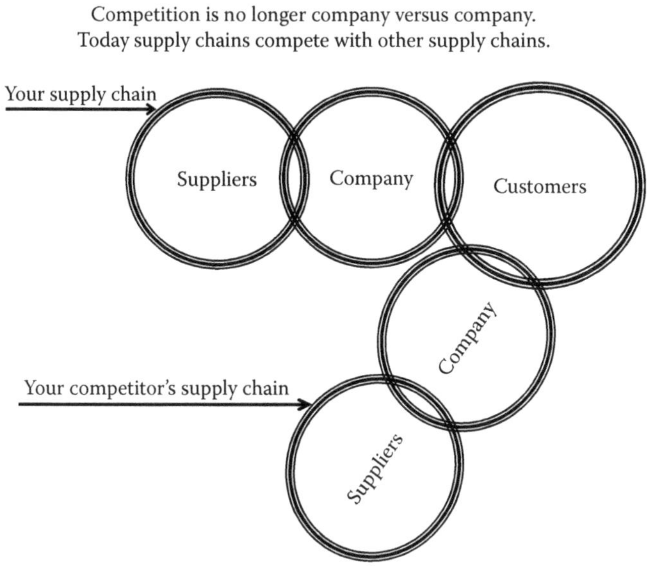

Competition is no longer company versus company.
Today supply chains compete with other supply chains.

Your supply chain

Suppliers   Company   Customers

Company

Your competitor's supply chain

Suppliers

Figure 1.1   Competing supply chains.

Please do not use the word "project" when someone asks you what you are working on. "Project" implies that some day this will end, and we can all go back to our regular jobs, doing exactly what we did before. This will never end. The players may change over the years, but we will create a new culture in our supply chain, one of harmony, unity, and cooperation: a culture of continuous improvement.

> **TIP #9:** *Rightsizing inventory is not "just another project"* *with a start date and an end date; it has to become a new* *way of life for the company.*

You are all aware that our inventory at the end of the year was $40 million. The first question we need to ask ourselves is this: Does our inventory level and its location in our supply chain match our inventory strategy? We should be positioning inventory to give us a strategic advantage in the marketplace.

Inventory as a Strategic Advantage

It's important to know why inventory exists in our supply chain. Because our product lines are sold into three distinctly different markets, we cannot have a "one size fits all" inventory strategy. Table 1.3 shows our annual

Table 1.3 Woodstock Annual Sales

Division	Sales ($)	Year End Inventory ($)
Flashlight Division	60,000,000	28,000,000
Spotlight Division	20,000,000	8,000,000
Beacon Light Division	10,000,000	4,000,000
Total	90,000,000	40,000,000

sales, broken down by division: 67 percent, Flashlight Division; 22 percent, Spotlight Division; and 11 percent, Beacon Lights. Our strategy for this year is to increase our share of the flashlight market by 10 percent and increase our share of the spotlight market by 15 percent annually. The beacon light business is a small portion of our total revenue, but it is very profitable. We forecast that sales will remain flat this year, with the exception of Field Service sales, where we forecast a revenue increase of $1 million, going from $10 million to $11 million. At some point we may spin it off because it is not considered a growth market for us (although it is a significant part of our core competency).

Make-to-Stock Inventory Strategy

Our Flashlight Division manufactures and distributes flashlights to commercial customers and distributors who sell to retail stores, from the large chains to independent hardware stores. Although making inventory that doesn't go out the door immediately goes against the principle of continuous inventory flow, the reality is that for now it is a necessity. We use a make-to-stock inventory strategy for this product line. A make-to-stock strategy is one where you manufacture to forecast and sell from the resulting finished goods inventory.

Put yourselves in the consumer's shoes. If you wanted to buy a flashlight to keep in your bedside table for emergencies, you would expect to go to a store, select one off the J-hook, pay for it, and be on your way home without a problem. However, consider this scenario: There are two different J-hooks on the wall in the store, each labeled with a different manufacturer's flashlight, and they are the same price and have the same features. One manufacturer's J-hook (Manufacturer A) is empty, and the other one (Manufacturer B) is full. What would you do? Would you go to the customer service counter and place an order for one flashlight from Manufacturer A and wait for the store to call you a week later to tell you that it had arrived? Of course not. All things being equal, you would take your hand and move it to the J-hook that was full (Manufacturer B), pull

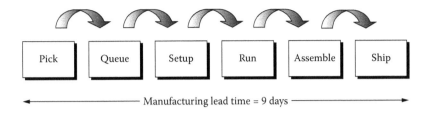

| Pick | Queue | Setup | Run | Assemble | Ship |

Manufacturing lead time = 9 days

Figure 1.2   Lead time as a sequence of process steps.

one off, and be on your way. Unless you were looking for some unique characteristic, the flashlight would be considered a commodity and you would expect it to be in inventory.

As Figure 1.2 shows, our lead time to manufacture and assemble a batch (product number 32750) of flashlights is five days (allowing for queue, setup, run, wait, and move time). Allowing two days to get it to our distributors and another two days for them to get it to their customers, we have a total lead time of nine days, door to door. No consumer wants to wait nine days to buy a flashlight when they need it now and it is available in many retail stores.

Because our total lead time is greater than the customer (consumer) lead time, we have to manufacture in advance of need and put the product in inventory. This strategy is called *make-to-stock*. How much to have in stock is a difficult question that our Sales link and our Demand Planning link struggle with all the time. Don't forget, we include batteries along with the flashlight, and the batteries have a shelf life to be considered. It wouldn't do for someone to buy a flashlight with dead batteries. Because of these issues, we decided to keep manufacturing the flashlight in-house, rather than go off shore. As 80 percent of our market is domestic, we wanted to keep control of the manufacturing and distribution.

Because we own and control the manufacturing and distribution of our products, we operate what is known as a *vertical supply chain*. If we outsourced any of the manufacturing or distribution, we would have a *horizontal supply chain*. One of the primary benefits of a vertical supply chain is that we have a high degree of control over our network. Once we decide to outsource manufacturing or distribution (horizontal supply chain), we will lose some degree of control. However, Sales tells us we might have to consider moving manufacturing off shore if we can't get our costs under control. Marketing, which sets our sales price, tells us pricing is becoming more of an issue every day. So our Flashlight Division faces its own set of inventory problems.

In an ideal world, we would not stock any finished goods but would manufacture to customer order. Wouldn't it be great if we could satisfy every customer order without carrying any finished goods in stock? Imagine production going right into cartons, moving to the shipping dock, and shipping directly to the customer, all in the same day! Wow! With a make-to-stock inventory strategy, the delivery lead time to the customer is very short. With this approach, the inventory must be positioned in our supply chain at a physical location close to the customer (at our distribution centers) or our distribution and transportation links must be able to deliver our flashlights directly from our manufacturing plant in New Jersey to our customers throughout the world. Ideally, we hope to improve our transportation response time to the point where we can eliminate the need for our three distribution centers, presently located in California, Texas, and Chicago.

Assemble-to-Order Inventory Strategy

Our Spotlight Division has a different inventory strategy. This is called *assemble-to-order*. We stock subassemblies of different size spotlights for the "special event" marketplace, the emergency vehicle marketplace, and the commercial and home marketplace. *Subassemblies* are partially manufactured products placed in inventory and assembled into the final configuration after receipt of the customer order. Typically, assemble-to-order products have many options to suit different customer requirements. For example, if a municipality wants a certain configuration of lights for its emergency vehicles, we will take the subassemblies out of stock and assemble the final product to their specifications. One municipality may require a four-color string of lights in a light bar and another municipality may require a five-color light bar. In this environment, we keep the standard component subassemblies in inventory and assemble the final product after receipt of the customer order.

Subassemblies are more costly to keep in inventory because not only did we pay for the raw material, but we also partially assembled the product, thus, adding value to it. We also have to pay for the labor long before we ship the order and bill the customer. The trade-off here is that we have more flexibility to respond to customer's unique needs in a timely fashion, and cash outflow will be greater. Overall, the delivery lead time to the customer with an assemble-to-order inventory strategy is longer than the delivery lead time in a make-to-stock strategy, because we have to add in the final assembly lead time, as shown in Figure 1.2.

Our supply-chain strategy is to deliver these orders directly to our customers, bypassing the distribution center, unless we are consolidating the order with other orders presently going to that customer. We do, however, keep a limited amount of standard assembled products at our three distribution centers for immediate delivery to our customers. Where the make-to-stock strategy is driven by forecasted demand, the assemble-to-order strategy is driven by actual customer orders. The subassemblies are driven by forecasted demand, and the final assembly is driven by the actual customer order.

Manufacture-to-Order and Engineer-to-Order Strategies

Our Beacon Light Division sells beacon lights that are used in lighthouses around the world. Today, this is mostly a replacement market with little growth. We call our strategy here a manufacture-to-order strategy or, in some rare cases, an engineer-to-order strategy, where we will actually design the light configuration for the customer. In the manufacture-to-order strategy, we keep very little inventory, limited to only the raw materials that are common to most beacon lights. This inventory is driven by a forecast. Only after receipt of the customer order do we go out and buy the unique raw materials needed. In the case of engineer-to-order, we don't stock inventory of any kind. We only buy inventory after the customer has approved the new design.

This division has one unique aspect of inventory management that the other two divisions don't face. It has a service department that goes into the field to repair beacon lights that malfunction. The field service group requires a certain amount of inventory be available on an emergency basis, because beacon lights must be functional at all times. We use a make-to-stock strategy for these replacement parts. This inventory is driven by a forecast, based on historical demand. The manufacture-to-order and engineer-to-order strategies require the longest delivery lead time. This is because, going in, we have no idea of what we are going to make and have to add the design element to the total lead time.

Because of this, we can say that the Beacon Light Division uses all four inventory strategies: make-to-stock, assemble-to-order, manufacture-to-order, and engineer-to-order. The supply-chain strategy for this product line is to ship the subassemblies directly to the customer site from our manufacturing facility in New Jersey. We then send a team of engineers to the customer site for final assembly and test. In the case of spare parts, we have third-party logistics providers who, for a fee, stock spare parts at strategic East and West Coast locations (close to airports) of the United States. Spare parts can be flown as needed anywhere in the world on a moment's notice. We also keep a limited amount of inventory at our own distribution centers and will ship direct to the customer or to our third-party logistics provider.

So there you have it. Each division has a different strategy when it comes to managing inventory. The total delivery lead time is getting shorter

Table 1.4   Woodstock Inventory

Division	Raw Material (%)	Work-in-Progress (%)	Finished Goods (%)
Flashlights	59	67	84
Spotlights	35	20	3
Beacon lights	6	13	13
Totals	100	100	100

and shorter as product life cycles continue to contract and customer's expectations increase.

As you are all aware, we took a physical inventory during our year-end shutdown. We were quite surprised to find that our book inventory was much lower than the actual physical inventory. This tells us our inventory record keeping throughout the year was grossly inaccurate. We will have to address this issue as soon as possible. The physical inventory gives us a good starting point, but unless we find and fix the reasons for inaccuracies, it will quickly become inaccurate again. However, our focus today is on matching our inventory position with our inventory strategy. Referring back to Table 1.2, please note that raw material includes sub-assemblies, and finished goods include spare parts for the Beacon Light Division. The numbers shown represent a good amount of data on the makeup of our inventory and where it resides in our supply chain.

Now, we have to turn this data into meaningful information. Does our inventory strategy match our inventory levels by location in the supply chain? Table 1.4 shows where our inventory resides in our supply chain. Does our inventory strategy for each division match our types of inventory (raw material, work-in-progress [WIP], finished goods)? Let's look at our flashlight make-to-stock strategy.

Table 1.2 and Table 1.4 show that 84 percent of our total finished goods inventory is for flashlights. Although the inventory is too high, it does match our strategy. But, as Figure 1.3 shows, only 46 percent of the flashlight inventory is in finished goods; it does not match our strategy. This also points out that the other 54 percent of the flashlight inventory is in raw materials and WIP. Because we can't do much about the finished goods, except to let sales know it needs to address it, we can focus on rightsizing the raw materials and WIP inventory for this division, which is too high and out of balance with our overall inventory strategy for this division.

Now, let's look at another strategy and inventory comparison. If you look at Table 1.4 for beacon lights, make-to-order strategy, you will note that 13 percent of all finished goods inventory is for this division, which

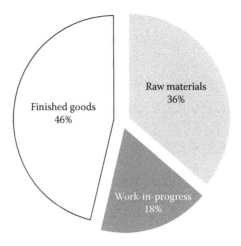

Figure 1.3 Flashlights inventory segmentation.

Figure 1.4 Beacon lights inventory segmentation.

seems to match the corporate inventory strategy. However, if you look at Figure 1.4, the beacon light inventory by itself, 50 percent of all beacon light inventory is in finished goods.

This does not match our inventory strategy. We should have a higher percentage of raw materials (spare parts) and a lower percentage of finished goods. Based on this information, we should attack the finished goods inventory first. In theory, we shouldn't have any finished goods for this division.

In the case of the Spotlight Division, Figure 1.5 shows that 75 percent of its inventory is in raw materials, and its inventory represents 35 percent

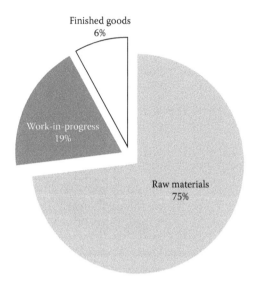

Figure 1.5 Spotlights inventory segmentation.

(Table 1.2) of all raw material inventories. This number is too high and does not match its inventory strategy.

Although the finished goods for this division are only 3 percent of all finished goods, it does represent 6 percent of all spotlight inventory, where the strategy calls for no finished goods inventory. So there you have it, our inventory levels by category do not match our inventory strategies by division.

> **TIP #10:** *Start rightsizing your inventory by aligning your inventory levels to match your inventory strategies by product or division classifications.*

Here is what we need to focus on to realign our physical inventories to our inventory strategies:

> **Flashlight Division:** Focus on reducing the ratios of raw materials and WIP to finished goods.
> **Beacon Light Division:** Focus on reducing the ratios of finished goods inventory to raw material and WIP.
> **Spotlight Division:** Focus on reducing the ratios of finished goods to raw material and WIP.

It is important to note that these actions won't necessarily reduce inventory levels but will shift location of our inventory levels in our supply chain so that they match our corporate strategies. Once we have done that, we can focus on reducing the levels of inventory in the supply chain.

> **TIP #11:** *Gather inventory data by type, location, and business segment. Compare it to the corporate inventory strategy. Any inconsistency in inventory and strategy must be addressed and corrected.*
>
> Unfortunately, not all of our supply-chain links understand the fundamental inventory strategies I've just cited. We need to educate everyone in our supply chain on the importance of aligning physical inventory to our corporate strategy.

Inventory: Asset or Liability?

That depends on who you talk to here at Woodstock. I'm not a financial guy, but no one here at Woodstock will argue the fact that in many real and tangible ways inventory is definitely an asset. Inventory enters our supply chain as an asset and, for accounting purposes, is recorded as an asset on our balance sheet. The balance sheet is a financial document where, on a periodic basis, we record what the company owns (assets) and what the company owes (liabilities). Table 1.5 is an example of a simplified balance sheet. Inventory is recorded as an asset on the balance sheet.

Hopefully, our assets far outweigh our liabilities. The difference between assets and liabilities is called owner equity. Put another way, if

Table 1.5   Balance Sheet

Assets	($)	Liabilities	($)
Cash	10,000	Accounts payable	10,000
Accounts receivable	40,000	Long-term loans	50,000
Buildings and equipment	85,000		
Inventory	40,000		
		Equity	
		Owner's investment	40,000
		Profit (prior years)	75,000
Total assets	175,000	Total liabilities and equity	175,000

Table 1.6   Income Statement

Income Statement ($)	
Revenue (sales)	200,000
Cost of goods	120,000
Gross profit	80,000
Other expenses	30,000
Net profit	50,000

your house is valued at $350,000 (asset) and you still owe $200,000 (liability) on the mortgage, your owner's equity is $150,000. Inventory remains on the balance sheet until it is shipped. At that point, it becomes part of COGS and moves to another financial document called the income statement, as shown in Table 1.6.

COGS is made up of three primary elements: material, labor, and overhead. Of course, I'm oversimplifying it, but you get the idea.

Now wait a minute, don't get excited and start yelling. I'll say it. "If the inventory is old, damaged, obsolete, discontinued, engineered out, has an expired shelf life, or is simply not needed, it becomes a liability. Feel better? As a rule of thumb, any inventory not needed to satisfy an immediate customer need can be considered a liability, with exceptions of course. This is an underlying principle of inventory management. It is a philosophy practiced by those who follow the concepts of just-in-time and lean manufacturing. The goal is zero excess inventories. No one ever gets to the end of that rainbow, but it is an ideal we strive to obtain.

Let me state the obvious: Inventory costs money. We have to pay for the materials, pay for the labor to transform the materials, and pay to store and ship the finished product. In a lot of cases we borrow money to buy the inventory, so we also have to pay interest charges on top of the amount borrowed.

> **TIP #12:** *Inventory is considered an asset on the company balance sheet. Inventory is a liability if you have more than you need to satisfy immediate customer requirements.*

As you may be aware, I've known some of our customers for years. Every once in a while they visit with us, and I take them on a plant tour to show them the latest additions to our manufacturing operation. As we are walking around, I always ask them the same question: What do you consider the perfect order? Let me share with you what they have said. I'll also share with you our internal sales and marketing view of the perfect order. This is an interesting point: If you ask ten customers to describe the perfect order, you will get ten different answers. However, many of the answers are common to all our customers. Here is how they see it:

The Perfect Order: Customer Expectations

1. **Shipped on time:** Their requested date; not the date we committed to ship, if different from the requested date.
2. **Received on time:** The date requested to arrive at their dock, not the shipment date, if different.
3. **Shipped and received complete**: All items ordered were shipped in the same shipment and arrived together.
4. **Perfect quality:** No defective parts in the shipment.
5. **Correct quantity:** No more or no less than was ordered.
6. **Requested carrier used:** Mode specified by the customer.
7. **Accurate documents:** All documents, including packing list, waybill, manifests, customs papers and advance shipping notices are in order.
8. **Shipment tracking mechanism in place:** Ability to easily track the shipment location while in transit.
9. **Packaged according to specifications:** Packing requirements were followed.
10. **Not damaged in transit**: The containers arrive in good condition.
11. **Correct invoice:** There are no mistakes in the invoice, and it arrives after the shipment in a timely, efficient manner, electronically if reasonable.
12. **Clearly defined reverse logistics policy:** Clearly defined instructions on what to do in the event that goods need to be repaired or returned.

Of course, it goes without saying that all customers want the lowest possible total cost. By total cost, I mean the cost of the item and all associated costs, such as transportation and handling. Our flashlights may have the lowest item cost to the customer, but if the transportation cost is too high, our total cost to the customer may be higher than our competition. Obviously, this is unacceptable. We need to analyze this further to find out if our total cost is higher than our competitor's total cost.

The Perfect Order: Woodstock Expectations

1. **Satisfy the customer's 12-point definition of the perfect order:** Do as they request.
2. **Customer order is easy to process:** Ideally, we receive the order electronically, and all required information is on the order or in our system.
3. **Customer order is profitable:** We can make and ship the product so that Woodstock makes money on the order.
4. **Customer pays on time:** They pay us on or before the invoice due date.
5. **No returns:** Customer keeps the entire shipment.

> **TIP #13:** *The perfect order must be considered from both the viewpoints of the seller and the buyer. The perfect order criteria must be measurable so that deviations can be corrected.*

The beauty of both lists is that all of the points are measurable. We can monitor how well or how poorly we are conforming to the "perfect order" criteria. Also interesting is the fact that every single one of these metrics relates to inventory, either directly or indirectly. Unfortunately, we haven't communicated this list to all the links in our supply chain. If you ask people in the 19 links to describe the perfect order, you will be surprised how many people couldn't name them all. This list should be documented and published to every link in our supply chain, and a monthly report should be distributed that measures our performance in each of these areas. The document should include a benchmark of where we are today and what our goal is for the rest of the year. At the same time, we should poll our customers to see how they view our performance in delivering the perfect order. Joe and Adriana are on the road right now meeting with customers and some of our key suppliers. I will be anxious to hear what they have learned. Now let's move on to another area we need to understand better.

Silos Versus Cross-Functional Supply Chains

A supply chain can be defined as a series of linked processes, often called a *network*, which delivers products or services to customers. A supply-chain network consists of information, product, services, processes, and cash that flow into and out of a supply chain. This flow is multidirectional, going both downstream and upstream. Here at Woodstock, our supply chain delivers both products and services. Put another way, we deliver inventory to our customers. We have problems doing this. The inventory problems we face at Woodstock are not new or unique to us. They are inherent supply-chain problems that go as far back in history to the invention of fire by the cave people. After all, once they discovered how to create a fire, they then needed a steady supply of wood (raw material) to keep their fire going.

Let me provide you with a simple example of a supply chain. I met a retired man recently who makes holiday decorations out of clothespins. He buys his raw materials such as paints, fabrics, and novelties at craft stores, manufactures the product in his home and sells them at craft fairs. This is a very simple supply chain, but a supply chain nonetheless.

On the other hand we have Henry Ford, who introduced us to mass production and the assembly line. Ford created a supply chain that grew to thousands of people located in multiple locations throughout the world. Ford achieved true vertical supply chain integration with the River Rouge complex in Detroit. So you see, supply-chains have indeed been around for a long time and can be very simple or quite complex. The point I'm trying to make is that supply chains are not a new concept and neither are the problems they face. The problems that Ford faced were the same we face today. These problems are

- Customer order delivery dates change: dates move up and dates move out.
- Customer order quantities change: Sometimes customers increase the order quantity and sometimes they decrease the quantity; sometimes they even cancel the order completely.
- Long lead times from our suppliers.
- Short lead times from our customers.
- Material shortages that disrupt manufacturing and distribution.
- Labor and machine capacities change.
- Price changes impact our costs.

> **TIP #14: *Successful supply chains have one characteristic in common; their ability to rapidly respond to change throughout their entire supply chain, not just one or two links in the chain.***

As you can see, one of the biggest problems supply chains face on a daily — no, make that hourly — basis is dealing with change. World-class companies have supply chains that can respond rapidly to change. If you can't respond in a timely manner and your competitor supply chains can — well, goodbye, you won't be around very long. For the most part,

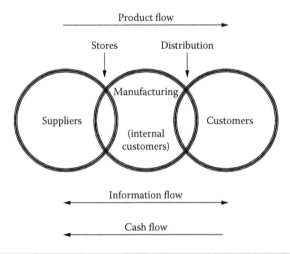

Figure 1.6 Supply-chain management.

managing a supply chain means managing inventory. Even a company recognized as a world-class manufacturer will fail if other links in its supply chain are weak. In its simplest form, a supply chain has three major links, as illustrated in Figure 1.6

On the left, we have suppliers who provide materials and services to a core company that adds value to the product or service and delivers it to a customer, as shown on the far right. The core company doesn't have to be a manufacturer. It can be a distributor who buys from a manufacturing company. In this case, the manufacturer is a supplier. The customer shown on the far right may not be a consumer (retail customer). The customer can be another distributor or manufacturer. This diagram would become more complex if we added more circles, as shown in Figure 1.7. I want to point out that one core company can have multiple configurations to depict its supply chain. For example, for some products the manufacturer is the core company itself. For other products the core company is just the distributor. You will see many variations of this configuration in various publications.

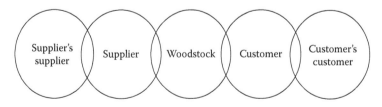

Figure 1.7 The extended supply chain.

Let's go back to Figure 1.6 for a moment: the three-circle configuration. Each one of these circles is made up of different business functions, processes, and activities performed by different people working in different departments. For example, all financial matters concerning the core company might reside in one department called the Finance Department. Depending on the size of the company, it might be one person (who also does work for another department), or it could be a whole slew of people, totaling in the hundreds.

Their responsibilities might include payroll, accounts payable, accounts receivable, general ledger, cost accounting, asset management, and the like. It would not include selling the product (Sales Department), making the product (Manufacturing), or shipping the product (Distribution). However, if the company is a one-person company like my clothespin guy, it could include all these functions. Each one of these departments is headed up by a manager who reports to a higher level manager. This organization can become very complex and very deep, depending on the size of the company. I have brought along a copy of our Woodstock organization chart for everyone (See Figure 1.8).

You will note that each department manager has a number of people reporting to him or her. In all, this chart represents the 300 employees of Woodstock. The popular term used today when referring to these departments is to call them *silos*. When you think of a grain silo, you picture grain flowing into the top of the silo. When needed, it flows out of the bottom or the top. It is not connected to other silos on the farm. Another popular term for this concept is *islands*. When you think of an island, you think of a piece of land surrounded by water on four sides and not connected to other islands. Figure 1.9 depicts the silo concept.

A poorly run supply chain is depicted by departments operating as silos or islands. These function as "entities unto themselves" and are not involved with what is happening on the other silos. Picture this scenario: A customer calls a sales representative to complain about receiving poor quality inventory. The sales representative goes up his or her silo and tells the local branch sales manager. This sales manager goes up the silo to the regional sales manager, who in turn tells the regional vice president of sales about the problem. Finally, the problem is reported to the corporate vice president of sales, residing in an office on the other side of the country, which is at the top of the Sales Department silo. The corporate vice president of sales tells the vice president of manufacturing (another silo) that they received a customer complaint. The vice president of manufacturing goes down the silo one level and tells the vice president of operations who in turn tells the plant manager. The plant manager then tells the floor supervisor, who eventually tells the worker who made the product. This worker is at the bottom of the Manufacturing silo. So

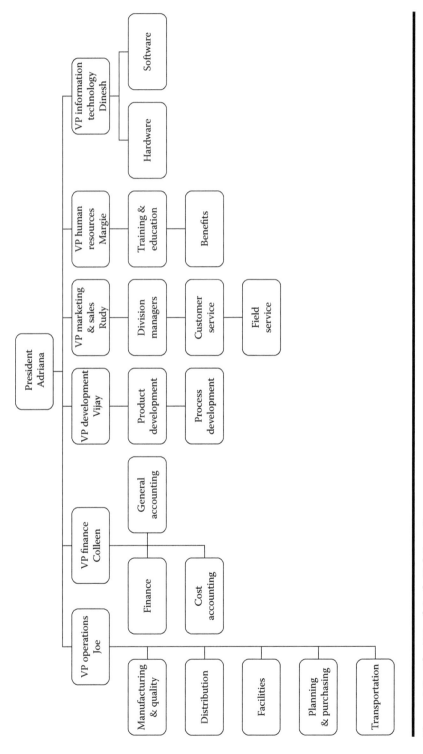

Figure 1.8 The Woodstock Lighting Group.

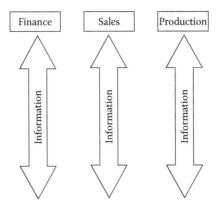

Figure 1.9   Organizational silos.

what we have is information flowing up one silo and eventually flowing down another silo. As you can see, if this happened in the real world it would take forever to respond to the customer's problem. The problem with information flowing up and down silos is that response time is poor and information might be misunderstood or miscommunicated. Obviously, it would have to be a very poorly run supply chain if this example were real.

The whole point of this is to show that supply chains cannot operate this way. They must become integrated and work as cross-functional work teams to respond to all the changes that take place in the entire supply chain. No single silo can do it all. When referring to these silos, I will now use the term *supply-chain link*. As I said earlier, each link performs a series of processes. Each link receives input from other links in our chain, and each link provides output to other links in the chain. This input/output can be information, cash, products, or a service. The input/output can flow both upstream (back through the supply chain to the supplier) or downstream (forward through the supply chain to the customer).

> **TIP #15: *A supply chain is only as strong as its weakest link; being world class in one link does you little good if your other links are weak.***

If you were to ask me how well our supply chain works today, I couldn't tell you. Oh, sure, each of our links has performance measures, and based on the individual link's performance measures, some are doing well and some are not doing so well. For example, we heard Arnie describe the perfect order. Of the 12 items listed for the perfect order, we currently measure only 2 of them: on-time delivery and product quality. The on-time delivery metric is used to track performance in our manufacturing and distribution links. The quality metric is used to track performance in our manufacturing link, because quality assurance reports into the manufacturing link.

But if we deliver a perfect quality product on time, have we shipped the perfect order? The truth is, we don't know. Today, world-class supply chains use key performance indicators (KPI) that measure how well the entire supply chain is doing. These KPIs are shared by all links in the chain and are closely tied to the companies' strategic plan. For example, the Supply Chain Council (SCC), a nonprofit organization that is open to all interested nonprofit and for-profit organizations, government and military agencies, consultants, and academicians has compiled a Supply Chain Operations Reference (SCOR) model that measures the perfect order as a KPI. SCOR® is a registered trademark of the Supply Chain Council, Inc. The formula is simple

Perfect order fulfillment =
Total perfect orders/Total number of orders

Well, if we applied that formula to the 12 perfect order (customer) attributes I spoke of earlier, our KPI is pathetic. In December of last year, we shipped 2500 customer orders; and Customer Service informed me that it had received 140 complaints from customers who were not happy with their shipments for one reason or another. Using the formula, our KPI would be

2360/2500 = 94 percent

I'm not even sure the complaints were related to the perfect order criteria I cited earlier. Customer Service doesn't keep track of the reason for the complaint. By the way, that has to change also. The point is, even if I didn't apply the formula accurately, you will agree that 94 percent customer satisfaction is not a good thing. This has to change.

TIP #16: *Define the perfect order criteria and measure them. Communicate this to everyone in the supply chain.*

Based on the published agenda, I've used up all my time. It is clear to me that we have a long journey ahead. As a result of today's meeting, and for all future Harmony Team meetings, I suggest we do five things:

1. Communicate what we have learned to all supply-chain managers.
2. Publish a "to-do" list of tasks to be accomplished.

3. Publish a weekly report on inventory levels.
4. Construct an analytical model of how we will maintain the "right-size" inventory in the future.
5. Use the minutes to document the details of how the TIPS, tools, and operating philosophies were applied and the impact they had on inventory.

Inter-Office E-Mail

To: Supply Chain Managers   February 2
From: Harmony Team
Subject: Rightsizing Inventory
Current Inventory Level: $41 Million; up $1 Million since the 1st of the year

This e-mail is a summary of the discussions we had at our first two meetings. As you all are aware, we have embarked on an effort to rightsize our inventory throughout our entire supply chain. We have had our first Harmony Team meeting today and would like to keep you informed on our progress and planned activities. Under a separate e-mail, you will receive detailed minutes of the meeting. We ask that you communicate with your team members and keep them informed on the progress of the effort. This e-mail will summarize some of the key points discussed. Please see the minutes for details of the points highlighted here:

1. Our inventory level and location is not aligned to our inventory strategy.
2. Our perpetual inventory records are not accurate.
3. We need to agree on criteria for defining the perfect order from both the customer and Woodstock points of view.
4. We have adopted a philosophy that any inventory not needed to satisfy an immediate customer need should be considered a liability and reduced to a practical level.
5. We must change from a silo operating philosophy to a collaborative, cross-functional operating philosophy.

6. As we learn how to rightsize our inventory, we will construct an analytical inventory model to be used as a foundation for maintaining the rightsize inventory in the future.

7. After each meeting, we will publish a list of tasks to be accomplished.

8. Each of you is scheduled to meet with the Harmony Team in the near future. We ask that you come prepared to discuss your role and responsibilities related to managing inventory, the tools you currently use, and the tools that you would like to use in the future to help you manage inventory more efficiently.

Attached to this e-mail are the first building blocks for our inventory rightsizing model (Figure 1.10). The entire inventory planning process starts with the Business Plan.

The Business Plan is a high-level management document that drives the entire company. Typically, it is very financially oriented and includes such things as sales growth, marketplace positioning, capital expenditures, and general business positioning. An important part of the Business Plan deals with strategy. This is where management talks about "reducing inventory by 20 percent over the next two years" or "increasing inventory by 15 percent over the next 18 months." It identifies supply-chain strategies and inventory positioning in the supply chain, as we have discussed at this meeting.

So let's begin building our model by showing (Figure 1.10) that the Business Plan drives our entire inventory strategy, recognizing the fact that the customer inventory strategy is a major input to our inventory strategy. We will continue to add to this model after each meeting until we have a framework for rightsizing our inventory. The customer input to our inventory strategy will be discussed at our next meeting.

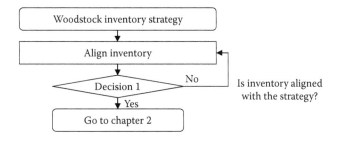

Figure 1.10 Woodstock inventory rightsizing model.

Applying the Tips, Tools, and Philosophies to Your Company

This chapter sets the foundation for rightsizing inventory. It is the first building block on your road to positioning your inventory correctly in the entire supply chain. I have suggested 16 TIPS in this chapter related to rightsizing inventory. Let's now discuss each TIP and how you can apply it to your company.

> ### TIP #1: *Communicate, communicate, communicate … with everyone.*

Arguably, the single biggest challenge you will face in turning your functional supply-chain silos into a collaborative supply-chain network can be summed up in one word, "communication." As a consultant, one of the first questions I ask a client (typically, the president) is, "What is your single biggest business issue that needs to be addressed?" More often than not, I get answers such as long lead times for materials, short lead times from customers, stock outs, and too much inventory. But if I ask the same question to people on the plant or warehouse floor, I get a different answer: poor communication. Because this is not a book about communication in general, I will keep it simple and to the point. I believe Joe, Jack, and Adriana took the right approach in addressing this issue. Here is a checklist of some things you can do to improve the communication issue:

1. Start at the top of the supply chain and communicate with everyone from the boardroom to the shipping dock.
2. When appropriate, use e-mail.
3. Where e-mail is not available, send out memos or post to bulletin boards.

4. Communicate in the appropriate language. One company I worked with translated a memo into Spanish and Polish (the predominate languages of employees in the plant).
5. Include notices in paycheck envelopes.
6. Communicate through the company newsletter.
7. Have the initial announcement come from the highest level executive in the company.
8. When reasonable, communicate face to face.

Using Woodstock as an example, Joe and Jack met face to face with Adriana and explained the issues and a plan of action. Adriana then sent an e-mail out to all supply-chain managers letting them know what was going on and why we were doing it. Jack and Joe then met face to face with all supply-chain managers to get their input. At the end of the meeting, the Harmony Team sent out an e-mail keeping everyone informed about the inventory rightsizing effort. All supply-chain managers were also asked to inform their employees. The following is an example of an initial announcement memo:

To: All Employees
From: Adriana, President
Subject: Rightsizing Our Inventory

The past two years have been difficult for all of us at Woodstock. However, we are working hard on many fronts to change this, and I am excited and optimistic that it will happen. One of the areas we are addressing is managing our inventory better.

I am pleased to announce that we have formed a cross-functional team of employees to focus on this issue. This team is lead by Arnie, our Plant Manager. The charter of the team is to rightsize our inventory. Our goal is to

1. Reduce inventory levels
2. Realign inventory in our supply chain
3. Increase inventory throughput in our supply chain

The team cannot accomplish these goals without your help and input. Many of you will be contacted directly for your ideas and suggestions. Because it's not practical for the team to meet with all 300 employees, I ask that all of you communicate any suggestions you have to any member of Arnie's team. The names of the team members will be announced shortly. All ideas are welcome and will be considered. Working together as a team, we can make this happen. Thank you for your help.

TIP #2: *Someone in the company must become the champion, recognize that change is needed, and take a leadership role in making it happen.*

A champion is someone in the company who is passionate in his or her belief that rightsizing inventory is a good thing for the company and believes it can happen. In the case of Woodstock, Joe isn't the champion. He is a reluctant participant, at best. I would say that for now, Adriana is the champion of this effort. She's the one who took action and believes it can happen. I would have preferred it be someone in a lower position who would be visible every day. As time goes on, you will learn that Arnie has become the true champion of the effort. He is the perfect candidate. Why is having a champion so important? Before I answer that question, let me provide you with a checklist of champion qualifications:

1. Well respected by employees throughout the supply chain
2. Has excellent (verbal and written) communication skills
3. Knowledgeable in how your supply chain currently operates
4. Knowledgeable in state-of-the-art supply-chain techniques and technologies
5. Outgoing and personable
6. Good management skills
7. Believes in the effort
8. Has reasonable expectations (obtainable goals)
9. Has been with the company for a period of time (at least two years)
10. Enthusiastic and optimistic

I have just described the traits of most successful leaders. Now I can answer the earlier question. People look up to such a person and will follow his or her lead. It is contagious, and they get caught up in the champion's enthusiasm. They say to themselves, "if Arnie believes we can do it, then maybe I can help make it happen." There is the old saying, "There are those who lead and those that follow; all others get out of the way." Having a champion is important. Initially, you might think that Jack would be a good candidate because he brings an outside perspective. In truth, he lacks three of the ten criteria. He doesn't pass the test of numbers 1, 3, and 9 for obvious reasons.

> **TIP #3: *Executive management must be committed and involved for change to take place.***

Your inventory rightsizing efforts will be less than successful without the support of your highest level management. This doesn't just mean that they send out the initial notice announcing the effort and then walk away. By commitment and involvement I mean:

1. Participation at various team meetings
2. Open door policy
3. Periodically communicating status to all employees
4. Ensuring cooperation from all links in the chain
5. Keeping the stakeholders informed
6. Helping the team cut through corporate red tape
7. Demonstrating support on a continual basis
8. Removing politics from the equation

> **TIP #4: *If you want to learn anything, ask questions … lots of questions.***

Do not be afraid to ask questions. The only stupid question is the one that goes unasked. One of the reasons we put people on the team who don't know an operation that well is because they aren't embarrassed to ask questions. They aren't expected to know all the answers. The checklist here is shorter but just as potent:

1. Challenge everything.
2. Don't take anything for granted.
3. Continue to ask questions until you are satisfied with the answer.
4. Ask why, as many times as necessary.
5. Move on to another question when you are satisfied with the answer.
6. Go back to step one, and repeat the process.

> **TIP #5: *When starting out on an inventory rightsizing effort, you must first benchmark where you are in terms of current inventory levels by category and location in the supply chain.***

This is an important part of the inventory rightsizing effort. If you don't know where you are today, how will you know if you are successful or not? One of the things that Woodstock did right at the beginning was that it provided details of its inventory levels by division, type, and location, as shown in Table 1.1, Table 1.2, and Table 1.3. Here is a checklist to follow:

1. If you cycle count and have an inventory accuracy of 98 percent or higher, you can start with the book inventory.
2. If number 1 is broken down by division, type (raw material, WIP, and finished goods), and location (manufacturing warehouse, distribution center, and product design) in the supply chain, you can start with the book inventory.
3. If you don't meet the criteria for numbers 1 and 2, you should take a physical inventory.
4. If you don't usually take a physical inventory until year end, and it is early in the year, start anyway, knowing the numbers you are using may be wrong.
5. Publish the starting inventory status, and continue to make the data available on a regular basis to all supply-chain managers.

> **TIP #6:** *Rightsizing inventory is the responsibility of everyone in the supply chain, and performance metrics should be shared by all links in the supply chain.*

You can't rightsize your inventory if different silos have different performance measurements. I learned this the hard way. Let me give you an example. I was a purchasing manager for a textile company, and I was measured on having a favorable purchase price variance. In other words, if the standard price was $2 per linear yard for gray goods, and I was able to buy it for $1 per linear yard, I had a favorable purchase price variance. If I did this often enough, at the end of the year I was awarded a bonus. I spent a great deal of time looking for the best deal. Once I purchased gray goods at considerable savings because the yarn had a lot of "knots" in it, and the vendor wanted to move it. Looking at price alone, it was a good deal, so I bought it. However, because of the knots, the knitting machine kept stopping as the yarn wouldn't go through the needles on a consistent basis, resulting in poor productivity. Because production had low productivity, it didn't achieve a favorable production variance. I had a favorable purchase price variance, but it came at the cost of manufacturing productivity. Needless to say, I got chewed out and was told to never do that again.

To avoid this happening in your company, do the following:

1. Assign the same performance measurements to all supply-chain managers.
2. Clearly communicate what the performance measurements are.
3. Assign metrics that are realistic and achievable.
4. Provide the tools and resources necessary to help achieve performance measurements.
5. Monitor performance on a consistent basis; don't wait until the end of the quarter or year to let them know how they are doing.

> **TIP #7: *Pick a team, establish goals and objectives, benchmark where you are, and identify shared performance measurements. Communicate this to everyone.***

In the case of Woodstock, none of the Harmony Team members are inventory experts per se, except maybe Jack. The team is not skewed to one particular silo. You may have also noticed that several important links are missing from the Harmony Team. As I have said earlier, there are too many links to have them all represented on the team, and not all supply-chain managers will fit the criteria discussed earlier in this chapter.

Thus far, Woodstock has done a good job of benchmarking where it is and selecting a team to rightsize its inventory. What they have not done yet, and what you will learn in later chapters, is to set specific numeric goals and objectives. It has stated that it has to rightsize its inventory, but it has not clearly defined it in terms of numbers. I believe this is the next step in the process. Knowing where it is and picking the team were necessary steps before establishing specific goals. Too often management sets inventory goals without having a plan in place to accomplish the objectives.

Woodstock started the year with $40 million worth of inventory. The Harmony Team's plan is to:

1. Understand the role and responsibilities of all links in the supply chain
2. Understand the inventory-related problems in each link
3. Educate all employees on points one and two
4. Establish specific inventory goals and objectives
5. Constantly communicate upstream and downstream in the supply chain
6. Use the appropriate tools, techniques, and technologies to rightsize inventory

You will note that establishing specific goals and objectives is mentioned as the fourth step in the process. Realistically, you must understand the roles and problems within each link before you can correctly rightsize inventory. Many inventory experts say that a focused effort on rightsizing inventory will result in an inventory reduction of 25 to 40 percent over the course of the effort. I too, agree with this statement. However, because Woodstock is like so many small companies with limited resources, a more realistic goal would be a 15 to 20 percent reduction in total inventory, along with a gradual shift of inventory location in the supply chain. This would equate to an inventory reduction of $6 million to $8 million in the first year — a good start.

> **TIP #8: *Delegate authority, accountability, and responsibility to those who can best accomplish the task of rightsizing inventory in the supply chain.***

Adriana, the president of Woodstock, has clearly defined who is responsible and accountable (all supply-chain managers) and has delegated the responsibility to Joe and the Harmony Team. The team members were selected because management believes they are the ones who can best accomplish the effort. What's left unsaid is that while management has done this, it is their responsibility to support the team in whatever is necessary for it to accomplish its goals. The key points here are:

1. Remove politics when selecting the team.
2. Pick people who can best accomplish the effort.
3. Management must provide support and encouragement.
4. The team should be prepared to spend 25 to 35 percent of its workday on the effort.
5. The daily operating environment cannot suffer because of the effort.
6. Team members should delegate their daily workload where possible.

> **TIP #9: *Rightsizing inventory is not "just another project" with a start date and an end date; it has to become a new way of life for the company.***

TIP #9 may be one of the most difficult TIPS to implement. A manufacturing company is a dynamic environment. People leave, get fired, or move on to another position in the company. The company could be bought or buy another company. There are too many variables to mention. Here are some points to remember:

1. Seek small successes.
2. If someone leaves the team, replace him or her immediately.

3. Publicize successes.
4. Recognize team members, supply-chain managers, and employees for their efforts.
5. Keep all employees informed.

> **TIP #10:** *Start rightsizing your inventory by aligning your inventory levels to match your inventory strategies by product or division classifications.*

> **TIP #11:** *Gather inventory data by type, location, and business segment. Compare it to the corporate inventory strategy. Any inconsistency in inventory and strategy must be addressed and corrected.*

A good place to start your inventory rightsizing efforts is to align your physical inventory to your inventory strategy. This is so obvious, yet many companies miss this one. These TIPS focus on the inventory you already have. We know it exists — but does the inventory location match your strategy? That is the question we are trying to address here. The ideal environment would be to have no inventory, and buy it and make it as needed. But we have a long way to go to get there.

A good example of a mismatch is the $4 million of inventory that exists in the Beacon Light Division. The strategy here is make-to-order or engineer-to-order, yet 50 percent of the inventory for this division is in finished goods. Only $.5 million has been identified with finished goods for Field Service. This point could have been missed if we just looked at the fact that only 13 percent of the finished goods inventory was for the Beacon Light Division. What Woodstock should do is focus its efforts on reducing or eliminating the Beacon Light Division finished goods inventory. This exercise would show you where to spend your limited resources. The key points are:

1. Do not spend a great deal of time on this exercise.
2. Look for the obvious mismatches in alignment and focus your efforts in rightsizing those inventories.
3. Find the root cause as to why the inventory is in the wrong form, and implement a policy to prevent it from getting out of alignment again.
4. Publish monthly reports that show inventory location and value.

> **TIP #12:** *Inventory is considered an asset on the company balance sheet. Inventory is a liability if you have more*

than you need to satisfy immediate customer requirements.

This TIP addresses the philosophy of carrying inventory and speaks to the whole inventory rightsizing effort. The entire effort begs the question, "Do we need this inventory?"

> **TIP #13:** *The perfect order must be considered from both the viewpoints of the seller and the buyer. The perfect order criteria must be measurable so that deviations can be corrected.*

The perfect order is defined earlier in this chapter. The seller's criteria are as important as the customer's. The key points to address here are:

1. Understand how the customer is measuring your company.
2. Understand what is important to your company.
3. Develop measurable criteria and publish it to all employees.
4. Constantly measure your company's performance against both criteria.
5. Establish flags in your process that alert everyone to unsatisfactory performance.
6. Establish action plans to bring the performance measurement back in line.

> **TIP #14:** *Successful supply chains have one characteristic in common; their ability to rapidly respond to change throughout their entire supply chain, not just one or two links in the chain.*

Your ability to respond to changes in supply and demand will be one of your keys to success. There are several key points to address:

1. Measure your current lead times and throughput times in each link of your supply chain.
2. Communicate this to all links in your chain.
3. Benchmark the best practices for each link of known successful supply chains.
4. Establish improvement goals for each link.
5. Work toward improving each link to meet these goals.
6. Sustain the improvements.

TIP #15: *A supply chain is only as strong as its weakest link; being world class in one link does you little good if your other links are weak.*

Identify the weakest link in your supply chain, and improve it. Once you have improved that link, another link will become your weakest link. Identify it and improve it. Continue this process on an ongoing basis. To identify your weakest link, look for the link that has:

1. The most inventory
2. The longest cumulative lead time
3. The longest throughput time
4. The poorest customer (internal and external) satisfaction
5. The worst comparison to a best-practice company

TIP #16: *Define the perfect order criteria and measure them. Communicate this to everyone in the supply chain.*

Seek to understand how the customer is measuring their satisfaction level of doing business with your company. Equally important, understand how the stakeholders in your company are measuring your success. You can meet the external customer's expectations 100 percent, but if your company is not meeting your stakeholder's expectations, you won't be in business very long and satisfying customers becomes a moot point. The perfect order criteria defined in this chapter should be compared to your performance, and where mismatches occur, every effort should be made to correct them.

Table 1.7 and Table 1.8 account for the inventory movement related to the topics covered in this chapter along with normal inventory fluctuations. They will be updated at the end of each chapter based on the application of the tips, tools, techniques, and philosophies learned.

Table 1.7 Inventory Starting Baseline (×1,000,000)

Month end	January 31
Forecast	7.2
Orders	5.8
Total starting inventory	40.0
Start FG inventory	15.5
+Production @COGS	4.1
–Shipments @COGS	3.9
End FG inventory	15.7
Start WIP inventory	7.5
+Material issues	3.4
+Labor and overhead	0.8
–Production @COGS	4.1
End WIP inventory	7.6
Start raw inventory	17.0
+Material purchases	4.1
–Material issues	3.4
End raw inventory	17.7
Total ending inventory	41.0

Table 1.8 Total Inventory Target (×1,000,000)

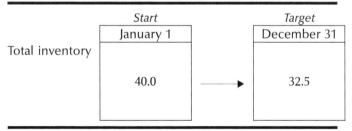

	Start	*Target*
	January 1	December 31
Total inventory	40.0	32.5

Chapter 2

Is the Customer Always Right?

February 14, Harmony Team Meeting
Woodstock Inventory: $41 Million

My name is Maria and I am manager of customer service at Woodstock Lighting Group.

I have been here ten years and it isn't getting any easier. Joe is one pain in the neck and has the personality of a rock. He needs to think before he acts and goes off on one of his tangents. I don't know how Eddie, Cyndie, and the rest of his people can stand him. I'm glad he isn't at the meeting. He would be disruptive and try to show everyone how smart he is. Thank goodness for Adriana and Arnie. They make a good buffer for us, and I'm glad they are involved. I hope this meeting doesn't take long. I've got a date later with a new guy I met the other night, and he is really neat. I want to get out of here on time, so that I can go home and change before my date. He's taking me to a new restaurant I've heard about but never been to.

Maybe I should go back into sales. I've heard through the grapevine that they are changing the sales compensation plan and it is going to be more attractive to sales people. When I was in sales I didn't have to deal with the internal politics or other self-serving nonsense. I find managing people to be a challenge today. Everyone here is under pressure and has too much work to get done. They get cranky and irritable at the most trivial of things. I think we should have classes here on stress management. Maybe

45

I'll talk to Human Resources about it. I know I could use it! Oh well, speaking of stress, I should get back to work.

Is the Customer Always Right?

No. The customer isn't always right. I can speak with authority because I am a customer and I know I'm not always right. I remember not long ago, my husband and I bought an exercise machine. It was one of those deals where it was noted that "some assembly was required." We've all been there, right? You guessed it. I got to the end of the job (five hours later) and had two pieces left over. I didn't have a clue where they were supposed to go. We spent another hour reviewing the instructions and I'll be darned if we could figure it out. I called the customer service number and actually got to speak to a real person. I started venting and complaining that the instructions were poorly written and that they omitted part of the instructions.

The customer service representative calmly asked me the model number and I gave it to him. He politely informed me that those parts were for a different model number. He went on to say that they pre-packaged a kit of parts that could be used on various models and that the two parts were to be used if we had purchased another model. He pointed out that this was written at the very top of the assembly instruction sheet. In our excitement to put the machine together, we quickly scanned the instruction sheet and had missed the part about the different model numbers. So, I was a customer and I was wrong. We don't like to publicly say it; we whisper it among ourselves. Some of our customers should only know what we say about them behind their backs. However, in the business world, we wouldn't be in business long if we took the position that the customer isn't always right. We should always keep an open mind and address any customer complaint from the viewpoint that customers are right, and most of the time they are. Satisfying our customer's needs is one of two reasons we are in business; the second is to make a profit for our stakeholders.

> **TIP #17: The customer isn't always right, but if you want to keep customers, you should do all you can to satisfy their requirements in a professional, businesslike manner.**

(Note: TIP = team important point.)

We live in an age of decreasing customer loyalty, increasing customer choices, deregulation, changing competitive boundaries, and "stealth -

like" Internet competitors. To stay ahead of the curve, we must become customer focused and willing to maximize the gathering and sharing of customer knowledge.

As we are in the business of providing products and services to our customers we have to get it right the first time. Our customers expect the products (inventory) we ship them to meet their expectations. They expect to receive the right product, in the right quality, in the right quantity, at the right time. Not too much to ask, is it? No, it is not. So every time we don't meet customer expectations, they get upset and we face the potential of losing a customer. It is hard enough trying to get new customers, so it is criminal to lose one we already have.

Know Your Customer — Keep Your Customer

It's very competitive out there today, and customers demand value for their money. If we don't provide value, they will go to another supply chain that will. Customer expectations have risen to a level where they require instantaneous information about their order and they expect delivery of our products in days, not weeks. Knowing what our customers want is an order qualifier today; anticipating their needs is an order winner. Order qualifiers are providing a quality product/service at the right price and at the right time. Without these order qualifiers, we can't even get into the game. On the other hand, an order winner is some characteristic that causes customers to buy our products/services, rather than someone else's.

> **TIP #18:** *Understanding the customers' needs is a good thing, but anticipating your customers' needs is an order winner that will help you sell more inventory.*

Let's discuss a few key attributes of customer expectations today. First of all, they expect us to be extremely flexible, respond to new orders quickly, and respond to changes in existing orders quickly. They may ask us to move an order in or ask us to delay an order and move it further out into the future. They may increase the order quantity or decrease the order quantity. The bottom line is we must become very flexible in our manufacturing and distribution links. We have to become customer literate. *Customer literacy* is knowing all we can about our customers. Some companies call this *customer intimacy*. It goes beyond looking at the internal quantitative data we have about our customers and what they have bought from us in the past.

Customer literacy is knowing what new products they have in development, what products they are phasing out of their product lines, and what their inventory strategy is for the future. We should be working with them on new product designs. Customer literacy is knowing their general business health. Do we even know if a major customer is in financial trouble? If our management knows, they certainly aren't telling us. I'm a customer service manager and my performance metric is based on accurately processing customer orders and answering their questions about the status of their orders.

I spend eight to ten hours a day on the phone with customers or other links in our supply chain, getting information and passing it on to our customers. I would love to anticipate our customers' needs and become proactive. The worse part of my job is dealing with our internal marketing and sales organization. They are even more demanding than the customers, and often quite rude. As I've known many of the customers for years, they call me up directly to get answers to their questions rather than contacting their sales representative. The sales reps get upset and don't like this. They want to be the ones talking to their customers, except of course, if the information going to the customer is "bad news"; then they are very happy we are the ones talking to the customer.

We waste a lot of time telling the sales reps what we already told the customer. There have been instances when the customer is given two different answers to the same question; this is a big problem and must stop. It confuses the customer, wastes their time and ours. This is a very good example of working as individual silos rather than one collaborative network. I strongly suggest that the Harmony Team work with us and the sales force to establish an operating policy and procedure that presents a clear and direct line of communication with our customers. We should consider providing every customer with a Woodstock company directory of who to contact for certain information. This will free up our sales force to focus on satisfying our customer's future needs, rather than on issues related to past and current sales.

The Customer's Customer

I have been talking a lot about the customer, but who is our customer? Is it the company we sell to or the person who uses our product? If you look at our three divisions, we have different definitions of who the customer is, and we need to understand this. Table 2.1 shows an example of our expanded supply chain. In the case of the flashlight division, our customers are distributors, and their customers are retail stores. The retail stores sell to the end users, who are downstream in our supply chain. Taking this a step further, when a product is scrapped, the recycling

Table 2.1   The Customer's Customer

Division	Our Customer	Our Customer's Customer
Flashlight	Distributors	Retail stores, independents, and chains
Spotlights	Municipalities	Health and safety professionals
	Entertainment industry	Event/trade show professionals
	Vehicle modifiers	Health and safety professionals
	Building contractors	Home/commercial building developers/owners
Beacon Lights	Governments	Lighthouse operators

company is further downstream. In some cases, the recycled material comes back to us as a raw material, closing the loop; interesting how that works.

Our strategy and planning must go beyond identifying our customers' needs. We must look at the ultimate end users of our products and get as much input about them and their marketplaces as we can. Including our customer's customer in our supply-chain planning is often called the *extended supply chain*. Figure 2.1 is a simplified version of our supply chain and looks like any other supply chain. However, Figure 2.2 is an example of our extended supply chain for the Flashlight Division.

A large part of understanding customer requirements will involve recognizing the trends, economics, and other market forces that impact the end user. We sell flashlights to distributors, who sell to stores, who in turn sell to consumers like you and me. We need to understand who

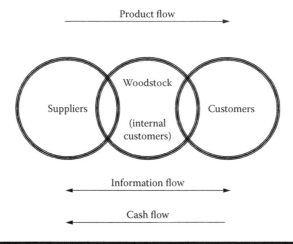

Figure 2.1   Woodstock supply chain.

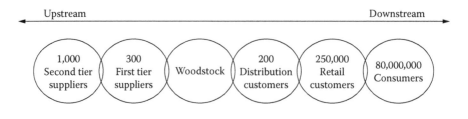

Figure 2.2 Flashlights supply chain.

our customers are, and we need to understand why the consumer is buying flashlights. Is it for emergency use? Are they going camping? On average, how many flashlights does the consumer own? We sell millions of flashlights. Are people replacing them or did they lose them?

Think about your personal life. Pens and umbrellas come to mind. I mean, come on, how many pens or umbrellas do you need? The truth of the matter is we probably buy these products because we have lost perfectly good ones. I think this applies to flashlights as well. We also need to understand what the end users like or dislike about our products. Their input will be important as we design new products. I don't know the exact numbers, but let's say, for example, that we sell 120 million flashlights a year to 200 distributors, who sell them to 250,000 independent and chain retail stores, who then sell them to 80 million end users.

Referring back to Figure 2.2, if we include all customers in the extended supply chain, the number of customers increases dramatically. So instead of 200 customers, we have 80 million customers. That's a great deal of customers. We can't possibly know why all the end users bought flashlights or how they like or dislike our products. I know that our marketing folks conduct surveys and have end user focus groups to look at this. In Figure 2.2, the extended supply chain shows only one link in the chain for Woodstock, and this link, as shown in Figure 2.3, is made up of many internal links that represent our total enterprise.

The challenge for us is to balance all these elements across both our internal supply chain and external supply chain. Is it reasonable to assume that you can have different supply chains for different product lines? The answer is a resounding yes! For example, spotlights for the emergency vehicle market are shipped directly to the end users and bypass the distribution centers. Spotlights for the residential and commercial marketplaces are shipped to our distributors, who in turn ship to the end users. Flashlights have a different supply chain. Our plant ships to our distribution centers, which then ship to the distribution centers of large chains, or in the case of small local retail stores, they make direct shipments to the stores.

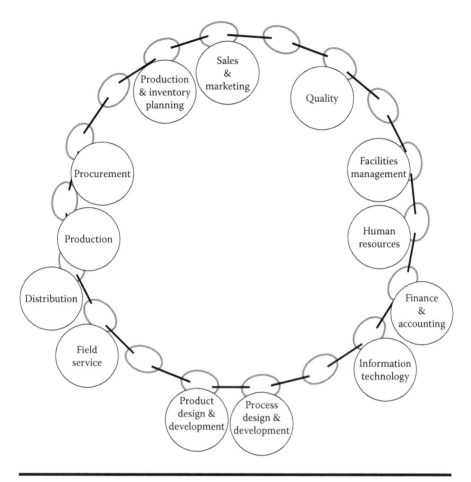

Figure 2.3   Woodstock internal supply-chain links.

If you look at our Spotlight Division, economic trends and predictions may be helpful when planning our inventory strategy. For example, one of our customer groups for this division consists of home and commercial builders. There is a great deal of data on new home/building sales, and trends that will be helpful in planning our inventory strategy for this customer group. If loan interest rates go down and new construction goes up, then there is a good chance we will sell more to these customers. On the other hand, if loan interest rates go up and new construction goes down, we may sell less to these customers. However, we may increase sales in the aftermarket by selling spotlights to customers who are remodeling their kitchens or bathrooms. These are good examples of why we need to understand and include our customer's customers in our extended supply-chain planning process.

TIP #19: *We must present ourselves as one united, collaborative supply-chain network to our customers and establish clearly defined lines of communication with them.*

I would like to understand our customer's inventory processing flow better. I don't know how they process and manage the inventory once it arrives at their dock. I would love to visit some of our customer sites and tour their facilities. I would love to meet with personnel in some of their links such as purchasing, material planning, and warehousing. It's ironic that my title is customer service and I don't know much about the customer at all. Typically, the only contact I have with the customers is with their purchasing agents and expeditors. I do, however, know a lot about our sales reps. I am personal friends with some of them, and they tell me they have no time to focus on the future. They are motivated by selling today's products, and as much of them as possible. A significant part of their salary is commission based, and if they don't sell now, they don't get any money now. It's all about this week, this month, and this quarter. Either the company has to change the salary structure in our sales link or find other people at Woodstock who can take the long-term view of customer literacy.

Have you ever wondered about all that "junk mail" you get in your snail mail and all that spam in your e-mail folder? We provide this information. How do we do this? With all those airline loyalty cards, credit cards, magazine subscriptions, Internet site visits, and yes, even your discount card at the grocery store. We lug these cards around, do all the work, and spend all the money. This allows companies to build databases about us, our preferences, and buying patterns. Right or wrong isn't the point, they just do it. It's called customer literacy.

TIP #20: *Know as much as possible about your customer: their needs, wants, problems, plans, and who else they buy from.*

Customer Relationship Management

Technology is available today that can help us achieve some level of customer literacy. Customer relationship management (CRM) is both computer software and a business philosophy. Let's stick with business philosophy. The whole idea is to know as much as possible about your customers. The objective of CRM is to know who your customers are and what their needs are, as well as to anticipate their future needs. The concept is to integrate all the information about a customer that each of our supply-chain links has. That includes such links as finance, sales, marketing, and all the others. In fact, there is a wealth of customer information in our field service link. Has anyone ever asked them what the customers are saying or doing? From a philosophical point of view, our sales link must shift from a product focus to a customer focus. We must know what our customer's plans are. We have to gather comprehensive information, not just data. We need to personalize every transaction and communication with the customer. In fact, the sales link should take people from the other links out to visit customers. We can turn data about customers into meaningful information by:

- Analyzing the data and developing customer needs by using proven analytical techniques and sound business models
- Benchmarking what our competitors are doing
- Finding out how our customers measure inventory (strategy, levels)
- Finding out what inventory measurement standards are used for their industry: Standard Industry Classification (SIC) codes
- Implementing enabling technologies (software)
- Disseminating customer insights learned throughout our supply chain
- Constantly talking to the customer

In fact, you should have customers on the Harmony Team. I'm a little surprised you haven't done it already. I know Joe and Adriana are visiting some key customers and suppliers, but that isn't going to tell us the whole story. They are probably only talking to other executives at their level. This won't give them the true picture of what's really going on with the customer. There is a downside to focusing on "too much data and too little information." We have to be careful not to get lost in the trees and not see the forest. Information and data are a good start, but we need to see the big picture. It's important to point out that as we are gathering information about our customers, they in turn are gathering information about us. This information transfer goes both ways. In this case, we are talking about supplier relationship management (SRM). Figure 2.4 shows the relationship of CRM and SRM in a typical supply-chain network.

With the advent of the Internet, a new reality has established itself: electronic customer relationship management (e-CRM), or as some people call it, E-business. This is software that tracks mouse click streams and has been designed to predict what customers will want before they know what they want. A company can go straight to a customer and suggest a particular product rather than sending out millions of solicitations to potential customers. If you have ever bought anything from a major online catalog retailer, you have experienced this. If you go to purchase something and they are out of inventory, they will suggest a similar product. What's also

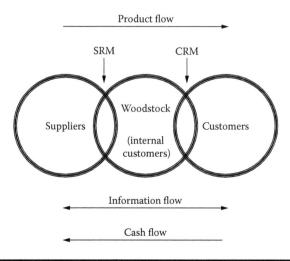

Figure 2.4 SRM and CRM in the supply chain.

neat about this is if an item is out of stock, they will tell you when it will be in inventory. Another example of e-CRM is online book stores. If you purchase a book, they will suggest other similar books by that author or about that topic. They will even tell you what other books people have purchased along with that book. This is inventory management at its best.

> TIP #21: *A successful supply chain knows its customers well and can anticipate their inventory needs. In some cases, it may be an inventory need that they don't recognize they have.*

Example of Inventory and e-CRM Working Together

A friend of mine provides a good example of inventory and e-CRM working together quite well. He has a horizontal supply chain with one supplier (who ships directly to the end user), himself (as the lone salesperson), and 2000 customers (end users). I call this a "virtual supply chain" and he calls it a "virtual franchise" (I like his term better). His whole food nutrition product line consists of fruit, vegetable, and grain products that are inventoried (condensed) into capsule, chewable, and gummy (for children) forms, a convenient and inexpensive way for any of us, age two through the elderly, to ensure we get our suggested number of fruit and vegetable servings each day.

My friend's role in this supply chain is to educate people on better preventive health from eating more fruits and vegetables. (I can hear my mother just as if it were today: "Eat your vegetables or no dessert. They're good for you.") The supplier does everything else. The supplier outsourcers the growing of fruits and vegetables (to farmers) and the manufacturing process of converting the fruits and vegetables into consumable format. The supplier then does everything else: storing, picking, packing, shipping (to the end user), billing, and collection. After the initial sale, the consumer can place orders directly with the supplier over the Internet. In fact, sometimes my friend isn't involved at all.

If a consumer hears about the product somewhere and visits the supplier Web site to place an order, my friend will get credit for the sale if it is in his territory. The supplier sets up an agreed-upon shipping schedule with the consumer. My friend gets credit for the sale, and on a monthly basis a commission check is electronically deposited into his checking account. Let's review this process once again:

■ He may or may not have direct contact with the customer.
■ He doesn't need to place orders with the supplier.
■ He doesn't see, own, or physically handle the inventory.
■ He doesn't need to keep track of the shipments.
■ He doesn't do billing or collection.
■ Commission checks are electronically transferred to his account.
■ He gets a commission statement once a month itemizing transactions related to his territory.

In theory, he could take a trip around the world and return a year later to a satisfied customer base, a satisfied supplier base, a satisfied stakeholder (himself), and a satisfied employee (also himself), completing the trifecta of the perfect order from the seller's point of view. Wow, was I impressed! Realistically, he wouldn't be in business long if he did ignore his supplier and customers for a year.

In summary, he has virtual inventory available at his disposal 24 hours a day, 7 days a week. This allows him the opportunity to succeed in direct proportion to the time he spends telling prospective clients about the benefits of his products. The Internet has become the crucial vehicle in enabling and accelerating the flow of inventory into and out of the supply chain.

Allowing Customers Access to Our Inventory Information

Something we might consider if we take an e-CRM approach is to have a two-way sharing of inventory information with our customers. Although it's important to know what inventory items a customer bought, it's equally important to understand what was used and how much is left in stock. Regarding our inventory, we could allow certain customers to access our inventory information system so that they can see what items we have in stock, available for sale.

We could take this a step further and let them access our master production schedule (MPS), so they can see what our manufacturing plans are. Of course, there is some danger in doing this. For one thing, if they see we have a lot of inventory on one particular item, they might not give us an order for it right away, seeing that we have so much. Another danger would be if they see we have a lot of inventory, they might try to see if they can get it at a discount because "they are doing us a favor." We could, of course, not show inventory quantity and simply say "available" or "not available." The big online retailers do this. If you are filling up a shopping cart, they will indicate "in stock" or "not in stock."

In the case of our Spotlight Division, I'm not sure how well this will work. I can see it working well for our spare parts sold to lighthouses through our Beacon Light Division and in our Flashlight Division. The way it works today is the customer will either call me up or contact the sales representative to find out if something is in stock. Sometimes, we play telephone tag, and if they don't get us right away, they could be contacting our competition. We'll never know if this is happening unless we can find a way of tracking this issue. One other point I want to make is if we do this with our spare/replacement parts, we would have to implement a standard operating policy (SOP). If a customer sees that we have inventory, would they have to call to request it? What happens if two different customers access the inventory data and both want it? If we give it to one customer what happens to the other? Can we have them electronically reserve it? We will have to work out the details and implement an SOP and maybe modify our computer software to take care of these concerns.

Asking Our Customers to Allow Us Access to Their Inventory Information

The other side of the coin is asking our customers to allow us access to their inventory and production information. Our salespeople would love this. From a salesperson's perspective it could save a lot of time and even help them anticipate customer needs, just as the CRM philosophy suggests. They could then spend their time looking into all of those other matters I talked about, such as finding out what their inventory strategy is and what new products they are working on. If we anticipate their inventory needs, we could let our planning and demand management links know, so that they can take that information under consideration as they develop their plans. Let's take it a step further and ask to see their production plans.

Most of our customers use materials requirements planning (MRP) software, and their planning horizon goes out for at least six months, if not longer. What great insight that would give us! I'm getting excited just thinking about it. I know a large manufacturing concern, not in our industry, that provides its suppliers with MRP output. Every Monday morning, the firm makes its MRP output available to its suppliers to see. All suppliers are given a password that gives them access to all the items the manufacturer buys from them. In this case, the MRP planning horizon goes out eighteen months. The suppliers can print this out and distribute it to all their supply-chain links so that everyone knows what the customer is doing and plans to do for the next eighteen months.

> **TIP #22:** *Don't keep inventory information a secret. Share it with your customers. Ask your customers to share their inventory information with you.*

When the Harmony Team meets with the other links, I hope you will discuss this topic with them. In the meantime, I'll talk with the powers that be in the sales link, get some input from them, and see if they will explore it with their customers. I know I will. In fact, as soon as I leave this meeting, I'm going to start making some calls. I'll provide feedback to Arnie, and if you like, I'll come back again to discuss it after I get a feel for how well this will fly. In fact, I know Rudy, our vice president of sales and marketing, is making a major effort to have our flashlights sold in one of the largest retail store chains in the world. This chain provides inventory data access right down to the shelf level in its stores. With their point-of-sale technology they can tell us in real time when an item is sold. They are making a big push to have suppliers use radio frequency identification (RFID) so that they can track inventory into and out of their stores, or for that matter, anywhere in their supply chain. Boy, talk about customer literacy, this is great stuff! Oh well, let's move on to another area of "Know Your Customer — Keep Your Customer."

Inventory Attributes of Customer Expectations

I understand that last week Arnie described the perfect order from the customer's perspective; that's good. I know this because after your meeting, you and Arnie sent out the minutes of the meeting to all supply-chain managers, and my boss in turn sent them to me. That's great communication. I hope you continue to keep everyone informed. Let's categorize customer expectations of the perfect order into five areas:

- Time
- Service
- Speed
- Flexibility
- Price

It should be noted that quality is not mentioned as a separate customer expectation. It goes without saying that the customer expects quality products and service. Without quality in all we do, we would soon be out of business. Because we have been around since 1942, I have to believe we are doing some things right, but if you listen to many people at Woodstock, you wouldn't think so.

> **TIP #23:** *Lead time is defined differently for each link in your supply chain. The most important definition is related to customer order lead time: from the time they ask you to ship the inventory until they receive the inventory.*

Time

On the surface, you would think that time and speed should be combined into one customer expectation. But there are differences. For example, if the customer requests that you ship the order three weeks from now and you comply, getting it there exactly three weeks later, then you were "on time." You can measure time. However, if the customer says ship the order as soon as possible, then we are talking about speed. This is a subtle but important distinction. Arnie told you the customer expects the order to be shipped and received on time, and this is true. In reality, the customer doesn't really care when you ship it, but he or she does care that it arrived at the site at the time requested. This is an important point. Lead time, although a simple concept, can be quite different for each of our three divisions. Our supply chain needs to understand this difference. Inventory in our supply chain has to be treated differently for each of our divisions. We can't take this customer metric lightly. All customers measure on-time delivery. Some customers measure it in more detail than others. There is a big difference between cumulative supply-chain lead time and customer delivery lead time. Cumulative supply-chain lead time deals with all those activities that have to be accomplished to make our product available to be shipped.

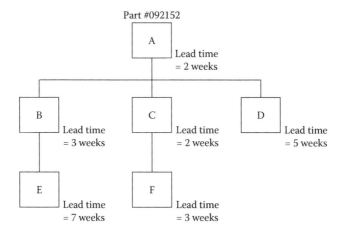

Figure 2.5 Cumulative manufacturing lead time.

Our Materials Management link is concerned with the longest cumulative lead time necessary to make a product available for shipment. For example, the longest cumulative manufacturing lead time of product number 092152 depicted in Figure 2.5 is shown as 12 weeks. That is, 7 weeks for part #E, 3 weeks for part #B, and 2 more weeks for part #A: 7 + 3 + 2 = 12 weeks.

If our planning horizon (the amount of time our plan extends into the future) only goes out 11 weeks, we would miss purchasing part #E in a timely manner. Unless we had safety stock of the component, part #E, we would be asking our supplier to expedite it. To make matters worse, we may have to pay a premium for the part and also may incur air freight charges. Knowing our cumulative lead time is important. Keep in mind that our customers only care about delivery lead time and not cumulative lead time. *Delivery lead time* is defined as the period from the time they give us the order until they receive it.

As demanding as customers can be, they are also reasonable. Some customers give their suppliers what is known as a delivery lead time window. For example, I know of one customer who uses a 15-day lead time window. An order is considered on time if it is received anywhere from 10 days early to 5 days late. This gives the supplier a 15-day window to be considered on time. In the long run, shipping 10 days early means we can bill our customer earlier and (hopefully) get paid 10 days earlier. The customer may also measure different product lines separately using the same criteria. They may define parts as A, B, or C, with As being the most important and Cs being the least important. Then they will grade the supplier accordingly. It may look something like this:

A parts: 20 shipments, 18 on time and 2 not on time, 90

B parts: 15 shipments, 10 on time and 5 not on time, 67

C parts: 18 shipments, 14 on time and 4 not on time, 78

On the surface, it looks like we are doing well (not great) on As and poorly on Bs and Cs. But the customer may apply a weighting factor and apply more weight to As and less weight to Bs and Cs. In the example cited previously, the supplier may receive a poor grade on As and a better grade on Bs and Cs.

> **TIP #24: We need to understand not only what inventory metrics our customers are using but also how they are using (calculating) it.**

Service

On-time delivery isn't the only attribute our customers are looking for. As Arnie mentioned, the perfect order has many service metrics, including having the correct paperwork, shipping in the correct container, and a clearly defined reverse logistics policy. We should be concerned about all four stages of service:

1. **Stage one — presales:** They expect our sales representatives to be well informed about the characteristics of our products and to quote achievable delivery dates. They expect to get instantaneous answers to their questions. Today we do this pretty well.
2. **Stage two — order placement and fulfillment:** After they give us an order they expect us to follow up and ensure that it is delivered on time. If we are going to be late, we should let them know and give them a new delivery date. They also expect us (and this is key) to honor any changes to the order that they require. We must be able to respond to any change requested by the customer. Today we are not good at this.
3. **Stage three — postsales:** This is after shipment follow-up. Today, we are terrible at this; especially our Flashlight Division. We don't have a procedure in place to follow up on how well our overall service was to our customer. Our sales representative may ask the customer if everything was all right with the shipment, but this is

done on an adhoc basis, with no formal feedback to other links in our chain except, "we shipped the order on time."

4. **Stage four — post postsales:** By this I mean, don't just follow up on particular shipments. Follow up on overall customer satisfaction with the entire order experience. What did we do wrong? How can we make it better? What did you like about the experience? Too often companies stop at stage three. The bottom line is: Are you really asking what we have to do to get more of your business? Stage four closes the loop so that we can enter the cycle at stage one again.

> **TIP #25:** *All stages of the sales cycle are equally important and should be measured throughout the entire supply chain.*

Speed

I alluded to the difference between an on-time and speedy response when I discussed on-time delivery. Speed is also measurable. It deals with how quickly we can react to something in our supply chain. Examples of speed include the following:

- How quickly can we ship a new order?
- How quickly can we give the customer or our suppliers information?
- How quickly can we design a new product?
- How quickly can our service department respond to a customer emergency?
- How quickly can our maintenance department respond to an unplanned machine downtime?
- How quickly can we ramp up production?
- How quickly can we ramp down production?

All of these are measurements of speed. World-class supply chains recognize that speed is an important differentiator for customers. All these attributes of speed are measurable. How many of them do we measure here at Woodstock, two or three? Who outside of the link measuring it knows what our performance in that area is?

Flexibility

It is difficult to separate speed and flexibility. They go hand in hand. For example, you would gain flexibility by cross-training the workforce on the factory floor, so that a person becomes skilled in knowing how to operate different types of machines. Being able to shift people around to different machines would give you flexibility in your capacity and capabilities. How quickly you respond to change, and move those people to other machines, would be the speed aspect of this attribute. Another example would be related to machine setup time. Machine setup time can be defined as the time the last piece of a part is made until the first piece of the next part is made. In other words, the amount of time needed to change a machine over from making part A to making part B. You can measure this as speed. But it does you little good to be very quick (speed) if you don't have an operator available to run the machine (flexibility).

Price

So far in this section we have discussed four major attributes of customer expectations: time, service, speed, and flexibility. All four are equally important, but it is the fifth attribute that ties it all together: price. You can have short lead times, speedy delivery, great service, and incredible flexibility, but if you can't provide all that at a reasonable price, the customer will look somewhere else. We live in a global economy. That means there is a great deal of competition out there looking to sell their inventory to our customers. If we can't offer our inventory at a reasonable price, our competition will take business from us. Because of the number of competitors offering similar products, we are not in a position to raise our selling prices on our products. We have to look at reducing our costs as a means of becoming profitable. The formula is simple:

Profit = Revenue costs

If you take costs as a category and look at cost of goods sold (COGS) as shown in Table 2.2, you will see that material cost is the largest component of COGS. In our case, material cost is 55 percent of COGS.

**Table 2.2   Woodstock
Cost of Goods Sold**

Category	Percentage
Material	55
Labor	15
Overhead	30
Total	100

This is an area we need to address, but I'm not going to discuss this now. We have other people more qualified than me who can give you input on this. I am only making the point that we must look to reduce our costs so that we can maintain/reduce our selling price to make a profit — something we haven't done for a couple of years.

Inventory Attributes of Woodstock Expectations

The five inventory attributes of customer expectations must be balanced against the three inventory attributes of Woodstock expectations:

- Customer satisfaction: We have met all 12 expectations of the customer's definition of the perfect order.
- Stakeholder satisfaction: The order was profitable to the company.
- Employee satisfaction: Processing the customer order was an enjoyable experience for employees.

Similar to the five attributes of customer expectations, the three attributes of the company expectations can be measured as well. There must be synergy between the customer and company measurements. What good will it do us to get a perfect score on a customer order if we lose money on every order and our employee turnover rate is 30 annually? I'm exaggerating. Actually, our employee turnover rate is quite low. It's somewhere around 10. The customer order is a contract, and similar to every contract there must be a benefit/reward for both parties.

The Balanced Scorecard

In 1992, Drs. Robert S. Kaplan and David Norton introduced the Balanced Scorecard (BSC). This tool can be used to measure supply-chain performance in different areas of the supply chain. What's unique about the BSC is that it offers a "balanced" perspective of supply-chain performance based on four elements:

1. **Customer:** This aspect offers a perspective of how the customer views our performance and looks at on-time delivery performance, satisfaction with customer service, and customer-related reliability issues.
2. **Financial:** Making money is not going out of style soon, it is still a key performance metric, and it is included as one of the four elements of BSC.

3. **Business process:** This element focuses on measuring such supply-chain goals as productivity gains, elimination of waste, and response time.
4. **Innovation and learning:** This element deals with product and process innovations and can include formal training programs for company personnel.

The BSC is a good set of metrics that we can use to measure our overall supply-chain performance. You should discuss this with Adriana as a tool we can use to measure our performance in the future. I realize that management will want aggregate performance measurements, and operations will want detailed item (physical) measurements. I believe we can use BSC to satisfy both areas. This will help us keep our Woodstock goals and objectives aligned with our customer goals and objectives.

We don't want to learn the hard way as one major equipment maker did. In 2001, it declared an inventory write-off of $2.5 billion of surplus raw materials (scrap), one of the largest inventory write-offs ever in the United States. This was a case of the customers and their suppliers not aligning their goals and objectives into one collaborative supply-chain network. There's an old saying that pops into my head every once in a while. I don't know who said it. If I did I would give them credit. One thing is for sure, it wasn't me. Let me present it as a TIP:

> **TIP #26:** *It's nice to know how good we are; we have to know how bad we are.*

Inventory Life Cycle and the Customer

Inventory is like a living and breathing entity. It's born (created), it grows, it matures, it ages, and alas at some point it dies (becomes obsolete). The six stages of the classic inventory life cycle are depicted in Figure 2.6. The customer should play an important role at every stage of the product life cycle.

Development Stage

First, let me identify the customer, who plays a very important role in this stage — not only the external customer who buys our product, but the internal one as well. This includes all 19 major links in our supply chain. However, let's start with the external customer. The customer should be involved at the very beginning and be part of our product development team. Who better knows what the end user is looking for in a product

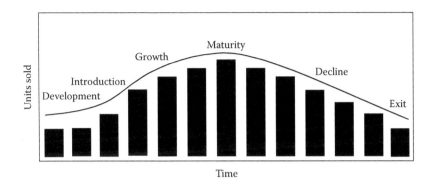

Figure 2.6 The six stages of an inventory life cycle.

than our customers? They can help us create form, fit, and function in our product design. Granted there is no immediate impact on inventory, yet everything decided in the design phase will have a significant impact in the other inventory life stages.

For example, take the Beacon Light Division, where we might create an entire light system, including electronic sensors. Our customers might tell us that they never use that particular part of the system, because it is too complicated or simply not needed. If we knew this up front, we could eliminate the sensor altogether, thus reducing the material and labor cost of the system. We wouldn't know this unless they are part of the process from the beginning. Our internal customers also have a lot to contribute.

Manufacturing might discover that it can reduce the number of different springs used in our flashlights from three different ones to one particular type. Product development (engineering) might have designed it with three different springs because the batteries fit really well with these, but manufacturing may find a better way of making the product use only one type of spring in all three places. Better yet, it may find a way of eliminating a spring and tell us that only two springs are needed. This means we could carry fewer part numbers in inventory, and maybe even less inventory. I bet if we took the time we could get meaningful design input from all links in our supply chain, including our suppliers. The concept of getting everyone involved up front is called *concurrent engineering* or *simultaneous engineering.*

> **TIP #27: *Get all supply-chain links involved in the product design phase. Decisions made in this phase will have a significant impact on inventory in all the other inventory life-cycle phases.***

Introduction Stage

During the introduction phase, we are just starting to roll out the product. In this phase, customers don't buy a lot of inventory. In fact, we sometimes give the product to customers on a promotional basis. During this phase, we begin to buy and make inventory. As it is a new product in which we don't have any history, we use a forecast based on demand for similar products. For the Flashlight Division (make-to-stock), we buy raw materials and produce finished goods for stock. This is in alignment with our inventory strategy mentioned at a previous meeting. Overall, aggregate inventory and sales are still low at this point in the product life cycle. Inventory stockouts may be high at this point because we haven't built up safety stock inventory.

Growth Stage

During the growth phase, both sales and inventory increase as more customers begin to buy the new product. Inventory begins to shift downstream in our supply chain and has to be carefully monitored. We have to be very careful in this stage because there is a high risk associated with stockouts. The customers in this stage have no brand loyalty, and if our product is not available they may switch to our competitors' products.

Maturity Stage

During this stage, sales continue to increase, but at a slower rate. It is at this stage in which inventory is the most volatile, and it can quickly get out of control. Inventory decisions made at this phase will impact decisions on how we deal with inventory during the last two phases of the inventory life cycle. Inventory should be held as far upstream in our supply chain as possible.

Decline Stage

As the market becomes saturated, sales decline, technology in the products may become outdated, and production drops off. Customers are watching their inventory levels carefully because like us, they don't want to be stuck with obsolete inventory. In this stage, we begin to reduce inventory in all three categories: raw material, work-in-progress, and finished goods. The one inventory area that is an exception to this policy is the spare parts inventory used by our Field Service organization. The life cycle for spare parts is now in the growth phase. It will be some time later that this inventory life cycle reaches the maturity, decline, and exit phases.

Exit Stage

When we get to this stage, all categories of inventory should be at zero. Our reverse logistics policy and strategy must be coordinated with our market exit policy. If we exit a market, do we want to continue to receive returns? We have to have a policy in place on how to deal with this well before we reach this stage in the product life cycle.

> **TIP #28:** *All categories of inventory must be aligned with the product life-cycle strategy and must be aligned well before moving out of that particular product life-cycle phase.*

Aligning Woodstock Inventory Levels with the Product Life Cycles

We have done an analysis of our inventory level as it relates to the product life cycle. Using annual dollar usage as the criteria, we looked at the top ten products in our product line and worked with marketing and sales to determine where they were in the product life cycle. Granted this was not very scientific, yet we were looking at the "order of magnitude." In other words, we were looking for any obvious mismatches between inventory levels and product life cycles. We then took the top 20 raw materials with the highest dollar value and ran a "where-used" report to determine if any of the high-value raw materials went into any of the top ten products. We found that ten of the raw materials (50 percent) fit those criteria.

Of the ten raw materials, we found two glaring mismatches between the raw material level and the product life cycle. Let's call them raw material A and raw material B. Raw material A goes into a flashlight that is in the decline stage of its product life cycle, yet we have a high-dollar value of the raw material inventory worth almost $150,000, an obvious mismatch. Raw material B goes into a spotlight product that just reached the market decline stage and is entering the market exit phase; another mismatch. This represents inventory worth another $75,000.

In fact, marketing wasn't even aware that although it was planning an exit strategy, there was still an open purchase order for new raw materials. How this happened we'll never know. The purchasing agent who placed the order is no longer with our company. This was a $5,000 purchase order and, fortunately, we were able to cancel it. So there you have it. It may not be scientific, but it does help us focus on reducing the $225,000 raw material, and it provided us with a sanity check on product life cycles. We have made everyone aware of this issue. Sales and manufacturing are working together to move this inventory out of our supply chain as soon as possible.

> **TIP #29:** *Focus on high-value inventory items first. This will have the greatest impact on aligning inventory in your supply chain.*

Inventory and Customer Service Levels

I can't conclude this presentation without offering some insight on how inventory, or the lack of it, affects our level of customer service. There are two general concepts of inventory used here at Woodstock. Concept number one: The higher the level of customer service desired, the higher the level of inventory in our supply chain. Concept number two: the more complex our supply chain becomes, the higher the amount of inventory in our supply chain. I wish this weren't true, but until we can get our act together there is a direct correlation between customer service level and inventory level that we maintain. Having excess inventory isn't always related to customer service levels, and we can't blame our customers for a lot of our inventory problems.

> **TIP #30:** *High inventory levels cannot always be blamed on the need for safety stock, because of customer uncertainty. More often than not, other problems cause the high levels of inventory.*

This inventory isn't just in one category. Because of the uncertainty of supply and demand, we keep a lot of inventory. Instead of looking at inventory from the traditional viewpoint of raw material, work-in-progress, and finished goods, let's look at it from a functional viewpoint. In other words, besides the need to fill customer orders, why does inventory exist in our supply chain?

Why Inventory Exists in the Supply Chain

Other causes of high levels of inventory are discussed in the following paragraphs:

1. **Safety stock inventory:** Safety stock, sometimes referred to as buffer inventory, is kept because of the uncertainty of customers (demand) and suppliers (supply). We keep safety stock of finished goods in our Flashlight Division because we don't want to have a stockout condition on a customer order. When finished goods are shipped to a customer, we need to replace the quantity shipped out, or we will eventually run out of finished goods. We keep safety stock of raw materials so we won't run out of them when it is time to replace the finished goods. In other words, safety stock exists at the raw material and finished goods level as a buffer against the uncertainty of supply and demand. You've heard from others that as a general rule we should have no inventory beyond satisfying immediate customer needs. If we were to follow that principle, we would have no inventory at all — but we have inventory worth over $40 million. However, it's not all because of safety stock. It's also because of the other functions of inventory, which follow.

2. **Lot size inventory:** Some of that $40 million inventory exists because of the lot size rules of our manufacturing plant and some of our suppliers. For example, if we need 500 lenses for a customer order and it is a purchased part, our supplier may require that we buy a lot size of 1000; the price will be tripled if they have to break the lot size. So after using the 500 to satisfy the customer order, the other 500 go into inventory. Again the impact of satisfying a customer requirement results in more inventory that has nothing to do with safety stock.

3. **Anticipation inventory:** Another function of inventory to protect against a stockout on a customer order is called *anticipation inventory*. Twice a year we shut down our manufacturing plant (July and December) for one week, so that our employees may go on holiday. As a common practice, we increase inventory levels just before these shutdowns so that we will have ample inventory to satisfy customers when we return. Our concern is that we won't be able to satisfy new customer orders when we open again for production.

4. **Transportation inventory:** This is sometimes called *pipeline inventory* and is defined as inventory in transit. This can be raw materials in transit to our manufacturing plant, or finished goods in transit to our distribution centers across the country. The greater the distance (geography) to the plant or distribution center, the greater the quantity of inventory in the pipeline. We buy quite a few components overseas, and this adds to our total inventory.

5. **Hedge inventory:** Sometimes we buy/make inventory based on some potential event that may or may not occur. For example, if we hear that there might be a shortage of a particular raw material

that is critical to our product line, we may buy more than we need just in case this shortage does occur. We may get word that a key supplier may close its doors for good, and few suppliers provide this product, so again, we may buy more than we need for the foreseeable future.

6. **Work-in-process buffer stock:** Don't confuse this with the buffer stock I referred to when I spoke of raw material and finished goods inventory stock. In this case, our manufacturing plant has extra inventory between manufacturing processes to protect against uncertainty in our manufacturing process. For example, spotlight assembly and test is a work center in our plant that we consider a bottleneck. A bottleneck is a manufacturing resource whose capacity is less than the demand placed on it. As a general rule, we never want the bottleneck work center to run out of work; hence the need for extra buffer inventory.

7. **Distribution inventory:** We have three distribution centers and the inventory in each of these centers pretty much mirrors the inventory of the others. It is a statistical fact that our total inventory, including safety stock, could be less if we only had one distribution center.

8. **Inventory planning rules:** This is one of my favorites. Let me define this by using an example. Suppose that when you went home Friday night, you had ten generators (Beacon Light subassembly) in inventory and no customer orders for them. You're in good shape on this item, right? Now suppose you run MRP over the weekend. Planning can explain what this is when it meets with you. But for now let me say it is a planning technique that tells us what parts are needed for a product we plan to make, how many of those parts are needed, and when those parts are needed. We don't use this tool yet, but planning is working hard to implement it. So remember we had ten in stock and no customer orders for it. However, your MRP rule is to always have 25 in safety stock. So now MRP says you are 15 short and you need to make them. Now suppose you gave MRP another rule that says, every time you make this part, you need to make 50 of them (for whatever reason, probably financial). When you come to work Monday morning, MRP will tell you to expedite an order for 50 as soon as possible. So here you are with ten in stock that you don't need, and you're being told to rush a new order for fifty. And guess what? It goes through that bottleneck work center I mentioned earlier. I have found planning rules to be a big problem here at Woodstock.

9. **Inaccurate inventory record keeping:** This is another good reason why inventory exists. We recently had a good example of this. Our perpetual inventory transaction system indicated that we were out of stock on part #92152, and we needed to buy 5,000 of them @ $2.00 per unit for a total of $10,000. So purchasing placed an order for 5,000 pieces, and they have just come in. The year-end physical inventory that we just took shows that we have 15,000 of these in the storeroom. This part has a very small footprint and was hidden behind a different part that has a much larger footprint.

   If you ask Jose, the storeroom manager, why our records didn't show this in stock, he will tell you he doesn't know. He will give you lots of probable reasons for this. He told me that the shipping and receiving department is understaffed and it is often rushed to get shipments out; received goods to be put away are cast aside at the time. He has no space left because of all the stock. And one more for good measure, he doesn't do cycle counting on a regular basis. So you see there are a lot of probable causes for this. The bottom line is that everyone was surprised by the results of the physical inventory.

10. **Lack of inventory accountability:** No one, yet everyone, is responsible for the high level of inventory that exists. Sounds confusing, huh? Well, let me explain. Up until now, the level of inventory was not a part of anyone's performance measurement. Therefore, no one is responsible. However, it seems as if everyone has been involved at one time or another. Sales keeps pushing for more and more finished goods. Manufacturing doesn't want to run out of work, so it makes stuff just to keep the machines running. On top of that, purchasing keeps bringing in stuff because it is measured on having a favorable purchase price variance. Buying large (lot size) quantities helps purchasing achieve this — and they get a bonus for doing it! I could go on and on, but I won't. The point is, everyone is responsible for causing our inventory level to be at record levels. Therefore, no one, yet everyone, is responsible for inventory levels being what they are today.

TIP #31: *Inventory levels will remain unabated and uncontrolled until accountability, responsibility, and shared performance metrics are assigned, measured, and communicated to all links in the supply chain.*

I see that Pat from finance and accounting is presenting at the next Harmony Team meeting. She will provide you with some good insight on what it is really costing us to have so much inventory.

Inter-Office E-Mail

To: Supply-Chain Managers   February 14
From: Harmony Team
Subject: Rightsizing Inventory
Current Inventory Level: $41 million (no change since February 2, but up $1 million since the first day of the year)

Discussion Summary:

We have made some small progress since our last report. We have begun to align our inventory levels with our inventory strategy. Unfortunately, it doesn't show in the numbers yet. The sales department has been a big help by starting to work off the beacon light finished goods inventory, which didn't match our inventory strategy at all. Purchasing has begun to look at the flashlight raw material and work-in-process inventory, which as you now know was at 46 percent of the total flashlight inventory, another mismatch between inventory, levels, and inventory strategy. Thanks to all for working together on this. Today, we received some great education from Maria in customer service. She pointed out some discrepancies between our product life cycles and our inventory levels. The following is what we learned along with some to-dos (the details will be distributed to all as part of the meeting minutes):

1. Even though customers aren't always right, we should make every effort to satisfy their needs.
2. We will adapt a business philosophy of CRM, where we will learn as much as possible about our customers so that not only can we satisfy their current needs, but anticipate their future needs as well.
3. Human resources (HR) will coordinate education and training programs for employees on CRM.

4. IT will start to look for CRM application software that will help us become "customer intimate."
5. We will adapt an extended supply-chain approach, which includes our customer's customers.
6. We will begin to share inventory information with our customers.
7. We will focus our efforts on the five inventory attributes of customer expectations and the three inventory attributes of Woodstock expectations (see minutes).
8. We will seek to understand how customers measure our performance.
9. We are in the process of aligning our inventory levels to match our product life cycles. We have already found two parts in which there is a significant imbalance. We have asked purchasing to continue looking into this.
10. Operations will work with HR to shift employees into the shipping/receiving department. Shipping says it is short-handed, and it is causing inventory problems.
11. We have learned there are many reasons that inventory exists in our supply chain, and we will have to look into all ten reasons.
12. As we continue this process we will need to assign responsibility, accountability, and shared performance metrics to all supply-chain processes.

These are the highlights from the meeting. If after reading the minutes you have any questions, please do not hesitate to stop by or call. Let's keep it up, we are making progress!

At the last Harmony Team meeting we published the beginning of an analytical inventory model (Chapter 1, Figure 1.10) that we should use as a guideline to right-sizing our inventory. We have added to the model in Figure 2.7. At this time, I believe we should include CRM as a major input to our inventory strategy. The inputs from CRM include the following:

- Customer orders/contracts
- Customer forecast of future inventory requirements
- Customer inventory status
- Customer inventory strategy

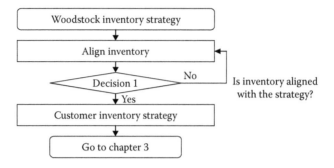

Figure 2.7 Woodstock inventory rightsizing model.

- Customer inventory plans
- Customer new product development
- Customer supply chain inventory logistics (how inventory flows through their supply chain)
- Methodology for integrating these activities into our inventory strategy and planning process

Sales and marketing will provide us with some more details on CRM. I know for a fact that forecasting customer requirements is a big problem, and I'm sure we will hear a lot about it when we meet.

Applying the Tips, Tools, and Philosophies to Your Company

In this chapter, I have added 15 more TIPs for rightsizing inventory and have expanded the inventory model to include customer requirements and expectations. The following discussion will review each of the TIPs and how you can apply them to your company:

> **TIP #17: *The customer isn't always right, but if you want to keep the customer, you should do all you can to satisfy their requirements in a professional, businesslike manner.***

Common sense tells us we should never be rude to customers no matter how angry they get with you. In Chapter 1, I discussed the perfect order from the viewpoint of both the buyer and seller. It is important that you understand your customers' and stakeholders' expectations and satisfy them, but that's not enough. It will do your company little good if only one or two links understand this. All links must share in understanding these expectations and meeting them. Here is a checklist you can follow:

1. Ask your customers what they consider the perfect order.
2. Ask your own management team what it considers the perfect order.
3. Identify the performance metrics your customer is using to measure your performance.
4. If it is a numeric measurement, ask how they calculate it.
5. Establish and measure your own performance to the customer's requirements.
6. Communicate all this to every link in your supply chain.
7. Take proactive measures to keep performance at the highest level possible.
8. Take reactive measures when performance is below the established standard.

TIP #18: *Understanding the customers' needs is a good thing, but anticipating your customers' needs is an order winner that will help you sell more inventory.*

You can anticipate your customers' needs by getting actively involved in their business. You don't want to become overbearing and bothersome, but you must first understand their needs before you can anticipate them. There are several ways you can do this:

1. Make visits to the customer, not just the buyer, and meet with other links in their supply chain. There are several important links in addition to purchasing:
   - Planning department: What tools does it use to plan inventory? How far out into the future do inventory plans go … ?
   - Product development: What new products is the department working on? What will the manufacturing process be … ?
   - Marketing: What is marketing's forecast for future sales? Are any products being discontinued (that include your products) … ?
   - Accounts payable: Are there any invoicing issues? Is your paperwork in order … ?
   - Manufacturing: How is your product used in manufacturing's product? Are there any issues with your product in the manufacturing process …?
   - Warehousing, distribution, receiving: Are they satisfied with the packaging? Are there any damage/return issues … ?

Several other points should be made here. It shouldn't be just the salesperson making these visits. If you're visiting the planning department, then take someone from your planning department. If you're visiting the manufacturing department, then take someone from your manufacturing department. People relate to those who understand their role in the company and they may help each other improve the process.

2. Invite your customer to visit your site — not just the buyer, but people from other links in the supply chain.
3. All findings should be communicated to the appropriate link in your supply chain.
4. Form a "Customer Anticipation" committee to review findings. Brainstorm to come up with ways to satisfy your customers.

TIP #19: *We must present ourselves as one united, collaborative supply-chain network to our customers and establish clearly defined lines of communication with them.*

You must be careful here. Too much communication can be harmful to your relationship. You cannot have three different people from your company calling the same person to ask a question. The customer will think you are disorganized and you may even get three different answers to your question. I have seen this happen more than once. You will be perceived as a very organized, professional company if you:

1. Develop and communicate a company policy of who should communicate with the customer on specific issues or questions.
2. Provide your customers with this policy and list. Be sure to include phone numbers and e-mail addresses.
3. Make sure there is a secondary person they can call if the primary contact isn't available.
4. Provide communication coverage based on your customer geography. If you are on the East Coast, consider your customers' needs on the West Coast.

Examples of inventory-related communication would be:

■ Inventory returns
■ Change of order status
■ Expediting a rush order
■ Damaged goods
■ Inventory quantity questions

For each of these, provide your customer with a contact name and ask your customer to do the same. Believe me, although this may seem a small point, it will be an asset as you try to rightsize your inventory.

> **TIP #20:** *Know as much as possible about your customers: their needs, wants, problems, plans, and who else they buy from.*

Most of this was covered in TIPS #18 and #19 discussed previously, but there is one more important point I would like to make here. So far I have talked about going direct to your customers to find out as much as you can about them. You can also get information about your customer from other external sources. Here are some examples:

1. Go to a credit rating agency to find out about their credit.
2. Attend conferences and meetings where representatives from their company are speaking.
3. Ask other customers (their competitors) about them.
4. Read articles about them in newspapers, magazines, and the Internet.
5. Visit their Web site.

> **TIP #21:** *A successful supply chain knows its customers well and can anticipate their inventory needs. In some cases, it may be an inventory need that they don't recognize they have.*

This TIP works particularly well if you have access to your customer's physical inventory or perpetual inventory records. I'm sure you have heard about the "bread person" who visits the supermarket early in the morning and removes the stale bread, takes inventory, and replenishes the shelf. Many manufacturing companies are following this practice today. One of my clients, a rather large electronics manufacturer, gave certain suppliers (truck drivers) badges that allowed the delivery person to go directly to the work cells and restock the inventory rack as needed. No paperwork exchanged hands on a daily basis. Once a month the supplier would invoice my client for goods delivered throughout the month.

If you have access to their perpetual inventory system, you can review their inventory levels and replenish based on a preapproved policy. I have known instances in which customers didn't think they needed inventory and the supplier was able to point out why inventory was needed.

TIP #22: *Don't keep inventory information a secret. Share it with your customers. Ask your customers to share their inventory information with you.*

To do this with your customer you have to have a true partnership. There is a lot of trust involved. In TIP #21, I spoke about your having, as supplier, access to your customer's inventory. If you really have a true partnership, you should allow your customer to access your inventory also. You have to be careful though; this can come back to bite you. You have to decide how much information to share. For example, should the customer have access to the total quantity you have available, or is it enough to say a product is "available," "not available," or "in stock"? The danger, as I pointed out earlier, is that if you have an enormous quantity on hand the customer may try to get a price break on the order. On the other hand, with a partner, there may be nothing wrong with that. I know I would be willing to consider a price discount if I had too much inventory in stock. Here are some thoughts to consider:

1. Allow only true partners access to your inventory.
2. Inventory information sharing should be both ways.
3. Decide how much information and what type of information you want to share.
4. Establish a policy of how and when the customer can access your inventory records.
5. Put procedures in place to ensure against two or more customers buying the same item at the same time. Don't think this won't happen.
6. Become proactive; if you have excess inventory you want to move at a discount (or full price), let your customer know about it.

TIP #23: *Lead time is defined differently for each link in your supply chain. The most important definition is related to customer order lead time: from the time they ask you to ship the inventory until they receive the inventory.*

Everyone has a different definition of lead time, but there is only one definition that counts — the customer's. This is what you can address here:

1. Ask your customers how they define lead time and the formula they use to measure you.
2. Ask all of your internal supply-chain links to define their lead times.
3. Publish an internal directory of lead time definitions.

4. Establish, measure, and report on all important lead time measurements, starting with the customer.
5. Ask your suppliers to provide you with their definitions and current lead times.
6. Establish a policy of who can change published lead times and when changes to lead times should be reported.
7. Look to reduce all lead times.
8. Be sure that all elements of lead time are considered. Don't forget to include the "paper processing time" and the "authorized approval time" elements.

TIP #24: *We need to understand not only what inventory metrics our customers are using, but also how they are using (calculating) it.*

Not all customers will use the same metrics to measure your performance. Some will place more emphasis on delivery time, whereas others may focus on fill rates. The following steps need to be taken here:

1. Ask your customers (using the 80/20 rule) what metrics they are using to measure their satisfaction with your performance.
2. Categorize their responses: on-time, complete, quality, etc.
3. Ask them to provide periodic feedback so there are no surprises.
4. Measure your performance against their criteria.
5. Compare their performance results with yours.
6. If the results are different, take action; ask the customer.
7. Establish internal warning signals if the performance metric dips to an unsatisfactory level.
8. Put procedures in place for corrective action to get the metric back on track if need be.
9. Communicate the performance results to all supply-chain managers.

TIP #26: *It's nice to know how good we are; we have to know how bad we are.*

One of the more difficult challenges I have faced as a consultant is convincing clients that they need to change matters when they are profitable and doing well. The typical response is that "if it isn't broke, don't fix it." In the dynamic business world we live in today, conditions can change quickly; a profitable company today can become unprofitable tomorrow. My advice to you is even if things are going well, there is always something that needs to be improved. No company is perfect; if you look hard enough and long enough you will find something that needs to be improved. Identify the weakest link in your supply chain and improve it. When you have done that, another link will rise to the surface as your weakest link. This is a never-ending process and should become part of your company culture.

> **TIP #27: *Get all supply-chain links involved in the product design phase. Decisions made in this phase will have a significant impact on inventory in all the other inventory life-cycle phases.***

Product design will be covered in more detail in Chapter 6, but there are some key points that should be made here.

1. Develop a matrix indicating supply-chain links (planning, sales, etc.), names of persons from the links who can contribute to the product design, and what category of inventory management they have an impact on (packaging, transportation, manufacturing, etc.). In the Woodstock example, 19 links were identified.
2. Meet with the persons identified in the matrix and get their input on new product design and improvements to existing products.
3. Do not attempt to meet with all 19 people at one time. Nothing will get done.
4. From the matrix, pick a core team that will be involved from the beginning to the end of the design phase.
5. Include external customers and key suppliers on your design team.
6. Consider using nondisclosure agreements for external supply-chain links (just in case).

> **TIP #28: *All categories of inventory must be aligned with the product life-cycle strategy and must be aligned well before moving out of that particular product life-cycle phase.***

The key to using this TIP successfully is in the timing. You don't want marketing to announce one day that product X is being discontinued tomorrow. You would want a market exit strategy in place well before the announcement. You should be planning one or two stages ahead in the product life cycle. The following suggestions relate to the six stages of the product life cycle.

1. **Development stage:** As new product ideas are being identified and developed, you should be looking ahead to the next phase (introduction) and answering these types of inventory-related questions:

- How much inventory will I need for stage 2?
- How will the product be introduced to the marketplace?
- What will the distribution channel be?
- What will the supply chain look like for this product?
- What is our inventory strategy going to be (make-to-stock, make-to-order)?

2. **Introduction stage:** During this phase, you should be looking ahead to the growth phase and answering inventory-related questions such as:
   - Can we ramp up production fast enough to meet demand?
   - Can we ramp down fast enough if demand doesn't meet expectations?
   - What alternative resources are available if internal capacity isn't sufficient?
   - Do we have supply-chain flexibility to cope with changes in demand?
   - Should we carry safety stock on this product and, if so, how much?

3. **Growth stage:** Looking ahead to the maturity stage, ask yourself these types of inventory-related questions:
   - Should we prepare a market exit strategy?
   - Should we enhance our product to keep it in the growth phase?
   - Should we change our supply-chain strategy?
   - Should we change our marketing strategy?
   - Should we decrease raw material purchases?
   - How can we use up existing raw materials and subassemblies?
   - Should we begin to reduce finished goods inventory levels?

4. **Maturity stage:** Looking ahead to the decline stage ask the following inventory-related questions:
   - Will we have to reduce/shift personnel in production?
   - Should we reduce selling price to move existing inventory?
   - Have all raw material contracts been satisfied, or are there outstanding balances on existing blanket orders?
   - How should we position the product in the marketplace?
   - Is an exit strategy in place?
   - How will customers be notified about the exit strategy?
   - How do we reduce/eliminate existing inventory?

5. **Decline stage:** You have now reached the point where you have decided that you will no longer invest in the product to enhance it, and are moving quickly to the exit phase. Inventory-related questions about the exit phase are:
   - How can we eliminate all existing inventory?
   - Have all customers been advised that the product will no longer be offered?

- Have all legal ramifications been considered?
- Has existing capacity for this product been assigned to other products?
- Has the workforce been reallocated?
- Have all marketing materials and programs been stopped?

6. **Exit stage:** By the time you get to this stage, all plans are in place and it just becomes a matter of execution.

What questions to ask, and at what stage they should be asked, is up to the individual company and the types of products involved. The key to this TIP is to think well in advance of the life-cycle stage your product is currently in and prepare plans to address it. Of course, you will need to recognize that demand for the product is changing and when the product is entering the next stage. I haven't discussed products that require ongoing support and spare parts. In Woodstock, they have the Beacon Light Division and the field service organization in place to support products well into the future. If you have such products, you will need to supply spare parts and components well beyond the exit phase. The key points here are to think ahead and recognize that you are entering a new phase of the product life cycle.

> **TIP #29:** *Focus on high-value inventory items first. This will have the greatest impact on aligning inventory in your supply chain.*

The greatest impact on reducing inventory and realigning inventory will be focusing on high-dollar-value items first. Of course, your situation may be different. You may have thousands of parts with low value, but the sum of these parts has a significant dollar value. In this situation, you may want to focus your efforts on those items. I had a client recently with just such a situation. Because theirs was a make-to-order environment with very little repeat business and limited finished goods, we focused on reducing raw material inventory. I'll address this TIP in two categories:

Large number of parts with low dollar value by item but large dollar value in total:

1. Run an inventory report by usage and list all inventory items with no activity (no transactions) for 12 months or greater. The theory here is if you haven't had any activity on the part for a year, what is the probability you will ever use it? It's kind of similar to your clothes closet. If you have clothes you haven't worn for a year, what's the probability you will ever wear them again? Be careful

here. Once you announce you are getting rid of inventory someone will invariably say, "Once you get rid of it we will need it." My client's answer was: "If you sell it in the future, we will make it again." That simple answer seemed to satisfy the sales force.

2. Run a "where-used" report to identify the "goesintos" (goes into). If the "parent" part was discontinued, then scrap/sell the goesintos. If the parent part is active, use the raw material up. If it is an active part but you have too much inventory, don't buy any more and use it up.

3. Ask product design if the part can be used in another product.

4. Ask the part supplier if it can take it back for credit or help you sell it.

Small number of parts with high dollar value:

1. Use the 80/20 rule to rank the inventory items.

2. Establish ABC classifications using some criterion such as "annual dollar usage."

3. Match inventory levels to inventory strategy and focus on inventories not aligned with the inventory strategy.

In Woodstock, the current inventory status (discussed in Chapter 1) meets the criteria of both scenarios presented here. The reader will learn how it addressed the inventory issue in subsequent chapters.

> **TIP #30:** *High inventory levels cannot always be blamed on the need for safety stock because of customer uncertainty. More often than not, other problems cause the high levels of inventory.*

Very few companies operate without safety stock. As you rightsize your inventory and improve your processes, you should be able to operate with minimal safety stock inventory. Other possible causes of having high levels of inventory are:

1. MRP lot-size rules
2. Minimum-buy requirements of supplier
3. Poor forecasting
4. Limited plant capacity
5. Excessive scrap and rework
6. Customer order cancellations
7. Long purchasing lead times
8. Long production lead times

This is just a partial checklist of causes that may drive up inventory. The key to this TIP is to seek the root cause of high inventories and address it.

> **TIP #31:** *Inventory levels will remain unabated and uncontrolled until accountability, responsibility, and shared performance metrics are assigned, measured, and communicated to all links in the supply chain.*

This TIP, more than any other, is a key to your inventory rightsizing efforts. It says a lot:

1. Assign accountability (who is responsible).
2. Establish shared responsibility and performance metrics (teamwork).
3. Monitor and measure performance.
4. Communicate, communicate, communicate.

Woodstock is a dysfunctional company right now, but you will note that (see Chapter 1, at the very beginning of the inventory rightsizing effort) it is taking the steps addressed in this TIP. Unless this TIP is implemented, your efforts will be minimally successful, at best. This has to start at the highest levels of management and must continue on an ongoing basis. Implementation of this TIP will help change the culture of the company for the better. Table 2.3 is the latest status of the Woodstock inventory and Table 2.4 shows the annual inventory targets by division.

Table 2.3   Inventory Balance
(×1,000,000)

Month End	31 Jan	14 Feb
Forecast	7.2	7.9
Orders	5.8	
Total starting inventory	40.0	41.0
Start FG inventory	15.5	15.7
+Production @ COGS	4.1	
−Shipments @ COGS	3.9	
End FG inventory	15.7	
Start WIP inventory	7.5	7.6
+Material issues	3.4	
+Labor and overhead	0.8	
−Production @ COGS	4.1	
End WIP inventory	7.6	
Start raw inventory	17.0	17.7
+Material purchases	4.1	
−Material issues	3.4	
End raw inventory	17.7	
Total ending inventory	41.0	

Note: FG = finished goods, COGS = cost of
   goods sold, WIP = Work-in-process.

Table 2.4 Inventory Segmentation Targets
(×1,000,000)

	Start	Target
Date	1 Jan	31 Dec
Total inventory	40.0	→ 32.5
		↓
Flashlights	28.0	→ 23.2
		↓
Spotlights	8.0	→ 6.5
		↓
Beacon lights	4.0	→ 2.8

Chapter 3

Having Inventory Costs the Company Money

February 25, Harmony Team Meeting
Woodstock Inventory: $40.9 Million

My name is Pat, and I'm director of finance for Woodstock.
I have been here for five years now, and it seems like twenty. When are they ever going to learn that inventory is at the very heart of our cash flow issue? I have been preaching this to my boss, Colleen, ever since I got here. But that's like preaching to the committed. She agrees with me. Joe seems to think that having lots of inventory solves lots of problems. I think that having lots of inventory hides lots of problems. If we had put the $40 million in the bank, we would have made more money than we did these past couple of years.

At my family's wholesale business we understood this concept, and before Uncle Billy sold it to that huge conglomerate, we were very successful. Of course, we were a small business with 14 employees; we communicated about everything, and we wore multiple hats. In addition to my duties as controller, I would help out in shipping when we got really busy. I enjoyed going to work and facing the unknown challenges of the day. Lately, here at Woodstock, I haven't enjoyed coming to work. The first thing I do is open the mail to see if any customers sent us payment, and the second thing I do is call the bank to see if there have been any electronic deposits to our account.

The job interview I had last week with that small wholesale distributor went really well. It was my second interview, and I believe they will make me an offer soon. My husband, Joe, says I should get out of here as soon as possible. I've started to bring the problems home with me, and it is affecting our relationship. I'm thinking I will accept the offer even if it's for less pay. The quality of my home life is more important than this job. That's just what it is, a job, not a career. Oh, well, time to start the meeting.

Having inventory costs the company money — a lot of money. We cannot afford the luxury of having $40 plus million in inventory. We have a long way to go. Let me share with you how bad it is. Unless inventory is drastically reduced immediately, we will run out of cash and have to borrow more money from our bank. No one wants that to happen. We have almost used up our line of credit, and if they call in the loan, we will be in real trouble. There is an old saying, "It takes money to make money." Well, we don't have any money. Most of our money is tied up in inventory. Our supply chain needs money for equipment, machinery, raw materials, supplies, operating expenses, payroll, transportation, warehousing, etc. The list goes on and on. One of the primary objectives of financial management is to manage our assets in such a way that we can achieve the highest possible profit for our stakeholders. If we look at money from a cash flow point of view, our cash inflow has to be greater than our cash outflow. Table 3.1 shows our cash outflow and inflow.

The only time we have true cash inflow is when we sell our products and services. Even then we have to wait 30 to 90 days for our customers to pay us. So, if our customers pay us on average in 60 days and we have to pay our suppliers in 30 days, you can see that our cash-to-cash turnaround is not good. On top of this, we have a weekly payroll to meet, monthly operating expenses, bank obligations, and all sorts of other costs to pay.

Table 3.1   Woodstock Cash Flow

Cash Outflow	Category
Raw material purchases	Accounts payable to suppliers
Work-in-progress inventory	Payroll — direct labor
Finished goods inventory	Inventory carrying costs
Salaries	Payroll — all other employees
Operating expense	Plant, office, other
Bank loan payments	Principal and interest

Cash Inflow	Category
Shipments	Accounts receivable from customers

Think of your personal cash inflow and cash outflow. Most of your cash inflow and outflow is recorded in your checking account. Your checking account becomes your record of what happened to your money: where it came from and where it went. When you get paid, your check gets deposited into your checking account as cash inflow (credit to your account). When you write out checks, you are withdrawing money from your account (debit to your account), and this is cash outflow. At the end of any given period of time — let's say a month — you can analyze your transactions for the month.

If your month-end checking account balance is greater than your beginning balance, then you have a positive cash flow for the month. You increased the equity of your account. If on the other hand, your month-end balance is less than your beginning balance, you have a negative cash flow for the month. After a few months of negative cash flows, what's going to happen? You will fall behind on your bills and have to look for alternative ways of getting cash, like dipping into your savings account or borrowing money. It is no different in the business world.

Budgeting to Monitor Cash Inflow and Cash Outflow

Analyzing cash inflows and outflows at the end of an accounting period is a noble and necessary task, but it is also a passive, reactive task. We must do a better job of monitoring cash flows. We have established budgets for the year, yet we don't do a good job of monitoring them on a daily or weekly basis. If we did so, we could make adjustments as they get out of balance. We need to track variances to the budget and report them on a routine basis so that we can take corrective action. In the future, I would like to see inventory as a budgeted item. We can set budget levels (value) for each of the links in our supply chain and monitor it. This would be a proactive change that will help keep budgets in line. It will show us where the money is going and what areas are over or under the budget.

We do monitor cash inflows a little better. We have an invoice aging report that shows all invoices due and past due. The report categorizes past dues in 30-, 60-, 90-, and 120-day periods. We even have one invoice past due by over 365 days, but that is an exception and a whole story unto itself.

Finance and Accounting: Role and Responsibility

One of the primary responsibilities of finance and accounting is to keep accurate and timely transaction records of all revenue and expenses (remember your checking account transactions). The second primary responsibility is to provide financial management and analysis reports, which can be used by our stakeholders, management, banks, and various government, tax, and law-compliancy agencies. We are the company scorekeepers; we watch the money and, in general, oversee the health and wealth of the company. We are sometimes called "bean counters" or "number crunchers," but we do much more than that.

Keep in mind that the numbers don't tell the whole story. There are outside factors such as the economy, changing customer requirements, new regulations, competitive strategy, and new emerging technologies. All these factors and others will impact how we analyze and use the numbers. Finance and accounting operates in a structured, formal manner that complies with good Generally Accepted Accounting Practices (GAAP). The numbers can be presented to make the company look good or look bad in any given year, but in all cases the numbers must be presented in a legal way.

In recent years, there has been a lot of press about companies presenting the numbers in a less-than-proper way. Company executives have been brought up on legal charges because of improper representation of the numbers. We must always strive to do it right and follow the laws and regulations, regardless of how bad the numbers may be. We are responsible for **managerial accounting and financial accounting.** *Managerial accounting* is providing the internal supply-chain links with financial information that will help them make intelligent decisions in their area of responsibility. *Financial accounting* is providing external supply-chain links with information about the company's financial health — past, present, and future.

> **TIP #32:** *Financial documents must be prepared in accordance with all laws and regulations, regardless of how bad they may make the company look. Inventory is a major component of financial reporting and must be presented as accurately as possible.*

(Note: TIP = team important point.)

Having said all that, there are two primary financial documents we use, and inventory is an important component in both. At present, we do not have balance sheets and income statements for each division. It would be great if we did, but we are not there yet.

Inventory and the Balance Sheet

The balance sheet is a financial picture of the business at a given point of time. It lists the company's assets, liabilities, and owner's equity. Assets

Table 3.2   Balance Sheet (×1,000)

Assets ($)				Liabilities ($)	
Cash			10,000	Accounts payable	10,000
Accounts receivable			40,000	Long-term loans	50,000
Buildings and equipment			85,000		
Inventory					
Flashlights		28,000			
Spotlights		8,000			
Beacon lights		4,000			
Total inventory		40,000	40,000		
				Equity	
				Owner's investment	40,000
				Profit (prior years)	75,000
Total assets			175,000	Total liabilities and equity	175,000

must always equal liabilities and owner's equity. That's why it's called a balance sheet. It answers the question of "What is our financial position at this point in time?" Table 3.2 is an example of a balance sheet; it was discussed earlier by Arnie.

Anything we own that has financial value is considered an asset. In our case assets are cash, accounts receivable, inventory, equipment, and company-owned facilities (including land), machinery, and other investments. Assets are classified as current assets or fixed assets. Current assets are assets that are expected to be converted into cash during a normal business cycle, generally within a fiscal year. Fixed assets are assets with a useful life of a year or more.

Inventory as an Asset

Examples of current assets are inventory of raw materials, work-in-progress (WIP), and finished goods, which we expect (hopefully) to turn into cash over the next 12 months. That new deburring machine we bought at the end of last year is considered a fixed asset, and we expect it to have a useful life of five years. Inventory is also referred to as a "tangible" current asset (it can be physically touched). There are different methods used for inventory valuation. Depending on the method chosen, the inventory asset can be reported as having either a higher or lower valuation. I'll discuss this in more detail later.

Among the assets reported on the balance sheet are cash, accounts receivable, and inventory. The whole idea is to turn inventory into cash so that money is freed up for other things, including buying more inventory. Don't forget the personal checking account analogy I spoke of earlier. So, if you look at our $39 million tied up in inventory, and let's say, for example, we reduce it to $19 million, we would have $20 million moved to accounts receivable, which becomes cash when the customers pay for it. Think of what we could do with $20 million. Cash is a great asset.

Inventory as a Liability

Raw material inventory that is purchased and received into our warehouse and is not yet paid for is recorded as an accounts payable on our balance sheet until the invoice is paid. For example, if we bought $20,000 worth of raw material from a supplier and we didn't pay for it yet, it would be entered as a current asset valued at $20,000 on the balance sheet. It would also be entered as a (accounts payable) current liability of $20,000 on the balance sheet. Thus, the asset and liability are in "balance."

Unfortunately, it is not as simple as I've just stated. Let's say you took $5,000 of the raw material and used it in production to make a finished-product. Then raw material inventory would be reduced by $5,000 and finished goods inventory would be increased by $5,000 plus the value-added content (labor), which, along with other parts, turns the $5,000 into, let's say $10,000. In other words, inventory doesn't remain stagnant in one category on the balance sheet. Hopefully, it moves from a raw material to WIP and, finally, to a finished product. Once it enters production and gets combined with other raw materials, it quickly loses its unique identity as a raw material. That's why from a balance sheet point of view, we look at the total aggregate value of assets and liabilities, but the transaction or audit records will keep track of the individual items in detail. The record keeping system that keeps track of these assets and liabilities is called the *general ledger of accounts* (the checking account analogy), and all financial transactions are recorded there. Many people, including our bankers, look at the balance sheet.

Financial Measurements

Two particular financial measurements related to inventory are important. They are the **current ratio** and the **quick ratio**. The *current ratio* measures a company's current assets against its current liabilities. *Current assets* are those assets that can be converted into cash in less than a year, and typically include cash, accounts receivable, and inventory. *Current* *liabilities* are liabilities that have to be paid off in less than a year, and typically include accounts payable and short-term loans. The formula for the current ratio is as follows:

Current ratio = Current assets/Current liabilities

Let's take our numbers and apply them to the current ratio formula. At the end of the year we had $40 million in inventory, $5 million in cash, and $25 million in accounts receivable. Our current liabilities at the time were $25 million. So our current ratio was as follows:

$70M/$25M = 2.8

Is the ratio of 2.8 too high, or is it too low? It depends on how you look at it. It is too low when the ratio approaches 1.0. When it gets close to one, we will barely be able to cover our liabilities, and it will raise a flag with our bank who lends us money against an established line of credit. If the ratio were too high, it might suggest that we were sitting on too much cash when we could have reinvested it in the company. So our current ratio of 2.8 is on the low side, but the good news is that it has been trending upward for the last two quarters. You might look at this and say we are in good shape — not great but good. This is where the quick ratio and inventory levels impact the current ratio. The quick ratio, also known as the acid-test ratio, is similar to the current ratio, except we subtract inventory from the equation. The formula is as follows:

Quick ratio = Current assets – inventory/Current liabilities

As everyone in this room knows, our inventory at the end of the year was $40 million. So, applying the quick ratio formula, we have a quick ratio of

$70M – $40M/$25M = 1.2

Now that's scary! As I said before, a quick ratio approaching 1 is trouble. This supports my earlier statement that we will soon run out of cash unless we sell off some of this inventory. The quick ratio clearly shows the impact that inventory has on our ability to pay our bills. Let's look at one more measurement before we leave this section: **total asset turnover.** This ratio compares total assets to revenue. Remember, revenue is income from sales. Total assets include current assets as well as fixed assets. Total assets include cash, accounts receivable, inventory, property, plant, and equipment (PPE), and other long-term assets. The formula for total asset turnover is:

Total asset turnover = Revenue/Total assets

Applying this formula to Woodstock, our total asset turnover is:

$90M/$85M = 1.05

Again, this is another financial measurement that tells us we are doing poorly. Oh, by the way, the $85 million of total assets is made up of $70 million of current assets and $15 million of fixed assets (PPE). Total asset turnover is a gauge of efficiency in the use of all assets. If we can reduce inventory as we must, then the total asset turnover will rise. These are useful tools in evaluating our company's performance. You can now understand how important it is for us to reduce inventory days of supply and increase inventory turns. Inventory levels have a major impact on the financial health of the company. Two more performance measures used to analyze the financial health of a company are the return on total assets and the return on inventory investment. Because we lost $2 million last year, it is not a pretty picture:

Return on total assets = Net annual profit/Total assets

–2M/$85M = –2.35% ROA

**Return on inventory investment =
Net annual profit/Average inventory**

–$2M/$35M = –5.71% ROII

> **TIP #33:** *Inventory moves into our financial reporting system as an asset on our balance sheet and remains there until it is shipped and billed to a customer (accounts receivable) or disposed of in some form or another.*

> **TIP #34:** *Inventory also moves into our financial reporting system as a liability (if we didn't pay for it yet) as part of the accounts payable on our balance sheet and remains there until it is paid for.*

We shouldn't leave the topic of inventory liabilities without discussing how raw material suppliers get paid. When raw materials are purchased,

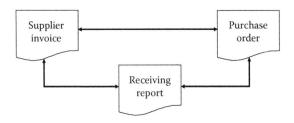

Figure 3.1   Purchase order payment three-way match.

a purchase order is created. We may or may not send a hard copy of the purchase order to the supplier. That depends on our relationship with a particular supplier. When the raw material is received, it is recorded into inventory, and an inventory receipt transaction is created by the receiving department. Finally, the supplier sends us an invoice for the raw material shipped. Before a supplier is paid, we do what is called a *three-way match*. As depicted in Figure 3.1, we match up the purchase order, the shipment receipt, and the invoice.

If all three documents are in agreement, we pay the supplier according to the terms on the invoice. We would like to get away from doing all this extra work. Companies today are eliminating this three-way match with some suppliers. If we have a true "trusting" relationship with our suppliers, we can do this also. The three-way match can also be done electronically. Although this may not directly help us "rightsize" our inventory, it will help us reduce our cost of doing business. At present we have two people who spend about 50 percent of their time performing the three-way match. At current salaries, this is costing us in excess of $50,000 per year.

Inventory and the Income Statement

Inventory will remain on our balance sheet as an asset until it is converted (transformed) into a finished product and sold to a customer. Once sold, the inventory moves to the income statement, sometimes referred to as profit and loss statement. The income statement reports revenues, expenses, and profits for a given period of time. This can be prepared monthly, quarterly, and annually.

We at Woodstock prepare a monthly income statement. Expenses are subtracted from revenue (income) and the result is the profit. Expenses fall into many categories and, in general, include all costs to run the business. Getting back to inventory sold, keep in mind that a finished product is defined differently for each of our divisions. For the Flashlight Division, a finished product is a flashlight, complete with batteries. For

Table 3.3 Income Statement (×1,000)

Income Statement ($)		
Revenue (sales)		200,000
Cost of goods sold		
Material	66,000	
Labor	18,000	
Overhead	36,000	
Total COGS	120,000	–120,000
Gross profit		80,000
Other expenses		–30,000
Net profit		50,000

our Spotlight Division, a finished product is a subassembly that the buyer will add to its product. For the Beacon Light Division, it could be a raw material (component or part) or a subassembly sold by our field service group, or a complete light system sold by our sales team.

Once the product is sold, it moves off the balance sheet onto the income statement as one of the three elements of cost of goods sold (COGS). Table 3.3 represents a financial presentation on an income statement. COGS is used to measure all the costs directly associated with making the products: materials, labor, and associated overhead. We all understand the material and labor portion of COGS.

It should be mentioned that overhead in our case includes the salaries of the planning, purchasing, and process design departments. Overhead even includes Joe's salary as vice president of operations. COGS is stated a little differently for retailers and distributors (wholesalers). These types of companies don't produce a product. They buy a product and then resell it at a higher price, often repackaging it. In addition to the item cost, their COGS may include freight transportation and repacking expenses. Getting back to Woodstock, we have to be careful how we report inventory in our financial statements.

Producing more than we sell can increase our profit picture — but did we really make a profit? The excess inventory (more production than what was sold) and its associated product costs are reported as an asset on the balance sheet, rather than as COGS on the income statement (until it is sold). Thus, it is recorded as a positive number (asset), rather than a negative number (expense). In a sense, these fixed costs will be part of the asset account and don't show up as an expense until they move to the income statement as part of COGS expense. This can lead to a misrepresentation of profit. No one should deliberately overproduce inventory for favorable accounting and reporting of an asset. Remember, sooner or later, that asset will have to be reported as an expense (when sold)

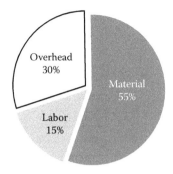

Figure 3.2 Woodstock cost of goods sold.

on the income statement. It may make the company's financials look good in one accounting period but bad in another. Let's get back to your personal checking account as an example. Suppose you deposited your salary checks into your checking account for a whole month and didn't write out any checks to pay bills. Well, someone could look at your account balance (asset) and assume you were in good financial shape. However, the next month you write checks to pay all your bills and you run out of money. You were only kidding yourself and didn't fool anyone. Figure 3.2 shows a breakdown of our COGS.

Our COGS for last year was $60 million: far too high for a company our size. Arnie probably already mentioned it, but I'll restate it in case you forgot. How slowly or how quickly inventory flows through our supply chain is an important aspect of rightsizing our inventory. If you look at the quick ratio cited earlier, we have to pick up the pace and move inventory out more quickly. The faster we move it, the sooner we will get the cash and improve this ratio. What I'm really saying is, we have to increase our inventory turns. Based on our average inventory and cost of goods sold, we turned our total inventory 1.7 times.

The formula is:

Inventory turns = COGS/average inventory

$60M/$35M = 1.7 turns

Inventory turns can also be calculated as:

Sales/inventory = Inventory turns

However, using sales rather than COGS can overstate the inventory turnover ratio, because the sales figure exceeds costs by the gross margin.

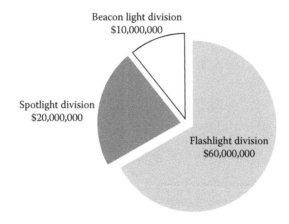

Beacon light division
$10,000,000

Spotlight division
$20,000,000

Flashlight division
$60,000,000

Figure 3.3   Woodstock sales by division.

Let's use the COGS/inventory formula, take this a step further, and calculate "inventory days on hand."
The formula is:

Days of supply = Days of the year/inventory turns

365/1.7 = 215 days of supply

From a financial point of view, this is not a good ratio. I realize, to you in operations, it has little meaning, because we have three divisions and multiple categories of inventory. Is this a true picture of our days of supply? I've done a little experimenting and estimating and have come up with some interesting numbers. I realized that our average inventory was $35 million throughout the year, and our year-end inventory was $40 million. Because we have no supporting data on the average inventory by division, I will use the year-end inventory to make a point.

There are several assumptions I used to come up with my numbers. I assumed COGS was related to sales by division. Let's take the Flashlight Division because that's our largest division. Total COGS for the company was $60 million, and sales for the Flashlight Division were 67 percent of all sales, as shown in Figure 3.3.

I assumed (arguably) that this corresponded to 67 percent of COGS, which represented $40.2 million in COGS for this division. Assuming the total year-end inventory for the Flashlight Division was $28 million (actual, not average) and COGS was $40.2 million, I applied the formula and came up with the following inventory turns for this division:

$$\$40.2/28 = 1.4 \text{ turns per year}$$

Taking this a step further, I calculated the days on hand and came up with the number of day's inventory on hand for this division:

$$365/1.4 = 261 \text{ days of inventory on hand}$$

Now let's look only at the Flashlight Division finished goods inventory and apply the same two formulas:

$$\$40.2/\$13 = 3.09 \text{ turns per year}$$

$$365/3.09 = 118 \text{ days of inventory on hand}$$

Now you might be wondering why I went through this mental exercise. We in finance look at the aggregate inventory and the aggregate inventory turns. From our point of view, we view low inventory turns as a sign that our cash-to-cash cycle (I'll explain later) is very poor, and overall inventory turns have to increase. You in operations, on the other hand, need to understand the details so that you can focus on areas where inventory turns are the lowest. If you compare our total company inventory turns and inventory days on hand to the Flashlight Division inventory turns and days on hand, you get a clearer picture of inventory turns and days on hand:

All inventory:
1.7 turns and 215 days of supply (100 percent COGS)

All flashlight inventory:
1.4 turns and 261 days of supply (67 percent COGS)

All flashlight finished goods inventory:
3.09 turns and 118 days of supply (67 percent COGS)

This approach gives us a more realistic picture of where we need to focus our attention. The average 215 days of supply for all inventory is a lot different when you compare it to the 118 days of supply for the finished goods, flashlights. However, we still need to dig into the details. In theory, 215 days of inventory means it takes 215 days for inventory to flow through our supply chain. In the aggregate, this tells us the big picture, but in reality, some inventory moves through our supply chains in days, and some inventory has been sitting here for years.

Having the numbers is a good thing, and it certainly gives us a benchmark to measure against, but we still have to manage the inventory at the item-level detail. As I said before, my numbers are off because I couldn't come up with realistic average inventory numbers by division. I'm merely trying to show you that if we can track COGS and average inventory throughout the year by division, inventory turns and days of supply will have more meaning to operations. If the numbers have more meaning, it will help in our efforts to rightsize our inventory.

> **TIP #35:** *Finance looks at inventory turns and days of supply in the aggregate, but for operations to address this issue in its inventory rightsizing efforts, inventory turns, days of supply, and COGS need to be broken down into inventory types and families at the item-level detail.*

I would like to make two more points before I leave this subject. You might be wondering why I used 365 days to calculate days of supply rather than just the 250 days or so that we normally work. The answer is that we are paying for and carrying that inventory every day of the year, whether we are open for business or not.

The other point I want to make is, when we look at COGS, we need to understand that inventory represents the greatest portion of that cost. Figure 3.2 shows 55 percent of COGS is for material, by far the highest cost, representing $33 million last year. Inventory levels and costs are the single biggest cash outflow we have, and it must be addressed and reduced, if we want to stay in business.

Inventory Carrying Cost

I started out by saying that having inventory costs the company money. So far we have learned that low inventory turns and high inventory days of supply are a drain on cash flow and cost us money. We also learned that inventory is the largest element of COGS, again, costing us a lot of money. Let's move on to a third area where having inventory is costing us money: carrying cost. My Uncle Billy, who was chairman of the board of our family business where I worked as controller before joining Wood-stock, once told me that carrying cost is a meaningless inventory metric. His argument was that we still had to pay for the space, people, insurance, etc., regardless of our inventory level. We argued about this all the time.

Let me share with you my thoughts on this topic. First of all, "carrying costs" can be defined as those costs associated with holding inventory in stock. This is usually defined as a percentage of the dollar value of the total inventory. This cost can vary from company to company, anywhere from 10 percent to 40 percent annually. What's important to understand here (and my uncle didn't get it) is whether we could get a better return on our investment if we spent the money elsewhere, rather than on inventory in our supply chain. Let me state the obvious: inventory costs money. It costs us money to buy it and look after it. Because most companies are not cash rich, they borrow money from the bank to do this. Thus, money costs money.

We pay interest on borrowed money, and we draw from a line of credit we have established with our bank. This money or line of credit might be best spent elsewhere, like buying newer, efficient machines that will improve our productivity and reduce the need to carry so much inventory. Carrying cost is not a one-time expense. It is an ongoing cost of doing business. Our carrying costs at Woodstock are 25 percent of the total value of our inventory. Our year-end inventory was $40 million. So, our carrying costs last year were

$$\$40M \times .25 = \$10 \text{ million}$$

It cost us $10 million last year to carry that $40 million. If we had invested that $10 million somewhere else, would we have a better return? That's the question. Keep in mind that this isn't a one-time cost. For every year we carry this $40 million, it will cost us $10 million to carry it. That's a great deal of money! What are some of these costs? There are three categories of carrying costs. Let's discuss them.

1. **Storage costs:** These costs can vary significantly, depending on your type of business and the value and size of your inventory. This cost category includes the cost for space, people, systems, and the equipment to move goods into and out of inventory. For example, if your product is a high-end watch brand well known as a piece of jewelry rather than a functional watch that you throw away when the battery goes dead five years later, your storage costs will be different.

   Let's refer to the high-end watch company as company A and the low-end watch company as company B. Which company would have a higher storage cost? If you guessed company A, you would be right. Company A's warehouse space might be a safe the size of a room where the watches are kept. It will spend more money on security systems and security guards. The procedures for entering and leaving a secured area might be complex and time consuming — and we all know that time is money. Let's say that you are a well-known manufacturer of high fashion designer briefcases and handbags. Which would require a more rigid inventory control system, the raw material or the finished product? In this example it would be the finished product. So you see, the value of the product is an important factor when we talk about space. The equipment cost is another part of the carrying cost. This will vary depending on the physical characteristics of the product and how your storeroom is laid out. In our case, the value of our products is a lesser issue than the cost of equipment and personnel.

Our storeroom shelves are over 20 feet high and we require forklift trucks that get to the top shelf. These forklift trucks require operators, and our maintenance department has to keep the equipment in running order. All this is part of the storage cost. We are lucky that our products don't require refrigeration, like some industries; this would add to the storage cost. The batteries we stock are in a climate-controlled room, which does add some to our storage cost. Even the computer system can be considered as part of our carrying cost. This would include the hardware, such as PCs, bar-code readers, and scanners, and software, such as our warehouse management system.

2. **Capital costs:** This portion of carrying cost is the amount of money we have tied up in inventory. We all know that our inventory is about $39 million. We had to borrow a good portion of this to pay for the raw materials and labor to make the finished products. As a result of this, we have to pay interest on the loans (line of credit) we have with our bank. Some of these short-term loans are coming due soon, and we will have a substantial payment due by the end of June. We will need to turn a lot of inventory into cash by then. It won't do us any good to move out $20 million worth of inventory if we are just going to replace it. We have to move it out and keep it out.

3. **Risk costs:** There is a degree of risk with carrying inventory. It can become obsolete, damaged, or we could have a pilferage problem. We have insurance to protect us against these risks, but the insurance cost is another cost we incur in carrying inventory. We need to look at this in more detail. The reasons that inventory becomes obsolete vary from company to company. Here are a few we should look at:

   ■ **No market demand:** The inventory is at the end of its life cycle, and the customers no longer want to buy it. I think we should look at any inventory item that hasn't had any activity for one year or more, consider disposing of it, and write it off our books.

- **Defective inventory:** Any inventory item that is damaged and cannot be repaired should be scrapped or recycled. I'm no chemist, but I do know we use a lot of plastic parts. Let's do an analysis of our damaged parts and see if it is possible to sell them to a recycling company. Rather than a total write-off, we would get some residual return and at the same time be environmentally conscious.

- **Technical obsolescence:** Some of our products may be technically obsolete. Let's have our sales teams review the finished goods inventory to identify products that have reached the end of their life cycle and see how we can move them out of inventory. The same is true for our raw materials. Let's have our product design team review the raw material inventory.

- **Design (engineering) changes:** I have been at meetings where our design team said it found a different part or component that would be better suited to our finished product. What about the inventory of the part that was replaced? Shouldn't we be looking for ways to work this inventory off?

- **Spoilage:** Fortunately, we don't have this problem, or do we? The only products that might be an issue are batteries. But I doubt it. Batteries today have a long shelf life, and unless some inventory fell through the cracks, I don't think this will be a big-ticket item for us.

Does anyone here know how much of our inventory is obsolete? I know there is a reluctance to admit that we have obsolete inventory. No one wants to see a large inventory write-off on our financial records. But truth be told, we are losing money and need cash to keep operating. If there is any way that we can move some of this obsolete inventory off the books and get cash for it, we should do it; we will be doing a good thing for the company.

As I said earlier, let's take our loss now rather than later. This needs to be explained to the sales team. Its immediate reaction will be to say "no." The team will want to keep the inventory "just in case" it gets an order for it. Another typical reaction will be, "the minute we get rid of the inventory, a customer will give us an order for it." My answer to that is, if the team gets an order for it after we scrap it, then we will make it. I have run a report indicating all inventory items where there has been no activity for 12 months or longer. This includes raw materials and finished goods. The oldest item is a raw material, part number 31918. We have 5000 of these (lenses) in stock, and the total value is $1000. Now you may say that $1000 isn't much, but Table 3.4 shows the complete list

Table 3.4 Inactive Inventory

Inactive Inventory	Raw Material ($)	Finished Goods ($)	Total ($)
Flashlights	1,800,000	1,100,000	2,900,000
Spotlights	1,200,000	350,000	1,550,000
Beacon lights	500,000	1,000,000	1,500,000
Total	3,500,000	2,450,000	5,950,000

of inactive items. This list shows that we have close to $6 million of inventory with no activity for a year or longer.

You want to rightsize our inventory, right? Well, this is a great place to start. I recommend that the Harmony Team study this in detail. I think you will be surprised by your findings. Here is a good way to look at it. We live in the northeastern part of the country and experience the four seasons of weather change. Typically, we go through our wardrobe each time the season changes and get out the appropriate clothing for that season. My husband is the type who doesn't like to throw out anything. He will keep rotating the same clothes year after year, even though he may not have worn it for five years! He keeps saying that he will go on a diet and fit into it some day. I'm just the opposite. I say, if I haven't worn it for this season, then get rid of it. That's the mentality we have to apply to our inventory here at Woodstock.

> **TIP #36:** *Analyze your inventory for activity. If there hasn't been any activity on an item in inventory for 12 months or longer, consider disposing of it. This includes raw materials and finished goods.*

> **TIP #37:** *There is a direct relationship between the level of inventory carried, and the cost of carrying inventory. When the inventory level increases, carrying cost increases; when the inventory level decreases, carrying cost decreases.*

Inventory Valuation

One major accounting decision we in finance have to make is how to measure the value of our inventory. As I've stated earlier, inventory remains on the balance sheet as an asset until it is sold and then moves to the income statement as part of COGS. The amount of this expense (COGS) depends on the accounting method we use. Likewise, the inventory value that still remains on the balance sheet as an asset depends on the accounting method used also. There are two popular inventory valuation methods used today: first in–first out (FIFO) cost sequence and last in–first out (LIFO) cost sequence. There are other methods, which I'll discuss later.

LIFO and FIFO seem to be the most popular. Item costs are entered into the inventory asset account in the order acquired, but they do not have to be taken out of the inventory asset account in the same order. The different methods address the order in which item costs are taken out of the inventory asset account but have nothing to do with the physical act of moving inventory into and out of stock. For example, if you bought 500 pieces of raw material A in January and 200 pieces in February, you don't have to physically use up the January material before using the February material. These techniques only address how you record the value of inventory movement, not the physical movement itself.

The FIFO Inventory Valuation Method

With the FIFO method, you charge out the item cost to COGS expense in the order in which you acquire the goods. Let's use light housing frame part number 5867 as an example. Suppose we bought this part as follows: January: 100 pieces at $25 each; February: 100 pieces at $30 each; and March: 100 pieces at $35 each. The total cost for the quarter is shown in Table 3.5.

For the quarter, we use 250 pieces and follow the FIFO inventory valuation method. Inventory expense would be $7250 (recorded on the income statement as part of COGS); the remaining 50 pieces would go into inventory at $35 each for a total of $1750 (recorded on the balance sheet).

The inventory asset account on the balance sheet and the COGS expense on the income statement are in balance, and all is right with the accounting world. FIFO is an ideal method for several reasons. The actual physical movement of goods typically, but not always, is on a first in –first out basis and matches the accounting method rather nicely. In this way, the ending inventory, 50 pieces in my example, reflects the most recent purchase cost and, therefore, is very close to the replacement of this item (currently $36 each).

When item costs are rising, as in my example, companies try to follow a first in–first out sales price strategy. That way they try to hold off a price increase a bit longer. They might wait until they have sold off all the lower cost inventory (January and February) before raising prices. On the other hand, they might want to raise sales prices before reaching the higher-priced goods so that they can make greater profit margins.

Table 3.5 FIFO and LIFO Valuation Example

Month	Units Purchased	Cost Each ($)	Total Cost ($)	FIFO Usage	FIFO Value ($)	LIFO Usage	LIFO Value ($)
January	100	25.00	2,500	100	2,500	50	1,250
February	100	30.00	3,000	100	3,000	100	3,000
March	100	35.00	3,500	50	1,750	100	3,500
Subtotals	300		9,000	250	7,250	250	7,750
Quarterly usage on income statement					7,250		7,750
Remaining inventory on balance sheet					1,750		1,250
3-month total cost					9,000		9,000

The LIFO Inventory Valuation Method

With this inventory valuation method, you charge out inventory based on the last item you purchased first and then work backward until you have the total cost for the number of items sold. Using this method, inventory expense would be charged as shown in Table 3.5. You will note, using the LIFO method, inventory is recorded at $500, which is lower than when using the FIFO method, and COGS is recorded at $500, which is higher than when using the FIFO method. In this example, using the LIFO method will result in higher cost. The remaining inventory will have a lower valuation, but will be further apart from a realistic replacement cost. So that's the trade-off: inventory (asset) valuation versus COGS (expense) valuation.

> **TIP #38:** *Select an inventory valuation method that best reflects the true value of your inventory and conforms to GAAP guidelines.*

When inventory costs are rising, the LIFO method maximizes your COGS expense deduction for determining taxable income and will help minimize taxable income. By taking out product cost and charging it to COGS expense, you minimize the inventory cost value. The pitfall in doing this is that your inventory cost value can very quickly become out-of-date, especially in our business where our products have very long shelf lives. If inventory items have a very short life cycle, then the gap between LIFO and FIFO will be less and the accounting method will not have as great an impact. However, we only get to use one method of inventory valuation at a time.

We have been using the FIFO method here at Woodstock, and we have no plans to change it right now. If we switched to the LIFO method, we could reduce the value of our inventory substantially, but it would be misleading. It would not reflect the true replacement value of our inventory. However, we found some cases where our current inventory value is higher than the current product replacement cost. For a few items, it is even higher than our selling price. I am going to recommend to Adriana that we decrease our product cost to the lower of the two, so that we recognize our inventory loss now, rather than when the product is sold.

> **TIP #39:** *Inventory valuation must be realistic and reflect the true value of your inventory. Consider adjusting the value of your inventory downward if it falls below the current replacement cost or the current selling price of the product. Take the loss earlier rather than later.*

Besides LIFO and FIFO, which are the two most popular inventory valuation techniques, there are other cost techniques and considerations:

Average Cost Valuation Method

The average cost method averages the acquisition cost of a material over a period of time. This provides some balance between COGS expense on the income statement and the inventory asset on the balance sheet. If we don't want to go with LIFO or FIFO, this is a method we should consider.

Standard Cost Valuation Method

Using the standard cost technique, a single value (standard) is selected for an inventory item, typically for a period of one year. This standard is based on some average of past usage and estimated future cost. Companies then compare this standard cost to actual costs and report the difference as an inventory variance from standard.

Actual Cost Valuation Method

This method attempts to capture actual inventory costs as they occur. For raw materials this is relatively straightforward. However, if you manufacture sub-assemblies like we do, it becomes a more difficult process. Once we take a raw material and add some value to it (labor and overhead), we would have to capture the new value when it is put into inventory. Some industries use this method when inventory is tied to a particular contract.

Activity-Based Costing Method

This method focuses on the activities that create cost, sometimes referred to as "cost drivers." This approach attempts to assign costs directly to specific products rather than assigning costs across the board to a broad range of products. Unless you have the capability to capture and assign these costs, this is a difficult technique to implement. We aren't there yet, but I would like to do this someday.

Lower of Cost or Market (LCM) Inventory Valuation

Inventory valuation methods are subject to the LCM rule. This means that if your inventory depreciates in value, you must write your inventory

Table 3.6   Market Valuation for Part #52969

Spotlight Part #52969	
Category	Dollar Value
Product cost	30.00
+Selling cost	15.00
Total cost	45.00
+Profit margin	15.00
Selling price	60.00

down to the depreciated value. There can be many reasons why an item decreases in value rather than appreciates. Damaged goods are a good example. If inventory is damaged, it may not be worth what you paid for it, so you can't charge full price. In this case, we estimate how much we can receive for the item and create an allowance for the change. In other words, we would write down the inventory value to the net realizable value. As part of our inventory rightsizing efforts, we should analyze our inventory for the LCM and make the necessary adjustments and allowances.

Market Valuation

Inventory is typically valued at cost or market, whichever is lower. Yes, there are situations where market value can be less than cost. This loss in market value can be a result of market forces related to supply and demand. Depending on how we measure our market, a decline in market value will have different effects on our inventory valuations and income calculations. For example, let's look at one particular product, spotlight subassembly part #52969, as shown in Table 3.6.

Net Realizable Value Less Profit Margin

Any reduction in selling price will reduce the value of the inventory. In this example, any selling price below $60 will not cover the selling cost of $15, the profit margin of $15, and the product cost of $30. If we actually sell the product for $55, we will only recover $25 of the $30 product cost. The reduction in inventory value will reduce income by the equivalent amount in the current period. It allows the company to cover its selling cost and show a normal margin when the inventory is sold at another time.

Net Realizable Value

A decrease in selling price in excess of profit margin will reduce the value of inventory, but a decrease in selling price of less than the profit margin will not. Any loss in profit margin will occur in the future when the inventory is sold. There is a reduction of inventory value and income in the current period if selling price fails to cover product and selling costs.

Inventory Replacement Cost

Market value can be defined as replacement or reproduction cost, with limits based on selling price. A decrease in inventory replacement cost will reduce the value of inventory and the income for the current period. Future income will be increased as the lower cost inventory is sold. Market cannot be more than net realizable value. An inventory item for sale cannot be worth less than its current price, less the cost of selling it and providing a normal profit.

Variable Costing

Some companies like to value inventory at variable cost and assign all fixed costs as period costs. This is known as *variable costing* or *direct costing*. This practice of assigning fixed costs to inventory is called *absorption costing*. This can sometimes be misleading and may cause the company to produce at full capacity when customer demand isn't there, because inventory is absorbing fixed costs. This is based on the concept "the more we produce, the more fixed cost we will cover." Although this might be a useful tool for financial analysis, I'm not sure it is an acceptable technique for income and asset management measurements.

Manufacturing Cost Accounting

Another area we are responsible for is product cost accounting. This activity is where we try to capture all the costs associated with a product, and come up with a total cost for the product. This is an important activity because once the total cost of a product is known, the sales and marketing team can establish a selling price that meets the company criteria for profit margins. We had a product in our Spotlight Division not long ago that we really messed up on. We estimated our cost to be $24.50 per unit, and sales priced it at $42.50. The books showed that we were making a gross profit of $10 per unit sold. We came to find out that we used the wrong labor rate in the assembly work center. After we made the adjustment, our cost ballooned to $37.95 per unit and our gross profit dropped to $4.55 per unit. After deducting all other business costs such as sales and administrative expenses, we discovered we were actually losing $3.95 per unit. Here's the real impact. We had already sold 2,698 of those units, so we actually lost $10,657.10. To make matters worse, sales was committed to that selling price and couldn't change it for the rest of the year. We lost $50,756 for the year on that product. We must be sure that we are assigning the correct costs to our products.

> **TIP #40: *Cost accounting must capture the true cost of adding value to a raw material, so that finished goods are valued correctly for sales and marketing to establish selling prices that conform to company profitability guidelines.***

We in finance and accounting shouldn't be doing this alone. We have a cost accountant on staff who does this, but he should be working with all the links in our supply chain to get the true cost. The two groups that should be heavily involved are product design for input on the materials used and process design for the labor required to put the product together. Even purchasing should be involved. After all, purchasing goes out and buys the materials. I know you are looking at getting all of our supply-chain links to work together. This is one more area that the Harmony Team should look at. Figure 3.4 shows a typical bill of material for one of our subassemblies.

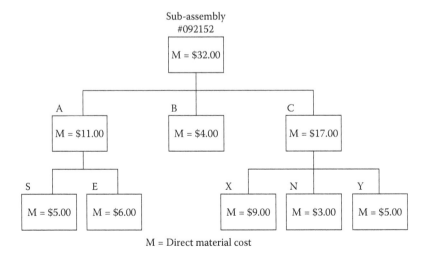

Figure 3.4   Direct material cost roll-up.

What we attempt to do in cost accounting is to assign material, labor, and overhead costs at each level in the bill of material and then roll up those costs to the finished product. This particular part is a subassembly that we ship to our customers, who then use our product to manufacture their product. Because this product has a lot of glass and other fragile components, we have to package it carefully. In addition to the manufacturing cost, we even capture the labor (time required to pack it) and material (carton, tape, inserts, bubble wrap, and peanuts) to pack it safely so that it doesn't get damaged in transit. Figure 3.4 shows the material cost for subassembly #092152. For example, subassembly A is a manufactured part that goes into subassembly #092152. It is made up of purchased materials S and E. The purchase cost of material S is $5, and of material E is $6. Therefore, the total material cost for part A is $11.

Likewise, the material costs of X ($9), N ($3), and Y ($5) are added up, and the material cost for part C becomes $17. Going up the bill of material, we add the material costs of A ($11.00), B ($4.00), and C ($17.00) and the total material cost (without labor and overhead) is $32.00. Now we need to add labor to parts A, C, and subassembly #092152, as shown in Figure 3.5.

Because parts S, E, X, N, Y, and B are purchased parts, no labor is added. It requires $1.65 of labor to manufacture part A, using purchased parts S and E. It also requires $2.55 of labor to manufacture part C from purchased parts X, N, and Y. It further requires $4.80 of labor to assemble parts A, B, and C. So, for part A, the cost of material and labor becomes

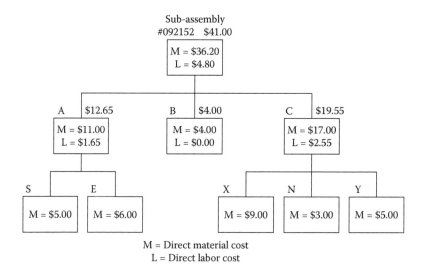

Figure 3.5 Direct material plus direct labor cost roll-up.

$12.65 (M = $11.00 + L = $1.65) and the cost of C becomes $19.55 (M = $17.00 + L = $2.55). The cost to assemble parts A, B, and C into subassembly #092152 is $4.80, for a total material and labor cost of $41.00 (A = $12.65 + B = $4.00 + C = $19.55 + L = $4.80).

In many cases, we are paying for the labor six months or more before the product is shipped to a customer. Then we have to wait another 30 to 60 days before the customer pays us. This hurts our cash flow. If we could keep the raw material in stock and add the labor further downstream in our manufacturing process, we would improve our cash flow. Granted, we have to pay labor anyway, but why not have them working on products that are going out the door immediately?

> **TIP #41:** *As a raw material moves through the manufacturing process, labor adds value and increases the cost of the item. If the item goes back into inventory, it goes back at a higher cost, thus increasing the total value of the inventory. If possible, delay adding value to a raw material until it can be shipped without going back into inventory.*

Inventory Accuracy

How can a financial person conclude an inventory presentation without discussing inventory accuracy? You know, every December is a time of the year we financial types dread. You would think, with the holiday season and all, it would be a happy time of the year for everyone. On a personal level it is, but on a business level it is a nightmare. Why? Because that is the time of the year when we take physical inventory. This process takes weeks to accomplish. We take one week preparing for it, another week to take the inventory, and then another two weeks to reconcile the inventory with our perpetual records. This is a total of four weeks. What is disheartening is the fact that, come January of the new year, it takes only about two weeks for it to get out of sync.

Every year we go through the same routine, and every year two weeks later, we are back where we were. I wonder why we bother. Actually, we have to do it. Our outside accountants and auditors require us to do it. We in finance take all the item counts and roll all this data up into an aggregate number that we use in our financial reporting. We aren't concerned about individual items. I know those of you in operations are. We are concerned with the total dollar value of the inventory, and you are concerned with individual item counts. If you remember, our year-ending inventory was $40 million, and our average inventory throughout the year was $35 million.

Table 3.7   Inventory Accuracy

Item Number	Perpetual Inventory	Physical Inventory
A	100	99
B	100	100
C	100	98

Our total inventory went up from the year before, and everyone was surprised. That's what caused Adriana to write her e-mail to Joe, and why you are tasked with rightsizing inventory. And let me say this, we can't possibly rightsize our inventory unless we know what it is. Inventory accuracy is a key criterion for successful supply chains. Inventory inaccuracy causes all sorts of supply-chain problems — not just immediate financial ones. At what point can we say our inventory is accurate? Well, the correct answer is when our physical inventory matches our perpetual inventory 100 percent. That should be our goal.

Table 3.7 represents three different inventory items. The perpetual inventory record says we should have 100 of each in stock. Well, we took a physical inventory, and the physical count was: item A, 99 pieces; item B, 100 pieces; and item C, 98 pieces. Based on this data, what is our inventory accuracy? Pretty good, huh? Would you say about 98 percent? Wrong. Our inventory accuracy in this example is 33 percent. Only one out of three inventory records are correct. In the aggregate, it looks pretty good. But what would you say if item B has a unit cost of .005 cents and item C has a cost of $150? It's not looking so good now. What if I said we could buy item B (which is a standard screw size) at the local hardware store and item A is purchased halfway around the world and has a 26-week lead time? What if I said we needed 100 pieces of item C right now to satisfy a major customer? Again, things look bleak. Inventory inaccuracy causes many problems; here are a few of them:

1. **Lost sales:** If you have a stockout because you don't have an item you thought you had in stock, you could lose a sale.
2. **Missed production schedules:** You set up a machine, assign an operator, and you are ready to go, but the material you thought you had isn't there.
3. **Lost capacity:** Now (see item 2) you have to do another setup on the machine and run a different product. While the machine is down for a new setup, you are losing capacity.
4. **Excessive expediting:** Someone has to spend time expediting the part you thought you had in stock. They could have finished a more constructive task, instead.

5. **Premium freight charges:** Now you have to ask your supplier to rush in the part, and as a result you may have to pay a freight premium.
6. **Premium item cost:** Your supplier may have to break down its setup to rush your job, and you may have to pay more for the part.
7. **High inventory levels:** You didn't know you had it, so it just sits there collecting dust and adding to your carrying cost.

The first six problems of inventory inaccuracy relate to not having an item in stock that you thought you had. The last problem relates to not knowing you had something in stock. This is just as bad as any of the other six for all the reasons I've talked about previously. Let's get back to defining inventory accuracy. I said the inventory accuracy in this example was 33 percent. In the real world, many companies apply a percentage range to inventory accuracy. For example, an inventory record may be considered accurate if it is within plus or minus 5 percent of the perpetual inventory record. If that were the case, then the inventory accuracy would be 100 percent (actually 99 percent). I'm not comfortable with that and neither should you be. We will have to agree on what constitutes inventory accuracy here at Woodstock.

> **TIP #42** *Inventory inaccuracy has a negative impact on the entire supply chain, can decrease customer service and productivity levels, and can increase costs. You must improve inventory accuracy.*
>
> **TIP #43:** *Each company must define the criteria used to measure inventory accuracy, measure accuracy against the criteria, and communicate all this to all employees in the supply chain.*

Just in case you hadn't heard, our year-end inventory was reconciled to our perpetual inventory. Using the criterion of total dollars of the physical inventory compared to the total dollars of the perpetual inventory, our inventory accuracy was 88 percent. The physical inventory was $40 million, and the perpetual inventory was $35 million.

Inventory accuracy: ($35/$40M = .875)

This is not good. If you looked at the details of individual items, you would find that accuracy at the item level was even worse. We didn't measure this, but I would bet it is somewhere around 70 percent to 75 percent. We need to improve our inventory accuracy. We can do this by using a technique called *cycle counting*. Cycle counting is a methodology of counting some inventory items every day rather than waiting for the end of the year. The concept behind cycle counting is to catch inventory inaccuracies immediately, rather than wait until the end of the year to count all items. Equally important with this concept is to not only correct the inventory record, but also find out (and fix) what is causing the inaccuracy to occur. Our warehouse link is looking into this, and I will let them explain to you how this works and what the plans are to improve inventory accuracy.

Inventory ABC Classification

Cycle counting is a great idea, and I'm glad that our warehouse folks are looking into it. However, not all inventory items need to be counted using this technique. For example, we use a great deal of standard size sheet metal screws in some of our product lines. These can be purchased from our local hardware store down the street or from one of the big chains located on the highway about two miles from our plant. We should categorize our inventory into groups by relative importance, with A items having the highest importance, C items with the lowest importance, and B items being somewhere in between.

The sheet metal screw I just mentioned should be classified as a C item and counted less frequently. On the other hand, we have some very expensive fabricated parts that cost in excess of $200 each. These should be classified as A items and should be counted more frequently. One method of categorizing our inventory might be based on annual dollar usage. Many companies do it this way. Table 3.8 is an example of using this technique. In Table 3.9, the data is resorted in descending dollar value, which shows part #5 to have the highest annual dollar usage. It is purely a coincidence that it is also the highest unit usage, also. Note that although part #4 has the second-highest dollar annual usage, it is only number 9 in annual unit usage.

We don't have to do it this way. We could instead establish a different criterion, such as long-lead-time items, difficult-to-get items, or even a high-risk supplier where we sole source.

I recommend that we classify our inventory into ABC categories and then decide on the degree of control we will place on them. For A items, we will have tight control and count them every month; for B items we will count once a quarter; and for C items, only twice a year. We may have to hire people to do this, but it will be money well spent to get our inventory accuracy up to acceptable levels. In the long run, we will save money. We can't truly rightsize our inventory if we don't know what it is. Let's do it. Well, that's all I have to say for now. I hope I have provided

Table 3.8 Inventory Sorted in Part Number Order

Item Number	Annual Item Usage	Item Cost ($)	Annual $ Usage
1	900	1.75	1,575.00
2	1,255	0.50	627.50
3	750	0.98	735.00
4	600	3.75	2,250.00
5	1,505	1.95	2,934.75
6	666	1.25	832.50
7	985	0.73	719.05
8	275	6.99	1,922.25
9	886	2.00	1,772.00
10	903	1.50	1,354.50

Table 3.9 Inventory Sorted by Annual Dollar Usage

Item Number	Annual Item Usage	Item Cost ($)	Annual $ Usage
5	1,505	1.95	2,934.75
4	600	3.75	2,250.00
8	275	6.99	1,922.25
9	886	2.00	1,772.00
1	900	1.75	1,575.00
10	903	1.50	1,354.50
6	666	1.25	832.50
3	750	0.98	735.00
7	985	0.73	719.05
2	1,255	0.50	627.50

you with a good understanding of our role and responsibility as it relates to inventory and also given you some good ideas on how we can go about rightsizing inventory.

Inter-Office E-Mail

To: Supply-Chain Managers   February 25
From: Harmony Team
Subject: Rightsizing Inventory
Current Inventory Level: $40.9 Million

Although the numbers don't reflect it yet, we are going in the right direction. Today we met with Pat in finance to discuss its role and responsibility as it relates to inventory. She did an excellent job in explaining inventory from a financial point of view. Following is a summary of some of the things we learned, along with some action items. As usual, the detailed minutes of the meeting will follow in another e-mail for your perusal. If you have any questions or insights you would like to share with the Harmony Team, please do not hesitate to contact any one of us.

1. We must reduce inventory immediately to improve our cash position (which is not good).
2. The only time we have real cash inflow is when our customers pay for the inventory we ship. All other inventory transactions effect cash outflow.
3. Finance will track inventory budgets and report monthly budget variances to all supply-chain managers.
4. From a financial point of view, inventory is considered an asset on our balance sheet. It remains there until it is sold and then moves to the income statement as part of COGS.
5. From an operations point of view, any inventory in excess of immediate customer needs should be considered a liability. We should question why we have it.
6. We learned that finance uses certain inventory ratios to measure our financial health. Although the current ratio is a good tool, the quick ratio (acid test) is more revealing and shows we are in trouble. Pat will distribute all the financial ratios we discussed for everyone to see on a monthly basis.

7. Inventory turns are terrible, and we discussed this before. However, Pat showed us another inventory turns-related formula that shows we have 215 days of inventory supply on hand. In other words, it takes us 215 days to turn over our inventory. Pat will publish this also.

8. On average, it costs us $10 million a year to carry inventory at our current levels. Not only does the inventory cost money to buy, it also costs us a lot to carry it in stock.

9. Pat explained the difference between LIFO and FIFO inventory valuation methods, and she will look into changing our GAAP reporting methodology. She would prefer to stay with FIFO but will explore the LIFO methodology.

10. Finance will look at our inventory from a LCM (explained in the minutes) point of view and, where appropriate, will write down inventory in accordance with GAAP principles.

11. Finance (along with process engineering) will review our item cost accounting details to see if adjustments need to be made.

12. Pat discussed inventory accuracy and defined it. Finance is concerned with the dollar accuracy and operations is concerned with the SKU (stock keeping unit) count. Pat estimates the dollar accuracy at 88 percent last year, and the SKU accuracy at 70 percent to 75 percent, although she couldn't justify the numbers at this time.

13. Because different items need different degrees of control and accuracy levels, we are going to use ABC analysis to prioritize our inventory and establish criteria for each category.

Our next meeting is scheduled for March 19 with sales and marketing. In the meantime, we will continue to work on the action items discussed with customer service (Maria) and finance (Pat). Attached to this e-mail is a continuation of our inventory rightsizing model (Figure 3.6) for your review and comments.

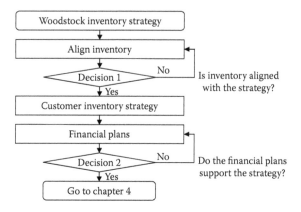

Figure 3.6   Woodstock inventory rightsizing model.

Applying the Tips, Tools, and Philosophies to Your Company

In this chapter, I have introduced 12 new TIPS and 10 formulas that can be used for financial performance measurements. Accounting and financial management are important elements of any supply chain, no matter how large or how small. Regardless of the size of your company, you must follow basic rules and regulations of inventory management. Certain financial documents must conform to GAAP.

> **TIP #32:** *Financial documents must be prepared in accordance with all laws and regulations, regardless of how bad they may make the company look. Inventory is a major component of financial reporting and must be presented as accurately as possible.*

Sarbanes–Oxley Act

As a result of the financial scandals at some public corporations and lack of corporate oversight that resulted in huge company losses, the Sarbanes Oxley Act, sometimes referred to as SOX, was enacted by Congress in 2002. The overriding intent of SOX was to protect investors by requiring public corporations to have better control over corporate disclosure, financial reporting, and corporate governance. The Securities and Exchange Commission (SEC) is responsible for the act and monitoring corporate compliance. There are two key provisions of SOX that have a particular impact on supply-chain management and inventory:

Section 401

In part, annual and quarterly financial reports are required to be filed with the SEC. Reporting companies must disclose certain material off-balance-sheet transactions, arrangements, and obligations (including contingent obligations). Other relationships of the issuer with unconsolidated entities or other persons that may have a material current or future effect on the financial condition of the company must be reported. In addition, changes in financial condition, results of operations, liquidity, capital expenditures, capital resources, or significant components of revenue or expenses must be reported.

Section 404

In part, this section of SOX requires that each annual report contain an internal control report that shall state the responsibility of management for establishing and maintaining an adequate internal control structure and procedures for financial reporting, and also an assessment, as of the end of the most recent fiscal year of the issuer. The effectiveness of the internal control structure and procedures of the issuer for financial reporting should be included.

Complying with Sections 401 and 404 of SOX goes beyond just recording a series of transactions. It must be a well-defined process that crosses links in the supply chain, from buying raw materials to shipment of goods to the customer, and all processes in between. Your service providers, such as third-party logistics (3PL) and fourth-party logistics (4PL) companies have supply-chain responsibilities to understand and comply with SOX requirements. SOX requires disclosure of risks and strategies that will go into effect in the event of a disruptive event, such as hurricanes, terrorism, or accidents.

Complying with SOX has a significant side benefit. Compliance with SOX will help you turn your inventory silos into a collaborative supply-chain network by defining and implementing inventory processes that cross supply-chain links. Everyone in the supply chain will be more aware of inventory levels, inventory accuracy, and inventory valuation. This can only make your supply chain stronger as you move forward to rightsize your inventory.

Additional Inventory Rightsizing Tips

TIP #33: *Inventory moves into our financial reporting system as an asset on our balance sheet, and remains there until it is shipped and billed to a customer (accounts receivable), or disposed of in some form or another.*

Inventory is an asset as long as it is used up for its intended purpose and in a reasonable period of time. What is considered a reasonable period of time? That is the question that must be answered by every supply-chain professional, and the answer will be different for each supply chain. As a general guideline, an inventory item may no longer be considered an asset (conceptually) under the following conditions:

1. There has been no inventory activity on the item for some pre-defined period of time (I suggest 12 months or more).
2. The inventory item is damaged and can't be repaired.
3. There is no market demand for the item.
4. The shelf life has passed or expired.
5. The value of the item has reached scrap value or less.
6. The item has been engineered out of the product and can't be used in another product.
7. The item has been engineered out of the product for health or safety reasons.

If any of these conditions exist, I suggest you consider getting rid of the item. Why keep it? It is only taking up space and costing you money to carry it in stock. To prevent any of these conditions from continuing, I recommend the following:

1. Establish a policy for inventory review (what, how).
2. Review inventory for these conditions on a predetermined schedule.
3. Have a plan in place to remove these items from inventory.
4. Before getting rid of the item, notify the appropriate supply-chain link.
5. Be prepared to be challenged by someone who wants to keep the item in stock.
6. Notify finance before scrapping large amounts of inventory.
7. Keep an audit trail of what you did with the item.

TIP #34: *Inventory also moves into our financial reporting system as a liability (if we didn't pay for it yet) as part of*

***the accounts payable on our balance sheet, and remains
there until it is paid for.***

Inventory not yet paid for is considered as part of your accounts
payable on the balance sheet and remains an accounts payable until it is
paid for (or in some cases, until returned to the supplier). Just as you
have an accounts receivable aging report, you can also have an accounts
payable aging report. It is important to keep an eye on the aging report.
This issue of paying invoices or not paying invoices can impact your
entire supply chain. All invoices should be paid on time and in accordance
with the stated terms and conditions. However, realistically, if you are
falling on hard times and can't pay your supplier on time, the following
might occur:

1. Your credit rating may be negatively impacted
2. Supplier relationships will suffer
3. Supplier may ask for cash on delivery (COD) for future shipments
   (further eroding your cash flow)
4. You may have to pay a premium for the next shipment
5. The supplier may not expedite your next delivery
6. Your supplier may cut you off
7. Word may get out to other suppliers that you are a bad risk

If you are going to be late (and I'm not suggesting that you should
be), at least let the appropriate supply-chain link know about it. I see
nothing wrong with publishing an accounts payable aging report internally to the appropriate people in your supply chain. If you only have
"n" number of dollars to pay bills, and you are late (the same amount
of time) on paying supplier A and supplier B, don't leave it up to the
accounts payable department to make the decision on who to pay. It's
not fair to them and in all probability, purchasing might make a better-
informed decision.

> **TIP #35:** *Finance looks at inventory turns and days of
> supply in the aggregate, but for operations to address this
> issue in its inventory rightsizing efforts, inventory turns,
> days of supply, and COGS need to be broken down into
> inventory types and families at the item-level detail.*

There is no universal rule for the number of times inventory should
turn or how many days of supply a company should have. It will vary,
industry segment to industry segment. Even then, just because your
competition turns inventory five times a year, is that right for your

company? The important thing to remember with this TIP is that different internal supply chains will measure turns and days of supply differently. For example, finance is concerned about the aggregate inventory and looks at inventory in terms of dollars. Manufacturing, planning, purchasing, and distribution look at inventory from an item point of view. These views are not in conflict, merely different. You should, however, have goals and objectives to satisfy both views. When establishing performance metrics, consider the following:

1. Find out what the standard and average is for each of your industry segments: the Standard Industry Classification (SIC Code). There is information available in the marketplace.
2. Find out (if possible) what your competition's inventory turns and days are.
3. Establish performance metrics that best suit your different industry SIC codes.
4. Publish your performance metrics to all internal supply-chain links.
5. Measure your actual performance to planned performance, and let all links know how you are doing.

> **TIP #36: Analyze your inventory for activity. If there hasn't been any activity on an item in inventory for 12 months or longer, consider disposing of it. This includes raw materials and finished goods.**

This TIP is similar to TIP #33, but I would like to add a few more points. If you don't have the tools available to create such a report, ask your IT folks to provide you with the information. In most cases, they will be able to do so. Before you make the decision to get rid of inventory, consider the following:

1. Ask all appropriate supply-chain links if there is any valid reason to keep the inventory.
2. Ask design engineering if the material can be substituted for an active material.
3. Run a where-used report to see if there is another use for the material in another product.
4. Ask the supplier if he or she will take it back. (The supplier may have a shortage and can use it for another customer; it doesn't hurt to ask.) There may be a restocking fee, but the value of the credit received will more than offset the fee.
5. Ask sales if there is another market for the product.

6. If it is a finished product, ask sales if it can sell it at a discount.
7. Ask if the product can be modified or converted into another product.
8. If it is a finished product you are getting rid of, be sure to use up or get rid of all corresponding raw materials that go into the product, if they can't be used elsewhere.

> **TIP #37:** *There is a direct relationship between the level of inventory carried and the cost of carrying inventory. When the inventory level increases, carrying cost increases; when the inventory level decreases, carrying cost decreases.*

Consider this scenario: In January you purchase all of part Y for the entire year, consume it month to month and, ideally, it is all gone by the end of December. You may have saved money on a "quantity buy" and your risk of stockout is considerably lower throughout the year. On the other hand, you have to pay for it by the end of February and have to carry the item in stock all year long. If you buy the item month to month, your carrying cost will go down, but your ordering cost will go up and your risk of a stockout is far greater. The point is that there are trade-offs in buying various quantities of material. In order to decide which approach you should use, you have to consider all costs and look at the total cost of acquisition. The following are costs to consider:

1. Ordering cost
2. Machine setup costs
3. Item cost
4. Carrying cost
5. Item demand patterns
6. Payment terms
7. Forecast usage accuracy
8. Item shelf life
9. Item obsolescence
10. Cash flow
11. Cash-to-cash cycle
12. Item inventory turns
13. Rarity of the item
14. Potential for price increase

There is no easy answer to the question of how much to buy and when to buy it. This list represents the things you should consider when answering this question. Some costs will go up and other costs will go down.

TIP #38: *Select an inventory valuation method that best reflects the true value of your inventory and conforms to GAAP guidelines.*

Careful attention should be given to the selection of an inventory valuation method. The most popular two are FIFO and LIFO. Once you have decided on a methodology, you will have to live with it for a while. It is not something you can change every day. As explained earlier in this chapter, a key consideration would be the replacement cost of inventory. When inventory replacement costs are rising, charging inventory out at LIFO will maximize the COGS expense and possibly minimize taxes, thus increasing profitability. The inventory valuation method chosen will have a greater impact on items with a long shelf life. If an item has a very short shelf life, then the gap between LIFO and FIFO will be less, and the accounting method chosen will have less impact. A very important point to be made here is that whatever method is chosen, you must comply with GAAP rules and regulations and SOX.

TIP #39: *Inventory valuation must be realistic and reflect the true value of your inventory. Consider adjusting the value of your inventory downward if it falls below the current replacement cost or the current selling price of the product. Take the loss earlier rather than later.*

Referring back to TIP #38 along with TIP #39, finance should not, by itself, decide on the accounting methodology to be used:

1. Multiple supply-chain links should provide input.
2. Purchasing can provide input on the replacement costs of items.
3. Use the 80/20 rule when looking at replacement costs.
4. Marketing and sales can provide input on future selling prices.
5. Your outside auditor should be a good source on which methodology to use.
6. Constantly monitor the value of your inventory to see if an accounting method change is in order.
7. Always, always follow GAAP guidelines.

Inventory Reserves

TIP #39 states that you should "take the loss earlier rather than later." By that I mean, if an item in inventory has no value, or its value is less than the cost to make it, and you decide to scrap or sell it below cost, you must still account for it. Many companies set up an inventory reserve account to deal with this inventory write-off or re-evaluation. A write-off may occur when the value of the inventory is less than its book value and, in some cases, the inventory item is no longer usable. Inventory reserve is an accounting entry, reducing earnings for the purpose of fairly representing the value of inventory on the balance sheet. This concept considers the fact that not all inventory will be sold to cover the cost of the product. If the cost of inventory exceeds the market value, the inventory value must be adjusted on the balance sheet. A company would not deliberately produce and stock an item in inventory at a cost that exceeds market value. Inventory reserves are typically stated and valued using either the cost or market value method, whichever is lower. It is misleading to carry an item in inventory with a value of say $5 each when it has no value in the marketplace and you have to actually pay someone to take it away. Don't wait.

> **TIP #40:** *Cost accounting must capture the true cost of adding value to a raw material, so that finished goods are valued correctly for sales and marketing to establish selling prices that conform to company profitability guidelines.*

You cannot correctly establish profitable selling prices without knowing what the item cost you. I have seen cases where companies thought they were making a profit on a product, and when they captured their actual cost they found out they were losing money on every sale. In this TIP, I state that cost accounting must capture the true cost. I am using the term *cost accounting* as an activity, not a job title. The goal is to capture all the costs to bring the product to market, not just the manufacturing cost. Once you have identified all the costs, you can then apply an appropriate profit margin on top of that. I'm sure you have heard stories about companies whose costs are greater than their competitions' selling price. Needless to say, those companies must change, or they will quickly be forgotten.

Standard Cost

Many companies establish a standard cost at the beginning of every year. The purpose is to establish a baseline product or order cost to the company and then compare actual cost to this standard. The difference between standard cost and actual cost is calculated, and the difference is called a *variance*, either favorable or unfavorable. Typically, companies don't change the standard cost during the year unless there is a dramatic change in the actual costs. Unfortunately, many companies don't do a good job of capturing the actual cost and make the assumption that the actual cost is pretty close to the standard cost. There is only one way to find out: capture your actual costs.

Current Cost

As the year progresses, costs will change. The current cost method captures the current cost of materials, labor, and overhead. For example, let's say you start out in January, and one of your primary raw materials costs $10 each. There is a shortage of this product in the marketplace, and by March the cost has doubled to $20 each. This may cause you to change your standard cost to the current cost. Of course, given the capability and time, you may want to compare actual cost to both standard cost and current cost and track the variances to both.

Average Cost

Another method calculates an average cost. Typically, this is a method using a weighted average, based on quantity, of an item's cost. This averaging considers both the LIFO and FIFO inventory valuation methods, and also considers labor and overhead in the equation. Once again, you can compare average cost to actual cost and report the variance. Like the current cost method, dramatic changes may occur during the year, and adjustments may have to be made to the average cost calculation.

Activity-Based Costing (ABC)

This method captures activities performed, accumulates these costs and then applies cost drivers to allocate these costs to products, orders, or projects. The concept is to apply overhead costs more realistically. If you can do this, you approach a true actual cost. For example, let's say you have a machining work center, and you are making a batch of 500 widgets in the work center. If you can capture the actual electricity used (overhead) in the work center to make that batch, you truly are capturing actual cost. Although ABC may be the most accurate of all the costing methods, it can be the most challenging to implement.

The key to using this TIP effectively is not in the cost accounting method used, but in capturing the actual cost of making the product. Once this is known, you can add on all other costs such as sales, general, and administrative (SG&A), and then mark it up to give your company a reasonable profit.

> **TIP #41:** *As a raw material moves through the manufacturing process, labor adds value and increases the cost of the item. If the item goes back into inventory, it goes back at a higher cost, thus increasing the total value of the inventory. If possible, delay adding value to a raw material until it can be shipped without going back into inventory.*

The point of this TIP is to delay adding value (labor) to a raw material or subassembly until a later time or a later step in the supply-chain process. If you add labor to a raw material and put it back in inventory as an intermediate product or subassembly, several things have occurred:

1. You have to pay for the labor well in advance of using the product.
2. You have committed to a particular configuration of the product. It can't be changed without adding more cost, assuming you can change it at all.
3. You will incur an inventory carrying cost.
4. You may have bought the raw material earlier than you needed to and have to pay for it earlier.
5. Making it early may hurt your cash flow.
6. You could have used the money elsewhere (opportunity cost).

You can help prevent this from happening by:

1. Delaying raw material deliveries until needed
2. Decreasing raw material delivery times
3. Designing products with modularity, so that adding value to a raw material can occur easier and closer to the customer delivery date
4. Designing processes so that value added steps can be combined and performed later in the process

> **TIP #42** *Inventory inaccuracy has a negative impact on the entire supply chain, can decrease customer service and productivity levels, and can increase costs. You must improve inventory accuracy.*

Inventory inaccuracy causes an enormous amount of problems, as discussed earlier in this chapter. In later chapters, we will come back to this topic again and discuss ways to improve inventory accuracy — in particular, the use of cycle counting. Some steps you should consider taking are the following:

1. Measure your current level of inventory accuracy by inventory category: raw material, work-in-process, and finished goods.
2. Assign inventory accuracy accountability to appropriate (and multiple) links in your supply chain.
3. Develop and implement a plan to improve inventory accuracy.
4. Continuously measure inventory accuracy, and report results to all supply-chain managers.
5. Identify and fix the causes of inventory inaccuracy.

> **TIP #43: *Each company must define the criteria used to measure inventory accuracy, measure accuracy against the criteria, and communicate all this to all employees in the supply chain.***

This TIP, although similar to TIP #42, focuses on one important difference: Different links in the supply chain will focus on different criteria. For example, sales will focus on the need for finished goods accuracy in units. Production, planning, and purchasing will focus on the need for raw material and work-in-process accuracy in units, and finance will focus on the need for inventory accuracy in all three categories, but in dollars rather than units.

Because the inventory is the responsibility of the entire internal supply chain, all links must be aware of and responsible for inventory accuracy across all categories and value measurements. The goal should be 100 percent inventory accuracy in the entire supply chain. The rules are simple:

1. Measure current accuracy.
2. Identify and fix causes of inventory inaccuracy.
3. Establish procedures to prevent causes from occurring again.
4. Communicate results to everyone.
5. Repeat the first step.

Table 3.10 represents the most current status of the Woodstock inventory, and Table 3.11 represents the inventory targets by division and inventory category.

Table 3.10   Inventory Balance (×1,000,000)

Month End	31 Jan	28 Feb
Forecast	7.2	7.9
Orders	5.8	7.4
Total starting inventory	40.0	41.0
Start FG inventory	15.5	15.7
+Production @ COGS	4.1	5.1
–Shipments @ COGS	3.9	5.0
End FG inventory	15.7	15.8
Start WIP inventory	7.5	7.6
+Material issues	3.4	4.2
+Labor and overhead	0.8	1.0
–Production @ COGS	4.1	5.1
End WIP inventory	7.6	7.7
Start raw inventory	17.0	17.7
+Material purchases	4.1	3.9
–Material issues	3.4	4.2
End raw inventory	17.7	17.4
Total ending inventory	41.0	40.9

Table 3.11   Inventory Segmentation Targets
(×1,000,000)

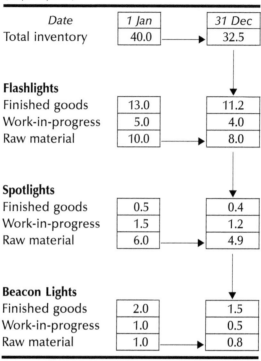

Date	1 Jan		31 Dec
Total inventory	40.0	→	32.5

Flashlights

Finished goods	13.0		11.2
Work-in-progress	5.0		4.0
Raw material	10.0	→	8.0

Spotlights

Finished goods	0.5		0.4
Work-in-progress	1.5		1.2
Raw material	6.0	→	4.9

Beacon Lights

Finished goods	2.0		1.5
Work-in-progress	1.0		0.5
Raw material	1.0	→	0.8

Chapter 4

Not Having Inventory Costs the Company Money

March 19, Harmony Team Meeting
Woodstock Inventory: $40.6 Million

My name is Rudy and I'm vice president of sales and marketing for Woodstock Lighting Group

Boy, I don't know if I'll ever get used to working here. It is unlike any other company I've ever worked for. The pressure and politics are the worst I've ever experienced. That reminds me, my wife is going to kill me if I don't get out of here on time today. It'll be just my luck that I'll get a call from an important customer at five minutes to five. Tonight is Trevor and Cameron's soccer game, and it's for the league championship. Afterwards, we promised Preston and the big guys we would take them out for ice cream. It's going to be a big family night!

I don't understand what Joe's problem is. They asked us for a forecast, and we gave it to them; then they completely ignore it and make what they want anyway. Why I bother, I'll never know. I'm just a nice guy, I guess. I am constantly making up excuses to our customers as to why we are late on their orders. I've got it down to a science: the raw material supplier delivered late; our production equipment broke down; we made your product, but the quality was poor and we have to make it again; you told us to rush your order for product A, so we had to reschedule your order out for product B; and my favorite excuse, "Didn't you get the message I left with your secretary? I had a question about your order and we were holding up production until we heard from you." Which excuse should I use with the next customer, excuse #1 or excuse #2? Oh, well, let me get started with these people so I can clean up my desk and get out of here on time.

Not Having Inventory Costs the Company Money — a Lot of Money

Our flashlight business is a commodity business, and if we don't have the inventory that customers want, they will go elsewhere to place their order. The same is true for spare parts sold by the Beacon Light Division. If it isn't in stock, they will go elsewhere. If we have stockouts often enough, not only will we lose orders, but in the long run we will also lose customers. Everyone knows we can't afford for that to happen. We in sales and marketing have two primary responsibilities, just as our title implies: We market and sell our product lines. What's the difference between the two? Well, marketing creates awareness about our products, and the sales team sells them.

Role and Responsibilities

Marketing

Marketing is responsible for market research, market demographics, and identifying market trends. Marketing visits retail stores (Flashlight Division), local governments, home and commercial building associations (Spotlight Division), and state and federal agencies (Beacon Light Division). Marketing also visits with our customers, large and small. The purpose of these visits is to identify market trends, customer needs, and regulatory changes. Marketing is also responsible for analyzing the competitive environment and knowing what our competition is up to. Here is a list of primary activities:

- **Market research:** Identify the marketplace: size, location, customer type, trends, market forces, requirements, impact of external factors such as economic conditions and government regulations.
- **Competitive analysis:** Identify the competition's strengths and weaknesses, market share, and pricing structure.

- **Marketing programs:** Create product line brochures and other marketing literature. Conduct customer focus group studies and get customer feedback about our products.
- **Advertising:** Product promotion through multimedia channels such as TV, radio, print, and Internet.
- **Promotions:** Create and implement customer incentive programs (along with sales).
- **Product line forecasts:** Along with sales and field service (spare parts), forecast product line sales for all products and services.

This is not all that marketing does, but it gives you an idea of what it does in relation to the sales team. The primary overlap with sales is in the forecasting. Of course, marketing also looks to sales for input on what the customers are saying and what the competition is doing. Marketing takes all this input and formalizes it into marketing plans. You might be wondering how marketing impacts our inventory rightsizing effort. Well, it does so in both direct and indirect ways.

In a very direct way, marketing input on product forecasts is part of our sales and operations plan. Our history has been, the higher the forecast, the higher our inventory. I'm not saying that's right, but it is a known fact here at Woodstock, particularly with our flashlight business where, as you know, we use a make-to-stock strategy. An inaccurate forecast can cause us to make too much or too little of a product, or make the wrong products and not make the right ones. We will spend more time on forecasts when we talk about the sales department.

I also said marketing impacts inventory in an indirect way. For example, after everyone agrees on the forecast (or so we think), we manufacture flashlights to meet the forecast. Marketing then must implement programs that help the sales team sell the product. If the marketing programs are weak or nonexistent, we will probably sell less and be stuck with a lot of inventory. I know for a fact this was the case when we came out with the new L-shaped camper's flashlight.

The forecast was aggressive. We forecasted to sell 500,000 SKUs in a 12-month period. So manufacturing went ahead and made 250,000 and put them into inventory. I don't know the actual cost, but let's say they cost us $0.55 each, which is probably pretty close. We invested about $137,500 in inventory. Marketing really blew this one. It didn't include it in our sales catalog and spent very little advertising it. The end result was we barely sold 100,000 SKUs.

At the end of the year, we looked at the results and wrote this product off as a loser. We deliberately didn't include it in the catalog the second year and had a zero advertising budget. The result is we sold less in the second year, about 50,000 or so, and still have 100,000 of these in inventory, with no marketing plans whatsoever.

I bet a good number of the 150,000 units we did sell to our distributors are still sitting on their shelves, because we didn't help them with product promotions and marketing materials. I think we should look at our inventory levels and analyze our marketing programs to see if there is a relationship between our inventory levels and our marketing efforts for specific products. My understanding is, we have categorized our inventory into ABC classifications. We will start with all A items and work our way down through the product lines.

> **TIP #44: Marketing has a direct and indirect impact on inventory levels and strategy. Typically, the higher the forecast (make-to-stock strategy), the higher the inventory level. Marketing programs and budgets should be set in proportion to inventory levels and inventory strategy.**
>
> (Note: TIP = team important point.)

As I mentioned earlier, marketing is not alone when it comes to developing the forecast. Almost every link in the supply chain has something to say about forecasts, some good and some bad. In the end, it is management judgment that is the final input to the forecast: Will the customer buy our product?

Sales

The sales team is the group that has direct contact with our customers and sells our products. Sales is on the front line, so to speak, and its success (or failure) will dictate how well or how poorly we move inventory through our supply chain. It is important that salespeople are knowledgeable about the products they sell. In the case of the flashlight products, the product knowledge required is less than what is required to sell beacon light systems. Here are some of their responsibilities:

- **Direct sales:** Contacting customers via phone, e-mail, snail mail, and direct meetings
- **Order processing:** Ensuring that customer orders are processed into the Woodstock customer order system; not directly, but through proper channels
- **Customer product forecasts:** Identifying customer requirements over a given period of time

- **Customer satisfaction:** Ensuring that customers are satisfied with Woodstock products and services
- **Customer problem solving:** Anticipating customer problems and following up on known problems
- **Sales forecasting:** Taking the customer product forecasts and developing product forecasts for aggregate product sales

Does sales have an impact on our inventory rightsizing efforts? It very definitely does. Given their way, salespeople would like to have lots of inventory available to satisfy customer needs whenever they receive an order. So we have a direct conflict with finance about inventory levels. As you've heard from finance, it wants relatively low levels of inventory because it costs so much money. Now you are hearing from sales that it wants relatively high inventory levels because, if it doesn't have it, the customer may go elsewhere.

Who does production listen to, finance or sales? This is a classic struggle that has been going on for some time. Now throw in some of the other links in the chain, and it gets more complicated. Take a look at Table 4.1, and you begin to see the challenges we face. The terms *high* and *low* are used in an ideal way. For example, when I say sales wants high finished goods inventory, I mean it wants to have the product in stock so that we don't have a stockout when the customer orders it. Ideally, they would rather have a high inventory of finished goods inventory. Because we have yet to reduce our lead times and manufacturing cycle times, we will have to live with these conflicting objectives longer than we would like to. We can all agree that once we improve our response times, all supply-chain links will want lower inventories.

Table 4.1   Woodstock Inventory Conflicts

Functional Silo	Type Inventory	Desired Inventory Level
Sales and Marketing	Finished goods	High
Manufacturing	Raw materials	High
Distribution	Finished goods	High
Finance	All categories	Low
Process Engineering	WIP	Low
Purchasing	Raw material	High
Stakeholders	All categories	Low
Customer Service	Finished goods	High
Field Service	Spare parts	High

As the expression goes, "We want to have our cake and eat it too." There aren't many companies out there that have solved this problem. Oh, sure, you will hear and read about a "world-class" company that has dramatically reduced inventory without sacrificing customer service; but they are few and far between. Most of us are struggling with this problem. Hopefully, the Harmony Team will put us in the world-class category; I certainly hope so. High inventory hides a lot of problems.

> **TIP #45: *Supply-chain links within a single supply chain may have conflicting inventory goals and objectives. You cannot rightsize your inventory until these conflicting objectives are resolved and balanced.***

Sales and Operations Planning

One of the ways that companies are dealing with all these conflicting objectives is by going through a process popularly known as sales and operations planning (S&OP). Essentially, S&OP is a planning process of integrating customer-focused marketing plans and all our supply-chain link plans into one homogeneous set of plans for our entire supply chain. It is a consensus-based process.

The process helps to reconcile all supply and demand conflicts at both the detail and aggregate levels. The planning horizon for this process should go as far out into the future as necessary to plan for acquiring the resources necessary to achieve the business plan for the near to intermediate terms. Once created, it is reviewed and adjusted on a weekly or monthly basis, depending on the nature of your business. If used properly, it links strategic plans with the tactical execution plans. It is used to monitor performance against the plans so that adjustments and improvements can be made on a continuous basis. From what I've read and learned, there are five stages of S&OP planning. Table 4.2 indicates the five stages. There is no question in my mind that we are at stage one. The closer we get to stage five, the more competitive we will be to reap the benefits of this collaborative planning process.

S&OP is a powerful tool that a company can use as a communication vehicle with all links in the supply chain. The benefits and rewards are huge:

- Improved customer service (internal and external)
- Inventory rightsizing
- Efficient operations (all links)
- Effective decision making
- Improved supply-chain communications

Table 4.2 Five Stages of Sales and Operations Planning

Level of Integration	Description
No integration	Each silo develops its own plans
Some internal integration	Some silos work together to develop plans
Full internal integration	All internal supply-chain links work together to develop plans
Customer integration	Customer plans are integrated with the internal supply-chain plans
Supplier integration	Supplier plans are integrated with the internal supply-chain plans

- Improved morale and teamwork
- Increased profitability and return on assets (ROA)

I think it's fair to say that S&OP can be viewed in three different ways: It is a philosophy (a way of doing business), a technique (a business operating process), and a computer (application) software. We will focus our discussion on the philosophy and technique aspects and leave the computer technology side to others. When attempting to balance supply with demand, we have to understand what that means. S&OP is about balancing sales (demand) with inventory (supply). The process will help us answer six significant questions about product family inventories over a specified planning horizon:

1. What is the demand for this product family?
2. How much inventory do we have?
3. How much inventory do we have to acquire?
4. When is the inventory required?
5. Do we have the resources to acquire the inventory?
6. Does the S&OP plan meet the objects of the business plan?

We have to decide what to buy and make and how much; I say "buy and make" because a manufacturing company has to buy raw materials and then make the product. A distributor on the other hand has to decide what to buy. Figure 4.1 illustrates this balance of supply and demand.

For those of you who are familiar with material requirements planning (MRP), you may think I'm describing that technique; but I'm not. We are not down to the SKU level yet. The S&OP is done at the product family level. What do I mean by product family? In the case of a manufacturer, which we are, a product family is based on the similarity of the manufacturing process, not the sales family. Let me illustrate this by an example.

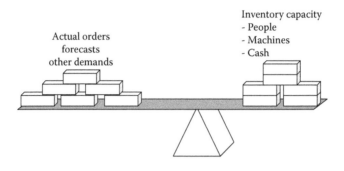

Figure 4.1 Balancing supply and demand.

Let's take a pharmaceutical company that manufactures aspirin, vitamins, and allergy medications. The sales families would be just the aspirin, vitamins, and allergy medications. You may or may not have different sales forces selling each of these product families. Now let's look at it from a manufacturing point of view. Figure 4.2 illustrates a manufacturing process that all three sales product families might go through. I may not have the process exactly right, but you will get the idea.

Operation 1 is the weighing of ingredients. Each ingredient must be precisely measured and weighed to a very strict formula governed by regulatory guidelines. Operation 2 is where all the weighed ingredients are mixed together in what looks like a big cake mixing bowl with huge rotating blades. This mixing and blending operation is sometimes called "product compounding." After the ingredients are compounded, the batch goes to Operation 3, where the compound is now compressed into tablets, which we are all familiar with.

Depending on the product, it may move onto Operation 4 when a coating is applied to the compressed tablets (making it easier to swallow). From there the product moves on to Operation 5, where it is bottled into various size bottles holding different quantities like 30, 50, or 100 tablets each. The process I described doesn't have to be continuous (occurring one immediately after the other). Depending on product shelf life, a

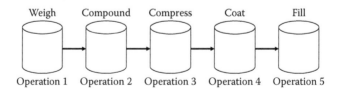

Figure 4.2 Manufacturing process example.

compounded product could be inventoried in this bulk state and later compressed into tablets. Similarly, the compressed tablets could be stocked (again, shelf life dependent) and packaged later.

Having provided you with a visual aid, I can now make my point. Each one of these operations is a manufacturing process that has capacity limitations for any given period of time. Let's take the compounding operation as an example. All products that have to go through this operation have a similarity of manufacturing process. Whether it is a vitamin, aspirin, or allergy pill (three separate sales families), they all go through one similar manufacturing process. In this example, it is the compounding operation. This is the definition of a manufacturing product family: similarity of the manufacturing process.

At this point in the planning process, we are planning at the aggregate inventory demand and supply levels by product families. Later on in the planning process, we will be developing another plan called the master production schedule (MPS). The MPS is also a supply and demand planning process, but at the detailed item level. I know that Cyndie in planning will explain this in detail when you meet with her. I bring it up now because it is important for us to understand that the S&OP plan and the MPS must be in balance with each other. Figure 4.3 illustrates where S&OP fits in the enterprise planning process.

S&OP Characteristics Related to Inventory

Let me share with you some of the characteristics of the S&OP.

- **The focus is on the customer:** You will learn later that two of the primary inputs are a forecast of external customer needs (for inventory) and a forecast of internal customer needs to produce and stock inventory. The process must be responsive to the customers' needs as they change.
- **Must be in harmony with the business plan:** The S&OP plan must take into account all of the elements of the business plan. It must be in agreement with the financial plan, cash flow, profitability, capital expenditures, facility planning, resource levels (people), equipment plans, and the like.
- **One integrated company plan:** It is used by all links in the supply chain to execute the business plan. The plan is visible and available to all links, and performance to plan is measurable by using dashboards and scorecards.
- **Rapid response to change:** The S&OP is not a stagnant document. The actual results must be compared to the plan, and change must

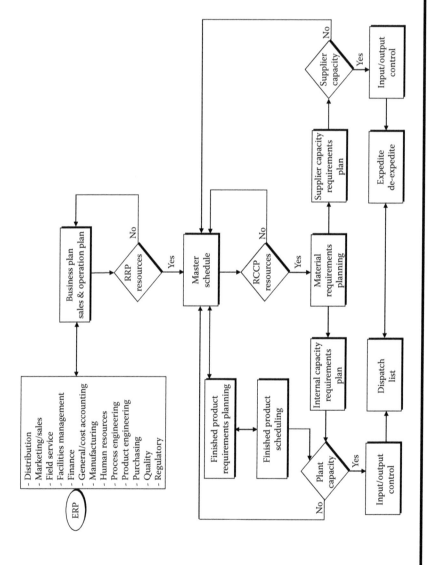

Figure 4.3   Enterprise planning process.

take place immediately. It must become a proactive planning process and not a reactive planning process. The S&OP will drive change on a continuous, as-needed basis.

- **Total supply-chain view considered:** The S&OP must be tightly coupled with the total supply chain to improve response time, operating efficiency, and flexibility. The total supply-chain costs to bring products to the market are a major element of the S&OP process.

Inventory Planning Zones

I know I've spoken a lot about making changes to the S&OP and how important rapid response is in today's marketplace, but, realistically, some changes are easier to make than others. All plans, whether it is the S&OP, MPS, or material or capacity requirements planning (MRP or CRP), have "frozen" periods where change to a plan will be difficult and costly to make, but the effect on inventory can be huge.

Change and its impact will vary industrywide and companywide. Conceptually, the S&OP is organized in monthly time buckets (periods) with a planning horizon of one year or longer. The general rule is that the S&OP plan should go as far out into the future as reasonable to acquire the necessary long-term resources. Examples of long-term resources that will take time to acquire are buying new capital equipment, adding another shift, or opening a new plant or distribution center. I will leave it to Cyndie to explain how planning zones work, but essentially it is a block of time in the planning process where it is reasonable or not reasonable to make changes to the plan.

> **TIP #46:** *The purpose of establishing inventory planning zones is to recognize the degree of difficulty to make changes and to allow enough time for all supply-chain links to react to the change in an economical, efficient manner.*

Balancing the Major Components of S&OP

As I stated earlier, the object of the S&OP process is to balance supply and demand and achieve the goals outlined in the business plan. The major components of the S&OP plan consist of

- Customer and forecast demand (demand planning)
- Inventory plans
- Production and distribution plans

- Resource requirements and availability
- Lead-time requirements

All these components must be in balance, and a change in any one of these elements will drive changes in the other components. We will go through several iterations of planning before we get it right. Figure 4.3 shows the closed-loop iterative process of change.

Demand Planning

Demand planning is at the very heart of the S&OP process, and it can be the most difficult to get right. It is the activity of planning demand for all products and services the company offers to internal and external customers. Demand is then evaluated against the resources we have. The inputs to demand planning come from many sources. Here are the primary ones that we should be looking at for Woodstock:

- **Customer plans:** This should come from our CRM process. It is the "voice of the customer." The more we know about our customers, the more accurate our demand planning will be.
- **Market intelligence:** We need to understand our buyers' customer needs. Our customers are mostly distributors and large retail chains (Flashlight Division). We also need to understand the market trends that are affecting the end users (consumers) in this market.
- **Competitive intelligence:** We need to understand our competitors, what they are doing, and what they are not doing that may affect our plans. We compete in a global marketplace, and new competitors are popping up around the world.
- **Internal marketing plans:** Our marketing programs and promotions will impact the demand for our products. We have 2 new flashlight products and 3 new spotlight products that will be released within the next 12 months. How much effort and dollars we put into promoting these new products will impact the demand for them.
- **Historical sales data:** We have been selling these and similar products since 1942, and we have a great deal of history on what we've sold in the past. Of course, we cannot assume the future will be like the past, because so many things have changed over the years. Historical data will give us a good benchmark to use, and we can apply mathematical formulas to this historical data to project future requirements.
- **Sales force:** Our sales representatives will have input on what they believe the customers will buy from us. They are in direct contact

with our customers. We can also get input from our field service personnel and our spare parts team in the Beacon Light Division.

Inventory and Sales Forecasting

Ah, we finally come to it … the forecast! The net result of looking at all these inputs is to develop a projection of demand, called "the forecast." Now, unless you are a company with five years' of order backlog, like an airplane manufacturer, you don't have the luxury of knowing what your customers will buy and when they will buy it. For that reason, we have to forecast the demand. Over- or underforecasting has a direct impact on inventory levels. Overforecasting will cause us to make more inventory, and inventory levels will increase if we don't sell it. Underforecasting will cause inventory levels to decrease, but may result in inventory stockouts.

Although all links in the supply chain have input to the sales forecast, it is the primary responsibility of sales and marketing to put it all together. The forecast is a process resulting in a formal input to the S&OP process. This forecast will cause purchasing to buy raw materials, manufacturing to produce finished product, and distribution to stock inventory.

> **TIP #47:** *Forecasting has a direct impact on inventory levels. Overforecasting may cause inventory levels to increase if it's not sold, whereas underforecasting will decrease inventory levels but may lead to stockouts.*

Of course there are other operational issues with over- and under-forecasting, but our focus today is on inventory. There are many issues that must be considered when developing the forecast. Let's discuss some of them:

1. **Forecast accuracy:** There is one accurate statement we can make about the forecast: The forecast is always inaccurate. I don't know of any supply chain out there today that has a perfect forecast. If we are lucky, we may get the forecast right for one or two products, but we will get most of them wrong.
2. **Product families versus specific SKUs:** We can more accurately forecast the total sales for a product family than we can forecast individual SKUs within a product family. But in the final analysis, we must convert the forecast into meaningful production units.
3. **Long term versus short term:** Forecasts are more accurate in the short term than they are in the long term. In other words, we can forecast this month's sales more accurately than we can next

year's sales. But for long-lead-time items, we must forecast the demand required to cover the cumulative lead time.

4. **Degree of accuracy:** Forecasts work better when planning for a range of forecast accuracy rather than an absolute number. For example, using plus/minus 10 percent rather than 100 percent accuracy.

5. **Forecast change:** I referred earlier to inventory planning zones. I worked for a company once that was having a bad financial year. It got to the 11th month of the year and it was off by 35 percent. They adjusted their forecast downward and made 95 percent of their adjusted forecast! They weren't fooling anyone but themselves. However, market conditions do change, and we must be as responsive as we can to adjusting and changing market conditions.

6. **Forecast accountability:** Although sales and marketing have primary responsibility for developing the forecast, all links in the internal supply chain should have input to the forecast and strive to meet the level of the forecast. Remember what I said earlier: Everyone is responsible for inventory rightsizing; because the forecast has a significant impact on inventory, it must be monitored and adjusted as necessary and realistically.

7. **Sales force incentives:** We should conduct a careful analysis of sales force incentives. I know if I were a salesperson (which I was) I would focus on selling the products that rewarded me the most financially. It is important that sales incentives be aligned to forecast numbers and inventory levels.

8. **Forecast assumptions:** Be careful about the assumptions used in developing your forecast. Using only historical data for existing products is not necessarily the right thing to do. We cannot assume the future will be like the past.

9. **External factors:** We need to also consider factors outside of our direct control like environmental, government, and regulatory issues that could affect our forecast.

I don't want to dwell on these issues too much. I am merely trying to make the point that forecasting is a difficult task and needs to be watched carefully. World-class companies have the ability to respond to changes in a timely manner. Those companies that can will have a greater chance of rightsizing inventory than those that can't.

> **TIP #48: *The ability to rapidly respond to forecast changes will greatly improve your ability to rightsize your inventory.***

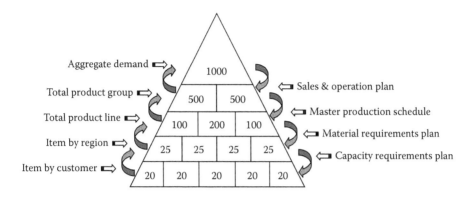

Figure 4.4 Forecasting and planning levels.

One of the points I should have made earlier is about forecasting in dollars versus forecasting in units. Our sales and marketing team feels more comfortable forecasting in dollars rather than in units. Our operating links need to plan for inventory in units. Keep in mind that we are still at the S&OP level where we are dealing with product families; so we are not looking at individual SKUs yet but need to convert dollars into product family units. It would be great if our Sales Team could forecast in units rather than dollars. I'm going to ask my team to do this.

You can help me by providing our sales history in units rather than dollars. This will give the team a benchmark to work from. There are several ways we can develop the forecast. Figure 4.4 demonstrates a bottom-up and a top-down approach to forecasting. We need to do both, then compare the two methods and agree on one set of numbers.

Customer demand variability has a significant impact on the entire supply chain. Even a small variability in end customer demand will expand successively upstream through the supply chain. This is known as the bullwhip effect, and the amount of variation grows at each link upstream from the end customer.

Basic Forecasting Techniques

Intrinsic forecasting techniques deal with historical data from past sales performance. This is known as *time series models*. I will briefly describe some of the time series techniques we are looking at implementing here at Woodstock.

Table 4.3   Woodstock Product Forecast

Month	Product	Forecast
January	#120417	20
February	#120417	30
March	#120417	40

Naïve Forecasting

This is a very simple concept, and one that we have used in the past. There is not much to it and, quite frankly, when we have used it in the past it has proven to be inaccurate more often than not. Naïve forecasting assumes that demand in the next time period will be the same as the demand in the last period. This technique doesn't allow for fluctuations in demand such as seasonality. We have decided that this isn't a technique for us.

Moving Average Forecast

Unlike the naïve forecast, where you use the most recent period to forecast demand for the next period, the moving average technique uses the average demand from a series of preceding periods. As the current period passes, the earliest period is dropped from the calculation and the most current past period is added. This dropping and adding of periods is why it is called "a moving average." Let's look at an example, as shown in Table 4.3:

Using a three-month moving average, the forecast for April would be

April forecast = (20 + 30 + 40)/3 = 30

So, in this example your new forecast for April would be 30 units. Now let's say, for whatever reason, you actually sold 50 units for April. You would drop January from the calculation and add April to calculate the May demand. Now the calculation looks like this:

May forecast = (30 + 40 + 50)/3 = 40

The forecast for May is 40 units. This is a very simple formula and is somewhat more realistic than the naïve method. However, there is a drawback. The moving average forecast lags the trend. Although the trend shows the May forecast is 10 units greater than the April forecast, you will note that the sales trend has been increasing by 10 units every month since January (20–30–40–50), and if this pattern continues in May, the May actual will be closer to 60 than 40. This is why we say that the moving average lags behind the trend and is hard to detect. The more time periods used, the more it will lag the trend. However, it does filter out random variation. For this reason, we have decided that this won't work for us at Woodstock.

Weighted Moving Average

A weighted moving average will provide a more realistic look at detecting trends. This places more dependence on the most recent periods and less on earlier periods. Using the data we used earlier to calculate the May forecast, we now place more weight on April than we do on February:

May forecast = (F 1 × 30 + M 2 × 40 + A 3 × 50)/6 = 260/6 = 43

You will note that the May forecast of 43, calculated from the weighted moving average, is higher than the 40 calculated using the simple moving average, although it still lags the trend. The difficult part here is in deciding which weights to use in each period. For that reason, I am not comfortable using this technique for Woodstock. Let me discuss another technique, which I believe will be more appropriate for us to use.

Exponential Smoothing

Exponential smoothing is similar to the weighted average moving forecast, but takes the calculation a step further by adding a smoothing constant. The exponential smoothing formula uses three factors: the last period's forecast, the last period's actual demand, and a smoothing constant, which is a number between 0 and 1 indicated by the Greek letter alpha (α). The formula is as follows:

**New forecast = Previous period forecast +
α(Last period demand – Last period forecast)**

NF = PPF + α(LPD – LPF)

The equation produces a weighted average of the previous results. There is no need to recalculate data from a number of preceding periods; the calculation does it for you, eliminating the need to maintain data from a number of preceding periods. Let's go back to our January, February, and March forecasts. Using the simple moving average, we calculated April as follows:

April forecast = (20 + 30 + 40)/3 = 30

Now let's use the weighted moving average:

April forecast = (J 1 × 20 + F 2 × 30 + M 3 × 40)/6 = 200/6 = 33

Now we will use the exponential smoothing formula with an alpha constant of 4:

April forecast = 40 + .4 (50 − 40) = 44

Note that with each succeeding technique, the April forecast moves closer to the trend. However, exponential smoothing still lags the trend but not by as much. The higher the constant, the more weight is given to the actual demand from the preceding period. Determining the best smoothing constant to use is critical for using this technique successfully. This may be accomplished by trial and error until we are satisfied that it is as close to reality as possible. There are other forecasting techniques available, such as double smoothing and seasonal indexing, but this is where we should start. We are in the process of implementing a forecasting system utilizing exponential smoothing. It should greatly improve our forecasting accuracy, which shouldn't be difficult because we don't have a forecasting tool in place today. Today, we mostly look at what we've done in the past and estimate a percentage increase over the preceding year's sales. It will take us several months to implement, but later in the year it should help us in our inventory rightsizing efforts.

> **TIP #49: Selection and successful implementation of a forecasting tool will greatly improve your chances of right-sizing your inventory.**

Other Sources of Demand Planning

As I've stated earlier, a forecast of customer requirements is an important element of the S&OP process. But there are other sources of demand for inventory that have to be taken into consideration when developing the S&OP. Here are some of those other sources:

- Research and development (R&D): Our R&D folks are constantly taking raw materials and finished goods out of inventory to conduct experiments. We must take into account their needs when forecasting demand.
- Destructive testing: Our quality team takes samples from inventory and puts parts through a process to determine product line cycles. Over the course of a year the team takes and uses hundreds of parts. These parts were bought and made based on customer use.
- Spare parts: We really have a problem with this one. We buy and make parts that go into our beacon light product line as part of the finished product. Some of these parts are also sold as spare parts through our service department. We should forecast this demand separately.
- Special promotions: We give a lot of products away as part of our marketing program. This is especially true in our Flashlight Division. Twice a year we have a promotion that we offer to our large retail customers. It is a classic "buy one, get one at half price" deal. We need to put these promotions in our forecast.
- Intracompany requirements: There is a lot of inventory transferring going on between our three divisions (and our service department). These intracompany requirements should be forecasted.

TIP #50: *All sources of demand must be considered when planning for inventory supply and demand at the S&OP level.*

Monitoring the Forecast

We know that no matter what we do, the forecast isn't going to be perfect. We can only hope to achieve a degree of forecast accuracy. We will measure actual demand against the forecast and publish the results. This should not be a passive activity. We should use the monthly results as a proactive tool and make adjustments as necessary. Table 4.4 shows data for the last six months of the last fiscal year: the actuals versus forecasts for our light bar product #070250.

Note that the cumulative variation for the six-month period does not equal zero. Bias exists in this forecast because we consistently undersold the forecast for four months in a row. If we had the same cumulative variation for the six-month total, but the period-to-period variation alternated from overselling to underselling the forecast, we could say that there is no bias in this forecast, but it exhibits random variation. It's time we let all supply-chain managers know how the company is doing month

Table 4.4   Forecast Sales Versus Actual Sales

Month	Sales Forecast	Actual Sales	Cumulative Variation
July	5,000	4,800	200
August	5,000	5,300	100
September	9,000	8,670	230
October	8,000	7,987	243
November	7,000	6,955	288
December	6,000	6,125	163
Total	40,000	39,837	163

to month. I will start to publish the sales results monthly to all supply-chain managers.

Inventory and the Production Plan

We have discussed demand planning as one of the major inputs to the S&OP. The next step is to develop a production plan. A production plan is a document (plan) that establishes the overall level of production required to satisfy the company's business plan, which includes the demand planning element, already discussed. The production plan is sometimes referred to as the *operations plan*. In this step of the S&OP process, we take the sales forecast by sales product family; if it is in dollars, we convert it into units based on the similarity of the manufacturing process, as I stated earlier.

This is no small task, but it doesn't have to be as daunting as it first appears. I remember in my last job, my boss literally developed a production plan on the back of an envelope while we were out to lunch. Six months later I looked at what he wrote on that envelope, and he wasn't that far off! Now I realize that the S&OP process has gotten more sophisticated; there is software to help us go through this process in a formal manner. In my opinion, we are looking for a ballpark estimate of how close or how far off we are from meeting the requirements of the business plan.

We should keep it as simple as possible and look at manufacturing processes that may be bottlenecked, based on the demand planning portion of the S&OP. I know that Arnie, Cyndie, Eddie, and the process design team are familiar with our product lines and can develop a production plan based on the similarity of the manufacturing processes. I will provide the forecast in units rather than dollars, and that should help. In time, this should help improve the forecast accuracy. Let's face it — it can't get any worse!

The production plan is a great tool and will help us in more ways than one. It can be used to help us

- Control and rightsize our inventory levels
- Maintain customer service levels
- Identify where and when resources are required (labor, equipment, materials, and cash)
- Balance supply and demand

Production Plan Principles

1. It should go as far out into the future as needed to obtain the resources necessary to meet the requirements of the S&OP.
2. The planning horizon is usually 12 or more calendar months.
3. The buckets of time are usually monthly.
4. It is established for product families based on the similarity of the manufacturing process.
5. It is used to satisfy a variety of management objectives.
6. At the end of the production plan process, supply and demand should be in balance. The process iteration continues until they are.
7. All of the internal supply-chain links must be in agreement on the numbers represented in the production plan. It is literally a contract between all links in the supply chain.
8. The production plan drives all subsequent planning processes.
9. The production plan should not be over/understated. It must be realistic and achievable.
10. Actual production plan results must be documented and communicated to all supply-chain links.

As you can see, this is a powerful tool if used correctly. I would like to demonstrate just how this tool can work to satisfy many business objectives.

Woodstock Business Plan Scenario

I don't know if you are aware of it or not, but our business plan has many requirements and restrictions that you need to know before you can develop a production plan. There is a hiring freeze, which means that we can't hire any more direct labor personnel. There is a capital expense freeze, so we can't buy any more equipment. It further states that no overtime is permitted unless absolutely necessary to satisfy a major customer requirement and that all overtime must be approved by Joe or Adriana. The business plan states that we must meet the sales forecast without increasing inventory levels. In fact, the business plan states that overall inventory levels must be reduced by 10 percent in value by the year-end. The business plan further states that we cannot outsource or subcontract any production or distribution work this fiscal year. You cannot develop a realistic, achievable production plan without knowing all this.

> **TIP #51:** *The business plan is a major input to the S&OP process; a realistic, achievable production plan cannot be developed without knowing and following the guidelines that are established in the business plan.*

> **TIP #52:** *The production plan, as part of the S&OP process, is an important tool that, if used correctly, can help us rightsize our inventory.*

This scenario tells us a great deal about how we will do business this year. I hope you were aware of it. March is almost over, and if this is the first you are hearing about it, that is a shame, and management, which includes me, should be embarrassed. Developing a production plan is not my area of expertise, but my team and I have worked offline with Arnie, picked several sales product families, and converted the data into units based on the similarity of the manufacturing process.

We have chosen our fabrication work cell. As you may be aware, a work cell is the same as a work center or a work module. By definition, it is a place on the factory floor where work is performed to transform raw materials into different products. This is called the *transformation process*. The fabrication work cell takes raw material, in this case rolls of sheet metal, and stamps out lens cover frames, primarily for spotlights and beacon lights. These are housings that hold the lens in place — but you already know that. So we took the forecast (demand planning) and summarized all products that go through the fabrication work cell. We came up with the demand forecast, indicated in Figure 4.5.

The chart in Figure 4.5 is called a planning grid and is used to develop the S&OP. You will note that the planning horizon goes out 12 periods, called "buckets of time," and each bucket represents one calendar month. Note that the starting inventory is 60 units (Actually 60,000 units — 000 understood as omitted). We want to determine how much production we need each month to satisfy the forecast demand, and because adding production capacity (resources) and working overtime are taboo, we must

On hand: 60	Period: Months											
Family: fabrication	1	2	3	4	5	6	7	8	9	10	11	12
Sales forecast	60	60	60	80	80	80	50	50	50	90	90	90
Planned production	69	69	69	69	69	69	69	69	69	69	69	69
Planned inventory	69	78	87	76	65	54	73	92	111	90	69	48

Figure 4.5   Sales and operations plan.

make the schedule as level as possible. In addition to that, we want to reduce inventory on this product family by 20 percent, which we believe is realistic.

Wow, that's a big challenge — where do we begin? Well, surprisingly the calculations are relatively easy; it is the execution that might be difficult. If we reduce the inventory by 20 percent, it will go from 60 units down to 48 units, which will satisfy the inventory reduction requirement:

$$60 \times .20 = 12$$

$$60 - 12 = 48$$

So ask yourself, how much do we need to satisfy customer demand over this planning horizon? The answer is 840 units:

$$\textbf{Forecast demand} =$$
$$60 + 60 + 60 + 80 + 80 + 80 + 50 + 50 + 50 + 90 + 90 + 90 = 840$$

To determine the amount of production required, the formula is

$$\textbf{Production} =$$
$$\textbf{(forecast + ending inventory) – beginning inventory}$$

$$(840 + 48) - 60 = 828$$

To have a level production plan for this product family for the entire 12-month period, the formula is

$$\textbf{Monthly production} =$$
$$\textbf{Total production required/Number of months in plan}$$

$$828/12 = 69$$

Has this plan met the requirements of the business plan? Let's review the objectives:

1. Reduce inventory on this product family by 20 percent: Yes, inventory will decrease by 12 units by the end of the plan horizon.
2. Produce at level rate throughout the year: Yes, we will produce 69 units every month.
3. Satisfy customer requirements without reducing service levels: Yes, with this plan the probability of a stockout is minimal.
4. No overtime or capital equipment authorized. Don't know; we have yet to check resources available.

One issue I see here is that inventory will increase before it goes down, and we will have the added cost of carrying it in stock for a while.

> **TIP #53: *Do not attempt to drastically reduce inventory levels of active items until the impact on customer service levels is understood by all links in the supply chain. Plan to reduce inventory, then measure customer service performance. If there is no negative impact on customer service, plan to reduce inventory again.***

Not bad, huh? So there you have it. We have satisfied many management objectives with this plan, and (hopefully) the plan also meets our customer requirements. On paper we have balanced supply with demand — or have we? What is missing with this S&OP plan? You probably guessed by now that we haven't answered an important question: **Do we have the necessary resources to meet the production requirements for each period of the S&OP?**

Validating the Sales and Operations Plan

I'm really getting out of my element here, but with the help of industrial engineering and planning, we've come up with some ballpark numbers to verify the S&OP. We've taken what I will call a "bill of resources" and calculated the resources required to make one lens cover. Remember, we are at the product family level and not talking about specific products. The same is true for resources required. We are not talking about "machine #2, next Wednesday, and Mary working on the second shift." We are still looking at the forest and not the trees. So, here goes:

The fabrication work cell has two machines, and each machine requires one operator to run it. Three operations are required to complete a lens cover, and the two machines can perform all three operations, if needed (although dies are limited to two for each operation):

> Operation 1 — Stamp out the lens cover from a roll of sheet metal.
> Operation 2 — Punch holes in each lens cover, and punch out the center.
> Operation 3 — Bend the lens cover to form.

Because these are highly automated processes, a lens cover can be transformed in about 15 seconds of run (manufacturing) time. Remember, we omitted three zeros, so we are talking about producing 69,000 units each month. Roughly, the calculation goes like this:

$$15 \text{ seconds} \times 69{,}000 = 1{,}035{,}000 \text{ seconds}$$

$$1{,}035{,}000/60 = 17{,}250 \text{ minutes}$$

$$17250/60 = 287.5 \text{ hours}$$

$$287.5/20 \text{ days per month (average)} = 14 \text{ hours per day}$$

$$14/6.5 \text{ hours per machine} = 2 \text{ machines required}$$

Excluding machine setup time (which can be an issue), we barely have the needed capacity to meet this plan. We require two machines and operators and we have them. Machine operators are not the problem. Our people are cross-trained, and we could move someone in if the assigned operator is out. It is the equipment I am worried about. You know Murphy's Law: What can go wrong, will go wrong. If one of these machines breaks down, we will not meet the plan.

Do we need to buy another press machine or add another shift? The production people don't think so. But we may need to work an occasional Saturday or have overtime during the week. The maintenance people will have to stay on top of the equipment to keep it running smoothly, and our machine setup team will have to do machine changeovers quickly. We will have to get authorization from Joe to work overtime.

Is this a good plan? I really don't know, but it gives us a good set of data to discuss, plan for, and take action. That is the purpose of the S&OP: to see if supply and demand are in balance to meet the customer and company requirements. We are looking at the big picture and want to know if we need to get resources that may take a long time to acquire, like buying a new machine or adding a shift, or if necessary, to outsource production. I know the business plan doesn't allow for these options, but we need to know if we are in trouble because of these restrictions or not.

Executing the S&OP

That concludes my presentation on the S&OP process. We will work with manufacturing, planning, industrial engineering, and finance to begin this process here at Woodstock. We will ask the information technology (IT) team to begin looking for software to help us accomplish this, although I must point out that I think we should start out slowly and get the process down pat before we implement software to help us. We can't do this with every product family but, using the ABC approach, we will start out with our most important products and our most critical resources. Everyone can help identify the products and resources that are candidates for the S&OP process.

I do know that once we develop the S&OP, it can be used by the planning group to disaggregate the numbers and begin the execution process. This plan will be the group's primary input in developing MPS. The two planning processes must be in sync. I think you should bring in the planning team as soon as possible so that we can get it involved with our efforts. Once developed, we must monitor our performance to plan on a monthly basis and make changes, following the inventory time zone guidelines I discussed earlier.

> **TIP #54:** *The S&OP process plays a major role in your inventory rightsizing efforts. All other steps in the inventory planning process are guided by the inventory planning numbers established in the S&OP.*

That's it for now. We in sales and marketing have a lot of work to do; we all do. I know that we play an important role in our inventory rightsizing effort, and we will do whatever we can to make it happen. Thank you for your time.

Inter-Office E-Mail

To: Supply-Chain Managers   March 19
From: Harmony Team
Subject: Rightsizing Inventory
Current Inventory Level: $40.6 Million

We continue to make progress on our inventory right-sizing effort. Thanks to the input from finance, customer service, and operations, we have begun to implement some of the tools and techniques we have learned, and inventory is starting to go down. IT is working hard on helping us with application tools that will make our job easier as we continue to replace inventory with information. This week we met with Rudy from sales and marketing. We learned a great deal more and, once again, came up with a list of action items that will further aid our efforts. The details of the meeting minutes will follow in another e-mail. Here are the highlights of what we learned today, along with some action items:

1. Not having the right inventory in stock can be just as costly as having no inventory in stock.
2. It is very competitive out there; if we can't satisfy the customer's needs, the competition can and will.
3. Marketing plays an important role by conducting an analysis of the marketplace and providing input to the forecasting process.
4. Marketing programs, budgets, and efforts have an impact on inventory levels.
5. Our sales team not only sells our product lines but also has responsibility for forecasting customer requirements.
6. We are reviewing our sales team incentive programs to ensure that they are aligned with our inventory strategy.
7. We learned how to develop an S&OP plan.
8. We have decided on a forecasting technique and will begin using it to improve our forecasting accuracy. IT is looking at forecasting software packages, along with sales and marketing.
9. The S&OP plan cannot be developed by one supply-chain link alone. We have identified other links that should be involved, and you will be asked for your input into this process.
10. The S&OP is a critical planning step in our inventory rightsizing efforts. It drives all the lower-level detailed plans that follow.

11. Necessary guidelines for developing the S&OP exist in the business plan. The S&OP is the tool used to meet many management business objectives.
12. The primary inputs to the S&OP plan are the sales forecast of demand, inventory levels, and production levels. Conceptually, they must be in balance.
13. After developing the S&OP, it is compared for resources that may take a long time to acquire. If we don't have the resources, one of two activities must take place: either we have to get the resources to meet the plan or we have to go back and change the S&OP. Supply and demand must be in balance.
14. We learned about inventory planning zones and will develop and publish a document indicating the planning zones we will use, along with a set of standard operating procedures.
15. In addition to external customers, inventory demand comes from many internal customers.
16. We learned that the company business plan has many inventory-related topics in it. If you haven't seen it, we will e-mail you a copy. Every supply-chain link should be aware of the business plan details.

Attached to this e-mail is Figure 4.6, which is the latest edition of our inventory rightsizing model, for your review and comments. As always, I encourage you to ask questions, provide ideas, and communicate our progress to your team. We are also going to include a status report in our company newsletter, along with pictures of the various people involved in the inventory effort. We have set up a meeting with human resources to discuss the newsletter, which it is responsible for publishing. Our next meeting is with planning and purchasing; we anticipate many good ideas and action items to result from that meeting. Thank you for your time.

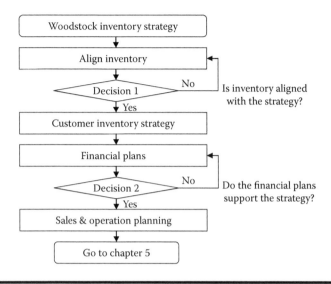

Figure 4.6   Woodstock inventory rightsizing model.

Applying the Tips, Tools, and Philosophies to Your Company

In this chapter, we have discussed the role and responsibilities of sales and marketing and have introduced 11 new TIPS on how these two silos can become part of a collaborative supply-chain network. Whereas sales and marketing has a responsibility on the demand side of the supply-chain equation, its actions (or inactions) have a significant impact on the supply side of the equation. All the TIPS, tools, and technologies in the world will not help if the sales and marketing plans aren't executed effectively. Careful attention must be paid to these two important links.

> **TIP #44:** *Marketing has a direct and indirect impact on inventory levels and strategy. Typically, the higher the forecast (make-to-stock strategy), the higher the inventory level. Marketing programs and budgets should be set in proportion to inventory strategy.*

Marketing plans and sales execution will cause inventory levels to rise and fall on a daily basis. Although we place a great deal of emphasis on these two silos, all other links in your supply chain have a vital role to play that will affect the execution of sales and marketing plans. High levels of inventory will hide a lot of problems in a make-to-stock supply-chain strategy. Underselling the forecast will cause inventory levels to rise, and when that happens:

■ Carrying costs go up because there is more inventory in stock.
■ Positive cash flow will slow down because items in inventory will turn at a slower rate.
■ Flexibility will decrease because you are using capacity to make items you don't need.
■ There will be rising pressure on sales to move the product.
■ Selling prices may decrease to move the product, and profit margins will suffer.

Overselling the forecast is not a good thing either. The inventory may go down, and that brings in another set of problems:

■ Inventory stockouts can occur.
■ Customers will be upset and they may cancel orders if you are late with delivery.
■ You can lose customers because of late delivery; once lost, it will be difficult to get them back.
■ You may pay premium prices to suppliers for raw materials that have to be expedited.
■ You may incur premium freight charges for inbound raw materials and outbound finished goods.
■ Breaking machine setups will decrease capacity and increase operating costs.
■ Because of the constant chaos, internal morale will suffer.
■ Manufacturing overtime may be needed, and this will increase operating costs.

As you have learned in this chapter, balancing supply and demand requires constant monitoring and adjustment. Although it appears to be a "no win" situation, it doesn't have to be. The forecast will rarely, if ever, be perfect. Assuming that this statement is a fact, there are several things you can do:

1. Improve the accuracy and timing of information when change occurs in the sales and marketing plans.
2. Improve your flexibility to change inventory levels in response to the forecast change.
3. If inventory levels increase because of an imbalance of supply and demand, don't wait until the end of an accounting period to deal with it.

4. Monitor budgets and plans weekly. Communicate budget and plan results as soon as possible and report the results to all supply-chain links.

> **TIP #45:** *Supply-chain links within a single supply chain may have conflicting inventory goals and objectives. You cannot rightsize your inventory until these conflicting objectives are resolved and balanced.*

To avoid these conflicting goals and objectives, take these important actions:

1. Use the sales and operations planning technique, discussed in this chapter, and have all appropriate supply-chain links sign off on it. It becomes an internal contract on which all links will perform.
2. Align supply-chain performance metrics with the S&OP.
3. Eliminate individual silo performance and reward programs, and implement shared performance and reward programs within your company.

This doesn't mean eliminating the traditional checks and balances necessary to run a business. These must continue in place. For example, although establishing shared performance and reward programs for meeting budgets and inventory goals is good, you still need finance to monitor and report the conformance to these plans, no matter how good or bad the results are.

> **TIP #46:** *The purpose of establishing inventory planning zones is to recognize the degree of difficulty to make changes, and to allow enough time for all supply-chain links to react to the change in an economical, efficient manner.*

Planning zones will be covered in detail in Chapter 5, when we discuss MPS. But planning zones must be considered when you develop the S&OP also. Essentially, planning zones are used to identify a period of time in your plan when changes to the plan cannot reasonably be made. Because changes to the plan will impact so many areas of your supply chain, companies also identify the level of authority required for a change to take place. You can apply planning zones to your S&OP as well. The S&OP process compares demand (orders and forecast) with supply (production and distribution) and identifies out-of-balance periods where you may have too much supply or too much demand, as the case may be.

In many cases, a period of time is required to bring the plans back to balance. This time period should be identified as a zone. To illustrate this, consider that today you are in month one, and the S&OP shows that, starting from month five (period five of the S&OP), demand is going to be greater than supply. If you decide that the solution is to add another shift, you may need two to three months to hire and train people to work on that shift. This gives you plenty of time. If, however, you decide you need to build another plant, the time frame will not be acceptable, and you would want some executive-level person making that decision. So if it takes two years to add an additional plant and three months to add a new shift, we are talking about two different zones and two levels of authority. We will discuss planning zones in a different context in Chapter 5.

> **TIP #47: *Forecasting has a direct impact on inventory levels. Overforecasting may cause inventory levels to increase if it's not sold, whereas underforecasting will decrease inventory levels but may lead to stockouts.***

Much of this TIP was covered in the discussion of TIP #44, but there are several important points that will be made here. Selection of the right forecasting tools and methodologies will have a positive impact on forecasting accuracy. A big challenge for many companies is in converting a dollar forecast into a unit forecast and a product family forecast into a unit forecast. Too often this conversion is left up to the operations link to deal with and, more often than not, it is the master scheduler performing this vital task. Forecasting accuracy can be improved by

1. Sales and marketing taking a greater role in converting the dollar and family forecasts into specific stockkeeping units
2. Selection of a proven computer-based forecasting application package
3. Using accurate historical data as input to the software
4. Applying sound and intuitive judgment to projected forecasting results
5. Getting forecasting input from customers
6. Getting forecasting input from all links in the supply chain
7. Applying top-down and bottom-up forecasting techniques discussed in this chapter
8. Applying a forecasting tracking signal that will monitor actual performance to forecast

Even after applying all these suggestions, there is a high probability that the forecast versus actual sales will be out of balance. My contention is that the best way to deal with the inevitable inaccuracy of forecasting is to improve your ability to respond to changing conditions. The best way to do this is to improve your supply-chain flexibility. The company that can respond to changing conditions quickly will help itself deal with forecasting inaccuracy. This comment leads us directly to TIP #48.

> **TIP #48:** *The ability to rapidly respond to forecast changes will greatly improve your ability to rightsize your inventory.*

Increasing your supply-chain flexibility will be a big asset in your ability to rapidly respond to changes in forecast. Here are some suggestions on how you can improve your flexibility:

1. **Reduce machine setup time:** This topic is covered in more detail in Chapter 5 but, conceptually, if you can reduce your setup time, you will improve your flexibility. If it takes you eight hours to setup a machine to run product A, production will want to run a large batch of the product before changing the machine setup to run product B. If, however, it only takes you three minutes to change over to run product A, production will be more willing to change the machine over to run product B. Under the long setup scenario, you may be making a product that is not needed right now, and you will be increasing inventory, inventory carrying costs and, in theory, reducing capacity in your plant.

2. **Reduce lead time:** If it takes you less time to make a product, then you can move on to the next product more quickly. The same is true for purchasing materials. If it takes you less time to acquire needed material, not only will you reduce the need to carry more inventory, but you will also improve your flexibility by ordering needed material more quickly.

3. **Improving supply-chain communication:** At times, a complex supply chain with many links is like an ocean liner out at sea. Once it has decided to change course, it is a slow, time-consuming process. Change in forecast usually starts at the furthest downstream link in the supply chain, and by the time information gets from the furthest downstream link to the furthest upstream link, much time has passed and unneeded inventory may be built. The ability to communicate accurately and rapidly will greatly improve your supply-chain flexibility.

TIP #49: *Selection and successful implementation of a forecasting tool will greatly improve your chances of rightsizing your inventory.*

Although intuition and "gut feel" are important aspects of forecasting, you will need a baseline forecast model to which you can then apply your qualitative instincts. Most software packages on the market today provide multiple forecasting models and techniques from which you can choose. You will rely heavily on qualitative forecasting techniques when historical, quantitative data is not available. Here are some suggestions on how to apply this TIP:

1. Get your IT link involved in the selection process.
2. Select at least three suppliers to review their software in detail.
3. Ask for product demonstrations.
4. Give them some of your actual data to apply their models to.
5. Visit/communicate with some of their customers (references) in a like or similar line of business.
6. Ask your suppliers and their customers the following types of questions: "What was the impact on inventory by using this software?"

TIP #50: *All sources of demand must be considered when planning for inventory supply and demand at the S&OP level.*

Actual customer orders are the most reliable and accurate input to the S&OP process (unless they are in the habit of canceling them). But there are many other sources of input that should be considered. Unless you have the luxury of working with an order backlog of at least a year's worth of orders, you will need to forecast all future demands for your products and services. The key word in this statement is *all*. Work with all links in your supply chain to determine the total demand for your products and services. Many companies and many industries have demands for their products that go beyond the external customer. Some were mentioned earlier in this chapter and are repeated here to reinforce the reader's learning experience:

1. Actual customer orders
2. Forecasted customer demand
3. Intracompany demand (from other divisions of the company)
4. Research and development (raw materials and finished goods)
5. Product design (raw materials and finished goods)
6. Quality control (quality assurance)

7. Destructive testing (cars)
8. Free samples (pharmaceuticals, textiles)
9. Marketing promotions (buy one, get one)
10. Field service (spare parts)
11. Company stores (employee discounts)

The above-mentioned inputs can be quantified, and a numerical value (projection) can be placed on them.

> **TIP #51:** *The business plan is a major input to the S&OP process; a realistic, achievable production plan cannot be developed without knowing and following the guidelines that are established in the business plan.*

Besides the quantitative numbers mentioned in TIP #50, there are other inputs to the S&OP process that are just as important, including business plan considerations and restrictions:

- Your company marketing strategy
- Customer's strategy and plans (CRM)
- Supplier's strategy and plans (SRM)
- Your company's resource strategy: people, plant, and equipment (increase/decrease)
- Your company's inventory plans (aggregate decrease/increase)
- Sourcing strategy: make/buy/3PL/4PL
- Financing strategy
- Manufacturing/distribution strategy

These inputs (and others) are just as important to the S&OP process as the quantitative numbers. It is the management's responsibility to see that these inputs are communicated to the appropriate supply-chain links. In my experience, this is one area that needs improvement in many companies.

> **TIP #52:** *The production plan, as part of the S&OP process, is an important tool that, if used correctly, can help us rightsize our inventory.*

The production plan section of the S&OP sets the overall production rates for a product family over a relatively long planning horizon, in monthly periods of time. This becomes the aggregate number of units that should be produced for that product family. The actual production of the individual items that make up that product family should not be greater than or less than the aggregate number. If you build more than the aggregate number of units, inventory may increase; if you make less than the aggregate number, the inventory may decrease. Of course, if sales increase in the former example and decrease in the latter, inventory change may be minimal.

The production plan sets the overall pace of production, and significant changes to the plan will have an impact on the business plan and inventory, in particular. The entire supply chain is being driven by the S&OP process, and if the S&OP changes, it must be communicated immediately upstream and downstream through the entire supply chain. Changes to the S&OP should only be made after receiving input from all links impacted by the change.

> **TIP #53: Do not attempt to drastically reduce inventory levels of active items until the impact on customer service levels is understood by all links in the supply chain. Plan to reduce inventory, then measure customer service performance. If there is no negative impact on customer service, plan to reduce inventory again.**

The operative word in this TIP is *active*. If the inventory is inactive, this TIP doesn't apply. I define inactive inventory as inventory items with no activity for 12 months or longer (unless you can justify keeping it). If it's inactive, get rid of it in a reasonable way that complies with GAAP principles (legally and documented).

In the case of Woodstock Lighting Group, it has far too much finished goods inventory of flashlights. In this case, steps should be taken to reduce the level of inventory. But as the TIP states, it should be a gradual process and customer service levels should be watched. In an ideal situation you should focus on reducing your raw material and manufacturing lead times, and this can be coordinated with your inventory reduction efforts. Conceptually, as you reduce lead times, you can reduce finished goods inventory proportionately. The ideal would be zero lead time and zero finished goods inventory.

> **TIP #54: The S&OP process plays a major role in your inventory rightsizing efforts. All other steps in the inventory planning process are guided by the inventory planning numbers established in the S&OP.**

Technically speaking, the business plan drives the entire inventory rightsizing effort. As a rule, it is rather general in nature and communicates a lot of information in dollars at a very high level. The S&OP is really the first opportunity to state inventory in terms of units, even though it is at the family level. The S&OP process is gaining in popularity, and there is now computer application software available that helps with the process. Having said that, there are still a lot of manufacturing companies out there that skip this part of the planning process.

The S&OP sets the guidelines on where inventory levels should be throughout the S&OP planning horizon. Because of that, extra care and effort should be spent in development of the important documents. All supply-chain links should be involved in the process, and the results should be reported and communicated to all supply-chain links.

What many companies do is take the sales forecast and go directly into a build schedule, omitting the production-plan part of the S&OP process. This is not a good idea. As stated earlier, the forecast is only one input to the S&OP process. Using this approach also eliminates the production-plan part of the S&OP, which is a vital link checking on resource availability. Table 4.5 shows the latest status of the Woodstock inventory, and Table 4.6 shows the inventory segmentation targets by ABC classification.

Table 4.5   Inventory Balance (×1,000,000)

Month end	31 Jan	28 Feb	19 Mar
Forecast	7.2	7.9	9.7
Orders	5.8	7.4	
Total starting inventory	40.0	41.0	40.9
Start FG inventory	15.5	15.7	15.8
+Production @ COGS	4.1	5.1	
–Shipments @ COGS	3.9	5.0	
End FG inventory	15.7	15.8	
Start WIP inventory	7.5	7.6	7.7
+Material issues	3.4	4.2	
+Labor and overhead	0.8	1.0	
–Production @ COGS	4.1	5.1	
End WIP inventory	7.6	7.7	
Start raw inventory	17.0	17.7	17.4
+Material purchases	4.1	3.9	
–Material issues	3.4	4.2	
End raw inventory	17.7	17.4	
Total ending inventory	41.0	40.9	

Table 4.6 Inventory Segmentation Targets (×1,000,000)

Date	Start 1 Jan	Target 31 Dec	A	B	C	Target Reduction
				Inventory		
Total Inventory	40.0	32.5	16.6	9.3	6.7	19%

Flashlights

Finished goods	13.0	11.2	6.0	3.0	2.2	14%
Work-in-progress	5.0	4.0	1.8	1.3	0.9	20%
Raw material	10.0	8.0	3.4	2.6	2.0	20%

Spotlights

Finished goods	0.5	0.4	0.29	0.00	0.15	20%
Work-in-progress	1.5	1.2	0.6	0.4	0.2	20%
Raw material	6.0	4.9	2.5	1.9	0.5	18%

Beacon lights

Finished goods	2.0	1.5	1.2	0.0	0.3	25%
Work-in-progress	1.0	0.5	0.3	0.1	0.1	50%
Raw material	1.0	0.8	0.5	0.0	0.3	20%

Chapter 5

How Much Inventory Should We Make or Buy?

April 15, Harmony Team Meeting

Woodstock Inventory: $39.5 Million

My name is Cyndie and I am the materials manager for Woodstock Lighting Group.

I wonder if this effort will require me to work more hours. I'm already putting in ten hours a day, and my husband is starting to question me whether it is worth the effort. Lately, he has been getting home earlier than I do, has to pick up our daughter at day care, and cook dinner. He isn't happy about that, and I'm starting to feel the pressure. But with all the downsizing going on in the manufacturing/distribution industries, I will have a hard time finding a job that pays as well as this — if I can find a job at all. Besides, it is close to home, and my boss is real good about letting me leave early to pick up the baby and take her to the doctor if she isn't feeling well. Lenny's company is thinking of relocating out of state, and if that happens I will have to find a new job anyway. So, sooner or later I will be out of this rat race. I better stop daydreaming and get back to work. I hope the company is serious this time. It seems like every time a new fad or buzzword comes out we get enthusiastic about it for a couple of months or so. and then it just dies a slow death, or the person who is the champion of the project leaves the company. I hope that doesn't happen this time.

How much inventory should we make/buy? That is the question we struggle with every day. It seems I spend more time with Eddie in purchasing than I do with my husband. I'm exaggerating of course, but there are days when Eddie and I are in constant communication. As you have heard from others, there are conflicting inventory-related objectives within the company. Sales wants lots of finished goods inventory, production wants lots of raw material inventory, and finance doesn't want any inventory! I guess you can say the biggest responsibility we have is balancing these conflicting objectives and keeping everybody happy.

But, you know what? It shouldn't be that way. We should all be in agreement about what our inventory management goals and objectives are. I realize this is exactly what the Harmony Team is trying to accomplish. From what I've seen and heard so far, you are doing a great job. Inventory is starting to come down and is being aligned with our strategy and our customer's strategy. We want to help also, and that's why I'm here today. I would like to give you a good understanding of our role and responsibility and provide some insight into the tools we are currently using that could be used more effectively than we use them today. I truly believe that between purchasing and planning, we can be an important part of the team effort to rightsize our inventory.

Role and Responsibilities

Our overall responsibility is to have the right inventory, in the right place, at the right time, and in the right quantities to satisfy our customer and company needs. That sounds pretty simple — but it's not. We are constantly replanning and changing things. I'll talk more about that later. Let me give you an overview of our tasks and activities:

- **Disaggregating the sales and operations plan (S&OP):** As you heard from sales and marketing, the S&OP is for product families, and doesn't tell us what specific end items to make. Our job is to take the S&OP and break it down into specific products to manufacture. We must ensure, however, that the sum of the items we make in production is equal to the aggregate numbers in the S&OP. The S&OP is for monthly periods of time, so we break it down into specific weeks, because our planning is based on weekly buckets of time. Again, the production we plan for on a weekly basis must equal the monthly numbers in the S&OP. So you see, the S&OP is the higher-level plan that we use to guide us on overall production requirements.

TIP #55: *The S&OP is the primary tool used to develop inventory plans for producing, purchasing, and stocking specific end products, spare parts, and subassemblies.*

(Note: TIP = team important point.)

■ **Master scheduling:** Based on the S&OP, we create a plan called the master production schedule (MPS). By definition, the MPS is a statement of production. It indicates to our manufacturing plant what products should be produced and when they should be produced. For the Flashlight Division, we master schedule-specific end items, like consumer flashlights, commercial flashlights, sport flashlights, night-glow flashlights, and so forth. For the Spotlight and Beacon Light Divisions, we develop the MPS for specific subassemblies, such as strobe subassemblies, flash strip subassemblies, etc.

TIP #56: *The MPS disaggregates the numbers in the S&OP, and the sum of the items in the MPS must be equal to the product family numbers in the S&OP.*

■ **Material requirements planning (MRP):** MRP is a technique that helps us manage production and material priorities. It also helps us determine what materials are needed, how much material is needed, and when the material is needed. MRP gets its input from the MPS. It is the primary tool used by Eddie and his team in purchasing to place orders with our suppliers, and it provides us in planning with the information we need to schedule and release orders to our factory floor.

■ **Capacity planning:** MRP answers three questions about material for us: what, how much, and when? It doesn't answer the question, "do we have the capacity in our plant to make it?" By definition, capacity is our overall capability to manufacture product. By capability, I mean do we have the resources (people, machines, equipment) to meet the MPS and MRP plans? We conduct two types of capacity planning: rough-cut capacity planning (RCCP) and capacity requirements planning (CRP). I'll discuss this, along with the other techniques, later on.

■ **Other inventory scheduling/ordering techniques:** We don't use MRP to plan for all materials. For some items, we use such tools as "min/max" (minimum/maximum), order point, and a "two-bin system." We will review these methodologies also.

■ **Replanning:** We spend about 70 percent of our time replanning the MPS, MRP, RCCP, and CRP. Why? Because change is an inherent part of our supply-chain process. Our ability (or inability) to respond to change accurately and rapidly will determine our success or failure as a company in rightsizing our inventory.

TIP #57: *The ability to react to change in a rapid and responsive manner will be a key to any inventory rightsizing effort.*

In a nutshell, these are the primary activities we perform. I should point out that the sequence in which I presented our activities, from the MPS to CRP, is the same sequence in which we plan. Figure 5.1 is a flowchart representing each step in the planning process.

You will note that there are arrows going back through the process to indicate that this is a closed-loop planning process, which was explained earlier. Different authors and textbooks present this flow in slightly different ways, but all these variations cover the basic concepts we spoke about here.

Replanning Because of Change

Supply chains are dynamic environments, so the one constant all supply chains face is change. I believe this is one of the most important things I am stressing today. If we are slow to change schedules and plans, we will be making the wrong products and inventory may increase, shipments to customers will be late, costs will go up, and production capacity will be lost. I think it's worth a few minutes to discuss the reasons for change:

1. Customers cancel orders.
2. Customers increase/decrease order quantities.
3. Customers change requested ship date; sometimes they want it earlier and sometimes they ask us to postpone delivery to a later date.
4. Customers ask for a different product than originally ordered.
5. Manufacturing has quality problems and product may have to be reworked or scrapped.
6. Manufacturing quantity produced may be different than the quantity requested on the manufacturing work order.
7. Manufacturing equipment breaks down and throws the schedule out of sync.
8. Manufacturing personnel are not available to perform a scheduled job.
9. Inclement weather causes manufacturing to shut down.

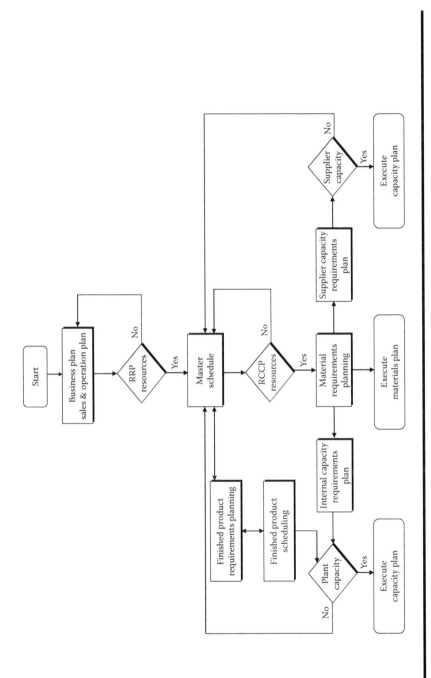

Figure 5.1 Woodstock planning process.

10. Utilities may shut off (blackout/brownout).
11. Manufacturing lead times are inaccurate.
12. Lot sizes are inaccurate.
13. Inventory stock records are inaccurate.
14. Bills of materials (BOMs) are inaccurate.
15. Supplier shortages.
16. Supplier late deliveries.
17. New "rush" orders.
18. Work stoppages.
19. S&OP and the MPS are not in balance.
20. Changes in personnel (new hires/reduction in force).

I've only mentioned 20 reasons for the need to replan. I'm sure there are many more that I didn't mention. The point I'm trying to make is that change will occur, there are many reasons for change, and dealing with change is a big part of our job. This is why every link in our supply chain must understand the role and responsibility of materials management. When changes happen, we need to know immediately so that we can adjust our plans accordingly. Too often, we hear about something that happened weeks ago, and nobody told planning about it! That's ridiculous and it has to improve. I suggest we do three things to improve our supply-chain communication about change:

1. Develop and publish a list of changes that will require us to adjust our plans (similar to the 20 items I discussed today).
2. Document and publish a procedure to follow in the event a change occurs (whom to contact regarding a specific type of change).
3. Develop timelines to communicate the change (i.e., machine breakdown: notify within one hour or sooner; customer order change in zone two: notify within five days or sooner).

I also think it would be a good idea to keep track of the types of changes that occur so that we can detect any pattern or trend. We might need to focus on those and get to the root cause of the change. We will also need to educate all employees on why communicating about a change is so important.

> **TIP #58: Develop, document, and communicate a procedure to be followed when changes occur. Educate all employees on the importance of communicating changes to the proper links in the supply chain.**

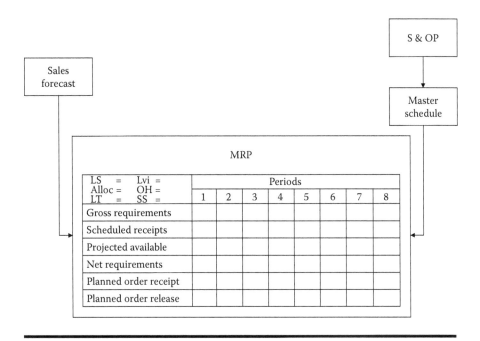

Figure 5.2   S&OP and master schedule relationship.

Master Production Scheduling

I personally believe master scheduling is the single most important activity we do. It is the foundation driving all other plans that cause us to buy or make inventory. What plan is more important than that? Although the S&OP sets the direction and overall production levels, it doesn't tell us which items in a product family to make, and that's an important part of our job. Many manufacturing companies use an MPS. They may not call it master scheduling; some companies call it production planning. According to APICS, the term production plan is synonymous with S&OP. But there are still a lot of companies that refer to the production plan as a statement of what they will manufacture. Figure 5.2 depicts the relationship of S&OP to MPS. Some companies use the sales forecast as a direct input to the MPS, and others use the S&OP process step.

Although the S&OP sets the overall guidelines for MPS, the actual inputs come from many sources. Not all companies have the same inputs. Figure 5.3 shows some of the primary inputs to MPS.

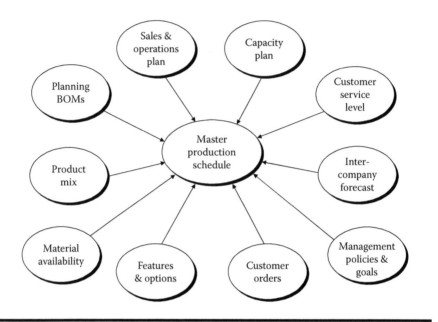

Figure 5.3 Inputs to the master production schedule.

Actual Customer Orders

Of all the inputs to the MPS process, who could argue that actual customer orders aren't the best inputs? I would think that make-to-order companies would have a higher percentage of actual customer orders than a make-to-stock company. But even a make-to-order company may have other inputs to the MPS process. A good example would be a company that manufactures capital equipment and also has a service department that sells/installs spare parts for its machines, similar to our Beacon Light service link.

Those spare parts would have to be scheduled also. In Woodstock, we master-schedule actual customer orders for the Beacon Light and Spotlight divisions: We also master-schedule subassemblies of spare parts. For the Flashlight Division, we master-schedule to forecast, because the lead time to make our products is greater than the delivery lead time given to us by the customer. But as a general rule, master-scheduling real customer orders is the best input to MPS. We do have to be careful though. I have known instances in which the customer gave us an actual order and we went ahead and built the product, only to have the customer cancel the order. Because this was an important customer, we canceled the order as requested and got stuck with the inventory. In fact, I think we still have the product in inventory and if I'm not mistaken it was about a $10,000 order. That reminds me, I want to check the inventory records to see if it's still in stock. We just received a new order from a different customer and I believe the product specs are similar. Maybe I can get the sales team to substitute that product for the new order. I realize that this was an exception — or was it? Does anyone keep track of this? If so, can we get a copy of that report?

Forecast

If the nature of your business is that your customer delivery-requested lead time is less than the time it takes you to manufacture the product, then you have a choice:

- Reduce the manufacturing lead time to something less than the customer-requested lead time, or carry inventory in stock.

As I said before, our Flashlight Division has this problem. It is impossible for it to make the product in a shorter lead time than the delivery lead time, so it has to build inventory in advance of actual customer orders. In this case, we rely heavily on the forecast. And as you heard from Rudy, "The one thing right about our forecast is that it is always wrong." I don't know statistically how wrong (maybe Rudy told you), but if you were to ask me to guess, I would bet it is about 60 percent to 70 percent accurate for the Flashlight Division and about 75 percent to 80 percent accurate for the other two divisions. Pretty bad, right?

That's one thing I would like to see: the actual sales to forecast numbers every month. Can you guys see to it that those forecast to actual numbers are published every month? We don't want the numbers so that we can point fingers and blame the other links; we want the numbers so that we can adjust the MPS accordingly. The forecasting inaccuracy works both ways. Sometimes the forecast is higher than actual sales, and in that case we are making the wrong things, building inventory, and wasting capacity.

Sometimes the forecast is lower than actual sales, and in that case we have to scramble to get the order completed. We call these orders *impact orders*, because they impact the whole supply chain. Purchasing, in particular, gets hit hard when we get an impact order. It has to pressure suppliers to get "stuff" in early (which doesn't help our supplier relationships). It may have to pay a premium to the supplier if the supplier has to break down a machine and do another machine setup. To add salt to the wound, it may have to pay a premium for airfreighting the materials in.

It also impacts our manufacturing plant staff. They may have to do additional machine setups and put aside other jobs they were working on. One of the issues the Harmony Team should look at is the total cost to the company of disrupting the MPS with a rush order. In fact, I will take that as an action item and do it myself. The very next impact order we get, I will look at the total cost to the company from schedule disruption. To prevent constant changes to the MPS, many manufacturing companies establish planning zones with different levels of authority required to make changes. Let me explain this in detail because I think it is something Woodstock should do.

Inventory Planning Zones

I know I've spoken a lot about making changes to the MPS and how important rapid response is in today's marketplace, but realistically, some changes are easier to make than others. All plans, whether they are the S&OP, MPS, or MRP/CRP, have realistic periods where change to a plan will be difficult and costly to make, and the effect on inventory can be huge. Change and its impact will vary industry by industry and company by company.

Our MPS is for weekly periods of time with a planning horizon of one year. The general rule is that the MPS planning horizon should go as far out into the future as our longest cumulative lead-time product, so that long-lead-time items can be acquired in a timely manner. Figure 5.4 illustrates three separate zones in the MPS.

A planning zone is a block of time in the planning process where it is reasonable, or not reasonable, to make changes to the plan. In my example, zone 1 is the closest in time, on the far left of this chart. This represents the current week and the next two weeks after this one. Changes to the plan in zone 1 will be costly to make because resources have been committed. Chances are we've already bought the raw materials, assigned resources (people and equipment), and booked actual customer orders. The only changes that should be allowed in zone 1 are emergency changes approved by Joe or Adriana.

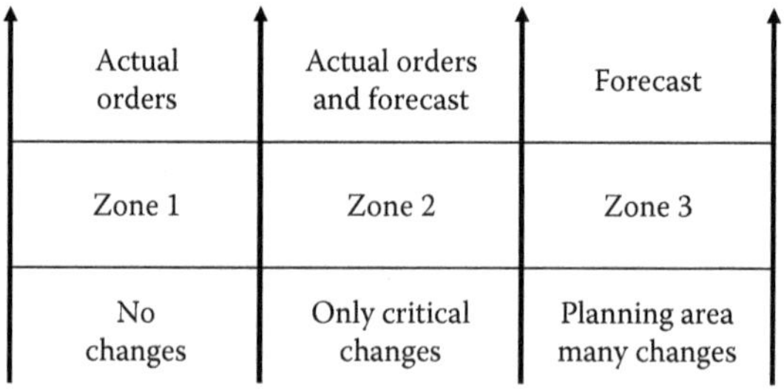

Actual orders	Actual orders and forecast	Forecast
Zone 1	Zone 2	Zone 3
No changes	Only critical changes	Planning area many changes

Figure 5.4 Planning time zones.

Zone 2 is represented by the next three weeks. In this zone (weeks four through six), changes are typically less costly to make. There may be enough time to reschedule machines, and raw materials may be rescheduled for another time. In zone 2, changes to the MPS may be made by Rudy, Arnie, or me.

Zone 3 is represented by the remainder of the planning horizon, which goes out the remainder of the year. In zone 3, changes, if justified, may be made by operating personnel as long as the change is within the guidelines established by our management team consisting of Adriana and Joe.

Obviously, the cost of change will be higher in zone 1 (the no-change zone) than it will be in zone 3 (the any-change zone). For now, I will look at the impact on costs in zone 1 only. I will report my findings back to the team in a couple of weeks, if not sooner.

> **TIP #59:** *Changes to the MPS in zone 1 can increase costs and inventory levels. Changes in zone 1 should be kept to a minimum and analyzed for the total impact to the supply chain.*

> **TIP #60:** *Every time an unplanned order (impact order) is expedited into the schedule, another order (or more) should be de-expedited.*

Other Independent Demand Items

I want to explain an important principle of inventory management: dependent demand versus independent demand items. Independent demand items are those items where demand for the item is unrelated to the demand for other items. A finished product, such as our small standard flashlight (sold as a unit of one to a package), is a good example of independent demand. When you look at the BOM in Figure 5.5, you will note that item #5867 is the finished product and there is no other demand in the BOM higher than item #5867. The same is true for item #52969. Therefore, the demand for item #5867 and item #52969 is independent of any other demand, and demand for them must be forecast.

On the other hand, a dependent demand item is related to the demand for another item. In Figure 5.6, the demand for parts #6167, #22596, #7250, and the light kit #103139 is related to the higher-level demand for item #5867. The demand for these parts is dependent on the demand for the finished flashlight #5867, and the demand for them can be calculated.

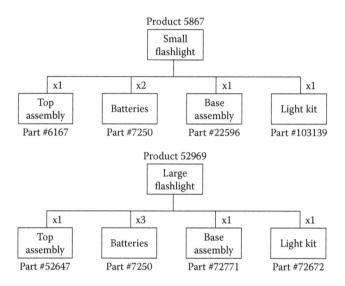

Figure 5.5 Single-level bill of materials.

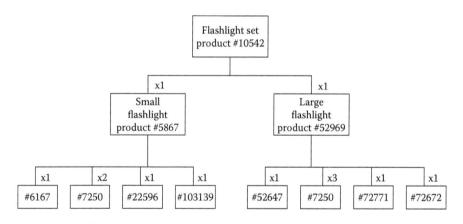

Figure 5.6 Multilevel bill of material.

For example, if the forecast (independent demand) for item #5867 is for 1000 units, then the demand for part #7250 is 2000 units (batteries), because it requires two units of part #7250 for every item #5867 made. Based on this example, we can say that the demand for item #5867 is unknown and needs to be forecast, whereas the demand for part #7250 is dependent on the demand of item #5867 and can be calculated.

Now, here is a good question: Can an item have both dependent and independent demand? The answer is yes, it can. You will see this illustrated in Figure 5.6, where item #5867 is now an independent item sold as part of a two-flashlight set made up of one large flashlight and one smaller flashlight.

The two-piece set, item #10542, is made up of item #5867 and item #52969. So in this example, item #5867 is dependent on the demand for item #10542 and can be calculated. Based on this example, we would master-schedule items #5867 and #52969 (when made to be sold as a single unit), and item #10542 (where item #5867 and #52969 are sold as part of a two-piece set). Later on, when we get to MRP, we will see that the lower-level demands can be calculated and summarized together.

All independent demand must be considered. We also run product promotions where we have a "buy one, get one" deal that we offer to our large retail customers. Although this is not a forecast sale so to speak, we still have to manufacture and ship the product even though it is not considered an item sold for profit. We also donate flashlights to various nonprofit organizations that use the flashlights to improve the quality of life for others. In our beacon light product line, we sell a finished beacon light that has a lens and prism set as part of its dependent demand. However, the lens and prism set is also sold as a replacement part, and thus has independent demand. I'm sure you can think of others, but I believe you get the point.

Restrictions and Limitations

Surprisingly, the MPS is used for other purposes beyond scheduling requirements. It is also a tool that can be used to control inventory levels, production levels, customer service levels, and capacity levels. Many of these restrictions and limitations can be found in the business plan. The business plan is the document in which companies state their strategy for the future, both short-term (one year) and long-term (three to five years). I am amazed by the fact that many people in our company don't know what is in the business plan. I can't tell you how many people I've spoken to who don't know. Just in case some of you don't know, I will highlight some of the points in the business plan that affect the MPS, and inventory in particular.

- There is a hiring freeze for this fiscal year. This means we won't be able to hire any more direct labor personnel in the plant, which in turn impacts our ability to increase our capacity.
- Although the plan doesn't call for plant layoffs this year, it does state that if people leave the company we will not replace them this year. This means not only will we not increase our capacity, but we may in fact have reduced capacity because of attrition.

■ There is no budget this year to purchase new capital equipment. The lead time to acquire new equipment is long, typically six months, and it will impact our capacity in the second half of the year (that is if we need it).

■ The business plan calls for an overall inventory reduction of 20 percent of the total inventory value at the end of the year. Because the inventory was $40 million at the end of the year, this means inventory needs to be reduced by $8 million. How many of our employees know that?

■ The business plan calls for increasing customer service levels by 5 percent over last year without increasing inventory levels. Now that's an interesting challenge.

I suggest as an action item that we cull out of the business plan all inventory-related topics and distribute them to all supply-chain managers so they can communicate what's in the plan to their team.

> **TIP #61:** *The contents of the business plan related to inventory management activities should be communicated to all supply-chain employees who have an impact on achieving those goals and objectives.*

I heard that Rudy explained to you how the S&OP could be used to reduce inventory levels; it is also true of the MPS. Remember, the sum of the items in the MPS must be equal to the product family total in the S&OP. Thus, it is a more detailed, item-by-item inventory reduction.

The MPS is also a tool that can help in establishing customer service levels. If you want to have a high level of customer service, one way to do this is to make more than is required for immediate use. This is particularly true for our flashlight products, which we make to stock. For example, if there is a high degree of uncertainty with the forecast, we may build more flashlights than the forecast calls for. Building extra inventory (safety stock) is the most desirable way to improve customer service. Until we get our act together and reduce our lead times to make the product, we will have to get approval from management, because it will be more than the S&OP shows in the aggregate. Who wants to explain this to management? I've just told you it wants to decrease inventory and increase customer service at the same time. What planet do these guys come from?

Developing and maintaining the MPS is an iterative process that never ends because of constant change. We redo our MPS weekly, usually on a Monday after the production meeting, when we review the results of the MRP computer run (which is done every Sunday) and look at our capacity.

Rough-Cut Capacity Planning (RCCP) and Capacity Requirements Planning (CRP)

The second step in the master scheduling process is taking a look at our capacity. We do this today by using spreadsheets. You would be surprised to learn how many companies pay all that money for sophisticated Enterprise Resource Planning (ERP) software and use spreadsheets for capacity planning. For now, this is the best we can do. There are two computer-based techniques available to us, but we don't use them today.

It is not my intent today to go into the details of RCCP and CRP, but let me at least provide you with definitions. There are plenty of great books written on capacity management, and I will be happy to provide you with references.

- **Rough-cut capacity planning:** This is the process of comparing the requirements of the MPS to the available capacity at our critical work centers. To us it would be our bottleneck work center (our CNC machines) and our gateway work center (our first operation at our first work center — compounding). The theory is that, if we don't have the capacity at our bottleneck work center and our gateway work center, why bother looking at all the rest of them? This doesn't mean that we don't have a need to look at all work centers because we are merely talking about the first review of capacity. The capacity at all other work centers has to be aligned to our bottleneck and gateway work center. Once we do that, we can look at all work centers using CRP.
- **Capacity requirements planning:** CRP is a detailed review comparing the planned requirements (workload) to the capacity at all work centers. I say all work centers, but in reality we don't have to look at all operations in detail. Whereas RCCP gives us some idea of the capacity available, CRP will provide more detail that may show capacity is not available at certain times.

Why is comparing the MPS to capacity so important to inventory management? For one thing, if capacity at a downstream work center is less than the capacity at the upstream work center feeding it work, work-in-process (WIP) inventory will build up at the downstream work center and potentially we could have late work orders. If you remember, our WIP inventory was $7.5 million at the end of the year. If we can balance (rightsize) our workload in the plant, work center to work center, then we have an opportunity to decrease the inventory buffer, which will reduce our overall inventory levels.

This balancing of load to capacity is an iterative process and requires constant attention. I suggest we talk to IT about activating the RCCP and CRP capabilities in our ERP system, so that we can stop using homegrown spreadsheets that take so much time to develop and execute. After all, time is money, and our time will be better spent on analyzing the data provided by these systems, rather than developing the data in a home-grown fashion.

> **TIP #62: Balancing workload (MPS) with available capac-ity is an important step in rightsizing inventory levels in the supply chain.**

Creating the Master Production Schedule

I have brought a copy of our most recent MPS to show you. You will note that Figure 5.7 shows the MPS for item #10542, the two-piece flashlight set I spoke of earlier. The demand comes from our forecast, because this is a make-to-stock item. I have dropped three zeros to make it easier to read. For example, the demand in period 1 is actually 50,000. As of Friday evening, we had 90 in stock. Because we are making this product well in advance of the needed date, no safety stock is required.

Product: #10542
Lot size: 100
On hand: 90
Safety stock: 0

	Periods								
	1	2	3	4	5	6	...	...	52
Forecast demand	50	70	60	50	50	60	0	0	0
Actual demand									
Projected available balance	40	70	10	60	10	50			
Available to promise (ATP)									
Master production schedule	0	100	0	100	0	100			

Figure 5.7 Master production schedule.

Every time we make this product, we make it in lot sizes of 100. I don't know how cost accounting and manufacturing engineering came up with this lot size number, but for now we have to live with it. We only make this product for six weeks out of the year, so this will be our entire production for the year.

We do this because this is a tough setup and takes one full shift to accomplish. Once the machine is set up to run, we want to make as many as possible. This is a terrible approach to planning production. Because much of this stock isn't needed until later in the year, I have been arguing with Joe to defer the final assembly until later in the sales cycle. This technique of "postponement" will prevent us from committing to the final configuration. We can stock them as item #5867 and item #52969 (see Figure 5.5 and Figure 5.6).

If the actual orders are less than the forecast, we can still sell them as single units without the additional cost of breaking down the configuration or selling them at a discount. These are two of our standard products, and we always sell a lot of them. Unfortunately, Joe is of the mindset to make them and be done with it. This is not a good approach, and I've told him so. Maybe you can convince him.

Because I don't think Joe is going to budge on this topic, I think you should talk to manufacturing engineering staff and ask them to focus on reducing the machine setup time. If we can find a way of dramatically reducing setup time, we would make smaller lots at a time and build them more often and closer to the actual date, rather than absorbing the high cost of carrying inventory.

> **TIP #63:** *Reducing machine setup time will allow for producing smaller batches of inventory more frequently and will help reduce the amount of inventory carried in stock.*

Now back to our example. Assume we had 90 units in stock on Friday evening when we went home and period 1 is Monday to Friday of the following week. This continues for a total of six weeks. I can give you a formula, but I would like you to think out the math logically. If we had 90 in stock on Friday and need 50 in week 1 for demand, then we will have 40 left in stock on Friday evening. Do we have to schedule any new stock for week 1? The answer is no.

If we have 40 in stock at the end of week 1 and need 70 for demand in week 2, do we have enough? No, we have 40 and need 70, so we will be short by 30 units. We can't build 30 units because of lot-size rules; we will have to make 100. If we make 100 and have 40 in stock, we will have a total of 140 for the week. We need 70 for demand, so that at the end of week 2 we will have 70 in stock.

This scenario of master scheduling continues throughout the planning horizon and results in an MPS. I have kept it simple because it is not my intent to teach you how to do it but rather to show you how the process impacts inventory levels. There are other considerations. For example, I haven't included safety stock as a planning rule. If I said we had to have safety stock of 50 units, then we would have needed to build 100 in period 1, because the ending inventory at the end of period 1 was only 40 units, which is 10 below safety stock. I also didn't discuss lead times. If the lead time for this product were 3 weeks, then we couldn't build the 100 units needed in period 2 in time. We would have to expedite this lot. I strongly suggest that we review all lot-size rules and operate under the philosophy that the goal is to make a lot size of 1 unit. Of course, this isn't realistic, but it is a goal to strive for.

> **TIP #64: *Constantly review and update your lot-size rules with a hypothetical goal of reducing all lot sizes to one.***

> **TIP #65: *The MPS must be realistic and achievable. If not, inventory will increase and customer service will decrease over time.***

Material Requirements Planning (MRP)

MRP isn't for everyone, and even those companies that use MRP don't use it for all items in their product line. Having said that, I believe MRP is an important tool and, if used properly, it can help us rightsize our inventory. I say that because even though we are using it I know for a fact that it is causing more problems than it is solving.

Let me start by providing you with a simple definition of MRP. It is a technique to calculate requirements for materials used in production. You don't need a computer to do it. My father was using MRP 40 years ago and didn't know it was called MRP for a long time. He used paper and pencil (and a lot of erasers!). He told me by the time he had finished it, it was outdated and he had to start all over again. What an exercise in frustration! So although it can be done with paper and pencil, it isn't practical or effective unless you are only planning for one or two simple parts.

Today, MRP is an application software that is part of an ERP computer system. It would be almost impossible and unrealistic to do it manually. We use the computer because it would be more timely and accurate than if we did it manually.

Figure 5.8 shows all the major MRP inputs and outputs. MRP answers three important scheduling questions for us:

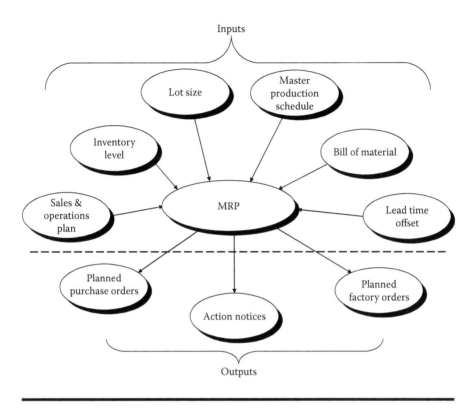

Figure 5.8 MRP inputs and outputs.

1. What parts/ingredients do we need to make or buy?
2. How many of those parts/ingredients do we need to make or buy?
3. When do we need to make or buy those parts/ingredients?

The answers to these questions have a major impact on our inventory levels. Let me quickly review the major inputs to MRP and explain why we are having difficulties with it.

MRP Logical Sequence

It isn't possible for me to teach you how to perform MRP in the brief time allocated to me today. But I would like to show you how it works. Don't focus on the math; focus on what the math is trying to accomplish. I recommend that personnel in all supply-chain links receive education on how MRP works.

We will use two different finished items that use the same battery, item #5867 and item #52969. Logically, the very first thing MRP needs to know is what to build; this comes from the MPS. You will notice in Figure 5.10 that we will require 100 units each in periods 2, 4, and 6 of item #5867, and 100 units each in periods 1, 3, 5, and 6 of item #52969. It is a given in this example that this input comes from MPS.

Now that MRP knows what to make, it next needs to know what parts and how many of each go into each of the two items. For simplicity, we will focus only on the battery, part #7250. Each part #5867 requires two D batteries and each part #52969 requires three D batteries.

Figure 5.6, explained earlier, shows a single-level BOM for each of the two flashlights. The highest level of a BOM is identified as the 0 level. The level immediately below it is called level 1. The battery is at level 1. Why is this so important? It is because MRP will review the material requirements level by level, starting with the 0 level and then reviewing the requirements at level 1 and so on, until it gets to the bottom of the BOM.

This is to ensure that all requirements for an item are captured in the sequence and quantity identified in the BOM. We are not going to plan for item #10542 in this example:

> **What independent items do we need to make?** Because part #5867 and part #52969 are at the 0 level in their BOMs, they are the independent items.
>
> **What dependent items go into each item?** The BOM, as shown in Figure 5.6, shows all the components that go into these two items, and the quantity required to make one flashlight. For every part #5867, we require two batteries, and for every part #52969 we require three batteries. Using part #5867 as an example, the MRP logic says that because we need to build 200 (planned order release) during this 6-week period, and each one uses two batteries, we will need a total of 400 batteries. This technique (calculation) is called a BOM explosion.

Independent demand quantity needed ×
dependent demand quantity

Part #5867: 200 × 2 = 400

Part #52969: 250 × 3 = 750

Total batteries required: 400 + 750 = 1150

Likewise for part #52969, we need to build 250 (planned order release), and each one requires 3 batteries, so the total number of

Product #5867

LS = 50 Level = 1 Alloc = 0 OH = 110 LT = 1 SS = 50	Periods							
	1	2	3	4	5	6	7	8
Gross requirements	100		100		100			
Scheduled receipts	50							
Projected available	60	60	60	60	60	60		
Net requirements			90		90			
Planned order receipts			100		100			
Planned order releases		100		100				

Product #52969

LS = 25 Level = 1 Alloc = 0 OH = 200 LT = 2 SS = 50	Periods							
	1	2	3	4	5	6	7	8
Gross requirements	100	100	100		100	100		
Scheduled receipts								
Projected available	100	100	50	50	50	50		
Net requirements			50		100	100		
Planned order receipts			50		100	100		
Planned order releases	50		100	100				

Product #7250

LS = 500 Level = 2 Alloc = 0 OH = 1200 LT = 3 SS = 200	Periods							
	1	2	3	4	5	6	7	8
Gross requirements	150	200	300	500				
Scheduled receipts								
Projected available	1050	850	550	550				
Net requirements				150				
Planned order receipts				500				
Planned order releases	500							

Figure 5.9 Material requirements planning grid.

batteries required is 750. Note that the gross requirements for part #7250 are shown by period in Figure 5.10.

Do we have any inventory in stock on part #7250? MRP will look to see how much is in inventory, if any. In Figure 5.9, you will note that we have 1200 (OH) in stock.

Do we have any on order? The scheduled receipt line in the grid doesn't show any batteries due in. (Note: on the top of Figure 5.9 we have a scheduled receipt for part #5867 of 50 due in period 1.) A scheduled receipt is an actual order and is scheduled to arrive in stock in the period shown.

After satisfying demand will we have any inventory left? Even if the answer is "yes, there will be some left in stock," MRP will ask another question.

Does the inventory remaining satisfy the safety stock requirement? If the answer to this question is yes, then the MRP system will post the inventory balance in the projected available balance column.

How much do we have to make (or buy if it's a purchased item) to satisfy demand or safety stock requirements? If, at any point during the previous two questions, MRP calculates a negative number, the system will tell us we have a net requirement. This means we must make some to satisfy the demand or safety stock requirements before we can calculate the projected available balance (PAB). The PAB must be a positive number.

When should I receive it into inventory? So now MRP says, "If you have a net requirement, you should plan on receiving some (planned order receipt) in period n."

When should I release the order? For example, Figure 5.10 shows 500 batteries should be received into stock in period 4, and the lead time to acquire the part is 3 weeks. The "planned order release" is in week 1, so that it will arrive into stock in week 4 (3 weeks later). The difference between the planned order receipt, and the planned order release dates is called the "lead time offset."

MRP Makes Recommendations

It's important to note that MRP doesn't automatically release orders to the factory floor or suppliers. MRP makes recommendations. It is up to us in the planning department to decide whether to execute the MRP recommendations. Our MRP system makes such recommendations as:

■ Release an order
■ Cancel an order

Product #5867

LS = 50 Level = 1 Alloc = 0 OH = 110 LT = 1 SS = 50	Periods							
	1	2	3	4	5	6	7	8
Gross requirements	100		100		100			
Scheduled receipts	50							
Projected available	60	60	60	60	60	60		
Net requirements			90		90			
Planned order receipts			100		100			
Planned order releases		(100)		(100)				

Product #52969

LS = 25 Level = 1 Alloc = 0 OH = 200 LT = 2 SS = 50	Periods							
	1	2	3	4	5	6	7	8
Gross requirements	100		100		100	100		
Scheduled receipts								
Projected available	100	100	50	50	50	50		
Net requirements			50		100	100		
Planned order receipts			50		100	100		
Planned order releases	(50)		(100)	(100)				

Product #7250

LS = 500 Level = 2 Alloc = 0 OH = 1200 LT = 3 SS = 200	Periods							
	1	2	3	4	5	6	7	8
Gross requirements	150	200	300	500				
Scheduled receipts								
Projected available	1050	850	550	150				
Net requirements				150				
Planned order receipts				500				
Lead time offset								
Planned order releases	500							

Figure 5.10   Bill of material explosion and lead time offset.

- Increase order quantity
- Decrease order quantity
- Expedite an order

There may be others, but these are the primary recommendations that we look at. MRP runs over the weekend, so every Monday morning we get together with Joe and Eddie in purchasing to review these recommendations and decide which ones to execute.

The Power of MRP

The real power of MRP is that it will combine requirements for the same part used in different products and at different levels in the BOM. Although this calculation could be done manually, it is almost impossible to do because of the number of calculations required. Not only will the computer do it faster, but it will also do it more accurately. Doing it by hand is bound to cause errors.

> **TIP #66: Executing the recommendations of MRP will have a significant impact on inventory rightsizing efforts.**

Data Integrity and MRP

MRP only works well if the data used for the calculations is accurate. This is where we are having our problems, and one of the biggest reasons why our inventory is out of balance and too high. There are four areas that we need to address to run MRP effectively:

1. **Inventory accuracy:** As you know, our inventory accuracy is somewhere around 88 percent. This is terrible. The inventory gurus will tell you that for MRP to work effectively, inventory accuracy must be in the neighborhood of 98 percent to 99 percent. Of course, the goal should be 100 percent. As you can see, we are way off. As a result, we are making things we don't need, and not making things we do need. There is no way we can rightsize our inventory without improving our inventory accuracy. We have begun to cycle-count our inventory. I'll leave it to our distribution team to discuss this with you.

   > **TIP #67: Inventory accuracy must be in the 98 percent to 100 percent range for MRP to function successfully. It will be almost impossible to rightsize inventory without this level of inventory accuracy.**

2. **Bill of material (BOM) accuracy:** I don't know how accurate our BOMs are. When you meet with the product design group staff you can ask them. This is one area where I think we function very well, because I don't get a lot of complaints about inaccurate BOMs. Similar to inventory, our BOMs should be perfect and 100 percent accurate. We should review our engineering change notice (ECN) procedure to ensure that our BOMs are kept up to date.

   Before I forget, and this doesn't have anything to do with BOM accuracy, it would really help get rid of some inventory if design engineering were to provide us with a list of item/part substitutes. There are times when we wait for a part to come in from a supplier but have a part in stock that can be substituted without impacting the end item's form, fit, or function.

   > **TIP #68:** *Have design engineering review the current inventory and provide a list of parts that can be used to substitute for the primary part as long as it can meet the criteria of form, fit, and function.*

3. **Manufacturing and purchasing lead time:** This is a real problem area for us. Lead times are a dynamic and ever-changing environment. Inaccurate lead times are causing us to make/buy products too early or too late. In either case, this is creating increased inventory levels and stockouts. We are wasting valuable capacity on making some products when they aren't needed until a later date. In other cases, we are starting setup or ordering material later than we should and have to go into an expedite mode to get the part on time. If it is a purchased part, we may have to fly it into our plant at a premium airfreight rate. This is equally unacceptable. I propose we establish an operating policy of determining when lead times should be changed in our MRP system. We should review all lead times (manufactured parts and purchased parts) once a quarter and make the necessary changes in our system. We should also have a policy where, if a lead time changes by five days or more, the change should be made immediately rather than waiting for the quarterly review. Is five the right number? I don't know, but it is a starting point; we can decrease it if that is working for us.

   > **TIP #69:** *Inaccurate purchasing and manufacturing lead times have a significant impact on inventory levels and require constant review and updating. An operating policy must be in place to ensure that lead times are current and up to date.*

4. **Lot-size rules:** We should also review our lot-size rules for all items, both purchased and manufactured parts. For the most part, I believe our MRP system operates with the lot-for-lot rule. This means that MRP will recommend only what is required to satisfy demand and safety stock. However, there may be some parts in the system that use the fixed-lot-size rule. This means that every time there is a requirement, MRP will recommend a fixed lot size that we entered into the system. In the case of our internal manufacturing, the fixed lot size was determined by our cost accounting and manufacturing engineering teams. They set this lot size based on certain parameters such as setup times, fixed costs, and associated overhead. In the case of purchased parts, the lot size is set by the supplier. You have heard from others how fixed lot sizes can cause our inventory to get out of balance and hinder our inventory rightsizing efforts. We should review all fixed-lot-size rules to see if we can change them to lot-for-lot. We will get a lot of grief from manufacturing over this because of some of the long machine setup times we have. But reducing setup times is one of the goals of the Harmony Team, isn't it?

> **TIP #70:** *Lot-size rules have a significant impact on inventory levels and should be reviewed and updated constantly. An operating policy must be in place to ensure this happens.*

As you can see we have a lot of work to do in this area. Data integrity is probably one of the biggest reasons that MRP fails in a lot of companies. If we improve the accuracy in these four areas, I know we can reduce inventory levels dramatically. We must get our data accurate and have operating policies in place to sustain the high level of accuracy required. As I said earlier, MRP isn't for everyone and shouldn't be used for all items we make or buy.

There are other ordering techniques we use such as minimum/maximum (min/max), order point, and the two-bin system. We will discuss these at another time. What is very important is that the four areas of data integrity apply to everything our supply chain does and should be taken very seriously.

> **TIP #71:** *The four areas of data integrity don't just apply to MRP; these four areas are important to all links in the supply chain.*

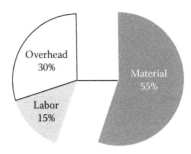

Figure 5.11   Cost of goods sold.

I hope they really understand what I've said about data integrity. Without fixing these areas our inventory rightsizing efforts are doomed to failure. I get frustrated when we run into problems because of inaccurate information, and I really have a hard time understanding why we haven't done anything about it or only make a half-hearted effort to fix it.

Purchasing

Eddie couldn't make it today. He is down in Englewood, Florida, checking out houses for his retirement; lucky him. As I've said before, I spend a lot of time with Eddie and have a good understanding of what goes on there, so I can give the team a good idea of what its issues are. Figure 5.11 shows purchased material as the highest element of COGS. Controlling purchased material costs is an important part of our inventory rightsizing efforts.

Role and Responsibilities

As with most purchasing organizations, the purchasing department of Woodstock is responsible for buying the right product at the right time, in the right quantity, in the right quality, at the right cost, and from the right supplier. However, because of the global marketplace and advent of the Internet, this has taken on a new meaning. Supplier information is just a mouse click away. That's the good news. The bad news (if you consider time) is that there is so much information out there it can become overwhelming. We are constantly looking for new suppliers who can satisfy all six of the "rights."

Unfortunately, purchasing here at Woodstock spends 95 percent of its time expediting materials it has already purchased, rather than finding and nurturing new suppliers who can become long-term partners. I'll share with you the issues our purchasing department faces on a daily basis:

1. **Constant changes to purchase orders:** As soon as we give a purchase order to a supplier we ask to change something on it; usually, the request date and order quantity. As I mentioned before, our MRP system is inaccurate, so we are constantly giving our supplier inaccurate data. I have actually seen purchase orders where we changed the requested date three or four times, only to go back to the original request date. This doesn't give us much credibility with our suppliers.

2. **Too much paperwork:** Current company policy dictates that we issue hard paper copies of purchase orders and amendments to purchase orders. This is a full-time job for two people on our purchasing staff who do nothing else except type, amend, mail, and file purchase orders. This is absolutely crazy. This is a non-value-added activity and should be eliminated.

   We must move to an electronic purchasing system. Eddie has been speaking with the IT team about this. The problem is that IT has a backlog of requests, and doesn't know when it can get to it. One thing is for sure: It's not in the budget for this year. Please help us by discussing this with IT members when you meet with them. We've got to find the budget to do this.

3. **Late payments:** We are constantly late paying our suppliers. We are supposed to pay most of our suppliers in 30 days, but on average we are running about 45 days. In rare cases, we are over 60 days past due. How can we expect our suppliers to cooperate when we are not living up to our end of the bargain? This is a real credibility problem for us. This also causes problems for us when we try to enlist new suppliers. You know that they are checking our credit rating. We had one new supplier who recently refused to give us credit and requested COD (cash on delivery) terms. How embarrassing!

4. **Just-in-time (JIT) delivery:** We have read so much about JIT deliveries where suppliers deliver their product several times a week and in some cases several times a day. I hate to say, "this won't work for us," because that's not a positive attitude and goes against the principles of change management. We have tried to implement this with several suppliers and they wanted to increase the purchase price to do it. Unfortunately, they said we don't buy enough products in large quantities from them to make it worth their while, without charging a premium. I think we should revisit this.

We have one item, an injected molded part, which we do buy a fairly substantial amount of from a local supplier. We currently carry about $500,000 of inventory in stock. We should look into developing a partnership to see if we can get the supplier to deliver on a JIT schedule. We should conduct a cost-benefit analysis to see if it would be beneficial to pay a premium for JIT deliveries. Like any other contract, there must be a benefit to both parties so that it is a win-win situation for both. I'll start to look at this with Eddie when he gets back.

5. **Erratic lead times:** The product is arriving late all the time. We can't predict when the material will show up. Suppliers don't tell us if they are going to be late. This really messes up our production schedule and causes us to be late on orders. This is one of the reasons we carry so much safety stock and why our MRP system doesn't work well.

   We can't follow up on every purchase order to see if it's on time. We process over 5000 purchase orders a year, and it isn't practical to do so. We need to implement a purchase order policy where suppliers must notify us if they are going to be more than three days late. The difficult part will be to get the suppliers to do this. I think we can do this with some of our key suppliers where we spend a lot of money.

   I recommend we establish a "supplier" day, when we bring in the key suppliers and give them some insights into our business. We should also show them our manufacturing processes, have them meet with our management and, in general, explain to them why it's important that they be on time with their delivery, and request them to let us know in advance if they will be late. I think this proactive communication will help.

6. **Excessive overshipments:** I don't know if it's industry practice or not, but our purchase order agreement says that suppliers can ship 10 percent more or less on an order. So naturally, what do some of them do? They constantly overship by 10 percent. If they do this with every customer, they are literally increasing their sales by 10 percent. I wish we could do it. Hey, maybe we do! I'll have to ask Rudy. Anyway, we should identify the suppliers who do this all the time and place orders for 10 percent less than we need, because they will overship and bring the order up to the quantity we actually need. Of course, you know what could happen if we do this. They could ship the exact quantity of the order, and we will have stockouts. We can't win!

Supplier Relationship Management (SRM)

Supplier relationship management can be defined as establishing an integrated partnership between the buyer and seller of products or services, where both parties obtain mutual benefits while satisfying marketplace needs. The SRM approach does not need to apply to all our suppliers but certainly should be used with a select group of suppliers who have the greatest impact on our supply-chain performance.

One of the key attributes of SRM is a greater sharing of information, to the point where we should consider integrating some of our business processes with them. Reduced costs and higher profit margins are commonly shared business objectives between Woodstock and our suppliers. SRM should be viewed as a strategic asset to Woodstock, and moving forward, it should be developed as part of our strategic plan. Thus, SRM is a long-term relationship with key suppliers to satisfy marketplace needs, by improving product design and quality, eliminating non-value-added costs, and focusing on those attributes that the customer is willing to pay for.

Strategic Sourcing

SRM is a philosophy of strategic sourcing with our key suppliers who have the greatest impact on our supply chain. These can be suppliers who we purchase the most materials from (dollars spent annually), provide products or services that are key elements in our final product, or contribute to our profitability and customer satisfaction. Suppliers who are identified as partners in an SRM relationship should be considered an internal upstream link in our supply chain; no different from all the other internal links in our supply chain.

SRM Characteristics

1. **Silo mentality removed:** Boundaries are removed and suppliers are no longer a separate silo in the supply chain. Cross-functional workgroups replace the traditional transaction-oriented relationship. Business goals between buyer and seller are realigned and business collaboration becomes a shared integrated effort.
2. **Improvement in product design:** Product design engineers from the buyer and seller work together to improve the product design to reduce costs, improve productivity in manufacturing, increase profitability (for both), and satisfy customer (marketplace) needs.
3. **Involvement from product conception to production:** Partners work together in designing new products. They work concurrently

and are involved in all phases of new product development. This includes product manufactured by both the buyer and seller.

4. **Technology sharing:** As new technology becomes available it is shared among partners for the benefit of both.

5. **Development of new processes:** Both parties can learn from each other about how their products are currently manufactured and provide input on how the processes can be improved.

6. **Sharing of business and strategic plans:** Long-term strategies related to new markets, new products, and new processes are shared.

7. **Profit sharing:** Any cost savings due to the partnership are shared between the partners. Equally important, any financial loss due to the relationship should also be shared.

8. **Open communication and information sharing:** Complete and open communications are established to the point where there is sharing and integration of computer-based data and information.

9. **Customer-focused relationship:** The focus is on satisfying the customer needs.

10. **A win-win relationship:** Both parties must receive benefits from the relationship. It cannot be skewed one way.

11. **Supply-chain eq. visibility:** The relationship is not just between purchasing and the supplier. In an ideal SRM environment, all links in the internal supply chain, including the external customer, interact with the supplier.

SRM and Inventory Management

What does SRM have to do with our inventory rightsizing efforts here at Woodstock? The answer is a great deal. Because purchased parts represent more than 50 percent of our COGS, it is one of our largest costs and presents a significant opportunity for improvement. The impact on inventory and the benefits are many. By working together we have the opportunity to:

- Reduce purchased part lot sizes
- Reduce purchased part lead times
- Reduce the number of parts needed in our products
- Standardize common parts in our products
- Receive JIT deliveries from suppliers
- Reduce cost of purchased parts
- Increase productivity in our manufacturing
- Increase capacity in our plant

All these benefits have common goals: increasing flexibility and reducing inventory levels in our supply chain. Although I have cited these as benefits to us, they are also benefits to our SRM partners when applied to their suppliers. I know Eddie is pursuing an SRM relationship with two of our key suppliers, and negotiations are taking place. Unfortunately, we won't feel the impact of this immediately; it will take several months to implement.

> TIP #72: *Because purchased material typically represents more than 50 percent of COGS, focusing on SRM with key suppliers will significantly improve inventory rightsizing efforts.*

Vendor-Managed Inventory (VMI)

One aspect of SRM I have deliberately kept separate is VMI. This operating philosophy will help us significantly in our inventory rightsizing effort. If we can get just one key supplier to work with us in a VMI environment, we will have dramatically improved our inventory rightsizing efforts.

One definition of VMI (there are several levels and definitions) is that it is an inventory management optimization technique. With the visibility of inventory levels and requirements of customers, suppliers maintain and replenish their on-site inventory, following a pre-established replenishment cycle. In some cases, the supplier retains ownership of the inventory until it is transferred to the customer site, at which point the customer is invoiced for the inventory.

With supply-chain visibility, the suppliers make and hold inventory in their warehouse until needed by the customer. Similar to all other aspects of SRM it must be a win-win situation for both the buyer and seller. Although it may cost us a little more for the materials, in the long run we will save money. The benefits to Woodstock are:

- Less in-house inventory
- Reduction in carrying cost
- Reduction in stockouts
- Less internal inventory management required
- Improved cash-to-cash cycle (paying for materials closer to use date)
- Increased opportunity cost (with the money saved used to buy inventory for the benefit of some other supply chain)
- Reduction in inventory shrinkage, obsolescence, and damaged goods

The benefits to our supplier are:

- Minimized disruptive expediting
- Long-term contracts with Woodstock
- Predictable annual demand
- Higher profit margins

Of the two SRM relationships, Eddie is pursuing a VMI program with our battery distributor. As you know, we buy a high volume of batteries in a variety of sizes, and we have problems controlling our inventory levels.

> **TIP #73:** *Implementation of a successful (and mutually beneficial) VMI program with key suppliers will benefit inventory rightsizing efforts.*

I can't stress enough how important the planning and purchasing links are to our supply chain. Not just because that's my job, but because we are right in the middle of all the upstream and downstream supply links. What we do or don't do affects all the other links in our supply chain.

That's all we have time for today. We still haven't covered such areas as supplier certification criteria, and several other ordering methods such as the two-bin system, order point, and the economic order quantity (EOQ) technique. We will have to save that for another day. I understand that your next meeting is with Michael, who is going to discuss product and process design. You will learn a lot from him; I know we have.

The product and process design links will play a significant role in our inventory rightsizing efforts. Too often they are not included in any discussions on inventory. When you consider that 60 percent to 70 percent of a product's cost is committed in the design phase, I'm very surprised no one asks for their input.

Inter-Office E-Mail

To: Supply-Chain Managers   April 15
From: Harmony Team
Subject: Rightsizing Inventory
Current Inventory Level: $39.5 Million

We are getting there, slowly but surely. A lot of the action items suggested by the various links in our supply chain are starting to show results. Finance has started to report and track budgets for each link in our supply chain. It has also written off some old inventory that we scrapped. The sales forecast has shown some improvement and we have categorized our inventory into A B C classifications.

We have begun to watch the A items more carefully and the results are starting to show. We are now using an S&OP and have established operating policies and procedures on how to use it. Equally important, we now have planning zones, should help keep schedule changes down. These and the other suggestions we implemented earlier are driving our inventory in the right direction. Our thanks to everyone!

Today we met with the planning and purchasing links and learned a lot more about how to rightsize our inventory. I will summarize the highlights in this e-mail, and as always, the details will be published in the meeting minutes and sent to all supply-chain managers. Meeting highlights and action items:

1. It is the responsibility of planning and purchasing to manage the six rights of inventory management. The right: product, time, quantity, quality, cost, and supplier.
2. It is the responsibility of planning to disaggregate the S&OP, develop the MPS, and run the MRP process.
3. Planning also compares capacity resources available to capacity required (load) and resolves differences.
4. Our planning process is very dynamic because of the constant changes in schedule. Planning spends up to 70 percent of its time replanning. It explained all the possible reasons for changes to the schedule.
5. We have implemented a new planning policy and divided our MPS into planning zones with levels of authority needed to made changes in each zone. This will help stabilize the MPS.
6. We have also published a list of 20 possible schedule changes and who to contact regarding the change. Because some changes are time sensitive, we have implemented a time policy for each change in each of the three planning zones.
7. We are establishing performance measurements for each category of schedule change so that we can

identify the most significant reasons for change and try to get the root cause of those changes.

8. We have found out that sometimes a customer will cancel an order after we have already built the product, and we get stuck with the inventory.

9. We have asked sales and design engineering to review our inventory for items that can be substituted without having a negative impact on the final product form, fit, or function. Sales will look into substituting products at the finished goods level. The focus, as always, is on meeting the customer's expectations.

10. We asked sales to review our order cancellation policy to ensure that we don't get stuck with inventory we made (customized) for a specific customer.

11. Actual sales compared to forecast values will be published every month to all supply-chain managers. This will help us adjust our MPS accordingly.

12. When we get an impact order (defined in the minutes) it should be communicated to all links in the supply chain.

13. From now on, we will look at the total cost of MPS schedule changes in zone 1 and will communicate the amount to all links.

14. We learned the difference between dependent and independent demand. Every link in our supply chain needs to understand the definitions of both. This will be part of the re-education program we are developing.

15. All product demand, beyond forecast and customer orders, needs to be planned for. We are asking all links to identify "other" product demands so that we can put them in our MPS.

16. There are strategies in our business plan that should be communicated to all links in our supply chain. We have asked Joe to communicate those strategies that have an impact on the supply chain.

17. The MPS can be used as a tool to maintain customer service levels. We are looking at that along with the sales link.

18. We have asked manufacturing engineering to review our current machine setup times. If we can reduce machine setups, we can reduce lot sizes and make less at one time.

19. We have also asked manufacturing engineering and cost accounting to review all lot-size rules to ensure that they are correct and meet the goals of our inventory rightsizing efforts.

20. MRP isn't working well and it is a big contributor to having the wrong inventory in stock. We need to improve our inventory accuracy and BOM accuracy to the 98 percent or 100 percent level. Design and manufacturing engineering will review all BOMs for accuracy, and manufacturing and distribution are implementing a cycle-count program to improve inventory accuracy (more on this later).

21. We need to audit our lead times in the MRP system and bring them up to date. We have established a review policy to do this.

22. MRP is a powerful inventory planning tool but is only as good as the information feeding it (garbage in, garbage out).

23. Purchasing will work toward an SRM supplier partnership with key suppliers.

24. Purchasing will work toward establishing a VMI program with our battery distributor.

25. Suppliers tend to overship us by 10 percent. This will be addressed by purchasing.

26. Purchasing will work with accounts payable to improve our payment schedule to suppliers.

Attached to this e-mail is the latest version of our inventory rightsizing model. Figure 5.12 shows the additions added after our latest round of meetings and actions. We ask that you provide the Harmony Team with feedback and suggestions on how we can further improve our inventory rightsizing efforts.

We encourage you to ask questions and make comments where appropriate. On May 8, we are meeting with Michael from packaging engineering, who will provide insight into the product design and product design supply-chain links. Thank you for your time.

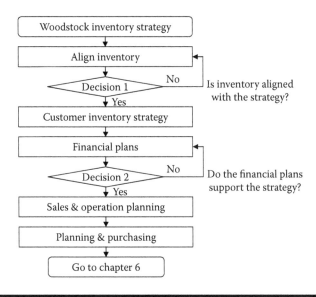

Figure 5.12 Woodstock inventory rightsizing model.

Applying the Tips, Tools, and Philosophies to Your Company

In this chapter, we covered the planning and purchasing supply-chain links. Nineteen new TIPS were provided for rightsizing your inventory, and examples of how to use the most popular tools were given. Whereas in Chapter 4, the emphasis was on the demand side of the supply and demand equation, this chapter focuses on the supply side. A discussion on how to apply the TIPS learned follows.

> **TIP #55:** *The S&OP is the primary tool used to develop inventory plans for producing, purchasing, and stocking specific end products, spare parts, and subassemblies.*

Although S&OP is developed for product families and not specific end products, the plan establishes guidelines on the aggregate inventory for a product family. The total of the disaggregated plan (MPS) for a product family must equal the aggregate quantity indicated in the S&OP. Looked at in that light, it does become the primary tool to develop inventory plans for specific end products. These are important points to be considered about this TIP:

1. Make sure all appropriate supply-chain links have input to the S&OP, including suppliers and external customers.
2. Don't try to make the plan perfect. Although the plan should consider all needs of the supply-chain links and conform to the requirements of the business plan, it looks at the order of magnitude of balancing supply and demand and should be treated as such.
3. The planning horizon should go as far out into the future as needed to acquire long-term resources such as new facilities and capital equipment.
4. Constantly monitor performance to plan and make adjustments when necessary.
5. The S&OP should be developed and approved by the highest-ranking supply-chain executives in the company.

> **TIP #56: *The MPS disaggregates the numbers in the S&OP, and the sum of the items in the MPS must be equal to the product family numbers in the S&OP.***

The disaggregation of the S&OP into the MPS is a process usually conducted by the planning department and should be considered as an operating agreement by which all supply-chain links will operate. When the plans are out of balance, either the demand or the supply must be adjusted to bring them back in balance. These adjustments may flow all the way back to the inventory planning model and the business plan.

> **TIP #57: *The ability to react to change in a rapid and responsive manner will be a key to any inventory rightsizing effort.***

The velocity (speed) of making changes to the entire planning process will be a key to your inventory rightsizing efforts. A very important point to consider when using this TIP: If values change in one plan, adjustments must be made to the other plans to bring them back in balance. For example, if the MPS calls for building more product than the S&OP does, then the latter should be adjusted accordingly. Likewise, the change may necessitate revising the business plan by having to acquire additional financing to build more product than previously decided.

> **TIP #58: *Develop, document, and communicate a procedure to be followed when changes occur. Educate all employees on the importance of communicating changes to the proper links in the supply chain.***

TIP #57 addressed the point that when changes are made all plans should be adjusted to bring them back in balance. To ensure that this happens, you should have a documented policy and procedure (in place and communicated) for all supply-chain links to follow. For example, if a significant change is made to the S&OP, but not communicated to the planning department in a timely manner, inventory build plans can quickly become out of balance.

> **TIP #59:** *Changes to the MPS in zone 1 can increase costs and inventory levels. Changes in zone 1 should be kept to a minimum and analyzed for the total impact to the supply chain.*

Because the MPS is a commitment to build as well as buy inventory, it is an important plan that will impact all supply-chain links. It cannot be treated as a silo activity. Your company should have an established policy on who can make changes in each zone of the MPS. Here is a general guideline to follow:

- **Zone 1 changes:** Only an executive-level manager should authorize changes. In a small company, this could be the company president. In large companies, it should be at the vice president level. The purpose is to raise the visibility of change in zone 1 because these will be the most costly to make. A new order inserted into the MPS may seem profitable, but because of the change, the order may in fact be unprofitable.
- **Zone 2 changes:** In theory, changes in zone 2 will be less costly to make and can be authorized by a director or manager-level person. This doesn't mean that changes in this zone are less important or that the personnel are less capable; it merely means that the decision making can be delegated to a different authority.
- **Zone 3 changes:** Conceptually, zone 3 is far out, so that changes in this zone will have the least impact on the supply chain. If you are using an MRP system, you can allow the computer to make changes as needed. This zone will represent planned orders, and the planners can use their judgment about whether they should react to MRP recommendations. Changes in this zone are typically made by planners and buyers.

> **TIP #60:** *Every time an unplanned order (impact order) is expedited into the schedule, another order (or more) should be de-expedited.*

This is an often-overlooked process. How many times has sales asked production to expedite an order and not tell production which order to reschedule out? Given an option, sales would like to satisfy all orders and not reschedule any of them out. An impact order will be defined differently for each company. As a general rule, an impact order is an order that may cause the following conditions:

1. Change to a machine setup
2. Premium charges for raw material
3. A premium for freight transportation (raw material in and finished goods out)
4. Need to work overtime
5. A bullwhip effect upstream and downstream in the supply chain
6. Postponement of scheduled orders
7. Impact on morale

Have a written policy in place stating that every time an order is expedited into the system, someone (defined differently for each company) must agree on which orders will be de-expedited. For this TIP to work effectively, the orders that are de-expedited must be rescheduled in your planning system.

> **TIP #61:** *The contents of the business plan related to inventory management activities should be communicated to all supply-chain employees who have an impact on achieving those goals and objectives.*

Far too many companies treat the business plan as a secret document, and its contents are communicated on a "need to know" basis. This is wrong. I realize that some information is sensitive and shouldn't be communicated to everyone. However, there is some information that is important for operating personnel to know, and therefore, it should be communicated. What's the point of putting a statement in the business plan that calls for a 25 percent reduction in inventory if you don't tell anyone? The following business plan information that may impact your inventory rightsizing efforts:

1. Reductions in inventory
2. Increases in inventory
3. New product introductions
4. Changes in customer service levels
5. Product life-cycle changes (market exit strategy)
6. Capital equipment expenditures and freezes

7. Employee hiring plans and hiring freeze plans
8. Implementation of new technologies
9. Inventory outsourcing plans
10. Changes in supply-chain configuration

TIP #62: *Balancing workload (MPS) with available capacity is an important step in rightsizing inventory levels in the supply chain.*

In this chapter, we discussed developing the MPS and then performing RCCP to validate the MPS. RCCP is a concept of analyzing your critical work centers to see if the workload (orders) is in balance with your capacity (resources). Typically, a company will look at a bottleneck work center. A bottleneck work center is one in which the demand for the resource is greater than the capability of the resource. You should try to improve the output of your bottleneck work center. If you can't, then all upstream and downstream work centers should be aligned with the capacity of the bottleneck, so that WIP flows at a constant rate.

TIP #63: *Reducing machine setup time will allow for producing smaller batches of inventory more frequently and will help reduce the amount of inventory carried in stock.*

Reducing machine setup time will greatly improve your flexibility to respond to change. Reducing setup times to minutes rather than hours will allow you to make smaller batches of inventory in a cost-effective way. Machine setup time is the time required to get a machine ready for a different part than the part previously completed. Setup time will be covered in more detail in later chapters, but for now it is important to note that reducing machine setup time will in theory increase your capacity. The following are important points to be considered when using this TIP:

1. Identify your bottleneck operation and improve it.
2. Look to reduce your longest setup times first.
3. Keep the machine running as long as possible during the machine setup (do as much external setup as possible).
4. Educate operators and machine setup personnel on the latest machine setup methodologies.
5. Benchmark your current machine setup time.
6. Establish goals for improving the benchmark.
7. Measure performance as compared to the goal.
8. Continually look for ways to improve setup times.

TIP #64: *Constantly review and update your lot-size rules with a hypothetical goal of reducing all lot sizes to one.*

Poorly defined or outdated lot-size rules will have an impact on your inventory rightsizing efforts. It will require that you constantly monitor and update lot-size rules on a continuous basis; this is especially true of purchased parts. In all probability, you have a better handle on internal manufacturing lot-size rules — or maybe not. For both purchased and manufactured parts, the following should be considered:

1. Establish a policy on when lot-size rules will be reviewed and updated.
2. Identify which links will make changes to the rules.
3. All information systems (manual or computer based) should be updated and in sync.
4. Communicate lot-size policies to all suppliers (for purchased parts).

TIP #65: *The MPS must be realistic and achievable. If not, inventory will increase and customer service will decrease over time.*

I have an old saying: "Lie to your planning system and it will lie right back to you — only faster." The computer is a wonderful and useful tool, but it is only as good as the data it is given to work with. There is another old truism: "garbage in, garbage out." If the MPS isn't achievable, what good is it? One of the reasons many companies have an unrealistic and non-achievable MPS is that they never reschedule the order backlog in their system. We spoke earlier about expediting and de-expediting. When you expedite you should reschedule the orders that you couldn't finish, for one reason or another. If you have a full load of work scheduled in week 1 of your MPS, and you also have a backlog from the week before, you are misstating your MPS and you will not achieve the plan for that week, and probably for many weeks thereafter if you don't reschedule the backlog.

TIP #66: *Executing the recommendations of MRP will have a significant impact on inventory rightsizing efforts.*

We spoke earlier about the fact that MRP doesn't automatically change orders. It makes recommendations, and it depends on human judgment whether you act on the recommendations. Not acting can be just as detrimental as taking action. If your system is making too many recommendations, or the next time you run MRP it is changing the recommendations back to what they originally were, it may be a symptom of a "nervous system."

If you are making changes to the MPS every day, or many times a day, you will have a slew of recommendations. You should be careful with this. If you find that you are making multiple changes to the same part and maybe returning to the previous recommendations, you will create a very unstable planning environment. This point goes back to freezing the MPS and zone 1. Every effort should be made to freeze the schedule in zone 1, and then you can better validate the MRP recommendations for that zone.

> **TIP #67:** *Inventory accuracy must be in the 98 percent to 100 percent range for MRP to function successfully. It will be almost impossible to rightsize inventory without this level of inventory accuracy.*

As explained earlier, different links will have different definitions of inventory accuracy and how it's calculated. The one fact in common with any definition is that inaccurate inventory causes many problems. If your perpetual system says you have more than you physically have, then you will experience stockouts and have unhappy customers and employees. If your perpetual system says you have less than you actually have, then it is hiding a lot of problems you won't see. What you will have in the latter example is an irate finance silo. They will notice.

> **TIP #68:** *Have design engineering review the current inventory and provide a list of parts that can be used to substitute for the primary part, as long as it can meet the criteria of form, fit, and function.*

There is a high probability that you have something sitting in inventory that you don't need for the product it was made/purchased for, but can be used as a substitute for a needed product. You can make this happen as follows:

1. Establish a material review committee consisting of design engineering, manufacturing, quality, planning, and purchasing.
2. The committee should meet at least once a month to review inactive inventory or items with a higher-than-needed inventory level.
3. Provide the inventory list to the committee members at least one week prior to the meeting so that everyone can come prepared to take action at the meeting.

4. If a crisis shortage comes up before the scheduled meeting, have planning review possible substitutes with design engineering on an ad hoc basis.

> **TIP #69:** *Inaccurate purchasing and manufacturing lead times have a significant impact on inventory levels and require constant review and updating. An operating policy must be in place to ensure that lead times are current and up to date.*

Many companies focus a lot of attention on getting their inventory and BOM records as accurate as possible. That is a true and noble task, but accurate manufacturing and purchasing lead times are just as important to your inventory rightsizing efforts. If lead times are actually longer than the system says, then the material will be late and you will have a stockout (unless you are carrying safety stock). If lead times are really shorter than the system says, you will probably experience an increase in inventory by making the product early or having purchased material arriving earlier than expected. To keep this from occurring you should:

1. Periodically review all lead times
2. Assign lead time review responsibility
3. Document date of change in the system
4. Make sure lead times are in sync between multiple systems (databases)

> **TIP #70:** *Lot-size rules have a significant impact on inventory levels and should be reviewed and updated constantly. An operating policy must be in place to ensure this happens.*

Similar to lead times, lot-size rules will have a significant impact on your inventory rightsizing efforts. Remember, you control and determine your internal supply-chain lot sizes. It is with purchased parts that many companies have difficulty controlling purchase quantities. This is particularly true if you are a small, infrequent buyer to the supplier. You may be able to reduce lot sizes by the following methods:

1. Simply explain your situation to the supplier. If you don't ask, you'll never know. What's the worst they can do? Say no.
2. Determine what your annual buy for the year is for that part and place a blanket order with multiple delivery dates throughout the year.

3. Conduct a cost analysis to determine if paying a premium for a smaller lot size will be offset by the cost of carrying the inventory in stock.

4. On internal supply-chain lot sizes, challenge the current lot-size rules to see if they make sense. Sometimes, it's just a communication problem.

> **TIP #71:** *The four areas of data integrity don't just apply to MRP; these four areas are important to all links in the supply chain.*

I call these four areas of data integrity the supply chain **"BILL of Integrity" (BOI).** BILL stands for:

Bill of material accuracy (B)
Inventory accuracy (I)
Lead time accuracy (L)
Lot-size rule accuracy (L)

An accurate BILL is critical to your inventory rightsizing efforts. Many companies will address these four areas when they embark on an MRP implementation. The consultants and software suppliers will advise them that MRP will not work effectively without a BOI, and rightly so. However, it usually stops there. Two points that will help you improve your BOI:

1. Don't just focus on the parts using MRP. Apply BOI to all parts and materials.

2. The BOI must be sustained on a continuing basis and not treated as a project with start and end dates.

> **TIP #72:** *Because purchased material typically represents more than 50 percent of COGS, focusing on SRM with key suppliers will significantly improve inventory rightsizing efforts.*

Considering the fact that one of the largest costs of most supply chains is the cost of material, it is an area that you should focus a lot of attention on. In today's competitive environment, the supply chain that can reduce these costs will have an advantage over its competition. Purchasing must move from being a reactive silo to a proactive cross-functional collaborator with other links in the supply chain. If you are spending 95 percent of the time expediting and only 5 percent of the time on true purchasing activities, you must reverse these percentages to be effective. You can start by focusing on key suppliers and establishing a true partnership with them.

> **TIP #73:** *Implementation of a successful (and mutually beneficial) VMI program with key suppliers will benefit inventory rightsizing efforts.*

VMI isn't a concept that can be used by all supply chains, and a VMI program will only work well if there are benefits to both the buyer and seller. For a VMI program to work effectively, consider the following:

1. Forecast for demand should be predictable and accurate.
2. VMI will work best with stable demand items.
3. Item quantity is significant.
4. The total cost of the VMI item should be considered.
5. The relationship is profitable to both parties.

This chapter on planning and purchasing is at the very heart of the supply chain, and successful execution of the topics covered will help you rightsize your inventory. Similar to all other links in the supply chain, they must move from a silo focus and become part of your collaborative supply-chain network. Table 5.1 shows the most current status of the Woodstock inventory, and Table 5.2 shows the excess inventory by ABC classification.

Table 5.1   Inventory Balance (×1,000,000)

Month end	31 Jan	28 Feb	31 Mar	15 Apr
Forecast	7.2	7.9	9.7	7.1
Orders	5.8	7.4	9.6	
Total starting inventory	40.0	41.0	40.9	40.3
Start FG inventory	15.5	15.7	15.8	15.3
+Production @ COGS	4.1	5.1	6.0	
–Shipments @ COGS	3.9	5.0	6.5	
End FG inventory	15.7	15.8	15.3	
Start WIP inventory	7.5	7.6	7.7	7.4
+Material issues	3.4	4.2	4.8	
+Labor and overhead	0.8	1.0	0.9	
–Production @ COGS	4.1	5.1	6.0	
End WIP inventory	7.6	7.7	7.4	
Start raw inventory	17.0	17.7	17.4	17.6
+Material purchases	4.1	3.9	5.0	
–Material issues	3.4	4.2	4.8	
End raw inventory	17.7	17.4	17.6	
Total ending inventory	41.0	40.9	40.3	

Note: FG = finished goods, COGS = cost of goods sold, WIP = work-in-process.

Table 5.2 Inventory Segmentation (×1,000,000)

Date	Start January 1	Target December 31	A	B	C	Excess	Obsolete
	40.0		19.9	11.2	8.9		
Total inventory		32.5	16.6	9.3	6.6		
Flashlights							
	13.0		6.7	3.5	2.8		
Finished goods		11.2	6.0	3.0	2.2		
	5.0		2.5	1.5	1.0		
Work-in-process		4.0	1.8	1.3	0.9		
	10.0		4.2	3.3	2.5		
Raw material		8.0	3.4	2.6	2.0		
Spotlights							
	0.5		0.3	0.0	0.2		
Finished goods		0.4	0.3	0.0	0.1		
	1.5		0.7	0.5	0.3		
Work-in-process		1.2	0.6	0.4	0.2		
	6.0		2.9	2.1	1.0		
Raw material		4.9	2.5	1.9	0.5		
Beacon lights							
	2.0		1.5	0.0	0.5		
Finished goods		1.5	1.2	0.0	0.3		
	1.0		0.5	0.3	0.2		
Work-in-process		0.5	0.3	0.1	0.1		
	1.0		0.6	0.0	0.4		
Raw material		0.8	0.5	0.0	0.3		

Chapter 6

How Can We Improve the Product and Process Design to Minimize Inventory Levels?

May 8, Harmony Team Meeting
Woodstock Inventory: $39 Million

My name is Michael, and I am a packaging engineer for Woodstock Lighting Group.

I really hope this inventory rightsizing effort works. I like working here and have made a lot of new friends. I told Butchie just the other night that as screwed up as the company is, I could spend the rest of my career here. I'm not one to change jobs every six months. The company was generous enough to sponsor my hockey team this season, and for that I am grateful. For the first time since I've been here, I really think we have an opportunity to get our act together, and we are becoming a team. I just wish people would stop complaining and talking about each other. I think we need to get rid of the politics constantly going on and start to trust each other more. If I say this openly everyone will deny it, but it's true. If everyone would expend the same energy on fixing the inventory problems as they expend figuring out how to get out of doing their job, we could be awesome.

Maybe my positive attitude will rub off on the Harmony Team and we can work together. I will do my utmost and hope for the best, but if I feel it's going to be business as usual, I'm getting out of here. Joe is the key to our inventory rightsizing efforts. He must set a good example by demonstrating a positive attitude and he must stop antagonizing everyone. Just because he chooses to work 12 to 14 hours a day, he shouldn't expect everyone to. I never understood that work ethic. Oh well, I guess I should focus on matters I can help change, and not worry about those I can't.

How can we improve the product and process design to minimize inventory levels? It's a good question and as I speak, we are aggressively pursuing the answer to that very question. Before I start, I want to note that our inventory went down, but not much. This shouldn't be a surprise to anyone. Once Cyndie, Eddie, and their teams reviewed and updated all the system lead times and lot-size rules, it was predictable. Materials requirement planning (MRP) is now generating realistic information. It is finding that on some items we have too much inventory and on others we don't have enough. So it has to bring the inventory into balance. In time, this will correct itself and the inventory will start to go down as the adjustments take effect. If they hadn't corrected the planning data, we would have continued to bring in the wrong inventory and our inventory rightsizing efforts would not be successful.

> **TIP #74:** *Any drastic changes in your MRP data may cause inventory levels to rise, until inventory is rebalanced and adjusted to the new planning requirements. Over time, it will begin to correct itself and decrease accordingly.*

(Note: TIP = team important point.)

Product Design and Inventory

If I had to guess, I would say that 50 percent to 70 percent of our product's total costs are determined in the product design phase. This is where we determine what parts and how many of them will be in our products. Product design will impact the type of packaging we use and could even affect our warehousing, transportation, field service, and warranty costs — and they are significant. On top of all that, product design will determine our selling costs and profitability. Do I have your attention? I hope so.

In times gone by, product design engineers could design a new product in their own little silo and then throw it over the wall for the rest of the links in our supply chain to figure out how to build it, price it, store it, and ship it. Not only was this poor communication among the links, but it was extremely costly and time consuming. In an age in which products have shorter and shorter life spans, Woodstock is put in the precarious position of being late to market with new products, and our ability to capture market share is compromised. Although a product should be designed to satisfy the customer's expectations, it is equally important that the product is designed to be manufactured efficiently, quickly, and at a reasonable cost. A poor design can impede productivity and increase manufacturing cost.

This focus on designing products to be produced efficiently and cost effectively is often called "design for manufacturability (DFM)" and "design for assembly (DFA)." Sometimes, the terms are combined and referred to as "design for manufacturability and assembly (DFMA)."

> **TIP #75:** *Product design has a major impact on inventory costs through every link in the supply chain. The design must become a cross-functional process with inputs from all links in the supply chain, including suppliers and customers.*

Product Design: Role and Responsibilities

I am going to take a different tack than my peers in the other links by speaking about product design's role working concurrently with other specific links in our supply chain:

- **External customers:** What better input can we get than feedback from our customers who buy our products and their customers who use them? We ask these customers what new generation of products they would like us to produce and what enhancements they would like to see in our current product offerings. We do this in a formal structure. Twice a year we have meetings with different customer groups to show them some of the new products we are currently working on and the planned enhancements to existing products.

    Along with sales and marketing, we have hosted this two-day event at three different locations across the United States. This is a great forum to get new ideas and suggestions. After these joint meetings, we visit some of the customers who attended, to view their operation. In many cases it is a distributor (flashlights), who sells our product to retailers. We analyze how they stock, pick, and ship our products to their customers.

In some cases, it is a subcontractor who is modifying a vehicle so that our light assemblies can be attached. We have even visited with the U.S. military to see how our flashlights and spotlights are used in the field. We ask our customers to share their insights into what new products they have on their drawing board. We even ask certain customers to participate in our product design teams.

- **Suppliers:** We can learn a great deal from our suppliers. Eddie or Cyndie has probably already told you we have scheduled "supplier days," when we invite some of our key suppliers (Eddie calls them partners) to visit our plant and take a tour of our manufacturing environment so they can see how we use their product. We hope to get ideas from them that will allow us to improve our product and reduce our costs. We in turn will visit their facility to see how they manufacture the products we buy from them. We may be able to improve both our products for our mutual benefit.
- **Warehouse and distribution:** We have been working with our peers in these two links to see how the product can be better designed for storage, packing, and shipping. In fact, we just had a meeting with them last week and have come up with a new-size carton that will allow us to store more cartons on a skid (pallets), without negatively impacting weight limitations and safety requirements. We are going to pass this new carton idea by our largest distributors to see if it will be useful for their internal operation.
- **Sales and marketing:** These are two more critical links in our supply chain. Sales can share with us what the customers are saying about our products, what's good about them, and how they can be improved. Marketing is always on the lookout for new product ideas and is out in the field visiting customers, taking surveys, and attending industry trade shows to find out what the latest and greatest is. We get a lot of good input from these two links.
- **Field service:** The people on our field service team are at customer sites all the time. In fact, they spend more time with the customers than our sales team and other internal links do. They know what problems there are in the field (with our products) and are a good source for value-added product enhancements. We consider the needs of all our customers, not just the large ones.
- **Manufacturing:** Because this link produces what we design, input is absolutely critical. What good is it for us to design the "best product in the world," if it can't be manufactured cost effectively?
- **Purchasing and planning:** Sometimes we design a new product and don't know if the parts we are using are standard off-the-shelf parts or custom made. The rule of thumb is we want to use

standard parts where possible (if it's cost effective). Purchasing personnel will know the answer to this question, and we are constantly working with them on this issue. Planning, on the other hand, needs to be involved because of lead time and lot-size issues. There are two principles at work here for planning. First, the greater the total number of parts designed into the product, the more parts planning has to watch and schedule. Second, the greater the variety of parts, the more parts planning has to watch and schedule. Put in another way, the fewer the parts, the less the scheduling; the more the standardization of parts, the less the complexity in scheduling.

■ **Information technology:** Although not directly involved in the design of new products, IT has been very helpful in identifying new tools and technologies that have made our job easier over the years. I hate to think of what it was like before we had computer-aided-design (CAD) systems. Since we upgraded our CAD system last year, we have increased our product design productivity by 25 percent. IT is constantly on the lookout for new technology to make our link more efficient.

■ **Finance and accounting:** You may be asking yourself, what does accounting and finance have to do with new product design? My answer is — a lot. After the product is designed (oops, I'm wrong; I meant to say, "as the product is being designed"), it has to evaluate all costs associated with the new product. It may find that the total cost to bring the new product to market is so high that we will lose money. Believe me when I say it; this has happened.

■ **Quality control and assurance:** Although we have consistently treated quality as part of the manufacturing link, I wanted to break it out in this part of our conversation because of the contribution it can make, particularly with product enhancements. One of its responsibilities here at Woodstock is to analyze returned goods. It has firsthand knowledge about quality defects in our products and helps us improve our current product line. This gives us some insight into what can potentially go wrong with a new product.

■ **Competitors:** Don't be so surprised. Yes, in a way, we interact with competitors. We buy our competitor's products and reverse engineer them. Reverse engineering is where we disassemble and evaluate our competitor's products. Our objective is to identify the characteristics of their product so that we can improve our products and manufacturing processes without infringing on our competitor's proprietary technologies.

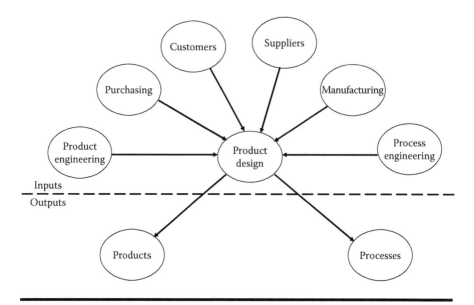

Figure 6.1 Product design inputs and outputs.

Working as a Team to Bring Product to Market

The bottom line is we interact with the entire supply chain from the very beginning of new product design. This "working together" has many names. Two of the more popular names are *simultaneous engineering* and *concurrent engineering*. Call it what you will, a product must be designed with consideration of the needs of the entire supply chain. Figure 6.1 illustrates this cross-functional approach to product design and enhancement. Not all inputs are shown in this example. This is just an example representing all 19 links in our supply chain. The two major outputs of process design are products and manufacturing processes.

Generally speaking, our responsibility is to design new products and to enhance existing ones. But what does all this have to do with rightsizing our inventory? The answer is — plenty. By working as a team we can impact inventory in several important ways. The inventory objectives would be:

1. Reducing the total number of parts in our products
2. Replacing unique parts with off-the-shelf parts
3. Combining parts so that there is less need for different part numbers
4. Designing parts for ease of handling and inventory storage
5. Reducing the need for rework and scrap

If we accomplish these objectives, we would have fewer part numbers and less inventory, and as a result could reduce the planning effort. I always thought companies that manufacture baseball caps were a good example of applying the principle of standardization. Years ago, they had to stock inventory on all different sizes of hats. I don't know how many sizes there were, but today we live in a one-size-fits-all world. They manufacture one size and use a Velcro-backed tab that can be adjusted to the precise size needed. This "mass customization" has greatly reduced the number of items they have to make, stock, and ship. What a wonderful, cost-saving idea.

> **TIP #76:** *Designing products collaboratively with other links in the supply chain can benefit your inventory right-sizing effort by eliminating or reducing the total number and variety of parts that have to be planned for and stocked in inventory.*

New Product Development Example

Let me share with you an example of a concurrent engineering project we are very close to finalizing. We have worked with many links in our supply chain to develop this new product, including two key suppliers and three of our customers.

The new product is a compact lantern that will be sold through our Flashlight Division. This compact lantern is styled along the lines of the old kerosene lanterns that have been around for years. Our lantern will operate with batteries rather than kerosene. It is lightweight, water resistant and comes with a canvas carrying case, rechargeable battery pack and a battery recharger. This product is unique because it is so compact and lightweight that it is easy and convenient to travel with on camping trips, picnics, beach parties, and hiking trips. It can also be readily stored in the home or office for emergency lighting use. Another unique feature of our product that distinguishes it from our competition is that it will have a remote control that will allow the user to turn it on and off at a distance. This will also help locate the lantern in the dark. Although the remote control is an important feature of the product, it won't be available for the first release. As you can see from Table 6.1, the initial design developed by our product design engineers had a total number of 56 parts, assigned 30 different part numbers.

That's a lot of inventory to buy, make, store, assemble, plan, and keep track of. Besides, it drives up the cost of the finished product. Now, I

Table 6.1   Compact Lantern Parts List

Part Number	Quantity	Unit of Measure	Description
1	1	Each	Lantern box
2	1	Each	Printed care instructions
3	1	Each	Product tag
4	1	Each	Tag holder
5	1	Each	Canvas carrying case
6	1	Each	Plastic top with logo
7	3	Each	Plastic o-ring: top
8	1	Each	Plastic shield
9	2	Each	Reflector
10	1	Each	Lantern base
11	1	Each	Prism
12	1	Each	Plastic bulb holder
13	8	Each	Bulb
14	1	Each	Light reflector
15	1	Each	Switch: off-high-low
16	2	Each	Plastic o-ring: bottom
17	3	Each	Insulated wire
18	2	Each	Contact boards
19	6	Each	Contact clips
20	2	Each	Rivets
21	0.01	Pound	Solder
22	4	Each	Screw
23	1	Each	Reflection donut: top
24	1	Each	Bulb plastic dome
25	4	Each	Battery pack
26	1	Each	Battery cover screw
27	1	Each	Plastic hook
28	1	Each	Plastic hook holder
29	0.001	Ounce	Glue
30	1	Each	Battery charger

don't want to get into a lot of details, but the goal of our concurrent engineering team was to:

1. Reduce the total number of parts
2. Use common off-the-shelf parts where possible
3. Standardize on fewer part numbers
4. Outsource some subassemblies

For example, the hanging hook and the hook holder that attaches to the lantern were originally designed as three separate pieces. We redesigned it using one mold, and now it is one piece rather than three. The original design called for six screws of three different sizes (two of each size). Working with our supplier and our own manufacturing people, we were able to reduce the total number of screws to three, all of the same size, and they are a standard size we can buy, if need be, at a local hardware store.

The original design of the light reflectors had four different parts of different shapes and sizes. Working with purchasing and our supplier, we were able to reduce the total down to two light reflectors of different sizes. We are working on getting it standardized to one size reflector.

Our customers were very helpful in giving us input to the design of the canvas carrying case. They came up with the idea of waterproofing the carrying case and adding a pouch to carry the battery recharger and an extra battery pack, thus making the new product more user friendly. These are just some of the examples of how the concurrent engineering effort helped us design a more cost-effective, user-friendly product.

Because of this concurrent engineering effort, we were able to reduce the total number of parts to 45 and different part numbers to 20. This resulted in an estimated material cost reduction of $1.50 per lantern. The labor cost to assemble the lantern was reduced by $0.50 per lantern. Based on the initial marketing forecast of 50,000 units for the first year, the total estimated material and labor saving would be $100,000 for the year.

This will accomplish two things: First, it will increase our profit margin, and secondly, if we reduce the selling price, we may sell more units. The cost saving that is difficult to measure is the amount of time that will be saved by planning and purchasing by not having to plan for and buy the 11 extra parts. There will be a savings in carrying cost because we will be carrying less overall inventory on this new product. I don't know what the saving will be, but it will certainly be a positive number. Imagine if we could do this with every product we make? The cost savings would be phenomenal.

This concurrent engineering effort will be continued for all new products. We are going back to the drawing board to review our current products to see if we can apply the same design concepts. One important point I failed to mention is that the supplier who came up with the idea of molding one plastic part for the hook instead of three will make a greater profit margin per hook, and eventually we will be paying less. This is an example of both parties benefiting from the partnership in the design phase. It is a win-win situation for both of us.

I believe the more we can get our suppliers to design our parts based on a collaborative effort, the better off we will be. Of course, this doesn't apply to all suppliers. To some suppliers, we aren't a big enough player for them to get involved with our design team. You can't have true collaborative product design without involving other links in the supply chain. In summary, a concurrent engineering approach should consider:

1. Minimizing the number of parts in a product
2. Minimizing the variety of parts in a product
3. Including all links in the supply chain that are impacted by the product design
4. Using existing resources: machines, equipment, skill sets, and processes
5. Designing for mass customization
6. Designing for product modularity
7. Using materials that will ease the production process
8. Using off-the-shelf parts rather than custom-made parts
9. Simplifying the packaging process
10. Simplifying the storage and retrieval process
11. Designing products for ease of repair and parts replacement
12. Designing products that are environmentally safe
13. Designing products that are environmentally disposable at the end of life
14. Designing products that consume less energy
15. Using lightweight materials that are ergonomically user friendly where possible to reduce transportation costs

One characteristic that I would like to talk about separately is designing products for "inventory postponement." This strategy calls for shifting product differentiation as far downstream in the supply chain as possible. This will be particularly appropriate for the new line of light bars we are making for emergency vehicles. We are replacing conventional light bulbs with light-emitting diodes (LEDs), which last longer because they have no filaments to burn out. These light bars come in many color combinations (options). We plan to manufacture subassemblies to stock and not commit to the final assembly until after receipt of the customer order. This will prevent us from stocking the wrong finished products, which would have a negative impact on our inventory rightsizing efforts.

> **TIP #77: Use an inventory postponement strategy that shifts product differentiation as far downstream as possible, so that final inventory configuration is committed when customer requirements are known.**

In the long run, concurrent engineering will bring us great benefits in our inventory rightsizing effort, but the impact on our short-term efforts will be minimal. There is one important task that design engineering can take on that will greatly enhance our short-term inventory rightsizing efforts: substituting parts that we have in inventory rather than buying new parts. I bet Cyndie covered this when she spoke about stockouts.

Substituting Part Numbers

We have just hired two interns who are "soon to be engineers," who will be seniors next year. They start in about two weeks. Their job over the summer is to analyze our existing inventory and look for opportunities to substitute the existing inventory in production, rather than buying new material. I know you are already aware of this effort, but I wanted to point out that I believe there is a significant opportunity to consume a lot of the inactive inventory.

It will be a tedious process. They will start out by looking at the inactive raw material inventory items with a value of $10,000 or greater. They will run a "where-used" report to see where the part was originally used and compare it to other product drawings. If they find something, they will check with planning (on active parts) to be sure it isn't committed to production at a later date in another product. I'd be surprised if Planning will need it because these items have been inactive for a year or longer.

This is a lot of grunt work. I don't envy them, but they will get it done. When you publish the minutes of the meeting today, please be sure to mention to all the other links that this effort will be taking place this summer. I will benchmark our current inactive inventory level when they start and report back to the team the results of this effort at the end of August.

> **TIP #78:** *Look to substitute existing inventory into a product, rather than going out to buy a similar part, if the substituted part can perform the same form, fit, and function to meet and satisfy customer expectations.*

Inventory Part Numbering System

As inventory variety increases, the number of part numbers used to identify inventory items increases. Although this may seem to be a minor issue, it can hinder our inventory rightsizing efforts as we increase the variety in our product lines. We have many parts that look the same to the naked eye but are unique in some way.

The general rule is that different parts should have their own unique item number and that a part number should be used only once. This can sometimes be a challenge for us. Our item identification codes are 12 alpha/numeric characters long (this currently includes three zeros to allow for expansion). Marketing says it wants to have a maximum item identification code of five alpha/numeric characters in the new product catalog it is working on for the Flashlight Division. This will make ordering easier for our customers. In some ways I agree. I have looked at four different catalogs published by major catalog retailers and the item codes range from five to ten alpha/numeric characters. To complicate matters, one of our major customers wants us to use its product number on our identification tags.

We have reached a compromise of sorts and will continue to use our 12-digit identification number for all internal operations. In the catalog, we will use the first digit and last four digits of the product item number. For example, our standard 7.25-inch flashlight is identified as item #A000632-5729. In the new catalog, this will be item #A5729. Our computer system will recognize the five-digit code and convert it to our twelve-digit item number for all internal use. In regard to our customers' request that we use their number, we will do so, but the tag will also include our internal number. So it appears that issue has been resolved (for now).

There are certain principles and conventions that should be followed with item identification. Let me summarize some of the more important ones for you:

1. Item codes should be unique, and each code should be used to identify only one item.
2. Item codes should be assigned and controlled by only one link in the supply chain. In our case it is product design.
3. Item codes should be as short as possible. Because item codes may have to be keyed into a record or written down, there is a high probability of error. The longer the item number, the higher the probability of error in translation.
4. Part numbers for discontinued products should no longer be used elsewhere. Customers may still have a product out years after we discontinue the item. This relates to beacon lights in particular.
5. Item codes should be uniform in size. All our parts have a 12-digit code, even though there are a lot of zeros.
6. The use of the 12-digit code allows for growth and expansion.
7. Avoid alpha/number combinations that may cause communication errors — for example, using the number 0 and the letter o side by side.

8. Create, maintain, and publish a list of active item numbers periodically, at least once a year.

> **TIP #79: A formal, structured part numbering system should be used. Item codes should be kept as short and simple as possible to eliminate the potential for translation errors, which may impede your inventory rightsizing efforts.**

Meaningful Versus Nonmeaningful Part Numbers

By definition, meaningful part numbers communicate some information about the part/product that helps with product identification. Nonmeaningful part numbers do not communicate any information about the part/product. Which is more appropriate? The answer is — it depends. There are advantages and disadvantages to both methods.

Meaningful part numbers are easier to understand and remember. This is particularly true when products come in multiple sizes and colors. On the other hand, you have to be careful you don't run out of numbers for a particular product line.

Nonmeaningful numbers will allow for growth and expansion and for the use of check digits to avoid data entry errors. The downside is they may be more difficult to use and remember. Woodstock decided years ago to use nonmeaningful part numbers because we wanted to allow for expansion and growth.

OK, now that I've explained (hopefully) the role product design can play in rightsizing inventory, I would like to move on to another important topic: the role of process design in our inventory rightsizing efforts.

Process Design and Inventory

Process design focuses on the processes used to make and move inventory throughout our entire supply chain. This encompasses how our work areas on the factory floor are laid out and the paths our products take through the plant and distribution center. The goal is to construct a process that is efficient and cost effective. To improve an existing process, we must first understand the details of how the current process functions today. The characteristics of an efficient plant layout and their effect on inventory are:

- **Process flexibility:** The ability to respond to ever-changing production requirements. Make only the inventory needed to satisfy current customer requirements.

- **Minimal production interruption:** Have a continuous flow of product through the plant without interrupting the transformation process. Minimize work-in-process (WIP) and reduce the amount of inventory sitting in queue.

- **Lead time reduction:** Reducing the total lead time will reduce the total cycle time and result in less WIP inventory.

- **Minimal material handling:** Reconfiguring the physical work center so that inventory movement and handling is minimized.

- **Reduction of WIP inventory:** Developing a transformation process that minimizes the amount of WIP inventory.

- **Improved process visibility:** Removing unnecessary inventory from the work center that isn't needed to improve visibility, so that inventory bottlenecks can be more readily identified and fixed.

- **Reduction in product rework:** Having operators inspect their own work so that damaged/poor quality inventory isn't passed on to a downstream work center.

- **Improved product quality:** Using signals to stop producing poor quality inventory so as to keep it to a minimum.

- **Elimination of production bottlenecks:** Rapid identification and resolution of inventory bottlenecks in the transformation process.

- **Use of cellular production layouts:** Improving physical plant layouts so that inventory throughput is improved.

- **Work cells organized to produce product families:** Reconfiguring plant layout so that instead of organizing machines and processes by similarity of the type of machine, they are organized into work cells configured based on similarity of the total manufacturing process of inventory product families.

- **Reduction in machine setup times:** Reducing the machine setup time to produce a different part, so that inventory lot sizes can be reduced and variety can be increased.

- **Utilizing poka-yoke techniques:** Mistake-proofing the manufacturing process so that errors in inventory production will be reduced or eliminated.

- **Elimination of non-value-added processes:** Conducting an analysis of the manufacturing process so that all non-value-added steps in producing inventory are eliminated.

- **Increase in production cycle time:** Reducing the amount of time to complete two discrete units of inventory.

- **Reusable, standardized containers:** Using standardized containers to make it more efficient to handle, move, and count inventory as it moves through the supply chain.

As you can see, the processes we design and use to manufacture our products have a significant impact on inventory.

Examples of Process Flow

If you think of your everyday lives, you are constantly involved in a process flow and probably don't even think about it. As you go about your personal chores, you become part of an inventory process flow. Here are some examples:

- Banking: When you go inside the bank, everyone gets in one line. You eventually get to the head of the line for the "next available teller." This helps avoid large queues so that you, the customer, don't get stuck behind someone with multiple transactions.
- Supermarkets: This is one of my favorites. You have lots of options:
  1. Ten items or less
  2. Fifteen items or less
  3. Cash only
  4. Bagger or no bagger
  5. Cash, check, or credit card
  6. Full service
  7. Self-checkout

  I don't know the details on the volumes of the full-service versus the ten-items-or-less line, but my guess would be that the latter processes more customers in one day and the former, more dollar value. What I find most interesting is that I am starting to like the self-checkout. Who would have thought that I would actually enjoy unloading my shopping cart, scanning the inventory, bagging the inventory, scanning the coupons, and scanning my credit card? This is an interesting inventory model. I'm doing all the work — yet I enjoy the process. Go figure.

  However, supermarkets still have some work to do. Have you ever been in a supermarket just before a potential snowstorm? I had this unfortunate experience this past winter. One would think the world was coming to an end. The checkout lines, regardless of the configuration I alluded to earlier, were unbelievably long and confusing. People were actually fighting with each other on who was in front of whom. It was so crowded that you move from line to line because of the bottlenecks at the checkout counters. This is an inventory process that is a candidate for improvement.

- Hardware stores: I saw a real interesting process improvement the last time I went to the hardware store. I had to buy a couple of loose bolts that were so small there was no place to put a bar-code tag. I thought to myself, "This is going to be a real frustrating checkout process." Low and behold, I was pleasantly surprised. The checkout associate had a template with bar codes and matched up the bolt size to the appropriate template and I was on my way. It didn't slow down the checkout process at all.

We in supply-chain management can learn from these examples. We need to learn to think outside the box when designing new processes in our supply chain.

Here at Woodstock, we have an opportunity to improve our process flows dramatically. If you recall, our year-end WIP inventory was $7.5 million. Although production process flow also impacts raw materials and finished goods, it is the WIP inventory that will be affected the most by improving the process flow. I believe we can achieve a significant reduction in WIP inventory before year end by improving our process flow. Keep in mind that it must be a collaborative effort between all the links in our supply chain. What good is a reduction in WIP inventory if all we are doing is pushing it upstream or downstream in our supply chain and having it sit there?

> **TIP #80:** *Pushing inventory to another upstream or downstream link in the supply chain will not solve your inventory rightsizing problem. It will only pass the problem on to another link in the supply chain.*

You can argue that at least if it remains in raw material inventory, we won't be adding labor costs to it, and that would be true. But for a total inventory reduction to occur, the inventory must be removed from the supply chain, not just pushed somewhere else. As we improve/develop manufacturing and distribution processes, we must also recognize that there will be constant challenges to be faced and resolved. Some of these challenges are:

1. Material shortages that impede the continuous flow of product through the work cell.
2. Product defects and scrapped product that stop or slow down production, which reduces capacity in the work cell.
3. Unplanned machine/equipment downtime must be kept to a minimum.

4. Maintaining process standards and methods as employees enter and leave the workforce.

> **TIP #81:** *Proper design of the manufacturing process has a significant impact on the total inventory in the supply chain, in general, and work-in-process inventory, in particular.*

Process Design: Role and Responsibilities

Design of our manufacturing processes, similar to all other activities in our supply chain, must be a collaborative effort between many links in our supply chain. We in design engineering can't do it alone. Process design goes by many names. Some of the more popular names are: manufacturing engineering, industrial engineering, or process engineering. Here at Woodstock we call it supply-chain engineering. Although the focus of my conversation today is on the manufacturing processes, our entire inventory rightsizing effort is all about re-engineering the processes we use in every single link of our supply chain. All of our meetings and analyses have to do with finding a better way of doing things in the total supply chain. That's why we call it supply-chain engineering.

If I had to describe our role in one sentence it would be: "to design supply-chain processes that reduce operating costs, increase inventory throughput, improve employee quality of work life, and satisfy internal and external customer requirements." That's it in a nutshell. If we do all these, we will be profitable. Our role is to work and communicate across functional lines, so that changes made in one area of process design do not have a negative impact on upstream and downstream supply-chain processes. We have to look at the big picture and cannot work as an island unto ourselves. That's why what the Harmony Team is doing is so important to the future of Woodstock.

We spoke earlier about performing concurrent engineering in the design of our products. The same is true when we discuss our process design. It must be done concurrently across all links in our supply chain.

> **TIP #82:** *Process design must consider the impact process changes in a work center might have on the upstream and downstream work centers in its path.*

> **TIP #83:** *Process design cannot take place in one inventory silo at a time. It must be a collaborative effort across all supply-chain links.*

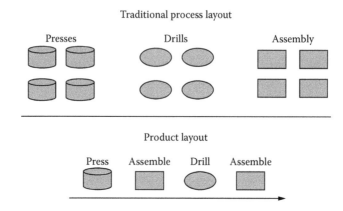

Figure 6.2   Product layout versus process layout.

Designing Work Cells

So far, in your conversations and meetings, everyone has referred to the different work groups on the factory floor as work centers. I would like to talk about the concept of organizing work groups into "work cells." The concept of work cells is to group resources (people and equipment) based on product families, using similar manufacturing processes. Figure 6.2 shows the traditional process layout and the new product layout. We are working with Arnie and his team to create a "super cell" on the lines of a product layout similar to that shown at the bottom of Figure 6.2.

This type of layout is ideal if the work center can be laid out in a U shape, as shown in Figure 6.3. Think of a conference room table with everyone sitting across from each other. Everyone sees what is going on across the table and can easily communicate with each other. What would happen if work center A is in one room, work center B in another, and there was a problem at work center A? As it's not visible, someone would have to go to work center B to tell them there was a problem and they should stop working. This will take time and the message might be miscommunicated.

The U-shaped work center is conducive to a continuous flow, and work-in-process inventory will be kept at a minimum. The ideal U-shaped cell will have cross-trained workers who can be moved around the work cell to balance workloads. The ability of workers to communicate with each other and provide immediate feedback is considered a big advantage of the U-shaped work cell.

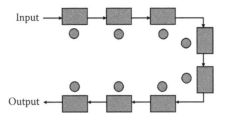

Figure 6.3 U-shaped work cell.

Balancing Work Operations and WIP Inventory

Let me give you an example of this workload balancing. Figure 6.4 shows an out-of-balance work cell. There are five different steps in the assembly process, starting with operator A and finishing with operator E. The manufacturing time for each operation is shown in Figure 6.4. The operation time of A is two minutes, and the operation time of B is one minute. You will note that there is no WIP between A and B. It has dried up. On the other hand, WIP inventory is building up between operation B and operation C because it takes three times as long to perform operation C as it does B. Moving on, WIP will continue to increase between C and D because D takes longer than C. WIP will start to decrease again between D and E because it takes less time to perform operation E. Eventually, WIP will dry up between these two operations. This goes against the principle of having a continuous flow of product through the work cell.

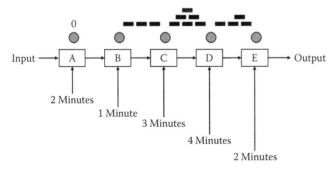

Figure 6.4 Out-of-balance workloads.

TIP #84: *Operations and inventory flows must be sequenced and balanced in a work cell, so that inventory flows on a continuous basis without WIP inventory increasing between operations.*

As operation D is the bottleneck taking four minutes, you might consider subordinating all operations to D's time. But that would increase the throughput time to 20 minutes instead of 12 (4 × 5) minutes. That wouldn't be a good idea. In an ideal world, all operations would be in sync and there would be no increase or decrease in WIP inventory between operations.

You might solve this problem by improving the processes of A, C, D, and E to match the process time of B. This would improve the throughput time to five minutes (1 × 5). Alternatively, you may move in more operators to A, C, D, and E to keep the line in balance. However, that would add to the cost. Adding people doesn't get to the root cause and solve the out-of-balance problem. One possible solution is to have the same operator perform operations A and B, which will take a total of two minutes each, but you would still be out of sync with C and D. Another approach would be to rearrange the assembly sequence.

One company I know of has come up with a unique approach to balancing workloads between operations in a work cell. It is a "cut and sew" operation, producing garments, mostly shirts, blouses, and slacks/trousers (pants for men and women). It is organized into six different work cells: two for women's blouses; two for men's sports shirts; and two for pants. It has put wheels on the sewing machine tables so that it can move them from work cell to work cell as needed, to keep the workload balanced.

Once moved to their new temporary location, the ·sewing machines are secured to the floor so that they can't be moved easily (safety concerns). Sewing operators are cross-trained to sew all of the garments. Once the line is back in balance, they move the machines back to their original location. As you can see, there are many variables that have to be considered, including operator fatigue time. The point is, you continue to experiment and try to get all operations in the work cell balanced so that work flows on a continuous basis, increasing throughput, and WIP inventory becomes zero. It should be noted that any tools and fixtures required in the operation should be located in or very near the work cell.

When we finish reorganizing our assembly operations into U-shaped work cells, we will achieve the following benefits:

■ More efficient use of floor space
■ Less material handling

- Reduced queues (WIP inventory)
- Visual production activity control
- Immediate communication and feedback
- Greater production flexibility
- Smaller lot sizes
- Improved quality
- Inventory moves one piece at a time
- Buffer stock is not required
- Workloads are balanced between operations
- Inventory flow is predefined
- Emphasis is on throughput and cycle time
- Provides visual control of the work cell
- All necessary tools and materials are close by

Facility Layout

We are thinking of organizing our light (spotlights, strobes, stripe bars) assembly area into U-shaped cells. Here is our big problem. The original building dates back to 1942 when Woodstock was first founded. The original plant was 75,000 square feet and 3 stories high; then 25,000 square feet (1 floor) were added in 1965. When the adjacent land became available in 1985, we added on another 50,000 square feet of single-floor space. So what we have to work with is a disjointed conglomerate of work flow and inventory movement. Figure 6.5 shows the three stages of facility development — not a pretty picture.

As you can see, today the offices are on the third floor of the original building. The second floor is used for the assembly of the beacon lights and spotlights and is the area we are changing to U-shaped work cells. The first floor houses our manufacturing work centers. It will be difficult to move that equipment elsewhere. The 25,000-square-foot addition is now the storeroom for inventory of ingredients and raw materials (there is some finished goods inventory there, too). The new addition made in 1985 now houses our robotic pick and pack operation for flashlights, including a state-of-the-art conveyor box sealing system and our finished goods inventory. We also ship and receive from this section of the plant. We have additional storage space off site that houses our finished goods inventory overflow and customer returns. Don't forget, we also have the distribution centers to deal with. I told Joe they should be closed down and we should ship directly to the customers from the plant. But you know Joe, he is thinking about it.

Due to our facility layout, inventory has to travel long distances, often crossing the same space many times. This extra movement doesn't add value to our products, but it does add cost. This layout is inefficient, and

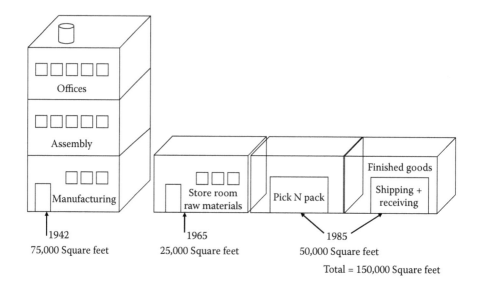

Figure 6.5 Woodstock facility.

we are looking for ways to reorganize the entire facility. Quite frankly, from our viewpoint, it would be a lot easier if we could just move into a brand new facility that was completely empty on the inside. This is a process design engineer's dream — but it's not going to happen. We just don't have the money to do it, so we will have to work with the space we have.

> **TIP #85: *Make use of existing space to store and move inventory more effectively, rather than look to relocate to a new facility.***

Value Stream Mapping

We are in the process of developing flow diagrams (process maps) of how product moves into and out of our facility. This procedure documents the flow (routing) that products take through our entire facility, from receiving dock to shipping dock. In addition to the product flow, we have documented the distance material moves and the time taken at each step. These flow documents are often called value stream maps. The objective is to identify non-value-added steps in the process and improve or eliminate them. For example, we documented the flow of sheet metal used to fabricate our spotlight assemblies. Figure 6.6 shows the flow diagram of the fabricated metal from raw material to finished product.

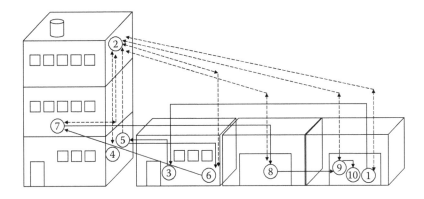

Figure 6.6   Value stream mapping.

The dotted line represents the paper/transaction (information flows), and the solid line represents the product flows.

The raw material is received (1), moved to the storeroom (3), moved to manufacturing (5), moved back to the storeroom (6), moved to assembly (7), moved to packing (8), moved to finished goods inventory (9), and eventually shipped out to a customer (10). You will note that the inventory (product) is moved eight times, transformed two times, and packed once. The product is touched 11 times.

Of the 11 times the inventory is touched, value is added only 2 times (manufacturing and assembly). You see there is tremendous opportunity to improve on this, but you need to benchmark where you are before you try to improve a process; otherwise, how will you know if you improved it or not? Keep in mind that some of the steps may still be necessary even though no value is added. For example, taking the sheet metal off the truck may not add value to the product, but it is a necessary step in the process — unless, of course, we could bring the press (200-ton press) onto the truck and transform it right there. I don't think so.

> **TIP #86:** *Use value stream mapping as a tool to help identify non-value-added steps in the inventory flow process. This should include the process step, distance moved, and the time required for each step in the inventory flow.*

Why? Why? Why? Why? Why?

As you go through your value stream mapping process, question every step in the process. One popular technique that has been used successfully in problem solving can be used in value stream mapping. Consider the question, "Why are we doing that?" Keep asking why until you can determine if it is a value-added activity or not. Here is how it works:

Process flow problem: There is too much WIP inventory between operation 1 and operation 2 in assembly work cell 200. Thus, operation 2 is determined to be a bottleneck. Relatively high inventory waiting to be worked on between operations is considered to be wasteful (and non-value-added) and should be reduced so that work flows between operations without waiting. Keep asking why until you get to the root cause of the problem:

Question: Why is there too much WIP inventory between operation 1 and operation 2?

Answer: Because the process times are not in balance with each other.

Question: Why are the process times out of balance?

Answer: Because operation 2 takes twice as long as operation 1.

Question: Why does operation 2 take twice as long to complete as operation 1?

Answer: Because it is more complicated to assemble.

Question: Why is it more complicated to assemble?

Answer: Because it was poorly designed.

Question: Why was it poorly designed?

Answer: Because the product was designed without consideration of the manufacturing process and flow.

Possible solution: Have design engineering and process engineering work together to redesign the product and process concurrently so that the process steps are in balance.

To summarize, the value stream mapping methodology is as follows:

1. Map the current process.
2. Benchmark where you are: touches, distance, time.
3. Brainstorm to improve the process.
4. Implement the improvements.
5. Benchmark the results.
6. If necessary, go back to step 3.
7. If successful, go back to step 1 and repeat the sequence.

Maybe I should amend the steps in value stream mapping to start with educating the workforce. In fact, I would strongly suggest that any process design effort should include education and training as the first step. Operators should understand the total process. I realize that a lot of what is going on in the inventory rightsizing effort has to do with a complete education program for all employees. I believe this is an excellent approach to all we do in the future here at Woodstock.

Takt Time and Inventory Production Rates

As I've said, we are going to reorganize our assembly work centers into U-shaped work cells, based on manufacturing product families. Our goal is to have a continuous flow of product going through the work cells, with a minimum of wait time and WIP inventory between operations. We are going to have a "single-piece flow" where one unit at a time is passed from assembler to assembler as each assembler completes his or her part of the total assembly process.

Conceptually, this will decrease process lead time and increase capacity. The idea is any process lead time saved can be used to produce more units. We are going to establish takt times as a measurement of finished goods inventory output. Takt time is a method of establishing production rates to match the rate of customer demand or, in the case of our make-to-stock products, forecast demand. It measures the rate at which a completely assembled finished product exits the work cell. It has been called the "heart beat" or "pulse rate" of a work cell. The formula is

$$\text{Takt Time} = \frac{\text{Available Production Time}}{\text{Customer Demand}}$$

Let me show you how this works. I will use the new compact lantern as an example. Right now the plan is to design a U-shaped work cell. Table 6.2 shows the number of assembly operations and the time required at each operation. You will note that the assembly of this product requires four assembly operators, with each operation requiring one minute to complete, for a total assembly time of four minutes per unit (for now, until the process is actually designed).

Table 6.2 Takt Time Example

Operation	Operation Time
A	1 minute
B	1 minute
C	1 minute
D	1 minute
Total takt time	4 minutes

The lantern can be made and sold in three color combinations:

Black/gray
Black/red
Black/green

They are packed and sold in lots of 24 per carton with a standard mix of 8 lanterns per color combination per carton. The forecast is 50,000 units for the first year of production and the test marketplace for the first year is the northeastern United States only. Our plan is to produce all 50,000 units in the first quarter of next year (January to March). If sales go as well as projected, we will go into full production by midyear and sell the product worldwide.

Getting back to our example, we will have two similar work cells with four operators in each work cell, working eight hours a day, five days a week. Allowing for two ten-minute breaks and one ten-minute "cleanup" at the end of the shift, the total available time is

$$8 - .5 = 7.5 \times 4 =$$
30 hours of total available time per day in each work cell

Computed in minutes, the total available time is 1,800 minutes (30 × 60 minutes) per day. Establishing two work cells will give us a total available time of 3,600 minutes (1,800 × 2) per day. I looked at the manufacturing calendar for the first quarter of next year, and excluding weekends and holidays, there are 63 work days. As the current plan calls for producing all 50,000 units in the first quarter, we will have to assemble 794 units per day (50,000/63). Applying the takt time formula, we calculate takt time as follows:

For both cells: 3,600/794 = 4.5   for one cell: 1,800/397 = 4.5

This means that one unit should exit the work cells every 4.5 minutes. Because our studies show that we can produce one unit every 4 minutes (see Figure 6.6), this is a reasonable assumption. As a precaution, we are going to assign one extra person as "floater," who will float between both cells and assist if any bottlenecks occur. Remember, this is a labor-intensive process with a minimal amount of training required to perform all four operations. The only tool required is a screwdriver, so equipment isn't an issue. If all goes well and sales come in as forecast, we will look to automate as much of this assembly work as possible. The product design team will also continue to look for ways to improve the product DFM.

We plan to install an electronic takt board system that will scan each unit as it exits the work cell, so that we can measure takt time required for actual production. If we fall behind we can add more people; if we get ahead of schedule, we can take people out and use them elsewhere in the plant.

Keep in mind that we have made certain assumptions. There is the "real world" and there is the "ideal world." In the ideal world, this is how it will happen. In the real world, we have to face reality, which says it won't happen this way. We assume that the customers will pull 794 units per day and we can ship them. You and I both know the customers won't order based on our assumptions. We must also be prepared to ramp up or ramp down production based on customers' ordering needs. Remember takt time is based on actual demand, and we have used forecast demand, not the best use of takt time, but it does give us an order of magnitude to plan for.

How does takt time relate to our inventory rightsizing efforts? It helps in the following ways:

- It gives us a benchmark and performance metric of how much inventory we need to produce in the given time.
- It allows us to plan material requirements to meet production requirements.
- Work-in-process inventory will be kept to a minimum.
- Inventory will flow on a continuous basis.
- We can adjust inventory levels based on takt time versus actual production.

Even if takt time isn't the right tool for this particular work cell, it is an excellent tool that we can apply to other work centers in our plant. Process design and takt time can work well together, which is the point of my conversation.

> **TIP #87:** *Takt time is a tool that can be used to monitor actual customer demand against actual production, so that adjustments can be made to keep inventory supply and demand in balance.*

Mistake-Proofing the Process

Mistake-proofing, sometimes referred to as "poka yoke," is a technique of preventing an error from occurring in a process to avoid product defects. In designing a new process, or improving an existing process, consideration should be given to preventing defects from occurring because of poor process design. Although primarily focused on machine setups, poka-yoke techniques can be applied to many areas in the supply chain. Mistakes that result in damaged or poor quality goods mean you may have to use more inventory to replace bad inventory — not a good solution to the problem. Some examples of mistake-proofing include the following:

- Color matching parts so that two like colors get assembled together
- Designing parts so that they can only be fit together one way
- Designing machine fixtures that can only be applied to a machine in one way, and will not move out of place during production

Mistake-proofing comes in many forms and shapes. It can be technology driven (hardware/software), procedural, visual, or manual tasks. I must point out that most times simpler is better. Let me give you an example of a supposedly mistake-proof method that failed in a highly sophisticated automated pick and pack environment. Product was picked by robots and placed in a bar-coded labeled carton that moved along a conveyor belt to a highly sensitive scale to verify the weight of the carton and its contents.

After scanning the label, the system calculated what the total weight should be, and then the carton would move along the conveyor belt to the box-sealing machine, where it was taped shut. After leaving the sealing machine the carton passed by a scanner, which verified that it was the correct weight, and then moved on to the shipping area to be packed on skids and moved out the door on to a waiting truck.

If the scanner indicated an incorrect weight, the carton would not move on to the shipping area. It would continue to travel on the conveyor belt to a quality assurance area where they would open up the box to verify the carton contents and correct if necessary. Sounds like a pretty good way to mistake-proof a process and catch errors, right? Here's where the story gets interesting.

One day, they ran out of the correct carton size and had to substitute a larger carton. Needless to say, every time a substitute carton passed by the scanner, it was flagged as having an incorrect weight and sent on to the quality assurance area for item verification. The scale was saying that something was wrong. The packed carton was a higher weight than it should be and possibly had more product than it should.

The net result was they had to open over 1000 cartons to verify the contents and then manually reseal every one of them. They couldn't recalibrate the scale because multiple robots were picking multiple products, packed in boxes of various sizes, and they all passed along the same conveyor system (and scale) randomly. Can you imagine the cost and time spent correcting a mistake-proof system? The moral of the story: keep your mistake-proofing process as simple as possible — and never, ever run out of packing boxes.

The goal of process design is to design processes where inventory flows in a continuous way throughout the supply chain. Similar to water flowing through a pipe, the design process should allow for a continuous, nonstop flow, maximizing throughput times and minimizing lead times. Any activity not adding value to the product should be questioned and minimized, or eliminated if possible.

Well, I guess that's it. I'm sure you will hear more about process design when you meet with the warehouse and distribution teams. I hope I was able to help. If you should need anything else, please do not hesitate to ask. I consider myself a team player and will help in any way I can.

Inter-Office E-Mail

To: Supply-Chain Managers   May 8
From: Harmony Team
Subject: Rightsizing Inventory
Current Inventory Level: $39 Million

You will notice that inventory went down since our last summary report on April 15. This is good news. Don't be discouraged; we are going in the right direction. Details about our last meeting with Michael on product and process design can be found in the minutes, which will be published at the end of the day. Following are the highlights:

1. Fifty percent to seventy percent of our product cost is determined in the product design phase.
2. Beyond manufacturing, product design impacts many supply-chain costs, including packaging, storage, picking, packing, and shipping.
3. We must move to a concurrent product design philosophy rather than a sequential design process. A sequential process is inefficient, prone to costly errors, and takes too long.
4. Concurrent engineering is a cross-functional approach to product design. We are getting all of our supply-chain links involved in the very beginning of the product design phase, including our external customers and suppliers.

5. Products will be designed with a focus on DFM and DFA.

6. We are also asking our buyers' customers (end users) to participate.

7. We have purchased our competitors' products and are reverse engineering them to gain an understanding of their product (part) content and assembly process.

8. Our design objectives include using fewer parts, using standard off-the-shelf parts, and combining several different parts into one.

9. Consideration will also be given to how we can improve product packaging for ease of movement through our supply chain.

10. Michael told us of a success story involving our new mini lantern and the benefits of our concurrent engineering efforts.

11. A real plus to our inventory rightsizing efforts will be designing future products using an inventory postponement strategy.

12. We have hired two summer interns who will be analyzing our existing inventory and providing us with a list of part numbers that we may be able to use as substitutes, without a negative impact on product form, fit, or function.

13. We will continue with our current nonmeaningful part numbering scheme but will simplify our part numbers for customers, making them 6 characters rather than the 12 characters we use internally.

14. We are redesigning our assembly work centers and converting them to U-shaped work cells.

15. Takt time will be used to monitor product output versus customer demand.

16. Pokayoke or mistake-proofing techniques are being built into the manufacturing processes.

17. Value stream mapping and brainstorming tools will be used to eliminate non-value-added process steps.

18. Reusable standard containers will be used in the new work cells.

19. We have set a goal to reduce WIP inventory 35 percent by year end (using the techniques mentioned here).

20. New process designs will consider the needs of the upstream and downstream work centers and work cells.

21. Work loads will be balanced from operation to operation in the new work cells.

22. Process design, along with other links in the chain, will look to improve the space utilization of our entire facility.
23. Studies are being conducted to understand how many times an item is touched and determine if we can eliminate the non-value-added touches.
24. We have learned that we need to keep asking questions ("why?") repeatedly to get to the root cause of a problem.

Attached to this e-mail is our latest version of our inventory rightsizing model. Figure 6.7 shows the latest additions. As always, we encourage you to ask questions and make suggestions on how we can further improve our efforts. Our next meeting is scheduled for May 29 when Orlando will discuss manufacturing and its impact on inventory.

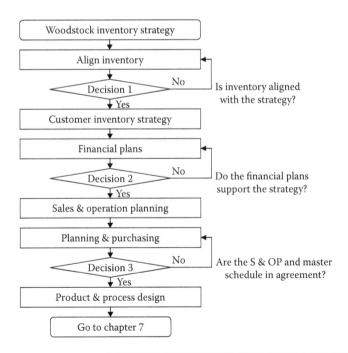

Figure 6.7 Woodstock inventory rightsizing model.

Applying Tips, Tools, and Philosophies to Your Company

In Chapter 6, we added 14 new TIPS and covered product design and process design. These two critical links focus on the demand side of the equation, but product design relies heavily on input from the demand side, in particular the input from customers on how to best design products that meet their needs and requirements. As you have learned, process design is a real challenge to Woodstock because of the old, antiquated facility it has to deal with.

I once consulted for a company with a facility similar to Woodstock's. But in this example, the company deliberately chose the facility. Under a state grant program it was able to obtain an old three-story manufacturing facility, right in the heart of a very populated city. The only means of transportation between floors was one old elevator that was converted from steam to electric. Needless to say, when the elevator broke down, nothing moved until it was fixed.

An analysis of manufacturing productivity showed that the company's overall efficiency was 66 percent of standard. Most of the inefficiency was attributed to the inefficient plant layout and poor process flows. A similar study would probably show Woodstock to be as inefficient. I point this out because some of the readers may face a similar set of circumstances and can identify with the challenges facing Woodstock. Let's review the TIPS and discuss how they can be applied to your company:

> **TIP #74:** *Any drastic changes in your MRP data may cause inventory levels to rise, until inventory is rebalanced and adjusted to the new planning requirements. Over time, it will begin to correct itself and decrease accordingly.*

Typically, with the initial implementation of MRP, inventory levels will rise. This is due to the fact that inventories may have to be rebalanced. You will need to buy things you thought you had enough of, and you will have to work off inventory (reduce) that you have too much of. In time, inventory will start to go down, and if you continue to use MRP effectively, you will see dramatic decreases in overall inventory levels. A reduction of 25 percent to 35 percent is not unheard of after 12 to 18 months. Even experienced MRP users will experience out-of-balance inventory levels if the "BILL of Integrity" (BOI discussed in Chapter 5) isn't correct. The BOI addresses four critical pieces of information that must be accurate:

1. Bill of material
2. Inventory records

3. Lead times
4. Lot-size rules

This accuracy won't happen on its own. It will require diligence and hard work. To ensure your BOI is at the highest possible level, I suggest you:

1. Establish performance standards (level of accuracy) that must be met.
2. Measure actual performance to standard.
3. Establish a policy and procedure to bring the BOI back to standard when it is out of the acceptable range.
4. Assign responsibility for each of the four BOIs of information.
5. Assign responsibility cross-functionally (more than one link held accountable).
6. Recognize teams (people) for outstanding performance.

> **TIP #75:** *Product design has a major impact on inventory costs through every link in the supply chain. The design must become a cross-functional process with inputs from all links in the supply chain, including suppliers and customers.*

Every single link in your supply chain can make a positive contribution to product design. The key points to be made here as follows:

1. Get all links involved to some degree. They don't have to be involved full time.
2. Get them involved early in the design phase. By early, I mean get them involved from the beginning.
3. Make sure to include your key suppliers and customers.
4. Find out what your competition is doing. Reverse engineer their products.
5. Mistakes made at the design phase will be less costly than if the product were made and shipped to the customer.
6. Most of your product cost is determined in the design phase.
7. Designing products with fewer parts will reduce costs and increase productivity.
8. Designing products with standard (as opposed to custom-made) parts will reduce costs.
9. It is imperative that the product as well as processes to make it are designed at the same time.

TIP #76: *Designing products collaboratively with other links in the supply chain can benefit your inventory rightsizing effort by eliminating or reducing the total number and variety of parts that have to be planned for and stocked in inventory.*

Most of the points related to this TIP were covered in TIP #75. However, I wanted to highlight some important points here. Although the focus on designing a product is on satisfying the customer requirements, your company still needs to make a profit. You can help accomplish this by:

1. Keeping the total number of parts in your product to a minimum.
2. Reducing the variety of parts in your product.
3. Using standard off-the-shelf parts rather than custom-made parts.

If you can achieve these three objectives, the following costs would reduce considerably:

- Cost of the part itself
- Cost of the labor employed on your product
- Cost of planning for it
- Cost of ordering it
- Cost of carrying it in inventory
- Cost of moving it
- Cost of transportation
- Cost of a stockout

No single silo can accomplish these objectives by itself. It will require a collaborative effort by the entire supply chain, including customers and suppliers.

TIP #77: *Use an inventory postponement strategy that shifts product differentiation as far downstream as possible, so that final inventory configuration is committed when customer requirements are known.*

The principle you want to follow using this TIP is, "Add value to your raw materials as far downstream in your supply chain as possible." Adding value too early in your process will cause you many problems you will have to deal with later. Consider this scenario: You buy raw materials and build a completed, finished product and put it into inventory. The sales forecast changes (downward) and you get stuck with the product. You have several choices:

1. Continue to carry it in stock in the hope that you can sell it at a later time. Now you are dealing with carrying cost.
2. Reduce the selling price to move it out of inventory. This will erode your profit margins, and in fact, you may lose money on the sale.
3. Reverse engineer the product. Take it apart and use the parts for some other product. This will add to your cost and also reduce your capacity. In all probability, you will lose money taking this step.
4. Scrap the product. This is a last-ditch solution. If you have to take this approach, one wonders if you had a market for the product in the first place. I have seen this happen, though.

How can you put off committing raw materials into a final product until later?

- Seek to decrease your raw material purchases lead time.
- Look to decrease your manufacturing lead time.
- Put off adding product options until the sale is made and the order is taken.
- Build your product modularly so that modules can be configured and added in the final assembly process.
- Seek to increase your manufacturing flexibility and response time.
- Increase your supply-chain velocity.

> **TIP #78:** *Look to substitute existing inventory into a product, rather than going out to buy a similar part, if the substituted part can perform the same form, fit, and function to meet and satisfy customer expectations.*

Too often in my experience I've seen a company expedite a raw material, pay a premium freight charge to fly it in, break a machine setup, work overtime, and then ship the part out at a premium freight charge — having all the time a perfectly acceptable raw material in stock that it could have used. To add salt to the wound, the substitute raw material was sitting around in inventory with no commitments for it. Don't let this happen to you.

Woodstock is taking a good approach to this issue. It is hiring a couple of summer interns who are going to analyze raw material and subassemble inventory to see if the slow-moving/inactive inventory can be used elsewhere. It will have to work closely with the experienced product design engineers as they go through this process. It will take a great deal of time to accomplish, but it is time well spent.

> **TIP #79: *A formal, structured part numbering system should be used. Item codes should be kept as short and simple as possible to eliminate the potential for translation errors, which may impede your inventory rightsizing efforts.***

There are several points to consider when applying this TIP:

1. Have only one supply-chain link assign new part numbers. In many companies this will be design engineering, but it doesn't have to be.
2. Have a formal process of requesting and assigning a new part number (or changing an existing one).
3. Use a part number only once. Do not reassign it to another part.
4. Develop and maintain a "part number master" within your formal system.
5. Develop and maintain a cross-reference list of sales part numbers and your internal part numbers.
6. Develop and maintain a cross-reference list of customer part numbers and your part numbers.

> **TIP #80: *Pushing inventory to another upstream or downstream link in the supply chain will not solve your inventory rightsizing problem. It will only pass the problem on to another link in the supply chain.***

In the early days of "just-in-time" (JIT), many companies attempted to push inventory back to suppliers, who in turn tried to push the inventory back to their suppliers. If every supply chain was able to push inventory back successfully, we would have pushed it back to our natural resources. Very few companies are able to do this. Henry Ford was an early (successful) pioneer of this concept. Unfortunately, it hasn't worked out all that well for others. There were several reasons for this:

1. In some cases, there wasn't mutual benefit to both parties.
2. The cost of JIT was prohibitive.
3. Stockouts were a serious problem.
4. Planning was complex and ever changing.
5. It was a big culture change to many companies.

If you can address these five points successfully, then JIT will work for you. However, within the internal supply chain, inventories must be balanced and rightsized. Pushing inventory back upstream will only cause the problem to shift to another link in the supply chain without resulting in this balance. It must be a coordinated approach and an integrated solution; internal and external customer service must not suffer because of it.

> **TIP #81: *Proper design of the manufacturing process has a significant impact on the total inventory in the supply chain in general and work-in-process inventory in particular.***

The objective of designing manufacturing processes properly is to eliminate non-value-added steps and improve the value-added steps, so that costs are kept low and efficiency high. The ideal process will have a balanced, continuous flow of product with minimal WIP inventory sitting in queue, waiting to be worked on. You can help accomplish this objective by:

1. Designing the product and the manufacturing process at the same time.
2. Making your suppliers part of the process design team.
3. Having your suppliers see and understand your manufacturing process, and how their product is transformed into your product.
4. Visiting your suppliers to see and understand how they build the raw material for you.
5. Staying on top of the latest technological advances in manufacturing productivity, including machine, information, and process technologies.
6. Benchmarking the recognized "best of breed" for that process.
7. Having customers involved in improving and designing your processes.
8. Conducting "process time studies" to ensure workload balances, and identifying process bottlenecks where WIP inventory has the potential to get out of balance.

> **TIP #82: *Process design must consider the impact process changes in a work center might have on the upstream and downstream work centers in its path.***

We spoke earlier of not pushing inventory back upstream in the supply chain because inventories would get out of balance and cause all sorts of problems. The same is true of manufacturing processes. If you change (improve) the process in one work center, you must analyze the impact on the upstream and downstream work centers. Why? Because it could cause a bottleneck at those work centers.

If an imbalance occurs, WIP inventory can build up or dry up, and in both cases, this would not be a good thing. It would result in stockouts and late orders, and an increase in WIP could also increase total lead times throughout the supply chain. To prevent this from happening, conduct an analysis of total process times of a product's routing through the supply chain. Communicate about any imbalances to all other links in the chain, and realign processes accordingly.

> **TIP #83:** *Process design cannot take place in one inventory silo at a time. It must be a collaborative effort across all supply-chain links.*

Product design and process design must occur concurrently, as mentioned in the Woodstock story. Mistakes caught in the early stages of development will be less costly. The days of designing a product and then throwing it "over the wall" to other links are gone forever. A side benefit not yet mentioned is that the total design time will be greatly reduced by not performing the process one step at a time. The general principle to be applied here is "get other supply links involved early and often in the design of both products and processes."

> **TIP #84:** *Operations and inventory flows must be sequenced and balanced in a work cell, so that inventory flows on a continuous basis without WIP inventory increasing between operations.*

We spoke earlier of balancing inventory and process flows in work cells, and we used an example of rebalancing in the Woodstock case study. In some cases, you may perform multiple operations in the same work cell. The obvious approach is that to balance workloads work cell to work cell, you must balance operations within a work cell first. To use this TIP effectively, the balancing of workloads cannot be made at the expense of the continuous flow of product through your processes. When you rebalance workloads, keep the concept of continuous flow foremost in your mind.

> **TIP #85:** *Make use of existing space to store and move inventory more effectively, rather than look to relocate to a new facility.*

If your current facility is an old building with many floors, you are at a disadvantage in trying to improve the flow of inventory through the facility, unless your manufacturing process requires multiple floors. However, if you own the facility and it is in a great location for transportation of products and easily accessible to employees, it might be worth redesigning, and every effort should be made to do so.

To make effective use of the space, begin by:

1. Creating process maps of how the product currently flows through the facility.
2. Eliminating/improving process steps by eliminating non-value-added steps.
3. Redesigning the new process on paper (computer models) before implementation.
4. Conducting a 5s campaign (Chapter 7).
5. Finding a place for everything and putting everything in its place.

> **TIP #86:** *Use value stream mapping as a tool to help identify non-value-added steps in the inventory flow process. This should include the process step, distance moved, and the time required for each step in the inventory flow.*

Value stream mapping (VSM) is essentially a process flow chart of activities/processes that occur in your supply chain. Once you have identified and agreed on the process flow, you can identify all non-value-added activities taking place and eliminate them, or in the worse case, try to improve upon them. Conceptually, the only activities left are value-added activities that the customer is willing to pay for. Once you have eliminated the non-value-added activities, you can then try to improve the value-added activities, making them more effective.

From my experience, the biggest challenge you face in developing value stream maps is getting everyone to agree on what the current process is. At this level of mapping you don't need to go into a lot of detail, but it should be detailed enough for everyone to understand the overall process. If more detail is needed, you can "drill down" through each activity and create sublevel process maps.

Challenge every activity. Don't take any process step for granted. Ask yourself, "Why are we doing that step?" Continue with this question until you are satisfied the step is needed; if not, eliminate it. Keep the people side of the equation out of the process. By that I mean, don't worry about what you will do with an employee if a step is eliminated. There are probably plenty of other (value-added) tasks for an employee to perform in other areas of the supply chain.

> **TIP #87:** *Takt time is a tool that can be used to monitor actual customer demand against actual production, so*

that adjustments can be made to keep inventory supply and demand in balance.

Takt time is a technique of matching production rates to customer demand. It sets the rate (pace) required to meet the demand. An example related to Woodstock was given earlier in this chapter. This is a technique popular with companies that have initiated a "lean production" environment.

Before initiating the use of takt time, have a program in place to bring the takt time back into balance when it lags behind the demand rate. The worst you can do is implement a takt time production environment, and watch as the system reports you are getting further and further behind, with no plan in place to correct the problem. Morale will suffer, and convincing employees to continue to try to meet the takt time will be difficult. Table 6.3 represents the most current status of the Woodstock inventory, and Table 6.4 shows a Pareto order of Woodstock inventory reduction.

Table 6.3   Inventory Balance (×1,000,000)

Month end	31 Jan	28 Feb	31 Mar	30 Apr
Forecast	7.2	7.9	9.7	7.1
Orders	5.8	7.4	9.6	7.7
Total starting inventory	40.0	41.0	40.9	40.3
Start FG inventory	15.5	15.7	15.8	15.3
+Production @ COGS	4.1	5.1	6.0	4.8
–Shipments @ COGS	3.9	5.0	6.5	5.2
End FG inventory	15.7	15.8	15.3	14.9
Start WIP inventory	7.5	7.6	7.7	7.4
+Material issues	3.4	4.2	4.8	3.9
+Labor and overhead	0.8	1.0	0.9	0.6
–Production @ COGS	4.1	5.1	6.0	4.8
End WIP inventory	7.6	7.7	7.4	7.1
Start raw inventory	17.0	17.7	17.4	17.6
+Material purchases	4.1	3.9	5.0	3.3
–Material issues	3.4	4.2	4.8	3.9
End raw inventory	17.7	17.4	17.6	17.0
Total ending inventory	41.0	40.9	40.3	39.0

Table 6.4 Pareto Order of Inventory Reduction (×1,000,000)

Date	Start 1 Jan	Target 31 Dec	Reduction
Total inventory	40.0	32.5	7.5
Flashlights raw material	10.0	8.0	2.0
Flashlights finished goods	13.0	11.2	1.8
Spotlights raw material	6.0	4.9	1.1
Flashlights work-in-process	5.0	4.0	1.0
Beacon lights finished goods	2.0	1.5	0.5
Beacon lights work-in-process	1.0	0.5	0.5
Spotlights work-in-process	1.5	1.2	0.3
Beacon lights raw material	1.0	0.8	0.2
Spotlights finished goods	0.5	0.4	0.1
Total reduction			7.5

Chapter 7

How Much Inventory Should We Make?

May 29, Harmony Team Meeting

Woodstock Inventory: $38.1 Million

My name is Orlando, and I am the assistant plant manager of Woodstock Lighting Group.

I've been working here for 15 years, and this is the first time I've been asked to participate in a group discussion other than with our own internal manufacturing staff. I wonder what that's all about. Usually Arnie does all the communicating with the other links in the chain. He likes to be the only one talking to outside groups. I don't know what he is afraid of. Maybe, he thinks I will say something stupid, or maybe he's afraid others will realize that I know a lot about what's going on and start coming to me for ideas and questions.

I started out as a machine operator in the machine shop and worked my way up to floor supervisor, and then assistant plant manager. I'm ready to be promoted to plant manager. I hope Arnie gets Joe's job soon, so I can move up. Joe doesn't have a clue about what's going on. We waste more time explaining things to him than it's worth. Arnie is more patient than me.

I think this whole Harmony Team thing is good for the company. The good news is it will give me a chance to interact with other people who I know by name but have never met. This will be good for my career. The bad news is that ever since Arnie took on the team leader role, he has been

261

inaccessible, and I've taken over many of his day-to-day tasks. Now I have to work 12 to 15 hours a day. It seems like I just get home and it's time to get up and go back to work again. I'm really tired, and this concerns me. I'm afraid I will make mistakes and use poor judgment.

Management might view this as a negative when the time comes to consider me as a candidate for the plant manager position when it becomes available.

How much inventory should we make? We constantly ask ourselves that question every day. Balancing supply with demand is an ever-changing formula, and we strive to get it right. However, as you can see from the amount of inventory in our supply chain, we need to reduce and "rightsize" our raw material and work-in-process (WIP) inventory. At the beginning of the year, we had $17 million in raw material inventory and another $7.5 million in WIP. Our raw material inventory alone was higher than our finished goods inventory, which was $15.5 million at the end of the year. Well, we are five months into a new year, and we are showing some improvement. You heard from Michael that we want to reduce WIP by the year end. We are working hard to do it. I believe we will make it happen.

I'm sure he mentioned to you all the process improvements we are making as we convert some of our work centers to U-shaped work cells. Today, I would like to discuss other aspects of manufacturing that are related to our inventory rightsizing efforts. The areas I will address will impact both our raw material and our WIP inventories. Our manufacturing environment is a mixture of a job shop and a flow shop.

The primary work centers are our pressroom W/C #201 and our machine shop W/C #301. The assembly work cells are on the second floor. Work cells #401 and #402 are for the light bars, and work cells #501 and #502 are for the new compact lantern product line. We also have one work center dedicated to beacon light assembly, W/C #101. The pressroom, W/C #201, has four presses of various tonnages. The machine shop, W/C #301, has six machines consisting of one lathe, one drill press, one sanding/deburring machine, and three CNC machines. The assembly work cells are mostly manual today, with very little automation. One of the challenges we face constantly is that our bottlenecks move around to different work centers and different machines from day to day.

> **Tip #88:** *In a job-shop manufacturing environment, the bottleneck operation is not stationary. It is constantly shifting from work center to work center and will create an imbalance of your WIP inventory.*

(Note: TIP = team important point.)

For example, last week the bottleneck was in the CNC area, where we had two machines down for unplanned maintenance. This week it was the pressroom, where we had a capacity overload on the 200-ton press. In both cases, the WIP inventory backed up and orders were late. This made a lot of people unhappy, least of whom were sales, who were pressing (no pun intended) for delivery on an impact order.

Role and Responsibilities

Our primary responsibility is to produce quality products and to meet the requirements of the master production schedule (MPS); but we do so much more than that. Here is a summary of our responsibilities:

- **Meet the requirements of the MPS:** Planning publishes (updates) the MPS on a weekly basis. We are measured on our performance to schedule. I don't believe this is a good barometer to measure our performance. There are too many schedule changes (during the week), and the sales team is constantly inserting new impact orders into the schedule.
- **Meet the requirements of the final assembly schedule (FAS):** In addition to the MPS, planning also publishes an FAS for the assembly work cells. We do a little better with the FAS than we do with the MPS. Most of the incoming orders are for customers, rather than a mix of customers and stock replenishment.
- **Effective utilization of resources to meet the MPS and the FAS:** In manufacturing, we consider a resource to be raw materials, subassemblies, machines, tools, jigs, equipments, or personnel (and money, budgets permitting).
- **Efficient deployment of personnel:** Assign personnel to work centers/work cells to meet schedule requirements.
- **Manage storeroom inventory:** We are responsible for storage and picking and moving materials into and out of the storeroom.
- **Manage WIP inventory:** Responsible for the levels of inventory in WIP (queue).

Today, I would like to focus on four areas of Manufacturing that have a major impact on our inventory rightsizing efforts:

1. Capacity management and inventory
2. Lean manufacturing techniques
3. Pull systems and inventory
4. Storeroom inventory management

Capacity Management and Inventory

Capacity management is the activity of balancing workload (demand) and resources (supply) to meet the priorities established in the MPS and the FAS. The major tasks to achieve this balance are:

> **Planning:** Establishing schedules and priorities
> **Execution:** Releasing work orders, assigning work
> **Monitor output:** Tracking work orders' progress through the plant
> **Control:** Adjusting supply and demand

In an earlier meeting, Cyndie spoke about developing the MPS and then performing rough-cut capacity planning (RCCP). Figure 7.1 shows the planning process and flow discussed by Cyndie.

We are discussing the decision point titled plant capacity (internal). If capacity and workload are not in balance, you have two choices: find the capacity to meet the MPS, or go back up the planning hierarchy and adjust the MPS. Conceptually, the last thing you want to do is adjust the MPS. Every effort should be made to meet the MPS as scheduled. No one wants to reschedule orders, particularly if they are actual customer orders. However, reality must set in, and the planning process must be followed. If you don't have the capacity to meet the workload for a given period, then orders will be completed later than scheduled. The condition is compounded if the late orders are not rescheduled. You now have an order backlog and, in all likelihood, an invalid MPS.

Why is balancing capacity and workload important to our inventory rightsizing efforts? If you have less capacity than demand, WIP inventory will increase. If WIP increases, total manufacturing lead time will increase. The result is that inventory will become unbalanced between work centers. If, on the other hand, you have more capacity than demand, WIP will decrease and eventually dry up. Although the decrease in inventory may be viewed as a positive condition, it may cause a work center to shut down. You will lose that capacity. Again, the result is that inventory will become unbalanced.

As shown in Figure 7.2, there is a direct relationship between lead time and capacity. Consider this scenario:

1. Demand for your product is greater than your capacity to produce it.
2. You can't catch up, and your backlog of orders grows.
3. As a result, it will take you longer to complete the orders you already have, so you have to increase the order lead time for new orders.
4. You tell your sales team to advise your customers that the lead time has increased.

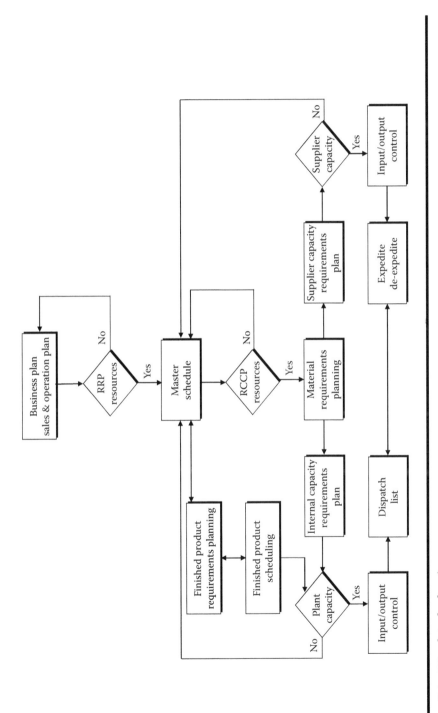

Figure 7.1 Woodstock planning process.

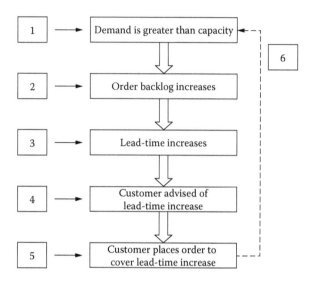

Figure 7.2 Lead time impact on capacity.

5. The customers, in turn, give you more orders because of the increased lead time. They want to be covered and not have a stockout.

6. The result of this process is you have more orders and your backlog grows again. What do you do? You again have to increase your lead time, and the customers give you more orders to cover the additional lead time. The process is now out of control and continues to repeat itself in a closed-loop, never-ending sequence. Someone looks at this huge backlog and decides to invest in additional capacity. You let the customers know you are catching up and will begin to ship their orders earlier than originally scheduled. Because the customers really don't need the orders earlier, they cancel them or postpone delivery to a future date. Now you have excess capacity and questionable orders on the books, all leading to higher inventories.

> **TIP #89: *If supply (capacity) and demand (workload) are not in balance, the change in inventory will negatively impact your inventory rightsizing efforts.***

Load Profile Report

A popular tool to analyze supply and demand is the load profile report. Table 7.1 is an example of this report.

Table 7.1   Woodstock Load Profile Report

Week	1	2	3	4	5	Total
Released orders	180	150	100	30	0	460
Planned orders	0	25	100	180	160	465
Total load	180	175	200	210	160	925
Capacity	190	190	190	190	190	950
Over/Under	10	15	–10	–20	30	
Cumulative	10	25	15	–5	25	

What you are looking at here is a planning grid, comparing the workload (orders and planned orders) to the available capacity (production) in our machine shop, work center #301. Let's calculate the available capacity first. The first data we need is the total available time in the work center. Capacity can be calculated (estimated) and then measured. It was mentioned earlier that we have three CNC machines in this work center. Each machine requires one operator. We operate work center #301 two shifts per day, five days per week. Thus the formula is

$$M \times H \times D = \textbf{Total available time}$$

$$\textbf{M = Machines} \quad \textbf{H = Hours (per day)} \quad \textbf{D = Days (per week)}$$

$$3 \times 16 \times 5 = 240$$

TIP #90: *Calculate capacity based on your normal work week. If you normally operate five days a week, then calculate your capacity based on five days. If you always operate seven days a week, then you can calculate your capacity based on seven days.*

As you can see, work center #301 has a total of 240 available hours. However, we can't base our capacity solely on this figure. It has to be adjusted for utilization and efficiency.

Utilization

Utilization is the time the machine is actively producing parts. The machine operator is available for 8 hours per shift. Lunch time was already eliminated. Employees are on site 8.5 hours per shift, and lunch time is 30 minutes; so we are down to 8 hours. Employees in our shop get two

10-minute breaks, and another 10 minutes at the end of their shift to clean up their work area and to wash up. The 30 minutes are deducted from the 8 hours, and we are down to 7.5 hours. There are always unforeseen activities going on, such as bathroom breaks, phone calls, and discussions with supervisors. We try to err on the side of caution and adjust out 30 minutes. I know that's a lot, but right or wrong, it's a reality here at Woodstock. So we are down to 7 hours per operator. Given these numbers, our utilization is 88 percent.

$$7/8 \times 100 \text{ percent} = 0.875 = 88 \text{ percent utilization}$$

Efficiency

Efficiency is actual output compared to the expected (standard) output. For example, if the standard is 30 minutes per piece going through the CNC center and we actually take 25 minutes, our efficiency is 120 percent.

$$30/25 \times 100 \text{ percent} = 120 \text{ percent efficiency}$$

On the other hand, if the standard is 30 minutes per piece, and it actually takes 35 minutes, our efficiency is 86 percent.

$$30/35 \times 100 \text{ percent} = 85.7 = 86 \text{ percent efficiency}$$

You will notice that efficiency in our first example was 120 percent, and in our second it was only 86 percent. This wide disparity does actually occur from time to time. In the former example, we might have had our best operator on the job, and in the latter we might have had a new operator with little experience, and thus the disparity. When estimating capacity available, we use the standard efficiency. If over time we consistently go over 100 percent, we look at the standard and adjust it (with approval of manufacturing, engineering, and cost accounting).

Based on historical data, work center #301 has an average efficiency of 90 percent, so I'll use that to calculate capacity. Now we have the total available time, efficiency, and utilization. Let's put it all together and see what we get:

Calculated capacity = Total available time × utilization × efficiency

$$240 \times 0.88 \times 0.90 = 190 \text{ hours per week of capacity}$$

This number is reflected in Table 7.1 on the line titled, "capacity." You will note that this load profile shows five weeks. That's because this

Sunday	Monday	Tuesday	Wednesday	Thursday	Friday	Saturday
1	2	3 · 1	4 · 2	5 · 3	6 · 4	7
8	9 · 5	10 · 6	11 · 7	12 · 8	13 · 9	14
15	16 · 10	17 · 11	18 · 12	19 · 13	20 · 14	21
22	23 · 15	24 · 16	25 · 17	26 · 18	27 · 19	28
29	30 · 20					

Figure 7.3 Woodstock shop calendar.

happens to be the month of August, which is a five-week month. This is probably a good time to point out that whether a month has four or five weeks is based on the company's fiscal calendar, established by Pat in finance and agreed to by the other links. Each quarter has thirteen weeks; thus, our fiscal calendar comprises four-, four-, and five-week periods in each quarter. We in production then take the fiscal calendar and develop what we call our "manufacturing shop calendar." This is based on the number of actual days the plant is open for business and functioning. Figure 7.3 shows our shop calendar for the month of September.

You will note that the month starts on a Sunday, September 1. The shaded square in the box is blank, indicating that it is not a work day. Monday, September 2, is also a nonwork day (Labor Day in the United States). Starting with Tuesday, September 3, you will see the number 1 in the box, indicating it is the first work day of the month. All work days are numbered sequentially. Figure 7.3 shows that there are 20 work days in September. The shop calendar usually starts in January, and work days are sequential and cumulative. If we work 240 days a year, the first work day is work day #1, and the last work day is #240. Sometimes the shop calendar continues for years. If it is a 4-year calendar, the last work day of year 4 would be work day #960 (assuming 240 work days per year).

Why is a shop calendar important? Without this input, our enterprise resource planning (ERP) system would be scheduling work on weekends, holidays, and other planned shutdowns. You can imagine the chaos this would cause.

TIP #91: *Make sure your shop calendar is adjusted each year to account for nonwork days. Failure to do so will hinder your inventory rightsizing efforts.*

Workload

So far we have talked about how capacity is calculated. You will note that I was very conservative in our estimates. Now let's talk about workload. Table 7.1 has two lines entitled, "released orders and "planned orders." This is what we call *workload*: the amount of work in standard hours that has to be done in the work center. Our system reviews each order and tabulates the amount of time required to complete each order. The numbers plotted on the grid in Table 7.1 reflect the workload in W/C #301. If you wanted to get technical, I could point out that, on a strictly monthly calculation, the first and fifth week would not have 190 hours because there is a monthly overlap. But this is how we do it today.

You can see that weeks 1 and 2 have excess capacity, week 3 is short 10 hours, week 4 is short 20 hours, and week 5 has excess capacity. On a cumulative basis, we have enough capacity for the month. However, we will experience some late orders in weeks 3 and 4. If you were a planner, what is the first thing you would do? Remember, we are at the end of May, and this load profile is for a future month. If your immediate reaction is to reschedule some of the load for week 3 to week 2, you might want to rethink. Why? You will note that the load in week 3 consists of 100 hours of released load and 100 hours of planned load. The planned load is just that: a planned load. It may or may not happen. More than likely, this information came from our MRP system as a planned order.

Going back up the planning grid, MRP got its input from the MPS. The MPS got its input from actual orders (among other inputs) and forecast. Well, if the 100 hours of planned input don't happen, we will actually have an excess capacity of 90 hours! So the first thing you want to do is validate the planned releases. If they are real, then we can talk about rescheduling orders into weeks 1 and 2. However, you may not be able to move the workload in because the raw materials may not be available, as you are a week early.

All this is food for thought. That's what planning is all about: looking at the information and making adjustments to balance supply and demand. The load profile is a good tool for other links as well. If you have another work center that is really backlogged, you may want to take a machine operator out of work center #301 and move him or her to the overloaded work center. Of course, this assumes the operator is cross-trained for the other work center. Even the human resources staff can benefit from looking at this chart. For example, if they were planning to show a safety video

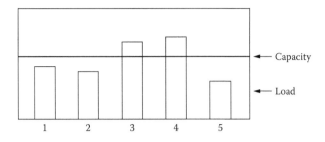

Figure 7.4 Load profile variation.

to employees in work center #301, they shouldn't schedule it for week 3 or week 4. It looks like the best time to show the tape would be in week 5, assuming the operators weren't moved to another work center. The point is, this report is a tool that can be used as a point of discussion in making decisions. The load profile depicted in Table 7.1 can also be displayed in chart format, as shown in Figure 7.4.

> **TIP #92: *Develop a load profile report by work center. Distribute it to all appropriate links in the supply chain so that each upstream and downstream link can use it as a tool to make decisions that impact inventory levels in the entire supply chain.***

Lean Manufacturing and Inventory

By definition, *lean manufacturing* is an operating philosophy that focuses on minimizing the amount of resources required by eliminating all non-value-added activities in the supply chain. Here at Woodstock, we have a lot of waste. Can any of you think of something we do almost daily that is wasteful and doesn't add value to our products or services? I bet each of you can come up with ten things we do that are wasteful, and everyone's list will be different!

I've heard that Michael spent considerable time discussing some of the process-flow improvements that are under way. He spoke about establishing U-shaped work cells, value stream mapping, takt time, and mistake-proofing processes. This is all part of our lean manufacturing initiatives; but getting lean is much more than that. It is a process of continuous, never-ending improvement. It has to become part of our company culture just like our inventory rightsizing effort. In fact, you really can't get the job done without some implementation of the lean concepts. We have a lot of waste here at Woodstock, and inventory is a big part of it. Consider these wastes and the impact on inventory:

Waste and Inventory

Defective parts: Making defective parts causes multiple inventory issues. If the defective part can't be reworked, it will have to be scrapped or sold as second quality. In effect, we will lose money on it. We have to use more raw materials to make the new part. If we don't have the raw material, we may have to pay a premium for it and might even have to pay a premium freight charge to expedite it. Having to make it again will require additional machine time and labor, which will add to the cost of the product and erode the profit margin. Using a machine to make the part again will also reduce our capacity. However, catching a defect before it goes out the door is a good thing, because the customer didn't receive it; otherwise, the cost of a defective part could be much higher — a lost customer.

> **TIP #93: *Producing defective parts will create multiple inventory problems, add to your cost, reduce profitability, and reduce capacity. Design processes to ensure perfect quality.***

1. **Wait time:** If a material is sitting in the storeroom or sitting in queue at a work center, it has the potential to become waste. If it sits too long without being used, it could become obsolete, damaged, or lost. If a machine operator has to wait for work, this too is wasteful. Conceptually, inventory should flow through our plant in a continuous flow, like water through a pipe. As material sits in queue to be worked on, WIP inventory will more than likely increase. This is one of our problems here at Woodstock. We have far too much WIP inventory waiting to be worked on.

> **TIP #94: *Balance workflows and production resources as much as possible so that wait time is kept to a minimum.***

2. **Moving material:** Any time we are moving material and not adding value to it, we are adding cost to it. You all know the problem we have with our antiquated plant layout and the issues we face with building #1 (the old three-story building). This puts us at a cost disadvantage. If we didn't have so many non-value-added "touches," we would be profitable; I'm convinced of it.

> **TIP #95: *Any time the product is touched without value being added is adding cost. All non-value-added touches are candidates for elimination.***

3. **Inventory itself**: Any inventory not needed to satisfy an immediate customer need is waste. High levels of safety stock are used to cover the uncertainty of supply and demand. We absolutely need to get a handle on it. Excess inventory is even worse. It is the inventory we have above and beyond established safety-stock levels. It's one thing to have safety stock, but to have inventory in excess of that is almost criminal!

> **TIP #96:** *Inventory not needed to satisfy an immediate customer requirement is considered wasteful and reduced or eliminated when possible.*

4. **Company politics and company culture:** What do politics and culture have to do with waste and inventory? I'll tell you. Our company environment is such that employees are afraid of getting yelled at, getting a bad performance review, looking bad to their peers (and bosses) and, in general, of losing their jobs. Everyone knows we are in trouble financially and doesn't want to be the one to go, at least not on the company terms. I bet that at least 50 percent of our employees are looking for other jobs — and doing a lot of the leg work on company time. The result of all this insecurity is that people protect themselves by having extra inventory in their area of the supply chain. "If I think I need two, I'll order four, just to be on the safe side." If everyone thinks that way, each silo will probably have two to three times the amount of inventory they really need. This affects employee morale, and we all know what happens when morale is bad. We become unproductive and waste even more time complaining about it than working.

> **TIP #97:** *Company politics is a complete waste of time and energy. Change the company culture and eliminate politics.*

5. **Inaccurate and untimely information:** This is one of the biggest wastes of all. We spend far too much time correcting inaccurate information. Not only does it waste time, but it causes our inventory to become out of balance. The other waste is untimely information. It takes us too long to get information from link to link in our supply chain. In today's environment of rapid response to changing customer needs, we cannot afford the luxury of waiting for information.

TIP #98: *To be successful in your inventory rightsizing efforts, information must be accurate and timely.*

6. **Waste of talent:** I can't tell you how many times I've seen Joe walking around the plant looking for a part that was supposed to be in stock. I have personally seen him do this for hours at a time! Do you know what this adds to the cost, to say nothing about his unproductive time? Many managers at Woodstock do this. We have stock clerks who are responsible for this. If they aren't doing their job right, then I suggest we explain what their responsibilities are and give them proper training on how to do their job effectively.

TIP #99: *Working outside your job description is admirable and shows teamwork, but it can be costly and wasteful. Delegate authority, and train employees to do their job.*

7. **Complexity:** I know the Harmony Team is looking at many areas of our supply chain, and I see that from time to time you publish new operating polices and procedures. I caution you to not make them too complex, because people will have difficulty understanding and executing them. If you do, this will cause more problems than it solves, and people will waste a lot of time that could be put to better use. A focus of our inventory rightsizing effort should be to keep processes and procedures as simple, easy to understand, and easy to use as possible.

TIP #100: *Complexity may cause problems and hinder your inventory rightsizing efforts rather than help them.*

You will need a plan for a lean implementation effort. You can't leave it to chance. Remember, you are looking to reduce waste. That waste can be in a product, process, or service you provide. You want to start in an area where you believe you can achieve success in a relatively short period of time. The success doesn't have to be large. Many small successes will be as rewarding as one large success. If you are on a lean implementation team for six months and still haven't achieved good results, you have picked the wrong place to start.

Not to be cynical, we could have started anywhere at Woodstock and achieved satisfactory results. That's how big our opportunity is. We have started on the factory floor because we have determined that is where the big savings will come from. You don't have to focus on one area exclusively. You can have multiple lean initiatives going on at the same time, but you must be careful not to cause chaos on the factory floor. Remember, you still have to produce and ship products out the door.

> **TIP #101:** *Begin your lean initiative in an area of your supply chain where opportunities for improvement are significant. For most manufacturing companies, this is usually the factory floor.*

This is the approach we are using:

1. Select an area to start: We have chosen the assembly W/C #401 and the machine shop W/C #301.
2. Select team members and a team leader: There will be two teams, one assigned to each work center. The makeup of the teams is a mix of personnel from manufacturing, distribution, and administration.
3. Conduct education on: what we are going to do, why we are doing it, and how we are going to do it (tools used).
4. Develop a schedule of when you are going to do it (start time and date, end time and date).
5. Take pictures and develop process flow maps on how product flows through the work center.
6. Establish timelines for each activity, including the wait (queue) time between operations.
7. When appropriate, measure the distances that products/resources move between each process step.
8. Benchmark the current performance in the work center (units of output, unit throughput).
9. Establish a criterion for the work center. For example, how much WIP should be in the work center: one hour of WIP or one day of WIP?
10. Conduct a good housekeeping campaign. Remove everything from the work center that isn't needed. For example, tables, benches, tools, inventory, empty cartons, etc...
11. Identify non-value-added activities in the work center.
12. Conduct brainstorming sessions to come up with ideas on how to eliminate the non-value-added activities, and improve the process so that there is a continuous flow into and out of the work center.
13. Convert work centers to the new flow.
14. Measure results of the new flow.
15. If satisfactory, look to improve the value-added steps in the process.
16. When you believe that the lean initiative in that area has been achieved (it's never over) for now, take pictures, publish results (storyboard, newsletter), and recognize the team for a job well done.

TIP #102: *If you want to achieve success with a lean initiative, you must have a plan in place prior to starting.*

This is the process we followed for W/C #401 (spotlight assembly). Figure 7.5 shows the work center before the lean initiative. Table 7.2 describes the lettering and number scheme depicted in Figure 7.5.

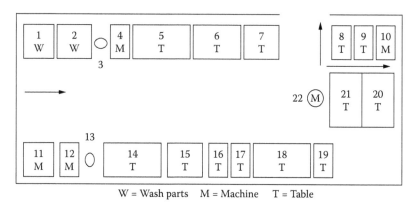

W = Wash parts   M = Machine   T = Table

Figure 7.5   Assembly work center #401 before lean initiative.

Table 7.2   Assembly Work Center #401 Description

Item	Description	Use
1	Cleaning bath	Parts cleaned
2	Rinse bath	Parts rinsed
3	Air gun	Parts blown dry
4	Table	Waiting area before moving
5, 6, 7	Assembly tables	Parts are assembled
8, 9	Cabinets	Small parts storage area
10	Drill press	Not used
11, 12	Rework areas	Drill holes, reassemble parts
13	Pole/column	File container for paperwork attached to column
14	Table	Waiting area for reworked parts
15	Computer table	Computer used for drawings, BOMs
16, 17	Cabinets	Storage for documentation manuals
18	Table	Storage for WIP inventory from Table 4
19	Tool table	Holds various hand-held tools
20, 21	Tables	Kitted jobs partially assembled, waiting for missing parts
22	Vise	Vise embedded in floor used for bending parts

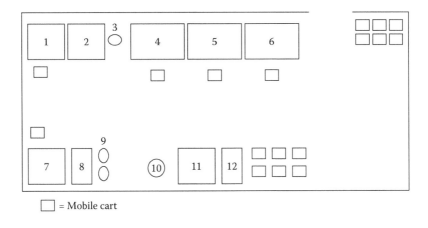

Figure 7.6 Assembly work center #401 after lean initiative.

Figure 7.6 shows the work center as it is today after the lean initiative. We still have a ways to go, but notice the progress we already made. We have gone from 22 work locations down to 12. We have eliminated all the tables that were holding WIP. Because we reduced WIP, we needed less space, and we also decided to replace the permanent storage tables with mobile carts, eliminating the need for several touches that don't add value to the product. A big space savings was eliminating the kitting operation (tables 20 and 21). We decided to eliminate kitting on jobs where all the parts were not available.

Tables 16 and 17 were eliminated because they held hard copies of the job description documentation. Because all the documentation was on the computer (table 15), there was no longer a need for the hard copies. Table 18 was the primary WIP inventory storage area. We eliminated this and put in mobile carts that could move about the work center. Each cart holds one job, and anyone walking into the work center can quickly see what the workload is in this work center. When we started the initiative, this work center had 5 days of WIP inventory, consisting of 63 jobs (work orders). On average, it could complete 10 jobs a day, so this represented 6.3 days of WIP. What is the point of sending in more jobs? They would only sit in queue. There are now only 30 jobs in the work center, about 3 days' worth of work. Our short-term goal is to get it down to 10 jobs (1 day of WIP) and take it from there. We aren't finished yet, but you can see we have made good progress.

The "good housekeeping" approach was great. We discovered a lot of stuff that had no business being in the work center. We also found a completely finished job under one table. One of the assemblers commented that just last week they had to expedite a work order for that very same job! Here they were, working hard and fast on the top of the workbench when there was a perfectly good finished part under the workbench not two feet away! Crazy, right? I bet this happens more often than we care to admit.

We are in the process of installing Andon Warning Lights in the pressroom, machine shop, and engineering, so that if assembly (second floor, building 1) detects a quality problem, it can signal production (first floor) and engineering (third floor) to stop sending parts and to focus on finding the root cause of the quality problem.

The primary tools used in work center #401 are screwdrivers, pliers, rubber mallets, wire cutters, and sheet metal cutters. Each operator keeps his own set of tools in a tool box under his work bench and locks it up at the end of the work day. Problems occur when he is not at work the next day. We can move cross-trained workers in from another work center, but they have to borrow tools from other operators because they don't have access to the primary operator's tool box. At times, either borrower or lender is waiting for the other to finish with the tool they are using. We are going to consolidate all tools into one tool cabinet. At the end of each shift, all tools will be put away and accounted for. The supervisor will have the primary key, and a spare key will be kept by me and Arnie.

> **TIP #103:** *When beginning your lean initiative, don't focus on eliminating inventory; focus on eliminating waste. A major benefit of eliminating waste will be the rightsizing of your inventory.*

Pull Systems and Inventory

One technique that will help us rightsize our inventory is to move from a "push philosophy" to a "pull philosophy" on the factory floor. I once worked for a company where the materials manager operated under the philosophy that when she left the office at the end of the day, she wanted a clean desk without any open "to-do" for the next work day. She was constantly releasing orders early and sending them to manufacturing without any regard for whether the plant could meet the delivery dates. Needless to say, this concept of pushing work orders without regard to production schedules caused havoc on the factory floor. It got so bad that when a customer called to check on the status of an order, we had to track it down on the factory floor. We spent just as much time looking for a copy of the order as we did looking for missing parts (not a good thing either).

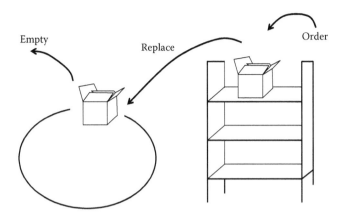

Figure 7.7 Two-bin system.

At Woodstock, our flashlight manufacturing is currently based on a push system from manufacturing to assembly. It's somewhat easier to control the spotlight and beacon light products because they are typically make-to-order and assemble-to-order. Because the flashlights are make-to-stock and the volumes are high, there is a tendency to push products downstream to another work center, whether they need the work or not. As you know, we mold the tops and barrels for our basic flashlights. We outsource the bulb assembly and kit the hardware (springs, contacts, and switches). The battery inventory is on the assembly work center floor and is the only item that is pulled into the work center based on a two-bin system. Figure 7.7 illustrates the two-bin system used for batteries.

A carton of batteries is on the factory floor. When the carton is empty, it is removed and replaced with a full carton from the storeroom. When the storeroom issues the carton to the factory floor, that is a signal for the warehouse to order another carton from the supplier. Of course, I am oversimplifying. There is more than one carton on the factory floor and more than one carton in the storeroom. But whether it is one or ten, the philosophy is the same.

All four of these components (top, bottom, bulb assembly, and hardware kit) come together in the assembly shop and are assembled by hand. Some day, when we can afford it, we need to automate this assembly process. If we can't, then we need to consider moving it offshore or outsourcing it. It's just getting too expensive to continue doing it in house much longer.

In an ideal manufacturing environment, all four major components would arrive at the assembly work center at the same time. Unfortunately this doesn't happen. We usually have too much of one part and a shortage of another part. It is rare to have the same quantity of all four components. It is hard for us to rightsize our inventory when we have this kind of imbalance going on in the plant.

> **TIP #104:** *Moving from a push manufacturing philosophy to a pull manufacturing philosophy will greatly benefit your inventory rightsizing efforts.*

To convert to a pull system from a push system, we need to start as far downstream in our supply chain as possible. Let's focus on the flashlight division because that represents our largest inventory investment and therefore becomes the best opportunity for aggregate inventory reduction. The furthest downstream point for this product line is our points of distribution to the customers, our distribution centers (D/Cs). Ideally, some day we can go further downstream to our customers, who are the actual distributors to the retail customers. We tried to implement a pull system with the D/Cs a few years ago, but it didn't work out very well. We advised them of our replenishment lead time, but they abused it. I think our sales team had a lot to do with it by pressuring them to ship their orders at the expense of other salespeople.

I believe it really failed for a different reason. We have three D/Cs located in California, Texas, and Florida. Each center operated autonomously and pretty much ordered what it wanted without regard for what the other centers needed or what the production schedule was at the plant. On some of the more popular products they would hoard inventory, even if they knew another D/C had a shortage. Management had to step in and force them to ship some of their safety stock to other D/Cs. It was absolutely chaotic.

Do you know we hired a consultant to look at this movement of goods between the D/Cs? The study showed one case where we moved finished goods from California to Florida, and a month later Florida sent the same goods back to California! I consider this a non-value-added activity. It adds to our transportation cost at a time when we are trying to reduce operating costs. The consultant estimated that we were spending over $100,000 a year in transportation costs moving goods between the D/Cs.

Since then, we have gone back to pushing products to the D/Cs based on the sales forecast for that region of the country. Off the record, I've heard rumors that we are going to shut the D/Cs down and ship directly from the plant. If it's true, I don't know where we are going to get the space. You all know the issue we have with space. Of course, if we didn't have so much inventory, we would probably have some extra room, but not enough to handle the current inventory at all three D/Cs. When you talk to Carlos in distribution, ask him. Maybe he knows if the rumors are true or not.

> **TIP #105:** *If multiple locations are pulling products from the same source of production, inventory movement must be coordinated and carefully planned for.*

For now we have decided to look at implementing a pull system in our manufacturing plant and put off the pull system at the D/Cs. In manufacturing, the problem with our push system is that it is based on schedules developed for each production and assembly work center. The minute the schedule gets disrupted, and this happens a lot, it gets out of whack, and we have late work orders. Due dates quickly lose meaning and planning has to regenerate a whole new schedule. Here is a real problem: We don't change the due dates on the late orders. After a while we have a backlog of orders, which backs up WIP inventory and creates a situation where we have inventory all over the place.

Last week manufacturing actually had to move WIP inventory up to the second floor because it ran out of room in the machine shop. On top of all this, new orders were released to the machine shop, which only compounded the problem. That's why, when we run MRP we get a slew of action notices that it is almost impossible to deal with. By definition, a pull system at Woodstock will be a *visual signaling system* where downstream work centers pull products from upstream work centers as needed. We are going to start by having spotlight assembly (W/C #401) pull products from the pressroom (W/C #201) and the pressroom will pull products from the machine shop (W/C #301). There are times when the machine shop is pulling products from the pressroom also. Figure 7.8 depicts the pull system concept.

The pull starts at the furthest point downstream, which, in this case, is the spotlight assembly (W/C #401). At the beginning of the shift, the

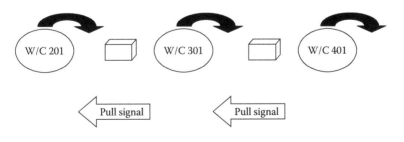

Figure 7.8   Product pull system.

bulb assemblies needed for that day will be pulled from the storeroom and staged in the W/C storage area. We are going to use a mixed lot schedule and make a lot size of 25 of each color lens in the following sequence: red, blue, and white. They can assemble 75 lights per hour (25 of each color). The spotlight frame comes from the pressroom (W/C #201) in multiple shapes, but in our example we are going to use part #81074. The assembly W/C #401 will pull 75 frames from W/C #201 at the beginning of the shift. Because the W/Cs are on separate floors, they will send a visual signal to the pressroom to send 75 frames.

We have decided (for now) to use lights as the signal between work centers. A light board will be installed in the pressroom, and each assembly area will have a different light code. For spotlights, the color used will be amber. Pressroom staff will have 75 lens frames made and sitting in storage in the work center (not the stockroom). When they see the amber light, they will move the 75 lens frames to the assembly work center. Once the 75 pieces are moved and the storage spot designated for the frames is empty, that is the signal for the pressroom to make 75 more lens frames and place them in the assigned storage space. The pressroom will not make any more of that frame until the 75 already made have been pulled by the assembly work center.

In the next phase of implementation, we will pull the components for that frame from the machine shop. The big advantage of this pull concept is that WIP for this part will never exceed 75 pieces, and the pressroom is only producing what will be needed to meet that immediate requirement. If we can get this to work well, we will reduce the lot size of the pull and continue to do so until the lot size is as small as reasonable. The concept is to have a lot size of one pulled when needed. I don't see us getting down to that small a lot size. Just controlling lot sizes of 75 pieces will be a big accomplishment for us.

> **TIP #106:** *When implementing a pull system, gradually reduce the lot-size quantity until you have achieved the smallest possible lot size. The ideal goal would be to produce a lot size of one.*

The primary advantages of moving to a pull system are the following:

1. Producing exactly what is needed to satisfy an immediate customer need (internal and external)
2. Eliminating as much paperwork as possible by using signals instead
3. Moving product only as needed — not before
4. Controlling the amount of WIP inventory
5. Gradually reducing the amount of WIP inventory

6. Reducing total product throughput time
7. Coordinating the movement of product through the supply chain

Because the lot size is predetermined, a standard size container can be used, eliminating the need to count the parts in the work center. Each container will hold the same quantity of parts. As you can see, the rewards of doing this successfully are significant. But there are risks. If the fabrication press breaks down, the assembly work staff may have to stop working as well after they finish the 75 parts in the work center. Because of this risk, Joe wants us to keep 8 lots (600 frames) in the storeroom to cover one day's production in the assembly work center (75 per hour; 75 × 8 = 600). This defeats the whole purpose of the pull concept. If he's worried about the press breaking down, he should focus on the maintenance of the press to keep it in good working condition. The maintenance crew can discuss this with you in more detail. For now, we have our hands full trying to convince Joe that safety stock isn't the answer to this problem.

Implementing a pull system in assembly and the pressroom will be relatively easy compared to the machine shop because they perform repetitive processes, which adapt well to a pull system. Products made once a year, like the new lantern product, will not be a good candidate for a pull system. Because assembly will be working on a repetitive schedule, no work orders will be issued to the floor. We are also going to install a takt time board to monitor the assembly work center output.

Storeroom Inventory Management

By way of definition, our *storeroom* is where we store raw materials, subassemblies, components, factory supplies, spare parts for maintenance, and office supplies. We try not to use it for finished goods. As you already know, the storeroom is in building 2, which is adjacent to our manufacturing plant. Every time we need something from the storeroom, we send a forklift driver over to get it. The building is only 100 feet away, but in inclement weather this becomes a problem. Every couple of years Joe talks about knocking down walls and attaching the two buildings, but it has never happened. There never seems to be any money in the budget for it. It becomes a particular waste of time when we have to move something from the storeroom to the assembly area, which is on the second floor of building 1. That's one of the reasons I support the pull system we are going to install in the spotlight assembly work center. Goods will go directly from manufacturing to the work center without having to be stored in the storeroom.

> **TIP #107:** *The storeroom is a good place to start your inventory rightsizing efforts. Inventory accuracy begins with the receipt of inventory into the storeroom.*

As we continue to reorganize the plant, we will look more and more at storing materials at the point of manufacture (in the work center needing it) or point of use (near the work center where it will be used). Once we get the WIP inventory down to a manageable size, we want to start doing this in the machine shop and press room.

Inventory is stored in the storeroom using two different stocking methodologies:

Fixed Storage Locations (Preassigned)

Storage locations are preassigned to part numbers and, when goods are received, they are put away into their assigned location. When the goods are picked, a "pick list" is generated with the location number where the goods are stored. Depending on the size, shape, density, and weight, we can control where the parts are stored. For example, heavy items like the rolls of sheet metal used for fabrication are stored on the floor, and lightweight items like the flashlight caps are stored on the higher shelves in the warehouse. Items that turn over frequently are stored near the staging area, and slow-turning items are stored at the farthest point from the staging area.

There are obvious benefits to using a fixed location system. It becomes more efficient for the stock pickers because they will quickly become familiar with where the parts are stored, and they won't have far to travel for the high-turnover parts as they are stored near the staging area. However, there are disadvantages. We frequently have more material to store than the assigned location will hold, so we have to go to an overflow location that, in most cases, is not close by and therefore more inefficient. Overall, the storing and picking activities are more efficient, but the aggregate space utilization is less efficient. We try to use a fixed location for fast-moving items and items of considerable weight.

Random Storage Locations

A random location method does not preassign locations to part numbers. With this method, as goods are received they are put away according to a predetermined criterion like size, weight, or quantity. Our computer system can take the shipment data and assign a location according to the criteria. The forklift operator then puts the goods in that location. In those cases where the computer doesn't have the capability to assign a location, the forklift operator will find the first suitable, available location, indicate the location on the paperwork, and advise the warehouse system where the goods are stored. When this happens, it sometimes causes us problems.

If the forklift driver doesn't write down the location clearly, it might get entered into the system incorrectly. For example, misinterpreting a 7 to be a 9, or a 3 to be a 5, may cause us hours of wasted time because the part wasn't where we thought it was. The benefit of using the random location method is typically a more efficient use of total storeroom space. The disadvantages are that part storage and picking may be less efficient, and it can cause the misinterpretation of part numbers I spoke about earlier.

Zoned Storage Inventory Locations

Fixed- and random-storage location systems focus on where the items are put in our storeroom. Zoned-storage location focuses on where we put personnel in the storeroom. We divided our storeroom up into three zones. Zone 1 is for flashlight inventory, zone 2 is for spotlight inventory, and zone 3 is for beacon light inventory. Zone 1 is our largest zone, and four stock handlers are assigned there. Zone 2 is half the size of zone 1, and zone 3 is about the size of my den at home (about 450 square feet). Two stock handlers cover zone 2 and 3 together.

Within a zone we use both random and fixed locations. The advantage of splitting our storeroom up into zones is that the personnel working in that zone really get to know their area well, and they have responsibility for their assigned zone only.

The Storeroom and Inventory Management

Following good warehousing concepts and procedures will greatly enhance our opportunity to improve our inventory rightsizing efforts. We have always had an "open door policy" in the warehouse. What that means is, any time someone needs materials, they can just go in and take what they need. And I do mean anyone. I have just discovered that Michael from our product design team took some preassembled light frames out of inventory to conduct destructive testing. Cyndie is furious. She needed these parts to complete a light assembly for a new customer. It will take two weeks to replace the raw materials and another week to manufacture and assemble. We promised customers we would ship it in one week. Now someone has to tell them we don't have the subassemblies and we will be two weeks late. I feel sorry for the sales representative who has to tell them. That needs to stop right now. We are going to implement a storage control procedure.

Yesterday we implemented an authorization control procedure where no one is allowed to enter the storeroom without the approval of the storeroom manager. I realize this is a bit harsh, but Joe is trying to take a stand on this. He is actually having signs made up that say, "Do Not Enter, Authorized Personnel Only" — do you believe it? He actually expects the requester to ring a bell and wait for someone to come and let him in. After he shows his request form, he will be allowed to take the goods. I have never heard of anything so silly. We are not dealing with controlled substances or high-value precious gems.

The company I used to work for had the inventory in what we called a locked storeroom. The room was literally locked up, and we had a counter behind a caged window where you went with your authorization form to take goods out of the room. The stock clerks would pick the goods and deliver them to the work center that authorized the movement. That is what we should do here. Our computer system is sophisticated enough to generate the pick list on the screen, and the storeroom can just print it out and deliver the goods to the required work center. There is no need for someone from the work center to waste time coming to the storeroom for the goods. I support the locked storeroom concept, but not to the extreme that Joe wants to go. A locked storeroom will protect against pilferage and help us maintain integrity of the inventory records — a big problem for us at Woodstock. We are going to ask Joe to modify the procedure as I have suggested today.

> **TIP #108:** *Establishing an authorized control procedure for goods moving into and out of the storeroom will greatly improve your opportunity to rightsize your inventory.*

I believe I covered the major points I wanted to share with you today. Michael told you about all the good things we have planned for product and process design. Those activities, along with what I have shared with you today, will greatly enhance our efforts to rightsize our inventory. Thank you for listening.

Inter-Office E-Mail

To: Supply-Chain Managers   May 29
From: Harmony Team
Subject: Rightsizing Inventory
Current Inventory: $38.1 Million: Down $1.9 Million
since the first of the year.

This e-mail represents a summary of the meeting we
had with Orlando about the activities going on in manufacturing. You will also note from Table 7.3 that actual
customer orders were greater than forecasted. This
helped reduce finished goods inventory. While WIP
remained relatively unchanged, we did reduce raw
material inventory, thanks to purchasing ordering less
raw material because of the changes in purchasing lead
time, and the fact that our summer interns have identified some raw material that were substituted for the
original part number. This shows that the things we are
doing are starting to pay dividends. We expect this
downward trend to continue for the rest of the year.
Product and process design are now working concurrently on all new products, have begun to look at our
most popular products, and are aggressively looking to
redesign the products and processes to reduce costs
and enhance our value-added activities. The following
are the highlights of our meeting. The minutes of the
meeting will be published tomorrow, and we ask that
you share them with your team:

1. Manufacturing is actively looking for ways to reduce
    the amount of raw material and WIP inventory in our
    supply chain.
2. The primary responsibility of manufacturing is to
    produce quality products and meet the require-
    ments of our MPS and FAS.
3. Manufacturing is also responsible for the effective uti-
    lization of resources, balancing supply and demand,
    and managing storeroom and WIP inventory.
4. We will use three different planning zones for our
    MPS and FAS. Different levels of authorization are

required in each zone. The purpose is to control the number of changes in the execution of our production plans. A policy will be published shortly.

5. We learned that there is a direct relationship between lead time and WIP inventory levels.

6. A load profile report showing a comparison of workload and capacity for each work center will be developed and distributed on a monthly basis.

7. We have learned how to adjust our total available capacity (resources: machines and personnel) for utilization and efficiency, and we will report the actual performance to planned performance.

8. Workload is calculated based on the remaining work to be done on released orders and orders that are planned to be released in the future.

9. The load profile report will not work effectively if lead times, routing, and work center data are inaccurate. (To that end, please look at the current data and advise us if you note any discrepancies.)

10. We have embarked on a lean manufacturing initiative. *Lean manufacturing* is a philosophy of eliminating waste in our supply chain. *Waste* has been defined as anything that doesn't add value to our product or services. (Please review your processes and let us know where you believe we have an abundance of waste that can be eliminated.)

11. We will provide education on the lean initiative to all employees. This education will include what a lean initiative is, why we are doing it, and how to do it.

12. A major good housekeeping policy is being implemented in each work center.

13. Major areas of waste have been identified, and we are seeking to reduce/eliminate the waste.

14. Our company will change from using a push-system philosophy to a pull-system philosophy throughout our entire supply chain. We are starting on the factory floor (work centers), and eventually we will move the pull system further downstream in our supply chain.

15. As much as reasonably possible, we will replace paper as a form of communicating product movement through the plant. Visual signals will be the primary vehicle to move product through our supply chain.

We have begun by installing Andon Warning Lights in some work centers.

16. There will be limited access to the storeroom inventory. We are implementing a locked storeroom concept so that inventory moving into and out of the storeroom can be controlled more effectively.

17. The storeroom will be divided into zones. Inventory clerks will be assigned to each zone, and they will be responsible for the inventory in their zones.

Attached to this e-mail is Figure 7.9, which is the latest version of our inventory rightsizing model. As always, we welcome your comments and suggestions. Our next meeting will be on July 2, when Carlos will discuss the activities of our distribution and transportation links.

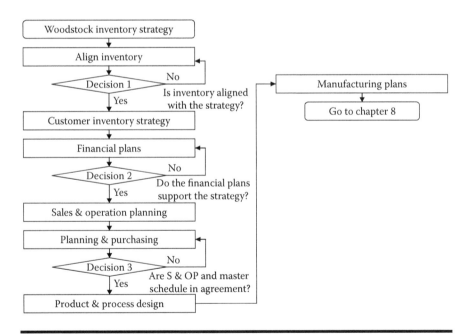

Figure 7.9   Woodstock inventory rightsizing model.

Applying the Tips, Tools, and Philosophies to Your Company

In this chapter, we covered the manufacturing supply-chain link and added 21 more TIPS on how to rightsize your inventory. In this section we will review each of the TIPS and discuss how they can be applied to your company. Before we begin, I want to emphasize how important a lean initiative can be to your inventory rightsizing efforts. I believe it is an important concept for companies to focus on as they try to reduce and shift the inventory in their supply chain. I cannot think of a more important philosophy to apply. Lean is all about eliminating waste. If you can reduce or eliminate the waste taking place in your company, your chances of continued success will be greatly improved. Those companies that cannot eliminate waste will have a hard time surviving in today's competitive global environment.

> **Tip #88:** *In a job shop manufacturing environment, the bottleneck operation is not stationary. It is constantly shifting from work center to work center and will create an imbalance of your WIP inventory.*

A bottleneck operation is one of the biggest challenges you must overcome to achieve a continuous flow in your plant.

1. Focus on eliminating the bottleneck. Once you do that, you will find another bottleneck somewhere else. Focus on eliminating that bottleneck. Continue this process until all bottlenecks have been eliminated.
2. Cross-train personnel so that additional resources can be added to the bottleneck operation until it is in line with the other operations. Then move the personnel on to the next bottleneck operation. In other words, move your resources around your plant as needed to relieve the bottleneck.
3. In some cases, you might be able to move machinery around your plant to address a bottleneck operation. Remember the example I cited earlier with the sewing machines on wheels in Chapter 6.
4. Until you can eliminate the bottleneck, all upstream and downstream operations from the bottleneck must be synchronized with the output of the bottleneck work center.
5. Conceptually, you never want to run out of work for the bottleneck work center. The worst thing you can do is have the bottleneck work center waiting for work. Until you resolve the bottleneck

issue, keep some buffer inventory in queue in front of the bottle-neck work center.

TIP #89: *If supply (capacity) and demand (workload) are not in balance, the change in inventory will negatively impact your inventory rightsizing efforts.*

You cannot balance supply and demand without first knowing what the supply and demand is for any given period of time:

1. Create a load profile report similar to the one shown in this chapter.
2. The load profile data must be accurate, otherwise you are wasting valuable time.
3. The report should go as far out into the future (planning horizon) as necessary to make adjustments to the plan to bring it back into alignment.
4. Before reacting to an overloaded condition, make sure you understand the nature of the workload (is it forecast or real orders) and the capacity.
5. Before rescheduling work to another period where capacity is available, make sure you have done everything reasonable to meet the demand. The last thing you want to do is change the order date, especially if it is a customer order.
6. If an out of balance (overload) continues to exist for a long period of time, you may have to consider getting permanent additional capacity (outsourcing or getting new equipment). However, before doing so, look at the long-term company plans (strategy, S&OP, CRM, etc.).
7. If an out of balance (underload) continues to exist for a long period of time, you may have to retrain workers and place them in other positions in the supply chain where overload conditions exist. If it is equipment related, you might want to consider keeping the equipment idle if not needed. Why make products you don't need?

TIP #90: *Calculate capacity based on your normal work week. If you normally operate five days a week, then calculate your capacity based on five days. If you always operate seven days a week, then you can calculate your capacity based on seven days.*

Only develop material and capacity plans based on your normal work week and your manufacturing calendar. Saturdays and daily overtime should only be used to catch up or work on a priority order and should never be counted on as part of your normal work week. If you consistently are working overtime (every Saturday and daily), you might want to consider adding a second shift (or third). The cost of additional personnel might be offset by not having to pay time and a half or double time. My experience has been that over sustained periods of continuous overtime, productivity decreases, quality decreases, and worker fatigue can cause potential safety issues.

> **TIP #91: *Make sure your shop calendar is adjusted each year to account for nonwork days. Failure to do so will hinder your inventory rightsizing efforts.***

If you mistakenly identify a nonwork day as a work day, your computer system (MRP) will generate recommendations for orders to be released that day and, when they are not, the next time you run MRP you will probably get an expedite message. If this misidentification of work versus nonwork days continues, you will create confusion as to what the real priorities are on the factory floor. Discuss the future shop calendar dates with your human resources link and your finance link. Typically, they will know years in advance what the company calendar looks like. One more important point I want to make here. If you plan for a complete plant shutdown for one to two weeks (vacation or holiday), make sure your customers are advised and are in agreement with the dates.

> **TIP #92: *Develop a load profile report by work center. Distribute it to all appropriate links in the supply chain so that each upstream and downstream link can use it as a tool to make decisions that impact inventory levels in the entire supply chain.***

I discussed the load profile report in tip #89. However, I do want to stress here that the report should be communicated to all supply-chain links. As I discussed in this chapter, even human resources can use this report to develop education plans. Although manufacturing will gain the greatest benefit from this report, other links (upstream and downstream) will also gain from seeing it. A load profile report should be reviewed and updated at least once a month, or more often if conditions warrant it.

> **TIP #93: *Producing defective parts will create multiple inventory problems, add to your cost, reduce profitability, and reduce capacity. Design processes to ensure perfect quality.***

Steps taken here should include the following:

1. Use a concurrent engineering strategy from the very beginning on new parts and products.
2. Reverse-engineer existing parts to see if parts can be eliminated or standardized.
3. Train operators on how to properly maintain their equipment and machines (routine maintenance).
4. Train operators on how to properly operate the equipment/machines.
5. Train operators on how to inspect their own work for defects.
6. Empower operators to stop production when defects are detected. Do not pass defective parts on to the next downstream operation.

> **TIP #94:** *Balance workflows and production resources as much as possible so that wait time is kept to a minimum.*

Wait time is a non-value-added activity that can be defined as the time a job is waiting to be moved to the next step. It could be waiting to be moved to another operation, work center, warehouse, or the shipping dock (if completed). I will define wait time in a broader sense. It can also be the time the job is sitting in queue, waiting to be worked on. Regardless of which definition you use, wait time should be kept to a minimum or eliminated completely. You can eliminate or reduce wait time by designing your processes so that products flow continuously. Reducing throughput time and lot size will minimize the amount of time a job will wait in queue. Reducing wait time will also help you reduce the amount of WIP inventory on the factory floor.

1. Try moving additional resources into a work center that has unacceptable wait time.
2. Reduce lot sizes.
3. Rebalance workloads at the upstream and downstream work centers.

> **TIP #95:** *Any time the product is touched without value being added is adding cost. All non-value-added touches are candidates for elimination.*

Not every product touch can be eliminated, but the total number of touches can be decreased:

1. Create process flow maps of how the product flows through a process.

2. Count the number of times the product is touched.
3. Identify the number of non-value-added touches.
4. Brainstorm for ideas/ways to eliminate those non-value-added touches.
5. Eliminate those non-value-added touches.

> **TIP #96:** *Inventory not needed to satisfy an immediate customer requirement is considered wasteful and reduced or eliminated when possible.*

This begs the question of why we are making more than we need to satisfy an immediate customer requirement. There are many reasons for you to do this. One of the reasons popularly given is that the customer order delivery time required is less than the time it takes us to make; therefore, we have to make it in advance and put it into inventory. Those of you with this environment need to focus on reducing your manufacturing time as much as possible. As you reduce your manufacturing lead time, you also reduce your safety stock (buffer stock) proportionally.

Companies that have a make-to-stock strategy will find this most challenging:

1. Look at your items and identify where you have excess inventory.
2. Try to reduce the lot size on your next order (make/buy).
3. Reduce your purchase or manufacture lead time.
4. Reduce safety stock levels gradually.
5. Keep your eye on customer service levels.
6. If customer service is not negatively affected, reduce your safety stock further.

> **TIP #97:** *Company politics is a complete waste of time and energy. Change the company culture and eliminate politics.*

I'm no expert on the human mind, but I do know this: As long as you need people to run your business, you will have some amount of politics in the company. I have never seen politics completely eliminated even in well-known world-class companies. What I do know is that spending time talking about your coworkers, having hidden motives (personal agendas) at meetings, and not telling your boss the complete truth about a certain situation are all a waste of time. They do not add value to your company and, in fact, they are harmful. Eliminating company politics and changing a company culture has to start at the top. Management must recognize the need for change and set a good example for all employees to follow. You can do five things to help change the company culture:

1. Keep employees informed on the current condition of the company.
2. Stop rumors and half-truths from circulating.
3. Treat everyone with respect.
4. Provide education and training to improve employee skill sets and morals.
5. Get all employees involved in your inventory rightsizing efforts.

> **TIP #98:** *To be successful in your inventory rightsizing efforts, information must be accurate and timely.*

In Chapter 5, I introduced the concept of the "BILL of Integrity." I believe it is worth mentioning again. The four areas of data accuracy that I have identified as important to your inventory rightsizing efforts are:

1. **B**ill of material accuracy
2. **I**nventory accuracy
3. **L**ead time accuracy
4. **L**ot-size rules

If the integrity of data in these four areas is accurate, then you have greatly improved your chances of rightsizing your inventory.

> **TIP #99:** *Working outside your job description is admirable and shows teamwork, but it can be costly and wasteful. Delegate authority, and train employees to do their job.*

Having the vice president (VP) of operations walking around the stockroom looking for parts (as Joe did) is not a good use of his time, and it sends a bad message to the employees whose job it is to store and pick parts from the storeroom. Unless it is a very small company with maybe five employees total, the VP shouldn't be doing this.

1. Assign accountability and authority to employees.
2. Give them the training and education necessary to do their job.
3. Provide them with the proper tools to do their job.
4. Have clearly defined job descriptions.
5. Measure employee performance.
6. Provide feedback to employees.
7. Don't do their job for them.

TIP #100: *Complexity may cause problems and hinder your inventory rightsizing efforts rather than help them.*

I have seen a lot of this. A company is having inventory problems, and it goes out and buys the most sophisticated application software available. It believes the software is the solution to its problem, but it isn't. Take MRP systems as an example. Software suppliers will pitch the fact that MRP will help you control inventory and establish inventory priorities. This is true, but the operative word in the previous sentence was "help." If you continue to do things the same sloppy way you did before and your BILL of Integrity is not accurate, all you are doing is automating your problem so that you can get bad data faster!

You cannot continue to do things the same old way and expect to get different results. In fact, more than once I have suggested to clients that they postpone the MRP implementation until they have their BILL of Integrity in order.

1. Don't write complex procedures that no one can understand or follow.
2. Don't buy and try to implement complex computer programs without providing education on why you are doing it and what you are trying to accomplish.
3. Don't buy and try to implement complex computer programs without providing proper training on how to use the software.
4. Throwing complexity (and money) at the problem isn't the answer.
5. Follow the mantra of the engineer: combine, simplify, eliminate.
6. After doing step #5, look to automate what's left.

TIP #101: *Begin your lean initiative in an area of your supply chain where opportunities for improvement are significant. For most manufacturing companies, this is usually the factory floor.*

You can start a lean initiative just about anywhere in your company, but you should start where the opportunity to eliminate waste is greatest. For most manufacturing companies, that is the factory floor. The cost of goods sold (COGS) is usually the highest cost of a manufacturing company. COGS is made up of material, labor, and overhead — material is usually over 50 percent of the total COGS. So follow the inventory.

However, if for some reason you have decided to start in the office, look for your most paper-intense supply-chain link. More often than not, there are a lot of wasteful activities associated with lots of paper.

TIP #102: *If you want to achieve success with a lean initiative, you must have a plan in place prior to starting.*

Don't expect your lean initiative to be successful unless you have a plan in place. Your plan should include the following:

1. Education program consisting of three types of education:
   - What is lean?
   - Why are we doing it?
   - How do we do it?
2. Different education for different employees:
   - Management education
   - Lean team members
   - All other employees
3. Pick areas to focus on (can be multiple areas at the same time).
4. Pick cross-functional lean team(s).
5. Pick team leaders.
6. Set guidelines as to what is off limits (personalities, raises, etc.).
7. Set criteria for each area chosen.
8. Provide work area for brainstorming.
9. Provide the lean team with the proper tools.
10. Establish time lines for each lean initiative. It's never over, but at some point you may want to move on to something else and then come back to that area at a later time.
11. Assign a management facilitator who can help the team accomplish its goals by removing obstacles.
12. Benchmark current performance.
13. Let all employees know what is going on, and keep them informed.
14. Have a plan to rotate all employees through a lean initiative so that everyone gets a turn.
15. Recognize lean teams for success.

TIP #103: *When beginning your lean initiative, don't focus on eliminating inventory; focus on eliminating waste. A major benefit of eliminating waste will be the rightsizing of your inventory.*

Although it appears that there is a dichotomy between TIP #101 and TIP #103, the goal of both TIPs is to eliminate waste. In many cases, companies have too much inventory. If you eliminate waste, you will be able to operate with less inventory in your supply chain. Inventory reduction is a benefit of getting lean and eliminating waste.

TIP #104: *Moving from a push manufacturing philosophy to a pull manufacturing philosophy will greatly benefit your inventory rightsizing efforts.*

Pushing inventory downstream will result in large WIP inventories. This is particularly true if the downstream work center can't keep up with the upstream work center providing it with work. The problem gets compounded if the receiving work center has a machine breakdown or quality issues. Before moving to a pull system, synchronize the production rates between work centers, as explained in Chapter 6. Pay particular attention to your exit work center. This is the last work center in an operation sequence, as opposed to the gateway that would be the first operation in the first work center of a product routing. The pull system will not work well without this coordination.

TIP #105: *If multiple locations are pulling products from the same source of production, inventory movement must be coordinated and carefully planned for.*

For example, you have two different work centers using the same part number coming out of the machine shop. Each work center requires different lot sizes. Work center A uses the part in quantities of 25 pieces to a lot, and work center B uses the part in quantities of 50 pieces to a lot. If work center B pulls at a rate twice as fast as work center A, the machine shop will have to adjust its output to meet the demands of both. Don't forget, in all likelihood your machine is making other parts for other work centers, so the coordination will require some trial and error. You should start the pull system at a work center where the demand is relatively constant and known.

TIP #106: *When implementing a pull system, gradually reduce the lot-size quantity until you have achieved the smallest possible lot size. The ideal goal would be to produce a lot size of one.*

Start your pull system with the same lot size previously used in the push system. Reduce the lot size by some factor (maybe 10 percent) and analyze whether the reduction impacts the flow of pieces out of the pulling work center. If the pulling work center runs out of work before the upstream work center can resupply it with a new lot, then you need to increase the throughput of the upstream work center to match the rate of pull from the downstream work center. If there is no noticeable impact on the flow between work centers, reduce the lot size again by some factor (maybe another 10 percent). Continue to go through this iteration until you have reduced the pull quantity down to a lot size of one.

I realize that for some products a lot size of one is unreasonable. The flashlight product line for Woodstock is a good example of a product that cannot reach a lot size of one. Go as low as you can. The goal of one is just that: a goal. You may never get there, but you can probably reduce your lot sizes to smaller quantities for many of your products.

> **TIP #107:** *The storeroom is a good place to start your inventory rightsizing efforts. Inventory accuracy begins with the receipt of inventory into the storeroom.*

Your furthest upstream process is receiving goods into your storeroom, which will be transformed into a finished product at some point in time. So that is where it all begins. What better place to start?

1. Develop a policy and standard operating procedure (SOP) for receiving, storing, and picking materials from the storeroom.
2. Identify a list of personnel who are authorized to be in the storeroom.
3. Send out a notice to all employees advising them of the new operating policies and procedures.
4. Educate and train personnel assigned to the storeroom.
5. Have a reprimand procedure in place for violators of the SOP.
6. Nothing should move out of the storeroom without some type of authorization (paper, signal, computer).
7. Keep a transaction log of all movement into and out of the stockroom.
8. Start a cycle-counting program.
9. Periodically conduct a good housekeeping campaign.

> **TIP #108:** *Establishing an authorized control procedure for goods moving into and out of the storeroom will greatly improve your opportunity to rightsize your inventory.*

TIP #107 mentions developing an SOP for the storeroom. Taking that TIP a step further, you will need an authorization procedure as part of the SOP. The policy should be clear, simple, and easy to follow. The upstream work center can pull goods from the storeroom without any personnel leaving the work center. Today, most systems generate a pick list that can be the authorization. The storeroom can have storeroom clerks deliver the material directly to the requesting work center, or it can be transported by some automated means like a conveyor system.

I will conclude this section with a brief narrative. A client told me that after the storeroom shutdown at the end of the normal work day, he had one work center working overtime. The work center needed some parts from the storeroom, but it was closed. Someone from the work center climbed over the fence and retrieved the needed parts. Because it was against company policy (for obvious safety reasons), they were afraid to report this event, and the transaction went unrecorded. I was told this was a frequent occurrence. Obviously, this caused inventory accuracy issues. What the person didn't realize was that at another time when someone went to pull that same part, it wouldn't be there, and a stockout would occur, maybe, even having to send everyone in that work center home for the day. However, if this company had excess inventory, it wouldn't have a stockout; it would only have an inaccurate inventory record that could be adjusted. That's why we like to say: "high inventory level hides a lot of problems." The moral to the story: follow the rules; they are there for a reason. Table 7.3 is the latest status of the Woodstock inventory and Table 7.4 shows the drivers of excess inventory.

Table 7.3   Inventory Balance

Month end	31 Jan	28 Feb	31 Mar	30 Apr	31 May
Forecast	7.2	7.9	9.7	7.1	5.9
Orders	5.8	7.4	9.6	7.7	6.8
Total starting inventory	40.0	41.0	40.9	40.3	39.0
Start FG inventory	15.5	15.7	15.8	15.3	14.9
+Production @ COGS	4.1	5.1	6.0	4.8	4.2
−Shipments @ COGS	3.9	5.0	6.5	5.2	4.6
End FG inventory	15.7	15.8	15.3	14.9	14.5
Start WIP inventory	7.5	7.6	7.7	7.4	7.1
+Material issues	3.4	4.2	4.8	3.9	3.5
+Labor and overhead	0.8	1.0	0.9	0.6	0.7
−Production @ COGS	4.1	5.1	6.0	4.8	4.2
End WIP inventory	7.6	7.7	7.4	7.1	7.1
Start raw inventory	17.0	17.7	17.4	17.6	17.0
+Material purchases	4.1	3.9	5.0	3.3	3.0
−Material issues	3.4	4.2	4.8	3.9	3.5
End raw inventory	17.7	17.4	17.6	17.0	16.5
Total ending inventory	41.0	40.9	40.3	39.0	38.1
Forecast	7.2	7.9	9.7	7.1	5.9
Orders	5.8	7.4	9.6	7.7	6.8
Total starting inventory	40.0	41.0	40.9	40.3	39.0
Start FG inventory	15.5	15.7	15.8	15.3	14.9
+Production @ COGS	4.1	5.1	6.0	4.8	4.2
−Shipments @ COGS	3.9	5.0	6.5	5.2	4.6
End FG inventory	15.7	15.8	15.3	14.9	14.5
Start WIP inventory	7.5	7.6	7.7	7.4	7.1
+Material issues	3.4	4.2	4.8	3.9	3.5
+Labor and overhead	0.8	1.0	0.9	0.6	0.7
−Production @ COGS	4.1	5.1	6.0	4.8	4.2
End WIP inventory	7.6	7.7	7.4	7.1	7.1
Start raw inventory	17.0	17.7	17.4	17.6	17.0
+Material purchases	4.1	3.9	5.0	3.3	3.0
−Material issues	3.4	4.2	4.8	3.9	3.5
End raw inventory	17.7	17.4	17.6	17.0	16.5
Total Ending Inventory	41.0	40.9	40.3	39.0	38.1

Table 7.4   Inventory Segmentation — Excess Inventory Drivers

Number	Excess inventory drivers
1	Forecast inaccuracy
2	Intentional safety stock
3	Supplier's minimum-buy requirements
4	Lifetime buy situations
5	Inventory in anticipation of a new product introduction

Chapter 8

How Much Inventory Should We Stock?

Harmony Team Meeting: July 2

Woodstock Inventory: $36.7 Million

Inter-Office E-Mail

To: All Employees   June 30
From: Adriana
Subject: Organization Announcement

It is with regret that I have accepted the resignation of
Joe as the vice president of operations. Joe has been a
loyal employee of Woodstock Lighting Group for the
past 15 years and he will be missed. We all wish him
well in his future endeavors.

Inter-Office E-Mail

To: All Employees   July 2
From: Adriana
Subject: Organization Announcements

I am delighted to make the following announcements:

Effective immediately, Arnie has been promoted to vice president of operations and will report directly to me. Arnie has been with Woodstock for 25 years and brings his vast experience to his new role in the company. I am excited and confident that Arnie will be a significant contributor to Woodstock's future. I ask that all of you support his efforts to make Woodstock a world-class company that we will all be proud of.

Effective immediately, Orlando has been promoted to the position of plant manager and will report directly to Arnie. Orlando has been with Woodstock for 15 years, and I know he will continue the excellent legacy that our manufacturing group has established over the years as the premier producer of quality lights. Orlando will also replace Arnie as the Harmony Team leader and continue with our company's ongoing effort to right-size our inventory.

My name is Carlos, and I am director of distribution and logistics for Woodstock Lighting Group.

Wow! What a surprise. I wonder if Joe quit or was fired. Well, it doesn't matter. The consensus is that he wasn't well liked and was more of a hindrance than a help. Every time we tried to do something positive, he would put obstacles in the way. Arnie and Orlando are cool guys and I'm excited about the things these guys can do without Joe getting in the way. The biggest problem with Joe was that if it wasn't his idea, he wasn't interested in pursuing it. Now maybe we can really get some things done. I'm going to give these guys all the support I can. I trust them to make good decisions that will help the company become profitable again. I know they will do everything in their power to prevent layoffs.

I've only been here three years, but I like it here. The money is good and I'm only three miles from the house. The company has been good enough to pay for my education, and I've only got one more year of college before I get my degree; then I'll see where things stand. If they don't do something about this huge inventory, we will all be out of a job. I think it's time everyone recognizes the importance of reducing transportation and warehousing costs. I am certainly going to do my best to explain the challenges and issues we have in distribution and transportation.

Role and Responsibilities

As director of distribution, I am responsible for the warehousing, picking, packing, and transportation of finished goods to our distribution centers, and in some cases, shipping directly to our customers. Here is an overview of what we are responsible for:

- **Logistics:** At Woodstock, we define logistics as the physical movement of product through our supply chain. This involves all internal movement of goods, from raw materials to finished goods.
- **Warehousing:** We are responsible for the finished goods warehouse (Building 4) located adjacent to our manufacturing plant in New Jersey. In addition to finished goods for the Flashlight Division, we also maintain the subassembly inventory for the Spotlight Division and the spare parts inventory for the Beacon Light Service Center.
- **Picking:** We pick and move goods to the automated "pick and pack" area and the shipping dock.
- **Automated Pick-and-Pack Center:** This is the high-volume pick-and-pack area for flashlights (Building 3). We have tried to automate this operation as much as possible.
- **Customer order picking:** We pick and pack goods for shipment to customers.
- **Transportation:** Our traffic department coordinates movement of product to our distribution centers, and in some cases, direct shipments to customers.
- **Reverse logistics:** We also coordinate the movement of all returned goods back upstream through our supply chain.
- **Inventory accuracy and accountability:** We are responsible for the data integrity of all our inventory records; perpetual and physical.
- **Cycle counting:** We are now responsible for cycle counting (buildings 2, 3, and 4) all inventory, not just finished goods. Until recently, we were only responsible for cycle counting finished goods.

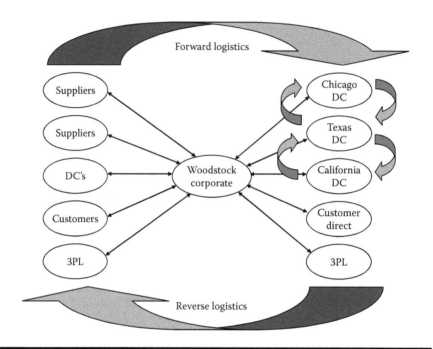

Figure 8.1   Woodstock logistics network.

- **Import/export documentation:** All activities (paperwork, customs, etc.) related to product moving into and out of the country.
- **Third- and fourth-party logistics providers:** We move goods into and out of our third- and fourth-party partners.
- **Government regulations:** We ensure that the movement of goods complies with all local, regional, and national regulations.

Figure 8.1 illustrates the Woodstock Lighting Group logistics network. You will note that the outbound (downstream) flow is entitled "forward logistics," and the inbound (upstream) flow is entitled "reverse logistics." The arrows going in all directions reflect the transportation (movement) of inventory through the supply chain. Conceptually, the more locations we have, the higher the inventory in our supply chain, and the more arrows (movements) we have, the greater our transportation costs.

> **TIP #109:** *The more inventory locations you have in your supply chain, the higher the aggregate inventory in your supply chain.*
>
> (Note: TIP = team important point.)

Our objective is to keep inventory flowing as much as possible. The ovals in Figure 8.1 represent inventory stopping points. Ideally, inventory will spend very little time at these locations, thus increasing the inventory turns for our products.

Logistics Goals and Objectives:

1. The timely (forward and reverse) movement of goods upstream and downstream through our supply chain.
2. The accuracy of our perpetual and physical inventory records.
3. Compliance with all government and customer shipping rules and regulations.
4. Maintaining a safe and healthy work environment for our employees.
5. Keeping inventory in a secure environment.
6. Ensuring as much as possible that shipments are not damaged during storage or shipment.
7. Consolidation of shipments to minimize costs.
8. Rapid response to changing customer needs.
9. Visibility of inventory requirements upstream and downstream in our extended supply chain.

> **TIP #110:** *Cycle counting inventory will greatly improve your inventory record (perpetual and physical accuracy) and will have a positive effect on your inventory rightsizing efforts.*

Logistics, more than any other link in the supply chain, has the greatest amount of interaction with all other links in the chain. It touches everyone from the receiving dock to the shipping dock. Logistics supports the actions of all other links in the chain and must understand the needs and requirements of the internal and external customers.

> **TIP #111:** *Movement of inventory between links in the supply chain must be coordinated on a daily basis. If not, your inventory rightsizing efforts will quickly dissipate into a chaotic situation.*

We started out with the idea of locating our distribution centers close to the customers. This business model needs to be changed. Think of it in terms of inventory. The more inventory locations we have in our supply chain, the higher the aggregate inventory in the supply chain. The higher inventory adds to the complexity of our planning process. This higher

Table 8.1 Woodstock Finished Goods Inventory by Location in $Million

Location	Flashlights	Spotlights	Beacon Lights	Total Inventory
Chicago	4.1	$0.1	0.0	$4.2
Texas	3.5	$0.0	0.0	$3.5
California	3.6	$0.1	0.0	$3.7
New Jersey	1.8	$0.3	2.0	$4.1
Totals	13.0	$0.5	2.0	$15.5

level of complexity has increased our cost of doing business. The major benefit of the old model (Figure 8.1) was that we could get product to our customers quickly, because the travel distance and time were minimal.

Transportation efficiency has improved dramatically over the years, and we believe we can deliver product to our customers just as quickly from one central location. I don't think a new business model of one centralized D/C will have a negative impact on customer service, and I truly believe it will reduce our overall inventory investment.

Table 8.1 shows four primary inventory locations: the three D/Cs and the finished goods warehouse at the plant. In total we have four inventory locations. At the beginning of the year we had $15.5 million of finished goods inventory dispersed at the four locations. Table 8.1 shows the distribution of our finished goods inventory by location.

As you can see, most of the finished goods are in flashlights. The entire beacon light inventory is here in New Jersey and very little of the spotlight inventory is in finished goods. As you are aware, we do have some beacon light spare parts sitting in third-party warehouses located at major airports, but it represents less than $100,000 in value.

Before we added the 3 D/Cs we kept $1.0 million worth of safety stock at our plant here in New Jersey. When we added the 3 D/Cs we used the following formula to estimate safety stock:

$$\textbf{Formula: } A = b/\sqrt{c}$$

Where A = safety stock @ each distribution center. B = safety stock for one distribution. C = number of distribution centers.

$$A = \$1.0/\sqrt{4} = \$1.0/2 = \$.5$$

$.5M × 4 locations = $2.0 million total safety stock

While total safety stock was increased to a total of $2 million, the safety stock at one location (the plant) was reduced by 50 percent. I don't know how it happened, but safety stock has grown to approximately $1 million at each distribution center. I believe that 1 or 2 of the distribution centers should be shut down and all inventory shipped from 1 or 2 locations. We will probably have to keep California and New Jersey. Or maybe we could turn the California D/C over to a third-party logistics provider (3PL). Even if we kept $1 million in safety stock at our two sites, we would be able to reduce safety stock by $1 million.

I presented this proposal to Joe last year but he rejected it. He said the higher transportation costs would offset the inventory dollar savings. I am going to revisit this topic and conduct a cost/benefit analysis of consolidating our warehouses. I think the study will show that while the cost of shipments to customers will increase, it will be offset by the elimination of transportation costs to the D/Cs. In effect, we have to look at the total cost of transportation and inventory carrying cost. At the same time, we cannot have a negative effect on customer service.

> **TIP #112:** *When determining the number of inventory locations (D/Cs) in your supply chain, you must look at the total cost of inventory and the impact on customer service.*

When conducting this analysis we will consider the following:

1. Transportation costs for shipments to the D/Cs
2. Transportation costs for shipments between D/Cs
3. Transportation costs for shipments to customers
4. Transportation costs for reverse logistics
5. Inventory carrying costs at each D/C
6. Inventory ordering costs and planning costs for each D/C
7. The aggregate amount of safety stock in our supply chain
8. The cost of personnel and equipment needed at each location
9. The relationship between inventory locations and the impact on customer service levels
10. Availability of efficient transportation where the D/C is located
11. Local government regulations
12. Tax considerations

Transportation and Inventory

Let's discuss transportation and its impact on our inventory rightsizing efforts. Transportation can be defined as the movement of inventory between locations in the supply chain. In a very narrow sense, this can be the movement of raw materials from the storeroom to the factory floor. In a broader sense, it is the movement of finished product to our D/Cs and customer sites. The objectives of transportation are to move inventory between supply-chain partners in a timely manner and at a reasonable cost.

Transportation can also be considered as a temporary warehouse location for inventory, whether it is in the belly of a plane, in a railcar, on a ship, or sitting in the back of a truck. As you are well aware, we presently have several trailers sitting in our yard that can't be unloaded because we lack storage space. We are using these trailers as temporary storage locations until we free up space in the warehouse. We are paying for the use of these trailers. This is not what I meant when I said "transportation can also be considered as a temporary warehouse location for inventory." Six months is not temporary!

There are legal aspects of inventory ownership that we have to consider in regard to the point that ownership or title is transferred from the seller to the buyer. The term associated with this transfer of ownership is called "free on board" (FOB). We use public transportation carriers (mostly trucks), and if our finished goods are shipped directly to customers they are shipped using one of two ways: FOB seller location: ownership of the inventory is transferred to the buyer the moment the shipment is delivered to the carrier; FOB buyer location: ownership is transferred when the carrier delivers the inventory to the customer.

Why is this important to our inventory rightsizing efforts? We shipped (transported) $90 million of product last year and over half of it was shipped FOB buyer location, which means we were responsible for the inventory until it was delivered to the customer. That's a great deal of money moving through our supply chain.

Modes of Transportation

There are five primary modes of transportation that can be used:

1. Railroad
2. Air freight
3. Pipeline
4. Water transport
5. Truck (motor) carriers

We use four of these. We don't use pipeline transport for obvious reasons. The primary use of pipelines is to convey crude oil and petroleum products. I wish we could. We wouldn't have to be concerned with packaging, pallets, and all the other associated shipping materials. Pipeline transport is unique in several ways. It is available to ship product 24 hours a day, every day of the year. Weather conditions are not usually a factor. On the negative side they have a high fixed cost to construct the pipeline, and the route (path) is fixed—offering limited flexibility.

Railroad

Rail is the primary mode of transportation we use to ship product to our D/Cs in Texas, California, and in some cases to Chicago. Rail is a cost-effective way of shipping heavy, large loads of inexpensive goods, like our flashlights, long distances at a reasonably low cost. We ship only full car loads by the mode. When the rail car arrives at the rail yard, we have a local carrier who puts the rail car on a flatbed truck and delivers it directly to our distribution center or in some cases directly to our customer (distributor). For the most part, weather is not a factor. On the downside, rail can be very slow when you consider all the stopping, coupling, and decoupling at switchyards, and their routing flexibility is limited to locations where there are railroad tracks.

Water Transport

Since we don't do a great deal of exporting (yet!), we use water transport on a limited basis. We ship to a distributor in Europe who is really a fourth-party logistics provider (4PL). They differ from the traditional third-party logistics provider (3PL) in that they subcontract some of the sorting, billing, and shipments to others. Like rail, water transport can handle large quantities of heavy goods at a relatively low cost. However, water transport is slow, and in recent years port accessibility can be difficult and tedious.

Air Freight

Unfortunately, we use too much air freight as I alluded to earlier. However, the bottom line is that it is the fastest mode of transportation, and it gets us out of a lot of trouble with customers. The cost of air transport is high and is limited in flexibility to the location of airports. Air freight regulations limit the weight and size of shipments. We rarely, if ever, ship flashlights by air. I do remember one time, when I first started working here, we air-freighted flashlights to a region of the country that was hit by a devastating hurricane. For the most part, it is our beacon light service department that used air freight to get spare parts delivered to customers. We use too much air freight flying in raw materials because of inventory shortages. Once that problem goes away, air freight costs will be less of an issue.

Motor Carrier (Truck)

Truck is the most flexible mode of transportation, and we use this mode a lot. Trucks can go wherever there is a road, and in some cases where there is no road, so to speak. However, weather can be a negative factor with this mode of transport. We don't own our own trucks; we don't want to be in the transportation business. For one thing, it's not part of our core competency, and for another, it wouldn't be cost effective. We do, however, lease one small panel truck we use to run errands and to make local deliveries. Having that truck available has helped us avoid a crisis on more than one occasion. When a machine breaks down, we send the truck to pick up spare parts so that we can get the machine back up in production quickly.

Inventory Shipping Costs

Generally speaking, it costs less to ship full truck loads than less than full truck loads (LTL). Full loads can be shipped directly to the consignee. With LTL, the shipment goes through a terminal where the goods are taken off the truck and sorted, loaded, and transported to the consignee, or another terminal. Obviously, because of the additional handling, there are additional charges. There are four primary costs associated with transportation:

1. **Handling costs:** The cost of terminal handling, cross-docking, and break bulk.
2. **Pick up and delivery costs:** Cost of the carrier pick up and delivery.
3. **Billing costs:** The cost of creating paperwork associated with the shipment: invoices, advance shipping notices (ASNs), shipment tracking, shipment tracing, claims forms, etc. These are either additional charges or built into the cost of transportation.
4. **Line-haul costs:** These are costs associated with fuel for the vehicle, drivers' salary, and the general wear and tear on the truck. The cost per ton (weight) will vary, depending on shipment weight and distance traveled. For example, let's use cost per ton. The formula is:

$$A = B \times C \div D$$

A = cost per ton B = line-haul cost per mile C = distance moved D = weight

For a shipment of 4 tons, traveling 500 miles, and a line-haul cost of $6 per mile:

$$\$6 \times 500 \div 4 = \$750$$

There is a direct relationship between transportation and our inventory rightsizing efforts. Inventory has to be transported through our entire supply chain, and the more times we move it and touch it, the higher our costs. Manufacturing and distribution lead times are impacted by transportation lead times. Typically, the greater the lead time, the more inventory we have flowing through our pipeline. Transportation is the vehicle (no pun intended) used to put inventory in the right place, in the right quantity, at the right time. How could it not affect our inventory rightsizing efforts?

Unfortunately, there are times when we are late on a customer order and have to ship by air freight. We conducted a study last year that showed 20 percent of our total transportation cost was for air freight. Our total transportation cost last year was roughly $2 million, so this means we spent $400,000 on air shipments. Not all of this cost was for shipments to customers. About 50 percent of it was for purchased raw materials that had to be flown in for one reason or another. The point I want to make here is that if we don't have the inventory available when needed, it impacts our cost. So our inventory rightsizing effort will affect our transportation cost.

> **TIP #113:** *Inventory stockouts have a negative impact on your transportation costs. Eliminating/reducing those (stockouts) will reduce transportation and handling costs.*

Stockouts cause us to back-order some customer shipments. Instead of one transportation cost per customer order, we can have two or three transportation costs per customer order. If we do that often enough, we will lose customers. It's difficult enough to get new customers without having the challenge of trying to win back a customer we already had. Our order fill rate is somewhere around 85 percent (per order). This is not good. This means that 15 percent of the order will either be back-ordered or cancelled. Remember, our standard flashlight product line is a commodity, readily available in the marketplace if we can't deliver. Every time we back-order we are adding to our costs: picking, packing, packing materials, and transportation.

TIP #114: *Stockouts result in back orders or customer order cancellations. Order cancellations can result in lost customers, and back orders result in higher transportation costs.*

Back orders are a challenge for even world-class companies. Just recently I placed an order with a major catalog retailer. I ordered two items. One was in stock and one wouldn't be available until two weeks later. As I wasn't in a rush to get them, I told the customer service person to hold the item that was available until the second item came in so that they could both be shipped together as one shipment. I was told that their "system" wouldn't allow them to do that. They would ship the available item at once and ship the second item separately when it came in. As there was no shipping charge to me, I didn't care; I was just trying to save them some money (nice guy that I am!). Can you imagine how much money they are spending on double freight charges?

Just-in-Time Delivery (JIT)

If you were to ask me what the difference is between JIT, lean, and the Toyota manufacturing philosophy, I would say, "very little, if anything." By way of definition, they all focus on the elimination of waste. However, adding the word "delivery" to JIT does have a different meaning. JIT delivery focuses on receiving raw material and delivering finished goods in a timely manner; that is, receiving the right material, in the right quantity, at the right time—sometimes directly to the factory floor. Some companies do this successfully, but we don't do it here at Woodstock. We did have a customer ask us to do this once but it was cost prohibitive. It was a small chain of hardware stores that wanted us to come in and stock their shelves once a week. But the volume was so small it wasn't worth it to us.

Of course, companies that can do this and do it well reduce the level of inventory they carry, and increase their inventory turns. The trade-off is having higher transportation costs. I worked for a large manufacturing company once that used JIT delivery with certain suppliers. It actually gave the truck drivers badges that allowed them access to the factory floor; they would go to the work center, check the stock, and replace the parts that were used with new inventory. They would leave a receipt with the work center supervisor and the supplier would bill our company once a month.

If you go with JIT delivery, you have to have a good relationship with your supplier. For one thing, the quality of the goods must be perfect as you typically receive a limited amount of material per delivery. JIT delivery usually ranges from one delivery per day to one delivery per week. In rare cases it can be multiple deliveries per day. If the quality is poor, or the supplier misses a delivery, you face the risk of a stockout and not having enough work for your employees. This actually happened at the company I worked for. The supplier's truck broke down and we didn't receive our expected delivery that afternoon, which was to be used on the second shift. We had to send six people home for the day because we didn't have any work for them. The company was generous enough to pay them for the day, but if this occurs on a regular basis, you will have higher costs and late orders.

> **TIP #115:** *JIT delivery is an effective tool to keep inventory levels low, but if your supply partner doesn't deliver quality product on schedule, it can cause a host of irrevocable problems.*

Material Handling

Handling inventory during transportation impacts our cost of shipment. Remember when goods are going from our plant to our D/Cs we have the task of loading and unloading our trucks. Most, if not all of our flashlights are prepackaged ready to hang on a jay hook in a retail store. The prepacked flashlights are placed in standard size corrugated cartons that hold from 48 to 144 assorted flashlights per carton. These cartons are then placed on a skid and a fork truck moves them on to and off of the trucks. So getting the product delivered safely and economically to the D/Cs isn't an issue for us. However, once it arrives at the D/C, we do have handling issues, which I will discuss later.

Warehousing and Inventory

I like to say, "We all live in a warehouse." I know that I do. If you think of your home as a warehouse, it makes a lot of sense. You buy things, you store things, and eventually you ship things out the door. Take your kitchen as an example. You go to the supermarket and you stock your shelves. During the week you take food products out of storage and consume them and dispose of the scraps (recycle). Sometimes the shelf life expires (this happens a lot in my house!). Once a week or so, you take inventory (cycle count) of what is left, make up a list (new order) and go to the store to shop for new inventory (purchase), and finally go home and restock the shelves. Like any other warehouse you sometimes damage goods (spillage, drop an egg, etc.) and you sometimes have a stockout. At least once a week we run out of something and I have to make a fast trip (expedite) to the convenience store to pick something up. On top of that I have to pay a premium for the item. Can you relate that to a supply-chain warehouse? I know I can.

Your clothes closet is another good example that you can relate to a warehouse situation. You go out and purchase new clothes, wear them for a while. One day you realize they are out of fashion (product life cycle), got soiled and can't be cleaned (damaged goods), or don't fit anymore (engineering change). So you just leave them hanging in the closet taking up space. Years go by and they are still sitting in inventory (low inventory turnover). Does this sound familiar? You bet it does.

> **TIP #116:** *If inventory sits in your warehouse unused for a long period of time, get rid of it. It's taking up space that can be used for active inventory or for some other activity.*

Warehousing cannot function as a stand-alone silo. It must be integrated into your entire supply-chain strategy. Warehouse activities must be coordinated with transportation, manufacturing, package engineering, and other supply-chain links. The objectives of warehousing are to store, pick, pack, and ship inventory in an efficient, timely, and cost-effective manner. Rapid response to customer needs must be the focus of these activities.

Getting back to our earlier discussion on reducing the number of D/Cs, I am serious about this. I don't suggest we do it all at once but over the course of a year or so. The present model has inventory redundancy and too much safety stock. Maintaining and staffing four warehouses also adds to our cost of doing business. I want to start by closing down the Chicago D/C by the end of this fiscal year, which ends on December 31. We will split that marketplace up between the New Jersey warehouse and the Texas D/C.

As most of the flashlight business is with large distributors or direct to major retailers, I am confident that full trailer loads can be shipped from Texas and New Jersey to meet the needs of our customers in that zone. It may be more difficult to shut down the California D/C and ship those customers from New Jersey. I propose we turn the California operation to a 3PL as I mentioned earlier.

Third-Party Logistics Provider (3PL)

By definition, a 3PL is a company that can manage all or part of our product break bulk, pick and pack, and ship operation. I have started to look into it and have found a 3PL on the West Coast that can provide the following services:

- **Freight consolidation.** They will take in full truck loads from us and consolidate small shipments (orders) into full truck loads of mixed product for different customers in one particular region.
- **Break-bulk large cartons** of flashlights into smaller lot boxes for shipment to customers.
- **Stockpile large quantities** of seasonal inventory (spotlights) in anticipation of product demand.
- **Postponement of final package assortment**. We can ship different colors in bulk and after we get the actual order from the customer, they can pick and pack the final configuration.
- **Reverse logistics.** They will accept customer returns and consolidate them into periodic shipments back to our plant or dispose of them as we see fit.

Warehousing is no longer simply a place to store inventory. It can be a value-added location with service provided by a third party. We will have to understand the total cost of outsourcing the distribution function to a third party. The benefits can be significant. We would no longer have to buy/lease space, hire employees, or run the operation. But the trade-off is that we will lose control of that activity and the total cost may be higher. As warehousing and transportation are not part of our core competency, we need to take a hard look at this.

Warehouse Automation

The pick and pack workcenter has two robotic pick and pack machines: one box-making machine and one sealing machine that also weighs the box contents. The machine is programmed to reject boxes when the stated contents do not equal the weight. Figure 8.2 depicts the flow of materials through the automated pick and pack operation. The finished goods warehouse has no automated equipment, and everything is moved by hand truck or forklift truck.

Automated Storage and Retrieval Systems (AS/RS)

I spoke to Arnie about this and asked him to ask Joe to consider my proposal to buy an automated storage and retrieval system (ASRS). Arnie gave me what I thought was a great answer to my proposal. He said,

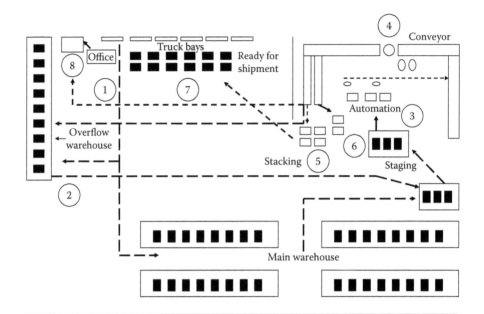

Figure 8.2   Woodstock pick and pack operation.

"Instead of spending a half million to automate the movement of inventory, we should spend the half million on ways to eliminate the need to carry so much inventory." He is right. If we can find a way to reduce our purchasing and manufacturing lead times, make quicker machine set-ups and smaller lot sizes, there would be a lot less inventory to move around. This is a case where automation is not the answer to our inventory problem.

Bar Coding

We have started to use bar codes on all incoming materials and manufacturing work orders. Finished goods are not currently scanned, but we plan to do so in the fourth quarter of this fiscal year. This will help with our inventory rightsizing efforts by eliminating the mistakes made in keying in data. We expect this to greatly improve our record keeping accuracy, which in turn should help us improve our inventory accuracy.

> **TIP #117:** *Rather than looking to automate the movement of inventory, focus your efforts on eliminating inventory so there is no inventory to move.*

Automated Shrink Wrap Machine

I remember taking a plant tour of a manufacturing company where a friend of mine worked. It was late in the day and the second shift was in full swing. Everyone was very busy, and there was a lot going on. When we got to the warehouse where they packed finished goods on skids, there was a guy with a roll of shrink wrap walking around a pallet full of boxes, unwinding the shrink wrap around the boxes as he was walking. I noticed off to the side that they had what looked like a state-of-the-art automated shrink wrap machine just sitting there, idle. I asked my friend why the man was performing a manual wrap when there was this wonderful automated piece of equipment just sitting there. He said: "Oh that thing. It constantly breaks down and takes forever to fix. We only run it when we have customers coming in so we can impress them with our sophisticated, automated equipment. After they leave, we shut it down and go back to our manual wrapping process."

Actually, I believe automation is a good thing. I wish we had an automatic shrink wrap machine. I'm embarrassed to say we do exactly what they did in my friend's plant; we shrink wrap by hand. The automation in our manufacturing plant has improved productivity dramatically. We are producing more products now, with less direct labor than we had just five years ago. The initial cost of the equipment was significant, but the payback time was equally significant—less than two years.

Automated Guided Vehicle Systems (AGVS)

Joe did approve the budget to put in an AGVS system in the finished goods warehouse. Now that Joe is no longer here, I hope Arnie continues with the project. Boxes and other material are loaded on these trucks, which operate without a driver. They will move along magnetic tape or optical tape in the floor, and we can program to send them where we want. The next step after that will be to automate the storage of items on high shelves to maximize the use of our warehouse space. Some day, I would like to get a "pick to light" system like those used in highly automated warehouses.

What does warehouse automation have to do with rightsizing our inventory? It helps us move, sort, and stock inventory in a safe, efficient way so that damage to goods is minimized, move times are reduced, and inventory handling is kept to a minimum. This will allow warehouse personnel to focus their time and effort on maintaining inventory count and location accuracy.

Picking and Pack Automation

We use printed orders to pick goods for customer orders and printed pick lists to pick components for final assembly. On the high-volume items, like the standard flashlight product line, we use the automated robots for picking and packing assorted colors and sizes into shippable cartons. We have two robot pick-and-pack machines that can pick and pack an average assortment of 48 flashlights per box every 30 seconds (each machine). Figure 8.2 shows the pick-and-pack operation.

So each robot is packing two boxes per minute (two robots × two boxes = four boxes per minute). The boxes are placed on a conveyor belt and moved to the box-sealing machine, which can attach labels, seal, and weigh six boxes per minute. After the boxes are sealed, they move on to a staging area where warehouse clerks remove the sealed cartons from the conveyor belt and load them onto skids. The skids are shrink wrapped and then transported to the shipping dock where the shrink wrap is removed (if going to different destinations) and the individual cartons staged for loading on the appropriate truck. Following the flow diagram in Figure 8.2 the activities and locations are:

1. Goods are received and placed into inventory.
2. Goods are picked for the day's production and placed in a staging area.
3. Automated pick-and-pack equipment.
4. Box-sealing machine.
5. Stacking on skid at the end of conveyor line.
6. Rejected boxes.
7. Staged and ready for loading onto trucks.
8. Office.

The automated packing and sealing are operations that are in balance from a capacity planning point of view. However, bottlenecks occur when the box machine jams up. The conveyor has to be stopped, and the box overflow from the picking machines has to be taken off the conveyor and put back on after the line starts up again. We are working with maintenance to see what can be done to stop the sealing machine from constantly breaking down. The other issue is we sometimes stage goods for production and find out later that we are missing one item on the order. The staged goods have to sit while other goods are rushed into production to replace the waiting order. Outside of those two issues, we have more than enough capacity to satisfy our customers' (internal and external) needs.

TIP #118: *Do not pick components for final assembly until you are assured that all components are available in inventory.*

To improve the flow of inventory and eliminate non-value-added steps, we are exploring the possibility of eliminating the staging step of the process and picking goods as needed to go directly into the automation line. Because we have so much excess capacity, we are actually thinking about becoming a 3PL in the pick-and-pack operation for noncompeting product lines. The big problem with doing this is lack of storage space.

Inventory Cycle Counting

Cycle counting is a procedure for physically auditing inventory on a predetermined (cycle) schedule rather than taking it once a year. This doesn't mean that you can automatically eliminate the annual physical inventory unless your financial auditors say it's okay to do so. The objective of cycle counting is to identify inventory errors and correct them. It is equally important that the cause of the error is identified and eliminated so that it doesn't happen again.

Understanding the Meaning of Inventory Accuracy

Inventory has been called "a necessary evil." It is hard to live with, and at the same time it is hard to live without. So we have to deal with it. I believe inventory accuracy is the single biggest challenge we face in our efforts to rightsize our inventory. Our entire supply chain is dedicated to buying, making, and shipping inventory to satisfy our stakeholders' and customers' needs. Who in this company isn't involved in managing inventory to some degree? Even our human resources link is involved. Its inventory is people. It also hires, trains, and educates people on various inventory management topics.

Inventory is also one of our largest investments and represents more than half of our cost of goods sold. The opportunity to become profitable again lies in our ability to get our inventory down to the right level at the right location in our supply chain. We cannot do this with inaccurate inventory records. Our goal must be to achieve 100 percent inventory accuracy and maintain that level each and every day of the year. A proven tool available to us that will help us achieve that goal is called cycle counting.

Table 8.2 Inventory Record Accuracy

Part Number	Perpetual Inventory	Physical Inventory	Difference
60702	125	125	0
81074	95	99	+4
51398	92	88	–4
Total pieces	312	312	0

> **TIP #119:** *You cannot sell products without managing inventory to some degree, and you cannot manage inventory effectively without knowing what inventory you have and what inventory you need. Cycle counting addresses the issue of what inventory you have.*

If we managed inventory the way Pat in finance manages our money, we would be in good shape. It's ironic that accounting can balance our checking account down to the penny, and yet our inventory, **which has a greater dollar value,** is so inaccurate. Granted, we have two or three people who manage the finances and hundreds of people who touch and move inventory. Still, that's no excuse. Our inventory is not only inaccurate, it's also high, and high levels of inventory hide many business problems.

> **TIP #120:** *High levels of inventory hide many business problems you may not even be aware of. Reduce the level of inventory in your supply chain to expose your business problems.*

Using an inventory accuracy tolerance of ±5 percent, our inventory accuracy last year was 88 percent. Without the 5 percent tolerance it probably was around 20 percent. Table 8.2 shows an example of inventory record accuracy.

In looking at this table, how would you evaluate the inventory accuracy for this inventory?

> Scenario #1: In the aggregate, we show 312 pieces in the perpetual (book) inventory record, and 312 are physically in stock. Based on total count, we are 100 percent accurate. However, it is not helpful, not even to finance. If the three-part numbers are different prices, the dollars would not be accurate. If the price were the same for all three part numbers, then the accuracy would be meaningful to finance. The chances of this happening are unlikely.

Scenario #2: Using a tolerance of plus or minus 5 percent, part #60702 is 100 percent accurate. Using the perpetual inventory as the benchmark, part #81074 shows 95 pieces in stock, and 5 percent represents 5 pieces (95 x.05 = 4.75 = 5). Anywhere between 90 and 100 would be considered 100 percent accurate, which it is. Part #51398 shows 92 pieces in stock and 5 percent represents a tolerance of (92 x.05 = 4.6 = 5) 87 to 97 pieces, which makes this part #51398 100 percent accurate. Under this scenario, all three parts would be considered 100 percent accurate. But again, if the cost basis were different it would have little meaning to finance.

Scenario #3: One out of three part numbers is 100 percent accurate. Measuring accuracy between part numbers, the inventory accuracy is 33 percent (1/3 = 33 percent).

Based on the above three scenarios, I recommend that we use scenario #2 and measure inventory accuracy with a tolerance of 5 percent plus or minus. There will be some exceptions. For example, the spare parts of reflectors and lights used by our Beacon Light Service Department should be measured without a tolerance, as these are critical parts needed on a moment's notice.

> **TIP #121:** *In order to determine your inventory record accuracy, you must first decide on a meaningful performance metric and communicate it to all links in your supply chain.*

Don't be lulled into a false sense of security. Measuring average inventory accuracy can be misleading. Referring to Figure 8.3, note that parts M, P, and S have an inventory accuracy of 96 percent each, yet the probability of all three parts being available when needed to make R is only 88 percent.

Probability = .96 × .96 × .96 = .884 = 88 percent

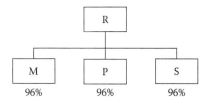

Figure 8.3 Available inventory probability.

> **TIP #122:** *Don't be lulled into a false sense of security with inventory accuracy in the mid-90s. The probability of a combination of parts being available when needed is still at risk.*

When calculating the overall inventory accuracy using scenario B, the calculation is:

**perpetual inventory accuracy =
total accurate records/total records checked × 100 percent**

Last year Woodstock counted 1,000 parts, and 880 of them were accurate (within tolerance):

880 ÷ 1,000 = 88 percent

It should be noted that finance is concerned about the dollar value of the inventory, but manufacturing and distribution are concerned about the unit accuracy of the inventory. Do you have to use the same tolerance for all parts? The answer is no. For various reasons you can set tolerances differently for different parts. The tolerance range would depend on:

- Annual usage of the parts (in units)
- How critical the part is to the product
- Lead time to replace the part
- Dollar value of the part
- Degree of difficulty to replace the part
- Potential for quality defects

To keep it simple, we may want to establish general rules related to A, B, and C part classifications, with A parts having the tightest tolerances and C parts with looser tolerances. As this is a relatively new concept for us here at Woodstock, we have started by using a 5 percent tolerance for all parts, with the exception of the spare parts for beacon lights noted earlier.

> **TIP #123:** *Don't spend a great deal of time analyzing tolerances for each part number. Pick some reasonable percentage and start there. You can make adjustments as necessary.*

Preparing to Cycle Count

Even though we decided on a record accuracy definition and established inventory accuracy tolerances, we couldn't just go on the floor and start counting stuff. For example, what do we do if an inventory record and physical inventory were out of balance. Who would adjust the record? What caused the discrepancy? Will/can it happen again? In fact, who is going to count, and how often? You see, there are many questions to be answered before we could begin.

We began by mapping the inventory process, from incoming raw material to finished goods going out the door. We also documented the inventory transaction steps related to each inventory movement. We wanted to understand where the opportunities for errors could occur and mistake-proof those processes as much as possible without hindering the inventory flow. One of the things we found out was that the same part number could be stored in multiple locations in the storeroom. We decided to consolidate the same part number into one area where possible. We accomplished this by coming in to work on a Saturday when things were quiet. We felt it was important not to disrupt the daily operations in the warehouse and finished goods warehouse.

We started out thinking we could use two cycle counters, and we wanted to fill those positions from within. We posted the cycle counter job position on the bulletin board in the plant and we were pleased to get four people who were interested. We selected two people: one person from receiving and one person who was a floater between work centers. This was a good start. Human Resources staff put together a cycle-counting education program, and they were trained in the mechanics of cycle counting. After the training (ten other people attended, including me) we designed a cycle-counting process and procedure.

As we were well into the new year, we didn't want to wait for the traditional year-end inventory so that we could start with a clean slate. We also couldn't afford the time to stop production for five days (that's how long it took us last year) and take a new physical inventory. We decided to jump right in and start cycle counting. Our ERP software provides the vehicle for us to do this. I'll let our Information Technology (IT) staff explain this to you. They will do a better job than I will. We systematically count inventory on a daily basis, and over the course of the year everything gets counted.

We have about 3000 different part numbers that have to be counted and have established the following count cycle:

A items: 600 part numbers: (3000 × .20); count once a month

B items: 900 part numbers: (3000 × .30); count once a quarter

C items: 1500 part numbers: (3000 × .50); count every six months

The results thus far have been rewarding. We have already increased our overall accuracy from 88 percent to 93 percent. We found that one of the biggest causes of inventory inaccuracy was that people were taking goods out of the stockroom without authorization. As you may recall, we now have a locked storeroom and that has helped a great deal.

Reverse Logistics

One last topic I would like to cover before I leave is reverse logistics. We have always accepted customer returns. I wish I could say, "With no questions asked," but that's not true. Rudy has a sales policy: "If your customer returns something, the sales credit gets deducted from your commission statement." Needless to say the sales people do everything in their power to get the customer to keep the goods. But times are changing. Adriana has said she wants a reverse logistics policy in place by the end of September.

Reverse logistics is the reverse flow of product back upstream through the supply chain. It can start with customer returns and go as far back as the suppliers we buy from. Goods come back from customers for various reasons: repair, refurbishing, damaged, recycling, or disposal. We are even considering taking back customer overstocks. Some companies are reselling returned products into secondary markets and are treating reverse logistics as a profit center.

Taking reverse logistics a step further upstream in our supply chain, we would like to sell back some of our excess raw materials to our suppliers. Maybe they can move them into their secondary market. It has to be a win–win situation for both parties. There are 3PL and 4PL logistics providers who have added reverse logistics to their services. As some of our flashlight returns are recyclable, they have to be disposed of properly, and we plan on using one of these companies because it specializes in that sort of service.

> **TIP #124: Consider outsourcing your reverse logistics function if it is not part of your core competency, or you lack the resources to properly dispose of returned goods.**

Reverse logistics can be one of the best opportunities to rightsize our inventory. We have so much excess inventory that still has value in other markets. I believe we can move a lot of product this way. I think Eddie should contact some of our key suppliers and see if we can work together to move some of the excess raw material back upstream. Rudy should set up a sales team to do nothing but sell our returned goods and seconds into new markets. On some of these items, if we just recover our manufacturing costs we will be doing well. I see it's getting close to the time to end the meeting. I understand Dinesh is scheduled to speak with you about information technology. He is a very bright guy. He and his team are really helping us replace inventory with information. If fact, they are a tremendous asset to our entire supply chain. I will close by saying that you can count on us in distribution to cooperate in any way we can to help with our inventory rightsizing efforts. Thank you for your time.

Inter-Office E-Mail

To: Supply-Chain Managers   July 2
From: Harmony Team
Subject: Rightsizing Inventory
Current Inventory: $36.7 Million: Down $3.3 Million since the first of the year

We met with Carlos from our distribution group and what follows in this e-mail is a summary of that meeting, including tasks to be performed. The detailed minutes of the meting will be published shortly and we ask that you share them with your team.

Note that inventory again went down in June from $38.1 million to $36.7 million. This represents a decrease of $1.4 million for the month. Sales were close to forecast but we weren't able to scale back production in time. July production will be reduced so we expect a dramatic drop next month. We were still able to reduce raw material inventory by $500,000. Some of the things that we are doing are starting to take effect. We are very pleased with our progress thus far.

1. Distribution is responsible for the warehousing, picking, packing, and transportation of finished goods to our distribution centers, and in some cases, directly to our customers.

2. Simply stated, it is responsible for the movement of inventory through our supply chain, from moving raw materials to finished goods.

3. Its business goals and objectives call for the timely (forward and reverse) movement of goods upstream and downstream through our supply chain.

4. Though all links in our supply chain are responsible for inventory (and inventory accuracy), they are charged with ensuring that everyone follows company procedures and that inventory record accuracy is at the highest level possible.

5. We are analyzing our distribution network and are considering shutting down one or two distribution centers by the end of the year.

6. Our largest distribution cost is transportation.

7. We are running out of space in our storeroom and finished goods warehouses. We are storing some raw materials on trailers in our yard.

8. Rather than looking for more space, the correct solution to this problem is to reduce inventory levels.

9. Because of the overall reduction in inventory, we are going to off-load those two trailers this week.

10. Our primary modes of transportation are rail and truck. Although we have used a lot of air freight in the past, we expect this cost to be reduced dramatically because of our inventory rightsizing efforts.

11. Inventory levels have grown in proportion to the number of inventory locations in our supply chain.

12. Our customer order fill rate is around 85 percent; this is not good. Our inventory rightsizing efforts will help us to improve our fill rates.

13. We have explored the possibility of offering JIT delivery to our customers but have ruled it out for now. It is not currently a cost-effective process for us.

14. We are exploring JIT delivery with some of our key suppliers. We are looking at the trade-off of higher cost per unit versus the cost of carrying inventory.

15. The pick-and-pack warehouse has automated equipment, but the finished goods warehouse does not.

16. Management has rejected the idea to buy an AS/RS system. It was felt the focus should be on reducing inventory and thus eliminating the need to automate the movement of inventory.

17. We have started to use bar-coding in our operations. This should improve our efficiency and eliminate data input errors.
18. The budget has been approved to purchase an AGVS system. This will improve our efficiency considerably.
19. A bottleneck in the pick-and-pack area has been identified, and maintenance is working with production to get this fixed so that it doesn't happen again.
20. We will no longer prestage materials unless all materials for the order are available.
21. We are looking to eliminate the staging area (non-value-added step) in the pick-and-pack room and move material directly to the automated equipment.
22. We have decided on a metric for measuring inventory accuracy. This is explained in detail in the minutes of the meeting. Please pass on to all of your team members.
23. We have developed a cycle count procedure and hired cycle-counting personnel who are performing this task on a full-time basis. Our goal is to move from an inventory accuracy of 88 percent at year end, to at least 99 percent by the end of this year. We are already making progress and inventory accuracy is currently at 93 percent.
24. We are looking to outsource our reverse logistics operation to a 3PL or 4PL as it is not part of our core competency.
25. We would like to operate reverse logistics as a profit center. We are working with Rudy and Eddie to see if we can start moving raw material inventory upstream to our suppliers and finished goods inventory further downstream into a secondary market.

Please review the minutes of the meeting and pass on the information to your supply-chain team. If you have any ideas on improving the activities mentioned or have questions about them, please do not hesitate to contact any member of the Harmony Team. Please see Figure 8.4 for the latest version of our inventory right-sizing model.

On a personal note, I am honored to be the new Harmony Team leader. Arnie and his team have done an

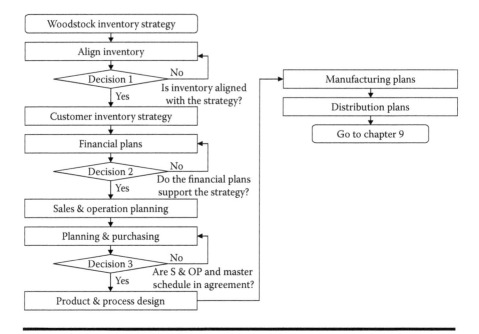

Figure 8.4 Woodstock inventory rightsizing model.

outstanding job and I look forward to being part of the team and continuing the legacy they have set.

Applying the Tips, Tools, and Philosophies to Your Company

In Chapter 8 we covered the distribution and transportation links, and added 16 more tips and several simple formulas to help you rightsize your inventory. Distribution is the furthest downstream link in your internal supply chain and the link that delivers product to your customers. As we discussed in this chapter there are many inventory costs associated with distribution and the most significant cost can be transportation. Let's review the 16 tips discussed in this chapter and find out how to apply them to your company.

> **TIP #109:** *The more inventory locations you have in your supply chain, the higher the aggregate inventory in your supply chain.*

If you have only one location that you distribute your products from, then you are probably okay. However, if you are experiencing difficulty in reaching your entire marketplace and experiencing poor customer service (on-time delivery), you may want to consider multiple distribution points. This doesn't mean you have to own the distribution points. You can outsource the distribution function to a 3PL or 4PL whose core competency is in the field of distribution and transportation.

On the other hand, if you have multiple points of distribution you might want to go the other way and eliminate some of them or, as discussed above, turn the function over to another party. Look at it this way, at every point of distribution you have safety stock, and the aggregate safety stock is going to be higher than if you only had one point of distribution. Keep in mind that turning over the distribution function to a third party will not eliminate the need for safety stock at its location. It might be lower than if you ran it, but it will not be eliminated.

My suggestion is to spend some time looking into a 3PL or 4PL relationship. Use the formula discussed in this chapter to see what the potential is to reduce safety stock.

> **TIP #110:** *Cycle counting inventory will greatly improve your inventory record (perpetual and physical) accuracy and will have a positive effect on your inventory rightsizing efforts.*

Those of you who have a high level (95 percent to 99 percent) of inventory accuracy are probably already doing cycle counting (that's why it's so good). For those of you with an inventory accuracy of 94 percent or less, you should seriously consider cycle counting. Some of you may not measure inventory accuracy at all and have no idea how accurate your inventory records are. But if you are experiencing a high number of stockouts you may find that the root cause of the problem is inaccurate inventory records. You should consider cycle counting if:

- Your inventory record accuracy is less than 95 percent.
- You are experiencing a high number of stockouts.
- You have extraordinarily long lead times to replace inventory.
- The value of the inventory is significant.
- The inventory item is critical to your finished product.

> **TIP #111:** *Movement of inventory between links in the supply chain must be coordinated on a daily basis. If not, your inventory rightsizing efforts will quickly dissipate into a chaotic situation.*

Moving inventory between supply-chain links is like conducting an orchestra; every piece must fit together at the exact time so that the end result is a coordinated effort of music, with a wonderful sound that is enjoyable to hear.

You cannot just develop a standard operating plan and procedure and then forget about it. Each and every business day you must communicate within and between supply-chain links to keep the flow of material moving from location to location, like a pipe with a liquid flowing constantly. When situations change you must react to those changes quickly. It's one thing to recognize that a change in plans has occurred; it is another thing to be able to react and adjust to the situation as quickly as possible. This is why we say visibility and flexibility are two characteristics of a world-class supply chain. To synchronize the flow of inventory through your supply chain:

- Monitor inventory levels daily.
- Review and adjust lead times as necessary.
- Establish inventory performance metrics.
- Formalize your inventory review procedure.
- Cycle count your inventory.
- Communicate with each other to avoid surprises.
- Respond to inventory changes quickly.

> **TIP #112: *When determining the number of inventory locations (D/Cs) in your supply chain, you must look at the total cost of inventory and the impact on customer service.***

Inventory costs money, not just the cost of the item itself. When determining the number of inventory locations in your supply chain, you have to ask yourself:

1. Can we supply the entire marketplace from one location?
2. How many locations do we need?
3. Where should the distribution locations be located?
4. Should we own or outsource the distribution link?
5. Will the total transportation costs increase or decrease if we have multiple locations?
6. Will total inventory investment increase or decrease if we have multiple locations?

You are the only one who can answer these questions. You have to look at the trade-offs between a single point of distribution and multiple points of distribution. The cost trade-offs you should consider are:

- Inventory cost
- Warehouse cost
- Transportation cost
- Lost sales cost

Estimate the total cost for each solution (single or multiple locations) before making your decision. Like all other business decisions, considerable weight should be given to the impact on customer service and company profitability.

> **TIP #113:** *Inventory stockouts have a negative impact on your transportation costs. Eliminating/reducing those (stockouts) will reduce transportation and handling costs.*

If you have inventory stockouts, one of three scenarios occurs:

1. Customer cancels the entire order.
2. Customer allows you to ship what you have and cancels the balance of the order.
3. Customer allows you to ship what you have in stock and allows you to ship the balance at a later date (back order).

Which option is the most costly to your company? If I had to guess I would pick scenario number one. However, if any of these options occurs often enough, you will lose the customer—the worst possible situation. It is difficult enough to get new customers, so you don't want to lose the ones you already have. If the stockout is because of a raw material shortage, you will have two transportation costs to contend with, to say nothing about the cost of multiple machine set-ups (stop making the current part and set up the machine for the new part, then go back to the original part), and the expediting attention required to rush the order through your supply chain.

How can you avoid stockouts?

1. Plan ahead.
2. Improve your inventory record accuracy by cycle counting.
3. Put procedures in place to ensure that suppliers deliver on time, and when they can't, to notify you well in advance of the material need date.

> **TIP #114:** *Stockouts result in back orders or customer order cancellations. Order cancellations can result in lost customers, and back orders result in higher transportation costs.*

Although similar to TIP #113, there is a subtle difference. This tip addresses scenario number 3 under TIP #113, where the customer allows you to ship back orders. Back orders cost money, but you already knew that. I did an analysis some time ago for a major brand name that sold its products through large, prestigious retail chains. The brand name, too, knew back orders were costing it money, but it didn't know how much. To find out the cost (estimate) we looked at:

1. The total number of back orders for the year, including the number of times a single order was back-ordered. One order could have as many as five back orders. At that time it was an acceptable policy with the theory being, "Put something on the shelf to be sold now, and not wait for a complete order." Given today's competitive environment, I'm not sure that would fly.
2. Average number of items back-ordered per order
3. Average cost of duplicate packing materials: boxes, peanuts, cartons, tape, etc.
4. Average paper cost: order, packing slip, pick list, shipping label, bill of lading, etc.
5. Average pick time per order
6. Average handling cost
7. Average transportation cost

In summary, we found that the company was spending millions of a year in back-order costs. We didn't even look at the cost of bringing the goods in from their suppliers (overseas). The morale of the story is that back-order cost could have a serious negative impact on your profitability. You need to understand what it is costing you to ship back orders to your customers. You might be surprised.

> **TIP #115: *JIT delivery is an effective tool to keep inventory levels low, but if your supply partner doesn't deliver quality product on schedule, it can cause a host of irrevocable problems.***

If you can implement a JIT delivery program with your key suppliers, you can reduce the amount of raw material inventory you carry in stock. Although the rewards are great (reducing inventory for the right reason is always a benefit), the risks can be just as great. In order for a JIT delivery program to work effectively, the following must occur:

■ The relationship with the supplier must be solid. By solid I mean a true, trusting partnership.

- There must be benefits to you and your supplier for this to work well.
- Supplier quality has to be perfect.
- Supplier delivery must meet your expected production schedule.
- Your planning process (as to when you need the materials) must be exact.
- Your internal inventory record keeping must be accurate.
- You must have a contingency plan in place if your supplier fails to deliver on time.

Start with the supplier you trust the most. It doesn't have to be your largest supplier or your most important inventory item. Get the bugs out of the system before moving on to other suppliers.

> **TIP #116:** *If inventory sits in your warehouse unused for a long period of time, get rid of it. It's taking up space that can be used for active inventory or for some other activity.*

This tip gives you a tremendous opportunity to reduce inventory. It's what I call the "low hanging fruit." Almost every company has some inventory sitting around that hasn't had any activity for some period of time. It's easy to identify but will take a lot of tedious work on the part of someone; however, it is worth it. Here is what I suggest you do:

1. Ask IT (or do it yourself, if you're able to) to generate an inventory aging report that identifies all inventory items where there has not been any activity for some specified period of time. I recommend one year or greater.
2. Develop a spreadsheet by category of inventory: raw material, subassemblies, and finished goods.
3. Ask product design to breakout the raw materials and subassemblies into two (where-used report) categories:
   - Those who have a BOM to identify what the part "goes into."
   - Those who have no BOM (you will find some of these!) and therefore no "goes-intos."
4. For those parts with a BOM "goes-into":
   - Find out if the upper-level BOM is still active, if so use it.
   - If not active, see if you can substitute it for a similar part.
   - If not, get rid of it: sell it (reverse logistics program) or scrap it.
5. For those parts without a BOM:
   - Ask product design if the part can be used elsewhere (substitute/replacement/new product).
   - If not, get rid of it: sell it or scrap it.

6. For finished goods:
   - Provide sales with a list of inactive items.
   - Provide sales with an incentive to sell them.
   - If not, get rid of it: scrap it.

It is important to keep finance in the loop when you are discounting the sales price or scrapping the product. You will have to keep an audit trail of all transactions so that finance can properly account for the inventory. It may have an inventory reserve account that can apply.

> **TIP #117:** *Rather than looking to automate the movement of inventory, focus your efforts on eliminating inventory so there is no inventory to move.*

As I stated earlier, automation is a good tool when applied for the right reason. Your focus should be on reducing the amount of inventory in your supply chain. If you can reduce your inventory enough, you may find that you don't need to automate the movement of it after all. Now that wouldn't be so bad, would it?

If the nature of your business is such that automation will improve the safety of your employees and is an enhancement to environmental concerns, then by all means automate if you can. But automation for automation's sake is a waste of money that could be best spent elsewhere in your supply chain to rightsize your inventory.

> **TIP #118:** *Do not pick components for final assembly until you are assured that all components are available in inventory.*

Many companies perform a process called "kitting." That is the picking of all the parts for a product (work order, production order) at one time, putting them in some type of bin or tote, and then moving them to the work center where needed (staging). If all the parts are not available to assemble, then the kit just sits there until they are. After a while, someone will come along and take a part out of the bin that they need to finish another job. This common technique is called "robbing Peter to pay Paul." I don't know where that expression came from, but it has been around for a long time. After a while you will have a lot of kits clogging up the aisles, and they are missing more than the original part. At this point chaos reigns. If this is happening in your plant my advice to you is:

- Put the partially completed kits back into inventory.
- Make sure you do the proper inventory transaction!

- Ask IT if the ERP system will allow you to run a phantom pick list. (A review to see if all parts are in stock before generating the actual pick list).
- Pick only those work orders where all the parts are available.

Of course, like most inventory requirements, your inventory records must be accurate. If they are not, then you are back to square one, picking orders where all parts are not available.

> **TIP #119:** *You cannot sell products without managing inventory to some degree, and you cannot manage inventory effectively without knowing what inventory you have and what inventory you need. Cycle counting addresses the issue of what inventory you have.*

Cycle counting is a proven method of improving your inventory accuracy. Success stories abound. However, before you actually start cycle counting you must have a plan of action in place:

1. Benchmark your current level of inventory accuracy. The best time to do this is when you take the annual physical inventory. However, if the year already started, don't wait. Take a random sample from a cross population of parts and establish an estimate of your inventory accuracy.
2. Identify personnel who will do the counting.
3. Decide if job is full-time or part-time.
4. Provide training and education to cycle counters.
5. If your ERP system has a cycle count program, make it part of the education and training program.
6. Identify what to count and when to count it (ERP will help with this).
7. Have a procedure in place to adjust records to match physical inventory.
8. Find the root cause of the inventory error and fix it so it doesn't happen again.

Number 8 above is very important. I like to tell my clients, "Don't focus on inventory accuracy. Focus on finding out what caused the inventory to be inaccurate, fix it, and inventory accuracy will take care of itself."

> **TIP #120:** *High levels of inventory hide many business problems you may not even be aware of. Reduce the level*

of inventory in your supply chain to expose your business problems.

Do not attempt to drastically rightsize your inventory levels all at once. It would be great if you could, but not at the expense of poor customer service and inefficient supply-chain operations. It could be a disaster. Follow the step-by-step approach taken in this book. The inventory model at the end of each chapter shows a logical flow and process you can follow. It is an iterative process. Rightsize inventory; take the time to understand the impact on customer service and supply-chain operations. If no negative impact results, repeat the cycle again.

As you begin to reduce inventory you will encounter problems. You must solve the problem that having less inventory has created. Once that is fixed and you can operate with this lower inventory, do it again; another problem will arise, fix it, and continue to rightsize inventory. It is going to be a never-ending process, but well worth the effort.

> **TIP #121: *In order to determine your inventory record accuracy, you must first decide on a meaningful performance metric and communicate it to all links in your supply chain.***

As you saw from the Woodstock case study, there are several ways to measure inventory accuracy. Woodstock chose scenario #2, as would most companies. There can be exceptions as were pointed out. Zero tolerance is the way to go on critical parts, as defined by your company. One thing is for sure: Operations measuring inventory accuracy in dollars would have very little meaning. Of course finance needs to measure inventory accuracy in dollars. Don't start out by making the tolerance too tight; you may never achieve it and get frustrated. After you have some experience with cycle counting, you can then tighten the tolerance to an achievable level.

> **TIP #122: *Don't be lulled into a false sense of security with inventory accuracy in the mid-90s. The probability of a combination of parts being available when needed is still at risk.***

As shown in the example in this chapter, if you have three parts in inventory, all with an inventory accuracy of 96 percent, the probability of all three being available at the time they are needed is 88 percent. If that part is needed to finish off a customer order ... well, you know what could happen. How high should the inventory accuracy be? The answer depends. I have worked with companies with a stated inventory in the 85 to 90 percent range that experienced very few stockouts. Of course you could argue that, in absolute terms, their inventory was high, well over the tolerance. Inventory inaccuracy doesn't always mean that it is lower than the tolerance range; it could just as well be inaccurate on the high side. I believe you should continue tightening your tolerances until stockouts are eliminated.

> **TIP #123: *Don't spend a great deal of time analyzing tolerances for each part number. Pick some reasonable percentage and start there. You can make adjustments as necessary.***

Because you are going to cycle count the part anyway and adjust the inventory record, that particular record will now be 100 percent. Tolerances are helpful as an overall measurement of the absolute (total) accuracy of the inventory records. I would recommend you start with a tolerance of no lower than plus or minus 5 percent and no higher than plus or minus 10 percent. If you start out with high tolerances, start to tighten them up until they reach 5 percent and then evaluate how tight you want to make them. Although zero tolerance is the goal, it will be difficult to achieve and maintain over time. However, it is reasonable and possible to have an accuracy in the high 90s (97 to 98 percent) and for some "A" parts, 100 percent accuracy.

> **TIP #124: *Consider outsourcing your reverse logistics function if it is not part of your core competency, or you lack the resources to properly dispose of returned goods.***

Effectively managing returned goods from customers and moving all materials back upstream in your supply chain is an effective way to help rightsize your inventory. You should consider the following:

1. Is reverse logistics part of your core competency?
2. Is it part of your business strategy?
3. Can it be a profit center for us?
4. Can we work with our suppliers to dispose of raw materials?
5. Can sales sell off our excess finished goods inventory in other after markets?
6. Should we outsource the reverse logistics function?
7. How should we organize to handle this function?
8. What changes do we have to make to our current customer return policy?

Management should put together a cross-functional team that can review and answer these questions. I don't know the answers to these questions for your specific situation. What I do know is that this is a great opportunity to rightsize your inventory and make money at the same time. You just have to focus your efforts, and you can make this happen. Table 8.3 shows the latest status of the Woodstock inventory and Table 8.4 is a list of the drivers of obsolete inventory.

Table 8.3 Inventory Balance (×1,000,000)

Month end	31 Jan	28 Feb	31 Mar	30 Apr	31 May	30 Jun
Forecast	7.2	7.9	9.7	7.1	5.9	9.0
Orders	5.8	7.4	9.6	7.7	6.8	8.8
Total starting inventory	40.0	41.0	40.9	40.3	39.0	38.1
Start FG inventory	15.5	15.7	15.8	15.3	14.9	14.5
+Production @ COGS	4.1	5.1	6.0	4.8	4.2	5.6
−Shipments @ COGS	3.9	5.0	6.5	5.2	4.6	5.9
End FG inventory	15.7	15.8	15.3	14.9	14.5	14.2
Start WIP inventory	7.5	7.6	7.7	7.4	7.1	7.1
+Material issues	3.4	4.2	4.8	3.9	3.5	4.3
+Labor and overhead	0.8	1.0	0.9	0.6	0.7	0.7
−Production @ COGS	4.1	5.1	6.0	4.8	4.2	5.6
End WIP inventory	7.6	7.7	7.4	7.1	7.1	6.5
Start raw inventory	17.0	17.7	17.4	17.6	17.0	16.5
+Material purchases	4.1	3.9	5.0	3.3	3.0	3.8
−Material issues	3.4	4.2	4.8	3.9	3.5	4.3
End raw inventory	17.7	17.4	17.6	17.0	16.5	16.0
Total ending inventory	41.0	40.9	40.3	39.0	38.1	36.7

Table 8.4 Inventory Segmentation—Obsolete Inventory

Number	Obsolete Inventory Drivers
1	Obsolete inventory inherited from a merger
2	Poorly planned product discontinuance
3	Engineering change order
4	Terminated supplier relationship
5	Missing parent–child link in the product structure

Chapter 9

What Information about Inventory Do We Need?

Harmony Team Meeting: September 21

Woodstock Inventory: $34.1 Million

My name is Dinesh, and I am vice president of information tech-
nology for Woodstock Lighting Group.

We get blamed for everything. Just because we have the latest in Enterprise
Resource Planning (ERP) software, everyone thinks our problems should
have gone away. I'm really getting tired of it. The users don't understand
that the system is only as good as the data going into the system. What's
that old saying: "Garbage in and garbage out."? Well we have plenty of
that going on. What's worse is that Adriana and the other executives view
our group as an expense, rather than a company asset that can help us
strategically and tactically.

I've been around the IT industry a long time, going back to the old
mainframe days where all information was centralized. Technology is
changing at a rapid pace, and I have all I can do to keep up with it. I get
a ton of magazines, e-mails, and newsletters about the latest technology,
but who has the time to read all that stuff? It seems like as soon as we have
installed the latest version of some technology, the suppliers are announcing
a new version. I'm buried. We are also having difficulty keeping these new

young people interested in what we are doing at Woodstock. IT has the worst turnover in the company.

My people are constantly asking me to go to management to get additional funding, so they can buy some new gizmo that just came out or attend a seminar on some new tools they think we can use. I just don't have the budget for it. So I'm right in the middle of things. I've got users complaining that we aren't giving them what they need, and I've got my people complaining that we should have more technology. Our major suppliers and customers are light years ahead of us in the use of technology, and if we don't keep up we won't survive.

Now it's inventory. Last year it was forecasting. I wonder how long this focus will last. I'll miss my good friend Joe. Now I don't have anybody to go to lunch with. It's bad enough I have to work with these people all day long, I don't have to eat lunch with them, too. Joe knew how to survive. He would just say yes to everyone and do what he wanted to do anyway. I've tried that, but I'm not in as powerful a position as Joe was. Even though we were both VPs, he controlled a lot more than I do. I don't know if people respected him or were afraid of him. I do know outside of me, he had very few friends here at Woodstock. I miss you, Joe.

Technology has changed dramatically over the years and so has the title of our department. We started out being called the data processing (DP) department, then it was the management information systems group (MIS), and today we are called the information technology (IT) team. Even though our name has changed we continue to perform the role of "keepers of the information," or should I say, "keepers of the data"? There is a difference between information and data, which I will explain as we discuss our role and responsibility in the supply chain.

Role and Responsibilities

Timely Movement of Data

Our supply chain is large in terms of geography and the number of users we support. In fact, if you count our employee automated attendance reporting system, everyone in the company is a user of our systems. Although the plant and distribution centers move product through our supply chain, we move data through our supply chain. Our customers are all users, upstream and downstream. We go as far as the extended supply chain, with the furthest users upstream being some of our key suppliers who we interact with (integrated systems) and the furthest upstream users being our customers (distributors), and in many cases, our customers — customers who interact with our sales and service teams.

Internet Technology Provider

We ensure that our entire supply chain has access to our systems through our data integration services. This includes the capability to enter customer orders and supplier orders, customer returns, and complaints. This Internet technology allows people to reach us from anywhere in the world, 24 hours a day, 365 days a year. Our responsibility is to ensure system access, security, and data integrity.

Supply-Chain Coordination

We coordinate data movement through the integration of various systems that allow for the downloading and uploading of data to each link in our internal supply chain, as well as to specified external links in our supply chain. This coordination revolves around predetermined schedules and sequences of data movement. The objective is to provide all members of our supply chain with the same information. Unfortunately, inventory data resides in several separate systems, and we have some difficulty keeping the inventory data in sync.

Real-Time Data

The Internet availability on a global basis requires that we move data on a real-time basis so that records are updated as transactions occur. When a customer order is entered, the inventory records must be immediately updated so that duplicate allocations do not distort the inventory availability records. This is a challenge for us. Not all of our applications run in real time. Some are batch updated at the end of the business day. So during the period of time before the batch update, the inventory records are out of sync.

Conversion of Data into Information

Some of our systems convert the data into report formats, but in many cases our end users can compile their own reports using data downloaded from our various applications. This becomes a particular challenge when they download inventory information. For example, if planning, manufacturing, sales, and distribution attend a meeting on inventory management at 10 A.M., they will go to the application they use most frequently to get their individual information. Well, at 10 A.M. our inventory tracking systems are not in sync and everyone goes to the meeting armed with different inventory information. This causes chaos and inevitably a heated debate follows about whose data is the most accurate.

> **TIP #125:** *When dealing with multiple inventory systems in your supply chain, you must identify which one is the primary inventory reporting system for the entire supply chain.*

(Note: TIP = team important point.)

Provide Information for Strategic Planning

Our management team uses the data in our systems to make plans that support the company's long range goals and objectives. For example, it uses historical data going back several years, along with current forecasts of supply and demand to develop our sales and operations plan, which was previously discussed by Rudy.

Provide Information for Tactical Planning

Information is provided to each link in our supply chain to generate, monitor, and report activities that support the strategic plans of the company. Information (data) must be synchronized and aggregated on a timely basis so that all supply-chain plans (tactical and strategic) support the company's goals and objectives. An example of this would be the financial budgets of each link in our supply chain.

Provide Information for Operational Planning and Execution

While the focus of strategic and tactical data is on analysis of data, the focus on operational data is on transaction reporting. In most cases our end users are responsible for the input of transactions, and we provide the computer programs that update the inventory records. For example, the planning department provides planning data for our MRP program (lead times, MPS, and lot sizes) and the engineering department provides BOM data. Our system takes that data and runs it through our MRP application and provides a basic report of "action notices."

> **TIP #126:** *The timing of inventory transaction reporting into the system is critical to maintaining accurate inventory records.*

Let me put it all together into one inventory-related example. From a strategic viewpoint, inventory for our flashlight division has a make-to-stock inventory strategy. That is, we buy raw materials, manufacture the flashlights, and put them into inventory. Our ERP system keeps track of the inventory to see if it matches our strategic plan (raw material or finished goods). As you heard previously, the flashlight inventory was positioned correctly from a strategic viewpoint.

From a tactical viewpoint, flashlight inventory is located at our distribution centers, our main plant, and some 3PLs. Our system monitors inventory at each of those locations, and our database keeps track of the separate inventory locations.

From an operational point of view, as transactions occur (orders and shipments), the inventory records at each location are updated and reported to our central inventory system, located here in New Jersey. So, in summary, we keep track of inventory at all three planning levels.

> **TIP #127:** *Although inventory reporting may be tracked separately for different supply-chain links, it should be aggregated into one system to monitor performance against company strategic and tactical plans.*

Data Warehousing

Our IT infrastructure consists of six different legacy systems, each purchased and implemented over the course of many years. This patchwork of six different databases is held together with a series of interface programs as depicted in Figure 9.1. These six legacy systems are defined as:

1. General accounting: Our oldest system. Performs general accounting functions such as general ledger, accounts payable, and accounts receivable. Interfaces with 2 and 5.
2. Purchasing: Purchasing department bought this stand-alone system to aid it in its purchasing functions. Interfaces with 1 only.
3. Computer-aided design: Stand-alone system; doesn't interface with others.
4. MRP II system: Used mostly for MRP; interfaces with 5 and 6.
5. Warehouse management system: Used by distribution centers for inventory management. Interfaces with 1, 4, and 6.
6. Forecasting system: Used for demand planning; interfaces with 4 and 5 only.

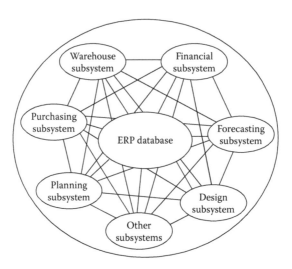

Figure 9.1 Woodstock system architecture.

Our most recent purchase is our ERP system, which will be the primary inventory system for our company. This will be our data warehouse where we will combine the data from these other legacy systems. This primary data warehouse will be the location of data for analysis, while the other databases will be used for reporting transactions in real time, which will be sent to the main data warehouse for updating the database once every hour. Our goal is to do this in real time some day.

We want this interaction between systems to be as seamless as possible so that all our supply-chain links can function without system interruption. Equally important is the timing of the information. Our supply chain must be able to respond to change quickly. We don't do this well today. It sometimes takes days for data to be transformed into meaningful information. I have proposed to Adriana that we move toward one centralized system for transaction reporting. Having one centralized inventory system will greatly enhance our ability to "rightsize" our inventory.

> **TIP #128:** *Inventory must be reported by its current location in your supply chain, so that you can effectively rightsize your inventory across supply-chain links.*

Objectives of Information Technology Inventory Management

- Collecting inventory transactions from each link in the supply chain

- Ensuring the synchronization of inventory data across supply-chain links
- Reducing or eliminating time lapses of inventory transactions
- Providing tools for the analyzing of inventory data
- Ensuring the integrity and security of inventory information
- Providing timely access of inventory information to all internal and external supply-chain links
- To some degree IT is responsible for inventory accuracy — in the sense that once reported, the data is maintained accurately. The accuracy of the data itself is the responsibility of the appropriate supply-chain link, which is charged with the inventory accountability.

> **TIP #129:** *Information technology is responsible for inventory data integrity once it is reported to the system. However, the actual transactions of inventory movement (physical movement) are the responsibility of the appropriate supply-chain link.*

Enterprise Resource Planning (ERP)

ERP can be defined as an application software suite, consisting of modules related to various business processes, which can be used as one common source of data storage and transaction processing. There was a time when there were literally hundreds of software vendors (suppliers) competing for the opportunity to sell their software (then called manufacturing resource planning [MRP II]) to manufacturers and distributors. The field of competitors has since narrowed to a few major vendors.

ERP systems offer the user the capability to plan at the strategic, tactical, and operational level. These systems are huge in the sense that they offer packaged solutions to most of the links in our supply chain. The company has the ability to pick and choose which modules are right. ERP systems are also available by industry-specific applications, using the terminology and applications unique to a specific industry classification (Standard Industry Classification [SIC] code). These systems allow you to conduct "what if" simulations. You can input certain data scenarios (without impacting the actual system data) to evaluate certain cause-and-effect situations. These ERP system models have been built on the basis of years of use and experience.

When we purchased our ERP system I made a silent commitment not to make major modifications to the software. I strongly believed (and still do) that we would benefit from the pure vanilla (as is, no changes) system. In time, after we truly understand the system, then we can look at changes, if they are warranted.

ERP systems impact inventory management in many ways. Here are some examples:

- **Finance and accounting.** General accounting of inventory transactions for accounts payable, accounts receivable, and the general ledger. Financial analysis and financial management of inventory assets.
- **Engineering.** Inventory BOM information and inventory routing, work center, and cost data.
- **Materials management.** Inventory planning and purchasing information.
- **Sales and marketing.** Inventory forecasting, sales history, customer master data.
- **Distribution.** Finished goods inventory levels and locations.
- **Manufacturing.** Raw material inventory levels and locations, WIP inventory tracking.
- **Service department.** Inventory levels, locations, and costs, BOM information.
- **Maintenance department.** Spare parts inventory levels and location. Spare parts supplier information.

> **TIP #130:** *Do not attempt to modify or customize the inventory management applications within your ERP system until you truly identify a real need to change it.*

As you can see, ERP systems have something related to inventory for all links in our supply chain. An argument can be made that human resources has a need for managing inventory also. After all, it manages our most important inventory asset — our employees.

Supply-Chain Management Systems

Software gaining popularity beyond ERP systems is supply-chain management software. This is sometimes referred to as supply-chain event management (SCEM) or supply-chain process management (SCPM). This software allows you to perform simulations and respond rapidly (if you have your act together) to unplanned events such as impact orders. Impact orders are orders not originally planned for that have the potential to disrupt the supply chain. It allows you to track inventory from raw material to finished goods through each link in your supply chain. The system will advise you when inventory is outside established inventory guidelines. By utilizing this built-in warning system, your supply chain can quickly collaborate to reduce the risk of inventory stockouts. This visibility occurs in a real-time dynamic mode so there are no surprises down the road. Suppliers, 3PLs, and your own plant will be able to adjust inventory levels more rapidly than the traditional approach of replacing inventory. I envision this software to gain in popularity. However, we at Woodstock have a long way to go before we consider using it.

Other Tools and Technologies

Bar Coding

This is a label applied to a part or package that is machine readable (usually scanned) and identifies the inventory item. You see these on products all the time during the course of your daily life. We are currently using bar-code labels on the cartons and the inventory package but not on the actual flashlights. At the present time we don't see the need to have the item itself bar coded, as the packaged flashlight is our finished product. We are also going to put bar codes on our work orders issued to the factory floor. The major benefits to us related to inventory management are that we can speed up data entry and accurately record inventory and work order movement. There will be far less inventory transaction errors when we bar code all inventory in our supply chain. This is a personal goal of mine.

Radio Frequency Identification (RFID)

RFID is a technology I would really like to use at Woodstock some day. Essentially, a smart chip is placed on the inventory item, which sends a signal that is picked up by a device that reads the item information embedded in the chip. Unlike bar coding, where you have to find the label to scan it, these devices can read the signal even if it's not visible. This will be great in the supermarket, too. We will no longer have to lift up that case of water or soda so that the checkout clerk can find the bar code and then scan it. You can track full loads of inventory that are in transit somewhere in our supply chain. This is a great thing. Again, this is a useful technology that will help us rightsize our inventory some day, but like some of the other technologies I've spoken about, we are not there yet. We need to get the basics down first.

> **TIP #131:** *Do not attempt to implement sophisticated technologies to help you rightsize your inventory until*

you have built a basic foundation of inventory management processes and procedures.

Electronic Data Interchange (EDI) and Electronic Data Transfer (EDT)

Essentially, this is the transfer of information via electronic means. There was a time when this required proprietary software, and customer orders, invoices, and shipping notices were sent this way. Today this has become a more open environment due to the advent of the Internet for such purposes. Wireless services have enhanced the use of this service even further. Virtually anyone, anywhere in the world, can electronically (if they have access) send and receive inventory information instantaneously. Of course, this is good and bad. Good in the sense that your inventory records are accurate and time sensitive — bad, if they are not. I don't have to point out which side of the coin we fall on, do I?

E-Business and E-Commerce

Internet technology has enabled Woodstock to sell our inventory to a broad base of customers around the world. This practice of electronic communication provides a business model where customers can obtain information about our products, order, and pay for them in a matter of minutes and in a cost-effective way. This business model also extends upstream where we can use the same model when dealing with our suppliers. The benefits of Internet technology allow us to reach a larger marketplace in a timely, cost-effective manner. We need to expand the use of this technology and leverage it as part of our corporate strategy. Equally important to us and our customers, the Internet allows us to communicate information at all levels and through all links in our supply chain.

Woodstock Web Site

We have been working with Rudy and Adriana to enhance our Web site with an online catalog offering our products (flashlights and residential spotlights) directly to the general public. Of course, it isn't realistic to expect someone to buy a flashlight valued at $2.59 (plus shipping and handling) over the Internet. We are focusing the catalog on the high-end (cost) spotlights for homes, and we will include some of our unique flashlights such as our batteryless flashlight, lanterns with remotes, walking stick lights, crank lights, and glow-in-the-dark flashlights.

Our strategy is that the consumer will buy our spotlights directly from us rather than a distributor. At the same time, we hope to attract those buyers who perceive the value-added uniqueness of our flashlights. We are currently conducting an analysis to determine the impact on our current sales model of selling directly to distributors. We need to determine whether we are just shifting the same sale from one selling model to another or whether we will obtain new customers through this new sales channel.

> **TIP: #132:** *Buying and selling inventory (products) over the Internet (through a Web site) can speed up the sales cycle, increase sales, and increase inventory turnover, but there are pitfalls to overcome.*

Our e-business strategy must go beyond just offering our products for sale through our Web site. It should include a tactical strategy of communicating with our extended supply chain: our customers and suppliers. Through our CRM and SRM strategies we hope to improve the flow of information through our entire supply chain. Our challenge is to replace inventory with information. If we can do that, we will have a positive impact on our inventory rightsizing efforts.

> **TIP #133:** *Replacing inventory with information will greatly enhance the opportunity to rightsize your inventory.*

Project Management

We have learned the hard way that when we (IT) are put in charge of an end-user application implementation, it typically fails to be implemented successfully. It is perceived as an "IT project," and the end users don't take ownership of it. Our end users have many daily chores and tasks on their plate and will focus their attention on those tasks that they are measured and rewarded on. Our initial MRP implementation is a good example. It took us over two years to implement, and we had many problems. Everyone blamed IT for the failure. We finally recognized our mistake and put Cyndie in charge of the project. It went fairly smoothly from then on.

> **TIP #134:** *Application software implementations should be managed by the supply-chain link most impacted by the application.*

I see that my time is up. I would like to leave you with a few comments. Our technology team should be considered a strategic asset to the company rather than a "cost of doing business." We can help the company by providing data and information that will strategically and tactically position Woodstock to become a world-class company. We impact every link in our supply chain and believe we can play an important role in our company's inventory rightsizing efforts.

Thank you for your time.

Inter-Office E-Mail

To: Supply-Chain Managers   September 21
From: Harmony Team
Subject: Rightsizing Inventory
Current Inventory: $34.1 Million

We continue to rightsize our inventory, thanks to all of you. You will note from above and Table 9.1 that inventory was down to $34.1 million by the end of August, and as we approach the end of September the downward trend continues. Customer orders in August actually exceeded the forecast by a small amount and all three categories of inventory went down for the month. This is due to all the things we have learned and executed since the first of the year. Not only is inventory being reduced, it is also being shifted in our supply chain to match our company strategy. We met today with Dinesh from our information technology team and learned many things that will help us as we further attempt to rightsize our inventory. What follows is a summary of that meeting, followed by our latest version of our inventory rightsizing model as depicted in Figure 9.2. The details of the meeting will follow in the minutes, which will be published shortly:

1. There is a difference between data and information. We gather statistics and other important pieces of data and store it in our database. This data is then extracted from the database and converted into information in the form of reports and documents for analytical purposes.
2. Every employee in our supply chain uses our IT services in one form or another.

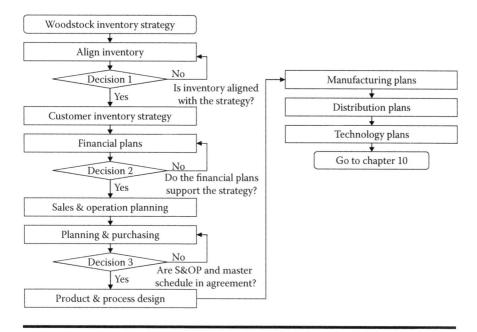

Figure 9.2   Woodstock inventory rightsizing model.

3. While manufacturing and distribution move product through our supply chain, IT moves data and information.

4. IT interacts with our extended supply chain, which includes customers and suppliers, and in some cases our supplier's suppliers, and our customer's customers.

5. Because of our Internet capability we are able to communicate with our supply-chain partners anywhere in the world, 24 hours a day, 365 days per year.

6. IT is responsible for ensuring system access, security, and data integrity.

7. IT coordinates and synchronizes the timely movement of inventory data through our supply chain.

8. It has been decided that our ERP system will be the primary and official record of our inventory status.

9. IT provides services and technology that help us achieve our strategic, tactical, and operational objectives.

10. Inventory data is stored in our "data warehouse" and can be extracted by end users for various inventory reporting.

11. IT is only accountable for inventory accuracy once it has been entered into the system. End users are responsible for the accuracy of the physical and book inventory transactions themselves.
12. No changes (modifications) will be made to any of our packaged application solutions until we truly understand how the software works; even then changes must be justified.
13. IT is looking into the next level of supply-chain software that will help us react to unplanned inventory changes by alerting us when inventory levels are outside stated parameters.
14. We are going to extend the use of bar codes in our company, and this will enhance our inventory-reporting accuracy.
15. We have decided that while RFID is an excellent technology, we have a long way to go before we can consider using it.
16. We are using EDI and EDT. They are working well for us by eliminating the need to pass paper back and forth. On the other hand, we are struggling to improve our inventory accuracy so the inventory information we pass back and forth will have more meaning.
17. IT announced that our Web site may soon include a sales catalog offering our spotlights and unique flashlights to the general public. This will be dependent on the analysis now being conducted by sales and marketing to determine if this will attract new business or if we will be taking business away from our distributors.
18. It has been decided that IT will no longer be the project leader on end-user application implementations. It will, however, continue in the role of facilitator, ensuring that the technology is used correctly.
19. IT should be considered as an asset to Woodstock. It should play a greater role in the development and implementation of technologies that will help Woodstock achieve its strategic, tactical, and operational objectives throughout our entire extended supply chain.

> If you have any questions, suggestions, or comments, please do not hesitate to contact any member of the Harmony Team. Our next meeting will be a joint meeting with maintenance, facilities management, field service, and human resources. We look forward to sharing their thoughts with you and your teams.

Applying the Tips, Tools, and Philosophies to Your Company

The reader will notice that the volume of pages in this chapter is the smallest thus far. This does not imply that IT is less important than the other links previously discussed. On the contrary, IT is on par with all other links in the supply chain. IT is such an integral link and so tightly woven with the other links that it is difficult to set it apart as a separate link. Much of the detail about its role in the supply chain has already been covered in other chapters. I do believe IT warrants a separate chapter. Without the IT link providing timely data and information, your company's ability to react to changing market conditions will be compromised and your inventory rightsizing efforts will suffer.

I have added ten more TIPs for you to use in this chapter. The following discussion will review these TIPs and how they can be applied successfully in your company.

> **TIP #125:** *When dealing with multiple inventory systems in your supply chain, you must identify which one is the primary inventory reporting system for the entire supply chain.*

When new technology is implemented, such as ERP systems, many end users still find the need to keep their legacy systems because they still find them useful and choose not to replace them for one reason or another. For some, it is just a question of time before they get rid of it. While legacy systems can run alongside your new ERP system, there will be a need for redundant data and information. Inventory data is one such example.

It is not uncommon to see inventory residing in an old MRP II system, a warehouse management system, and a demand planning system. The challenge is to keep all these redundant inventory systems in sync, hopefully for only a short period of time. But for some companies it is a new way of life, and the redundancy isn't going to go away.

When dealing with such redundancy:

1. Choose one application that will be the "primary" and "official" data warehouse for all company inventory data.
2. Establish detailed schedules of when this system will be updated with inventory transactions from other inventory systems in your supply chain.
3. Advise all links in your supply chain (extended supply chain) when the inventory records will be updated, so that everyone who has access to the data understands what the updated inventory record does and does not include.
4. Pay particular attention to inventory being offered for sale through an online ordering system (such as a Web site or sales entering orders from the field). These transactions may need to be updated in real time (as the transactions occur). You don't want to be in the position of "double selling" your inventory. Some companies I have done work for wish they had this problem to deal with.

> **TIP #126: *The timing of inventory transaction reporting into the system is critical to maintaining accurate inventory records.***

TIP #125 dealt with the timing of information and data that was exposed in a real-time environment with the extended supply chain. TIP #126 focuses on the routine, daily internal transactions that may be updated in real time or, in some cases, updated in a batch mode. A batch mode is when transactions are accumulated (batch) and on a predetermined schedule sent to the data warehouse to update the records.

What you have to be careful of here is that when reviewing the status of an inventory item, you understand that the inventory balance you are looking at may not be correct, because there are a "batch" of transactions against that inventory item waiting to process that will change the balance. You have to look at the (clock) timing of your inquiry to see if you have the latest information.

In a complex supply chain with multiple plants, warehouses, distribution centers, and 3/4 PLs, all inventory transactions must be synchronized. If the technology is available to update inventory records in real time, and the need to do so exists, do it.

> **TIP #127: *While inventory reporting may be tracked separately for different supply-chain links, it should be aggre-***

gated into one system to monitor performance against company strategic and tactical plans.

This TIP doesn't focus on the timing of inventory transactions but rather the aggregation of information into one system for centralized company reporting. At some point in time, corporate inventory performance metrics require aggregate inventory information. For example, finance will require the dollar value of the total inventory, and inventory management, for planning and operational purposes, requires that total units be reported. Inventory should also be aggregated by category: raw material, WIP, and finished goods. If you already have this data in one data warehouse, that's fine. If not, it should be.

Performance metrics dashboards are typically aggregated for management so that it can see at a glance the status of inventory all rolled up into a few numbers. This requires that you find a way of feeding this data directly onto computer screens. This can be accomplished by feeding information through a series of interfaces from various systems or feeding directly from the data warehouse of choice for the entire company. The former will work, but the latter is a more effective approach.

TIP #128: *Inventory must be reported by its current location in your supply chain so that you can effectively right-size your inventory across supply-chain links.*

This TIP deals with the movement of inventory through your supply chain, link by link. Inventory may be tracked through:

1. Raw material receipt
2. Raw material inspection (if required)
3. Raw material storage location
4. Raw material movement to your gateway work center (first operation at the first work center)
5. WIP inventory through operations and work centers. Some industries will not find this a necessary step, particularly if the operation times are short — usually if less than eight hours.
6. WIP completed
7. Finished goods to warehouse
8. Finished goods to final assembly (or packaging)
9. Finished goods to distribution center or warehouse
10. Finished goods to transportation company
11. Finished goods to customer

Not all companies will find the need for tracking inventory through all the steps mentioned here. However, it is important for all companies to know when a raw material arrives (step 1) and when it is shipped (steps 10 and 11). The rest are dependent on your need for the information. For example, planning and purchasing may require inventory item (by location) information on a daily basis, and executive management may require aggregate inventory (by location) on a monthly or quarterly basis.

To determine how often to report inventory by location, you have to answer two questions:

1. What is our need to capture information?
2. What is the cost and effort required to capture the information?

Of course, the need to capture information may win out over the cost to capture it. So cost might be a moot point. At the very least, you have to capture the inventory coming into your supply chain and the inventory going out of your supply chain. Keep in mind we are speaking about capturing information in units for operations and dollars for finance.

> **TIP #129:** *Information technology is responsible for inventory data integrity once it is reported to the system. However, the actual transactions of inventory movement (physical movement) are the responsibility of the appropriate supply-chain link.*

Inventory accuracy should be viewed from two perspectives: the reporting of the item as it moves through the supply chain and the integrity of the item information as it is accepted by the system and as it resides in the system. Inventory management systems have been around a long time and formulas are not rocket science.

However, a 7 and a 9 being misread by the person doing manual data entry will still be accepted by the system. The result will be inaccurate information being reported to the system. Is that the responsibility of IT? I don't think so. If you have two part numbers where all digits are similar except for that misread 7 instead of a 9, you are going to have accuracy problems, but the integrity of the data once reported will be fine. It will perform the mathematical equations exactly as programmed.

Cycle counting and bar coding will greatly enhance your data accuracy, but at any point in the transaction where you have human input to the data, you have to be careful. That is why we stress getting to the root cause of why an inventory record is inaccurate. I have seen many sophisticated and state-of-the-art inventory systems fail because an operator wrote down the wrong quantity on a work order. It can happen to the best. The challenge is to keep it to a minimum.

TIP #130: *Do not attempt to modify or customize the inventory management applications within your ERP system until you truly identify a real need to change it.*

Modifying your ERP system is fraught with problems:

- The cost to modify the system could be significant.
- The time it will take to modify the system could be significant.
- You may be modifying the system to do what you did in the past, but is what you did in the past the best way?
- The software supplier may not support the software once you modify it.
- If you don't document the changes you will have future problems.
- Upgrading to the next release of the software will be difficult or impossible.
- If (when) the person who did the modifications leaves, you've got problems.
- If you have other systems that the modified ERP system has to interact with, you will have issues to deal with when those other systems are upgraded.
- If the software supplier modified the system and it goes out of business or stops supporting the software, you will have problems.

So, you can see you really need to think twice (or ten times) before you decide to modify the system. Knowing all this, why do so many companies do it anyway? It's a good question, and I wish I had a good answer for you. When I ask this question, I usually get two answers:

- "Our business is unique, we are different."
- "The vanilla system doesn't satisfy the requirements of our ... link."

When buying a new ERP system I would suggest:

1. Look at industry-specific software. Many software suppliers have taken their vanilla system and modified it to fit specific industry niches. If they have done the modifications, it now becomes a standard software package for you.
2. Ask the supplier to put you in contact with their customers who are in a similar business and are using the vanilla system or their industry-specific system. Talk with them, visit with them.
3. Ask how the new software has helped them rightsize their inventory.

> **TIP #131:** *Do not attempt to implement sophisticated technologies to help you rightsize your inventory until you have built a basic foundation of inventory management processes and procedures.*

There is an old saying that goes something like this, "Continuing to do things the same old way and expecting different results is foolish," or words to that effect. If you have a poor foundation of managing inventory, don't expect your ERP inventory system to help you. On the contrary, you can expect to receive inaccurate information even faster than you did before.

Before implementing a new ERP system, look at your current method of processing inventory information:

1. Understand the requirements of all links in your supply chain.
2. Conduct a requirements definition.
3. Map the current inventory information flows.
4. Compare the results with the new ERP system to ensure that all requirements of the links have been covered.
5. If a current process is not covered by the new ERP software, see if the process can be eliminated.
6. If not, see if you can work around it.
7. Document the new way you will handle inventory transactions.
8. Get everyone's buy in.
9. Communicate the new inventory transaction foundation to all supply-chain links.
10. Having done that, you are now ready to implement the new ERP system, as is.
11. Work with it as is (pure vanilla) for at least six months so that everyone has had a chance to evaluate it.
12. Necessary modifications must be justified before making changes.

Of course, you may determine that modifications are necessary before you even begin. Although I don't usually recommend modifying the software, I do understand there are situations where it is necessary. You must understand the risks I pointed out earlier.

> **TIP: #132:** *Buying and selling inventory (products) over the Internet (through a Web site) can speed up the sales cycle, increase sales and increase inventory turnover, but there are pitfalls to overcome.*

The Internet has and will continue to redefine the way products are sold and move through your supply chain. If you are venturing out into this brave new world beware:

1. You must have visibility of your entire supply chain inventory (upstream and downstream).
2. Inventory transactions must be recorded accurately and in a timely fashion.
3. Your supply chain must be flexible and respond to change rapidly.
4. Inventory performance benchmarks and metrics must reflect these attributes.
5. You must have open communications throughout the entire extended supply chain.
6. Procedures and systems must be in place to handle both forward and reverse logistics.

Don't open your company up to this highly visible environment until you have addressed these six points to your satisfaction. If you don't overcome these pitfalls you're flirting with disaster and you could quickly lose any competitive advantage the Internet has to offer.

TIP #133: *Replacing inventory with information will greatly enhance the opportunity to rightsize your inventory.*

More isn't necessarily better when it comes to information. In fact, many system end users are on information overload. They get so many e-mails, memos and reports, it's almost impossible to dissect them on a daily basis. What happens is they will put it in a folder "to be read later" and never get back to it. The key to this TIP is getting a reasonable quantity of quality information to make inventory management decisions.

For example, if you don't have time to read all the information sent to you, then you surely won't have the time to analyze it. You may miss a key inventory figure or trend that would have caused you not to make a particular part for inventory because it wasn't needed. If you had the right information at the right time, then you could have reduced or eliminated the need for inventory. This is what I meant when I said information can replace inventory in your supply chain.

I once had a boss who used to send out a particular inventory report at the end of every month to almost everybody in the company. This was in the days when the only computer reports we got were on the old "green bar" paper. He had IT (the data processing department in those days) print out a slew of these reports, using up at least one full box of paper. One day he decided not to send out the report anymore just to see if anyone missed it. Low and behold he only heard from about 5 people out of the 30 or so who got the report. What is the moral of the story?

1. Identify what information the other links in your supply chain need from you.
2. Ask them how they are using the information in the report so that you might be able to enhance it.
3. Hard copy reports are passé.
4. Don't send out reports as an e-mail attachment if you have a company intranet.
5. Advise all supply-chain links where to find the information on the company intranet site.

> **TIP #134: Application software implementations should be managed by the supply-chain link most impacted by the application.**

I find that successful application software implementations are led by the end user most responsible for the functionality of the application. Although I must admit one of the most successful implementations I ever worked on had coproject leaders, one person from IT and one person from the end-user link. In this case it was an MRP implementation and the coleader was the director of materials management. As a general rule, IT should not be the project leader for an end-user application. If IT leads the project I have found:

■ The end users will not take responsibility for it.
■ It will be perceived as an IT system.
■ IT will have difficulty getting the end users involved due to other work commitments and other motivational factors, such as personal performance measures and department goals and objectives.

The end users are best skilled (or should be) to deal with the requirements of their link in the supply chain. After all, who should know the needs of the link best? Getting the end users to head up the project has the following advantages:

■ They know what their needs are better than any other link.
■ If it is part of their annual performance goals and objectives, they are motivated to get it to work successfully.

- As they interact with other links in the chain they will have a greater understanding of the implementation impact on the other links.
- They can provide the knowledge experts for particular operational functionality.

However, that doesn't mean that IT staff shouldn't be involved. On the contrary, the system won't work without them. They also know all the technical aspects of implementing the new technology, certainly not a job for the novice. IT should play the role of facilitator and act as an internal consultant on the project. Of course, it also goes without saying that the software supplier will also play an important role in the implementation.

Is the project leader role a full-time job? That depends on the complexity of the software and the size of the company. In large companies, it is typically a full-time job for some defined period of time. For example, I have seen high director-level personnel taken out of their daily job for 12 to 18 months to head up a project with the guarantee that when the project is over they will be placed in a position equal to or greater than the position they held before the implementation. They literally are moved out of their office — in some cases moved to another building.

Many small companies can't afford the luxury of having a full-time project leader. In most cases it is a part-time job while they are still performing the daily tasks. These implementations are usually less complex, and the number of people they have to interact with in the other links is somewhat less, too. That doesn't mean it's any easier to implement. In fact, if ERP is a new tool they have never used before, it can be a greater challenge than the large company has.

Who should be in charge of the inventory management functionality of the ERP implementation? After all, I have repeatedly stated that all links are responsible for managing inventory. The answer is that there will be different project leaders for different functionality of the system. For example, finance should be in charge of the inventory accounting applications, engineering for the BOM applications, purchasing for the purchasing applications, and planning for the MRP applications.

Regardless of who is in charge, it should be a cross-functional team working on the inventory application. As inventory touches all links in the supply chain, all links should be involved. The knowledge experts from these links can be called upon as needed. For large companies, these too will be full-time temporary positions.

Table 9.1 reflects the most current Woodstock inventory balances, and Table 9.2 shows the finished goods inventory turns based on the estimated annual cost of goods sold (COGS).

Table 9.1 Inventory Balance (×1,000,000)

Month end	31 Jan	28 Feb	31 Mar	30 Apr	31 May	30 Jun	31 Jul	31 Aug	30 Sep
Forecast	7.2	7.9	9.7	7.1	5.9	9.0	9.3	8.7	7.0
Orders	5.8	7.4	9.6	7.7	6.8	8.8	7.7	8.8	8.0
Total starting inventory	40.0	41.0	40.9	40.3	39.0	38.1	36.7	35.7	34.1
Start FG inventory	15.5	15.7	15.8	15.3	14.9	14.5	14.2	13.7	13.0
+Production @ COGS	4.1	5.1	6.0	4.8	4.2	5.6	4.7	5.2	5.5
−Shipments @ COGS	3.9	5.0	6.5	5.2	4.6	5.9	5.2	5.9	5.4
End FG inventory	15.7	15.8	15.3	14.9	14.5	14.2	13.7	13.0	13.1
Start WIP inventory	7.5	7.6	7.7	7.4	7.1	7.1	6.5	6.2	5.9
+Material issues	3.4	4.2	4.8	3.9	3.5	4.3	3.8	4.3	4.2
+Labor and overhead	0.8	1.0	0.9	0.6	0.7	0.7	0.6	0.6	0.9
−Production @ COGS	4.1	5.1	6.0	4.8	4.2	5.6	4.7	5.2	5.5
End WIP inventory	7.6	7.7	7.4	7.1	7.1	6.5	6.2	5.9	5.5
Start Raw inventory	17.0	17.7	17.4	17.6	17.0	16.5	16.0	15.8	15.2
+Material purchases	4.1	3.9	5.0	3.3	3.0	3.8	3.6	3.7	3.5
−Material issues	3.4	4.2	4.8	3.9	3.5	4.3	3.8	4.3	4.2
End raw inventory	17.7	17.4	17.6	17.0	16.5	16.0	15.8	15.2	14.5
Total ending inventory	41.0	40.9	40.3	39.0	38.1	36.7	35.7	34.1	33.1

Table 9.2   Woodstock FG Inventory Turns Improvement

Month end	31 Dec	31 Mar	30 Jun	30 Sep	
Inventory turns	4.3	4.3	4.6	5.0	
End FG inventory ($M)	15.5	15.3	14.2	13.1	
Annual COGS ($M)					66.0

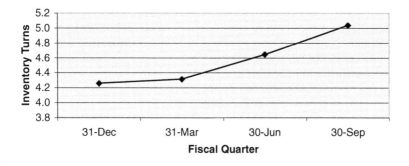

Chapter 10

The Unsung Heroes of Inventory Management

Harmony Team Meeting: October 31

Woodstock Inventory: $31.6 Million

Field Service

My name is James and I am the field service manager for Woodstock Lighting Group.

It's about time they figured out that field service can contribute to our inventory rightsizing effort. I've been waiting all year for them to call me in to discuss inventory. I was so mad I had a good mind to tell them to go pound salt. We should have been one of the first links they spoke with. Oh, well, I'm here now, and I will show them how much we are involved with inventory.

My girlfriend Louise tells me all the time that I should just quit and get on with my life. But I can't. I've made so many friends around the world that depend on me and my team. I enjoy working with the lighthouse managers. They are a unique breed and I find their stories and tales fascinating. There aren't too many of us left that understand the workings of a lighthouse. What am I going to do if I leave here? Service copy machines? How exciting is that? Although it is a noble career, it just doesn't have that sea coast aura and intrigue. Oh, well, I'm not going to quit. I like my boss Rudy, I have a great staff, and I've been all over the world. How many people can say that?

Even though we don't manage a large amount of inventory (less than $100,000), we can have a positive impact on our companywide inventory rightsizing effort. We interact on a daily basis with virtually every link in our supply chain. I have proposed to Rudy and Adriana that we expand our field service role to include the Spotlight Division. Some of our huge spotlights are leased/rented out for special events, like store openings, pep rallies, and the like. We are in the process of investigating it further and if approved, we should be in operation about a year from now.

Role and Responsibilities

Spare Parts Sales

We are a profit center and sell **inventory,** at a profit, to lighthouses around the world. Although the sales of new lighthouse systems have been declining over the years, our spare parts business has been rather steady with marginal increases each year. We have a sales forecast and we have achieved our sales goal for five years in a row.

Service Sales

We physically install roughly 25 percent of the **inventory** we sell. The other 75 percent of inventory sold is installed by the lighthouse itself or its designated third party. We also make money on providing consulting and maintenance services to lighthouses to enhance/upgrade their system. It doesn't have to be a Woodstock light system; we also service and maintain competitor systems. Around 35 percent of our lighthouse customers have service/warranty contracts with us. Some of the services we provide are covered under warranty, but many are not.

Interaction with Other Links in the Supply Chain

Sales and Marketing

Our three field service representatives and our two customer service representatives are speaking with or visiting with customers every day. In most cases (within the Beacon Light Division), we speak with the customers more than sales does. We have great insight into what customers' needs and problems are. We know when they expect to place orders, we can predict when the system will need servicing, and we sometimes know when they are planning to replace an existing lighthouse with a new one. All this information can be made available to our CRM folks. Although we don't expect to sell flashlights to them (at least not directly), there is the potential to sell some of our spotlights for use along the shoreline or for emergency purposes.

> **TIP #135:** *If you have a field service division, get it involved in your inventory rightsizing efforts; it has a lot to contribute.*

(Note: TIP = team important point.)

Product Design

We work with our product design link on the design of new products and the enhancements to existing products. Last year we came up with a new light reflector design that the company has applied for a patent on. Just last week I met with Michael about eliminating three parts from our new lantern light. This inventory reduction will reduce the lantern cost by 20 cents per lantern, a substantial savings. We are in the process of reviewing all of our existing flashlight and spotlight products (along with our beacon lights, which we constantly do) to see if we can apply the things we have learned from our customers to further reduce the number of parts in our products. This will help with our inventory rightsizing efforts.

Process Design

We are also working with our industrial engineers to see if we can improve the manufacturing process on beacon lights. Some of our customers have come up with ideas that we would like to apply here at Woodstock. For example, we mount an angle shaft, part #111604, to the rotating arm of the light fixture. When the part is installed at the customer site, the angle has to be turned 90° to fit on the armature. We suggested to manufacturing that this part not be attached at the plant. We ship it as a separate part and attach it at the correct angle at the time of installation. This saves manufacturing one operation in a very busy work center. It reduces our manufacturing cost and makes the installation process more efficient. This won't reduce inventory, but in the broader sense it is helping us to rightsize our inventory by having it at the right place at the right time.

TIP #136: *Field Service can help reduce inventory by assisting product design with the reduction of parts in your product.*

Suppliers

We interact with suppliers all the time. We can help each other improve our products so that the relationship is profitable for both of us and at the same time provide the customers with value-added enhancements. Our goal with suppliers is to eliminate parts (inventory) in their product and to use common, standard parts where possible. This, too, will enhance our inventory rightsizing efforts.

Distribution

As you know, we keep a small amount of inventory at depots near the major airports in the country. It is our responsibility to ensure that replacement lights and fixtures are shipped to customers on a moment's notice. We are measured on how well or poorly we do this. For domestic customers, our goal is to deliver product within 48 hours of receipt of the customer order. For international customers, it is within 72 hours of receipt of the customer order. Distribution is a big help with this. It maintains the inventory at the depots and arranges for the shipment. We are going to eliminate the need to carry emergency inventory at the depots and distribution centers.

All field service inventory will be kept at the plant in New Jersey, which is only 30 minutes from Newark Airport. Joe was dead set against doing this, but now that Arnie is in charge, it was one of the first decisions he made.

TIP #137: *Consolidating spare parts inventory into fewer locations can reduce the overall amount of inventory carried, without having a negative impact on customer service.*

Maintenance

Field service also interacts with our own internal maintenance department at our plant in New Jersey. Our personnel are experienced mechanics and can fix just about any machine we have. They help out the maintenance team any time they can. From an inventory perspective, we use quite a few parts that are the same and some that are similar (can be substituted). We are working with maintenance to stock only one inventory of those parts, so that inventory redundancy can be eliminated. This will help us reduce overall inventory (some, not a lot, but every bit helps) and make it easier to plan for and maintain. We are also working with facilities management to see if it carries similar parts in its inventory. You never know until you ask. Now that I think about it, we probably should look at taking a tool inventory. I bet we have a lot of redundancy there also.

> **TIP #138:** *Field service may share resources with other links in your supply chain. By combining resources you may be able to save money and improve operating efficiency.*

Technology Used

We currently use a stand-alone, PC-based application to keep track of our inventory and customer service records (warranty information). It doesn't interface with any of our six legacy systems. The plan is to bring all our information over to the new ERP system within the next six months. Until then, we have to continue bringing paper documents to each link affected by the field service transactions.

Inventory and Field Service

As you can see, we have a significant impact on inventory and interact with many links in our supply chain. When all is said and done, there is some inventory redundancy between maintenance and field service. The real impact on inventory will be on "undesigning" parts from our products, identifying where common parts can replace custom parts, and helping make our manufacturing process more efficient. We know a lot about the customers' inventory needs and problems. We can play an important role in our inventory rightsizing efforts.

Human Resources

My name is Aimee and I am manager of human resources for Woodstock Lighting Group.

I wonder why they asked me to meet with the Harmony Team. What does human resources (HR) have to do with inventory? Maybe they all want to get a bonus, or raise, or some type of award for doing this. I hope not; I'm not authorized to deal with that. Whatever it is — it better be important. I had to get up an hour earlier today so that I could drop Alyssa and Justin off at daycare to get here on time. Why can't they be considerate and schedule these meetings for later in the day?

I have been here for five years and really like the employees a lot. I get a lot of satisfaction out of helping them solve their personal issues related to company business. To be honest, I'm really glad Joe is gone. I had more complaints about him than any other manager in the company. He couldn't get along with anybody, except Dinesh. They were like two peas in a pod. I've actually had people come up to me to say how happy they were to see him go. I think some of them were trying to find out if Joe was fired or quit. I'll never tell.

Role and Responsibilities

As I was on my way to the meeting I was wondering what I could possibly contribute to our inventory rightsizing efforts. Then I got to thinking, I deal with inventory all the time, except my inventory is unique. My inventory is people. If I could use a corny analogy, we bring new people into the company (raw materials), sometimes we have to let people go (excess inventory, poor quality), and we maintain finished goods (satisfied, well-trained employees). Anyway, you get the idea. It's the latter I will focus my talk on.

Interaction with All Supply-Chain Links

We interact with everyone, regardless of what link they work in and what position they hold in the company.

Job Descriptions

We help the supply-chain managers develop job descriptions. Adriana recently told me all future job descriptions will include some role in managing inventory. She wants inventory management embedded into the culture of the company. Each position also includes performance metrics on which an employee's job performance is based. Just so you understand how important our inventory focus is, starting next year, everyone in a particular supply-chain link will share the same performance metrics related to inventory, whether it be inventory turns, inventory levels, inventory stockouts, etc. We are in the process of defining these metrics now with each supply-chain manager.

> **TIP #139:** *Individual performance measures (related to inventory) should be replaced by shared, team-based performance measurements.*

Salary and Benefit Administration

We match up job descriptions with the going salary rate for that position on a geographic basis, along with other job characteristics, such as experience and education. We now ask all prospective employees if they have any experience managing inventory, in any capacity. If so, we note it in their file as an asset to their skill set. Not having experience with inventory is not necessarily a negative attribute (depending on the job), but having experience managing inventory is considered a positive attribute.

Compliance with All Regulatory Agencies

We comply with all federal, state, and local government (and reporting) agencies.

Education and Training

This is where we can be the biggest help with our inventory rightsizing efforts. We are responsible for "Woodstock University," our own internal education and training facility. We develop the education and training programs, hire the instructors, and establish the schedules. Each Woodstock employee is required to have 40 hours of education or training per year. We maintain employee records to see that this happens. For specialized education and training we sometimes seek the recommendation (for instruction) from the supply-chain link requesting the training. I keep saying education and training (E&T). From now on I'll just say E&T.

What's the difference between education and training? **Education** mostly focuses on the "**What is it and why do it?**" aspect of a topic; and **training** focuses on the **"how to do it"** aspect. For example, as you know, we are currently installing a corporatewide ERP system in the company. All employees will receive varying hours of **education** on the **what** and **why** of it. Those employees who will actually work with the system will receive **training** on **how** to use it.

TIP #140: *Education and training has to be an important part of your inventory rightsizing effort.*

Woodstock University will have a complete curriculum of inventory-related courses delivered by classroom instruction, Webinars, self study, or video compact disc (CD). As part of our employee improvement program (and for advancement/promotion), each employee will be required to take at least 40 hours of education/training per year; including 8 hours on an inventory-related topic. So far we have identified the following courses and are working on the curriculum for each of them:

- Purchasing Inventory
- Managing Work-in-Process Inventory
- Material Requirements Planning
- Distribution Requirements Planning
- Bill of Material Structuring
- Cost Accounting for Inventory
- Inventory Forecasting
- Sales and Operations Planning
- Lean Concepts

As you can see, this is an impressive list of courses. As part of our employee new hire orientation program, we will show a 16-hour video CD on why maintaining a rightsize inventory is so important to the company. This isn't a case of "Can we afford to do this?" This is a case of "We can't afford not to do it."

Company Communications

One of the biggest challenges supply chains face today is communications. That is, having all employees know what's going on in the company. In the past, we have made a half-hearted attempt to publish a company newsletter once a quarter. Sometimes we did and sometimes we didn't. Last year we only published three newsletters. So far this year we have only published two, and the year is almost over. Well, that's going to change.

Starting January of next year, Adriana has stated she wants a newsletter published once a month, and she insists it include communications about the status of our company inventory. This is what she wants to see in the monthly newsletter:

- Total value of the company inventory graphed month by month, in dollars

- Total number of inventory stockouts in manufacturing, plotted monthly
- Total number of stockouts in distribution, plotted monthly
- Writeup on "Employee of the Month" for outstanding contribution to inventory management (who they are and what they did)
- A monthly "President's Message" (which she will write herself) on an inventory-related topic

TIP #141: *Human resources can take a proactive role in your inventory rightsizing effort by raising the visibility of the inventory effort through formal company communication channels.*

Adriana's goal is to change the culture of the company when it comes to managing inventory by raising the recognition and visibility of inventory throughout our entire supply chain. I think it is a good idea, and we in HR are looking forward to it.

We currently use the HR functionality that resides in our financial reporting system. Starting next year we will be using the HR functionality of the new ERP system. We will be the second supply-chain link to go up on the new system. Finance was the first, and it is almost ready to cut over to the new system. The new HR system will enhance our capability to serve our customers (all Woodstock employees) well. As you can see, HR is actively involved in our inventory rightsizing effort.

Maintenance

My name is Anthony, and I am the maintenance manager for Woodstock Lighting Group.

If it wasn't for my maintenance team, the company would be in a world of trouble. My guys can fix anything, and I am proud of them. Mark, Richie, and I have been together for over ten years, and we know what each other is thinking without saying it. The other links in our supply chain should be as lucky. I'm thrilled that Joe is gone. He was a real pain in the neck. He wouldn't let us spend one extra dime on preventive maintenance than was absolutely necessary. Arnie is a good guy, and he really understands the need to perform preventive maintenance. When outsiders come for a visit, they are amazed to see some 1960 vintage machines still running— and running well.

I'm looking forward to my honeymoon next month. I can't wait! Lorri is so understanding. She knows my job requires me to work evenings and weekends. It is the only time I can get at the equipment. It's not that bad though; it's quiet, and we don't get many interruptions. This Harmony Team thing is a great concept. It's not often we get asked for our opinion and ideas. My team and I are going to help in any way we can. Arnie and Orlando are great leaders, and I am confident that they will turn this company around. If anybody can do it, they can.

Role and Responsibilities

The role of maintenance at Woodstock is broad. We do a lot of interesting and important things. There is a fine line of difference between my team and the facilities management team. If I had to sum up our responsibility into one sentence, I would say, "Maintenance is responsible for keeping our machines and equipment in perfect working order without compromising the health and safety of our employees." But it can be much more than that. We can contribute to our inventory rightsizing efforts in many ways.

Machine and Equipment Maintenance

Needless to say, our machines and equipment make and move inventory. When they break down, they can't make and move inventory. That alone tells you that keeping them in good working order is important to our inventory rightsizing efforts. I will categorize maintenance into several types:

Planned Maintenance (Preventive Maintenance)

Planned maintenance is also referred to as *preventive maintenance* or *planned downtime.* We are all familiar with this type of maintenance because we do it (or should) as part of our personal life. For example, your car requires periodic maintenance to have the oil changed, tire pressure checked, engine tuned up, wheels aligned, etc. If you don't take care of these things, what will happen? Sooner or later your car will break down. If you are on vacation traveling cross-country and your car breaks down you will not be a happy camper. Well, it is the same thing with equipment. We have established a preventive maintenance schedule for all our equipment. We know in advance when the equipment needs to be shut down so that maintenance can be performed.

There are two types of preventive maintenance. There are those tasks that the machine operators can perform themselves, like changing the oil and general machine cleaning. We call these tasks *operator maintenance*. Then there are those tasks like machine calibration, changing belts, and inspecting gears that my team does. We call these tasks *technical maintenance*. Preventive maintenance is a good thing to do. As the schedule is coordinated with manufacturing, it has little impact on production schedules.

As a general rule, we perform (technical) preventive maintenance on weekends, and operator maintenance is performed at the end of a shift, Monday to Friday. If the work center doesn't have work, it will do it during the course of the normal work day. My job prior to coming here to Woodstock was in a confectionary plant, and every Friday during the summer was designated as "maintenance day." In the summer the plant operated certain workcenters on a 4 × 10 schedule; that is, they worked four days a week, ten hours a day, Monday through Thursday. That work center shut down on Fridays and the plant was "turned over" to maintenance for the day. This was a win–win situation for everybody. The plant workers got long weekends and maintenance got to do its work without interruption.

Unplanned Maintenance

Unplanned maintenance is when a machine breaks down unexpectedly during scheduled production time. This can be a plant's worst nightmare if the problem can't be solved immediately. Think of the inventory disruption if you had only one machine of that type, it broke down, and you couldn't get replacement parts, or it took a week to fix. The impact on inventory could be significant. Upstream workcenters would have to stop work because WIP inventory would build up. Downstream work-centers would have to stop because of the lack of work. Customer orders would be late and the problem would be compounded well into the future. That's why we do preventive maintenance — to keep the unplanned downtime to a minimum. We also keep a spare parts inventory of long lead time replacement parts. If we have to, we can make many of the replacement parts ourselves in our machine shop, but it would also disrupt their schedule.

Proactive Maintenance

This is our favorite task. Proactive maintenance, also referred to as *productive maintenance*, is where we work with the machine and equipment operators to improve the efficiency of the machines. The benefits are many:

- Machine flexibility is improved.
- Material handling is reduced.
- Operator ergonomics is enhanced.
- A continuous flow of material is achieved.
- Capacity is increased.
- Lead time is reduced.
- Lot sizes are reduced.

As you can see, this will have a major impact on our inventory rightsizing efforts. We don't do enough of this. Now that Arnie is our leader, he has told me he wants us to spend more time taking a proactive role in enhancing our plant efficiency.

> **TIP #142:** *Get your maintenance team involved in performing proactive maintenance. This will greatly enhance your chances to rightsize your inventory.*

Machine Setup Reduction

One proactive task that will provide us with many benefits is to reduce the time it takes us to change over a machine from producing one product to another. We have several complex time-consuming machine setups in our machine shop. For example, for some of our spotlight framed lenses we have to change out the tool, reprogram the machine and add an additional angle axle. This can take up to eight hours to perform. Naturally, once this setup is done, Orlando wants to make a ton of these so that he feels the setup time was cost efficient.

If we can find a way to reduce this setup time down to minutes, that would change a lot of things. For one thing, Orlando wouldn't mind making smaller lot sizes, and for another, our overall capacity would increase. Machine time is lost because a new setup is being done. While the machine is sitting, it is not making product, thus we have lost capacity.

> **TIP #143:** *Maintenance personnel should be part of a cross-functional team committed to reducing machine setup times.*

We are fortunate in that we have many talented people here who work on this. By combining their knowledge and experience into one group, I am confident that we can make dramatic improvements in machine setup times. I recommend we include:

- Maintenance
- Machine Operators
- Field Service
- Facilities Management
- Product Design
- Process Design

It also wouldn't hurt to get our suppliers and customers involved, when and where appropriate. Reducing setup times will give us all the benefits I spoke about when discussing proactive maintenance. Reducing lead times and lot sizes will greatly enhance our inventory rightsizing efforts. Perhaps the biggest benefit to Woodstock will be improved flexibility. Improved flexibility to change over production will allow us to rapidly respond to customer needs. This will make for satisfied customers, who may in turn give us more business.

> **TIP #144:** *Reducing machine setup times will increase capacity, reduce lead times, and decrease lot sizes, which could ultimately lead to increased sales and profits for the company.*

Machine maintenance and machine setup reduction aren't the only activities we are involved with that impact inventory. We are also involved in developing the layout for the new assembly work cells in Building 1. We are working with our facilities team and industrial engineers, getting ready to install the new AGVS system that Joe approved before he left. Our team may be small in size, but we are large when it comes to the contribution we can make to our inventory rightsizing effort. You can count on us to work with all links in our supply chain to make this happen.

Facilities Management

My name is Jon, and I am the facilities manager for Woodstock Lighting Group.

I've worked here for six months now, and this is the first time anyone other than Joe and Arnie has asked me to make a presentation on what we do in facilities management. I don't even know most of the people on this Harmony thing they are working on. For all I know, it's the company singing group and they are looking for a bass tenor to sing in harmony with the rest of the group. However, they said they want me to describe our role and responsibility as it relates to inventory. So apparently they aren't interested in my singing.

Talk about inventory. They've got so much inventory in this facility; someone could hide in it and not be found for months. That reminds me: I wonder if I should tell Arnie I saw one of the floaters taking a nap during working hours the other day? He was flat on his back, lying on a skid of cartons. I would have thought that wouldn't have been very comfortable, but it didn't seem to bother him, he was snoring away for a good half hour. He couldn't have a very important job if he wasn't missed for that long a period of time. Oh well, I'm no snitch, let someone else deal with it. Well, here I go ...

Role and Responsibilities

Most people think the only thing we do is see that the heat or air-conditioning is working, arrange for the plowing in winter, and turn the lights on and off. We do so much more than that. For one thing we keep the facilities up to code so that we comply with all health and safety regulations. I view this as the most important thing we do. However, we also work with many of the other supply-chain links to improve the storage and movement of inventory throughout our facility here in New Jersey.

Good Housekeeping (Part of the 5s Effort)

You are aware of the lean initiative Arnie and Orlando have got going on in the plant. Their supervisors are responsible for the 5s campaign in each work center, and we are responsible for keeping the general work areas clean and clear. We are like internal policemen. Sometimes we find inventory sitting where it shouldn't be, and we have to get the supervisor to get it removed. On more than one occasion, they have blocked access to a fire exit door. This is a clear violation of the safety regulations. This has happened a lot since I have been here. We have now painted those areas and designated them as "clear zones." Anyone stacking inventory or anything else in those zones will be written up.

One of our biggest problems is in the receiving area. When some raw materials are received in cartons, they empty the cartons and move the inventory to a storage location. That's the good news. The bad news is that they were haphazardly stacking the empty cartons in front of a fire door. That was a no-no, and we quickly solved that problem. The point I'm trying to make is that as inventory moves throughout our facility, it can sometimes leave a wake of debris that has to be cleaned up by someone — and that is typically us. The bottom line is, we are responsible for keeping the areas clear for the safe movement of inventory.

> **TIP #145: Get facilities management involved in your "good housekeeping" activities. It can contribute to the improved visibility of inventory, which is an important criterion in your inventory rightsizing efforts.**

Workcell Layout

We are actively involved with manufacturing and industrial engineering to improve our plant layout. As you know, we have an issue of material flow due to the original building designs. We are constantly trying to find ways to improve the flow and movement of materials through this hodge-podge. We are also building new workbenches for the new assembly light workcell on the second floor of Building 1.

Tool Room Inventory

We have a small machine shop where we make repairs and modifications to various pieces of equipment needed to maintain the facility in good working order. As this room is in the same building as manufacturing (Building 1, first floor), we keep all the unused tools, dies, and jigs. When the manufacturing workers need something, they come to us, and we move the needed tool to the work center. Don't ask me how this started. It's been done well before I got here.

I recommend that manufacturing moves all active tools to the appropriate work center and store them there. This will increase efficiency by not having to wait for us to bring the tools, and it will save us time by not having to manage inventory, which they should be responsible for. Furthermore, we can put that space to good use.

Shelving

We erect all the shelving used for storage of raw materials and finished goods. We are always working with the other links in our supply chain to find better ways to utilize our space. As you know, we are running out of space to put inventory in all our buildings. Just before Joe left, he asked me if we could build up our storage area so we had more space to store things. I told him we have gone as high up as reasonable for safety reasons. He and I argued over this, and I said I would quit before I would consider going any higher.

Truth be told, this was the wrong focus, anyway. I told him the focus should be on reducing inventory so that we wouldn't have the need for more space. I recommend we use a philosophy of "space denial." That is, we gradually reduce the amount of space to store inventory. Once we have effectively improved the utilization of that space, reduce it again. Continuously go through this cycle until we are operating with a reasonable amount of inventory. That's what I would do if I were you.

> **TIP #146:** *Don't focus your efforts on finding new space to put inventory. Focus your efforts on better utilization of the space you already have. Better yet, get rid of your inventory so you don't need the space.*

Weather and the Impact on Inventory

When it snows we have to plow the parking lot and the truck bay area so that inventory can be moved into and out of our facility. As our buildings aren't connected, we also have to ensure safe passage (for carts and people) between buildings.

There is a major leak in Building 2, and I told Joe about it. We need a new roof, but he said we couldn't afford it. At any one time, we have about $200,000 worth of inventory sitting under this waterfall. I told him we couldn't afford not to replace the roof. He still wouldn't budge. When it rains, we have to put tarps over the inventory. When you consider the costs of the tarps (these are big industrial tarps) and the labor cost to put them on and take them off, the roof would be half paid for by now.

> **TIP #147:** *Facilities management can help protect inventory from being damaged during storage and internal movement through your supply chain.*

Just last week, we had to scrap $3,000 of inventory because it got wet. I went to Arnie and he approved the expense for a new roof on the spot.

Matters got worse when I found out that the scrapped goods were needed for a customer rush order and couldn't be replaced for two weeks!

We have our own generator that we use when the city power system fails. This happens a lot in the summer when their electrical system goes on overload. By activating this system, we help keep the plant operating so that production can continue to produce inventory with minimum disruption. I'll close by saying that we can contribute a lot to our inventory rightsizing efforts. Please continue to call on us. We want to be part of this companywide team effort.

Inter-Office E-Mail

To: Supply-Chain Managers   October 31
From: Harmony Team
Subject: Rightsizing Inventory
Current Inventory: $31.6 Million U.S. Dollars

As the year begins to wind down, we have made great strides in our companywide effort to rightsize our inventory. Our inventory has dropped from $40 million at the beginning of the year to its current level of $31.6 million — a reduction of $8.4 million. We have accomplished our goal, even though sales is behind in the forecast by roughly $1 million. All three categories of inventory went down for the month. Because of more accurate planning information coming out of MRP, we were able to reduce production and utilize the finished goods inventory we had in stock. Sales also sold off about $50,000 in obsolete inventory. Product design continues to review slow moving raw materials as a replacement for BOM parts and was instrumental in using $25,000 worth of substitute raw materials to be converted into finished goods. Everyone is contributing.

This week we met with representatives from four of our internal supply-chain links. Although these four links aren't normally associated with managing inventory, we believe they are an asset to our inventory rightsizing efforts. Following is a summary of those meetings. Details will follow in a separate e-mail later in the week:

Field Service

1. They are a profit center, selling and installing inventory, having achieved their sales goals for five years in a row.
2. 25 percent of the inventory they sell, they also install.
3. They also provide consulting services.
4. They are in direct contact with our customers and provide input to our sales and marketing links.
5. In the future, their input will be used in the CRM system.
6. They work with product design to develop new products and to enhance existing products.
7. They have been instrumental in our efforts to eliminate parts in our products, and in other cases they have helped product design standardize on common parts.
8. They are working with our industrial engineers (process design) to improve the manufacturing efficiency by suggesting better ways to build our products that will add value to the products our customers buy from us.
9. They also interact with some of our key suppliers on improving the products we buy from them.
10. They have direct responsibility for managing the spare parts inventory sitting at depots near airports.
11. We are in the process of eliminating the depot inventory. All spare parts will be shipped direct to customers from our plant in New Jersey.
12. When they are not in the field, they lend their expertise to our maintenance department.
13. Several parts used by maintenance and field service are similar. They are looking to combine inventories, which will reduce the overall inventory previously carried by both links.
14. They are going to work with facilities management to see if they, too, use similar parts. If so, we can look forward to combining that inventory, also.
15. Their current stand-alone inventory management system will be eliminated, and they will start using the new ERP system within the next six months.

Human Resources

1. HR deals with our most precious inventory: our people.
2. Job descriptions: All future job descriptions will have a statement regarding that job's role in managing inventory.
3. We develop team performance metrics along with supply-chain managers.
4. We keep up to date on industry standards related to salary ranges for each position.
5. We are establishing "Woodstock University" for education and training programs. It is developing an education curriculum for each position that will have an "inventory education" element to it.
6. A preliminary list of inventory-related courses has been developed.
7. Our company newsletter will be revitalized, and inventory-related topics will be highlighted.
8. Adriana will have a "President's Message" in each issue, and inventory management will be the theme.
9. We will recognize an "Employee of the Month" for an outstanding contribution to inventory management.
10. Starting early next year HR will transition to the new ERP system.

Maintenance

1. Keep our machines and equipment in good, safe, working order so the inventory can be produced and moved as required.
2. Follow maintenance's established and published schedule of preventive maintenance activities.
3. Operators have been trained to perform routine maintenance on their machines.
4. They will react to unplanned maintenance immediately.
5. They will take on a proactive role in improving machine efficiency and operator safety.
6. Along with other links in our supply chain, they will focus on reducing machine setup time. They will start in the machine shop, which has several long setup times to contend with.

7. They will seek input from suppliers and customers in helping to reduce setup times.
8. Along with our lantern assembly team, they are developing a new layout of equipment to improve the work flow.
9. Installation of the new AGVS is planned.

Facilities Management

1. Actively involved in our good housekeeping campaign.
2. Keeps aisles safe and free of debris and unnecessary inventory.
3. Works with maintenance and industrial engineering to improve our plant layout, so that inventory moves in a continuous flow as much as possible.
4. Tools will be moved out of the facilities workshop and stored in the using workcenter.
5. Installs all shelving to store inventory.
6. Keeps the inventory maintained in a safe, damage-free storage environment. A new roof is being installed in Building 2.
7. Recommends we practice a "space denial" philosophy.
8. Maintains a backup generator system, so that in the event of a power failure, we can continue production.

We recognize the contribution these four links are making to our inventory rightsizing efforts. I suggest that each of you seek their guidance and counsel in helping achieve our collective inventory objectives. Figure 10.1 is our latest version of the Woodstock inventory rightsizing model. Please review it and offer any comments or suggestions you may have. At our next meeting, Arnie will discuss the total supply-chain effort to date and what we must do to sustain this new company culture of managing inventory.

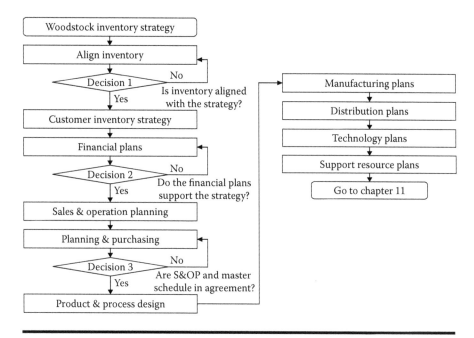

Figure 10.1 Woodstock inventory rightsizing model.

Applying the Tips, Tools, and Philosophies to Your Company

Too often, these supply-chain links are not involved in a company's inventory rightsizing effort. They should be. They have so much to offer. I once worked with a maintenance guy who knew more about inventory flow and management than anybody else in the company. No one had ever asked him his opinion on what should be done to make production and inventory movement more efficient. We got him involved and it was one of the most successful inventory rightsizing efforts I was ever involved with. Let's review the tips discussed in this chapter.

> **TIP #135:** *If you have a field service division, get it involved in your inventory rightsizing efforts; it has a lot to contribute.*

The field service people I have met and worked with seem to have the ability to fix almost anything. Give them a screwdriver and a pair of pliers and they get the job done. I've always been impressed with their product knowledge and their ability to interact with the customer. How to apply this TIP is simple: ask for their help. It doesn't have to be full time. Get them to meet with you and ask them questions. They know more about the customer than they think they do.

- Educate them on what questions they should be asking the customer.
- Provide them with sales education (soft sell).
- Consider rewarding them for selling products.
- Structure formal meetings with other supply-chain links such as: sales, marketing, product design, process design, and suppliers.

TIP #136: *Field service can help reduce inventory by assisting product design with the reduction of parts in your product.*

Field service personnel are out at the customer site almost every day touching and fixing your products. They know the strengths and weaknesses of your product. They may find that some parts you have included in your product aren't necessary. I had a client once who sold electrical replacement kits to OEMs. The kits included washers and lock nuts. While visiting the customer, field service observed the maintenance person using the old washer and nut rather than the new ones in the kit. When asked why, the maintenance person said it was easier to get on because they were already greased up and readily available at the point of installation and, besides, why waste a perfectly good washer and nut? End of story.

TIP #137: *Consolidating spare parts inventory into fewer locations can reduce the overall amount of inventory carried without having a negative impact on customer service.*

As we discussed with consolidating finished goods, you should also consider consolidating spare parts used by field service, facilities management, and maintenance. You may find that all three are using common parts. Consolidation into one inventory location will make it easier to control inventory and keep it more accurate. You may also achieve savings in storage space and safety stock inventory. Moving goods around the world has dramatically improved over the years, and storing goods close to airport hubs may not be necessary. You must be careful that consolidation of inventory doesn't have a negative impact on customer service. Of course, if you can eliminate the part from your product, there would be no need to keep the part in inventory at all, would there?

TIP #138: *Field service may share resources with other links in your supply chain. By combining resources you may be able to save money and improve operating efficiency.*

TIP #137 spoke about combining the inventory of diverse supply-chain links. This TIP addresses combining the actual personnel who perform these functions. Consider the following:

- If it makes good business sense that they be part of the same supply-chain link, by all means do so. This might work with a small company, but a large company may have trouble implementing this.
- If not part of the same supply-chain link, you can still combine their collective knowledge. After all, all three links have at least one thing in common (even if inventory is not common); they fix things.
- Get them together for a meeting at least once a quarter to discuss such things as new product design, and product enhancements and redesign.
- At the very least, make them aware of your inventory rightsizing efforts and ask them what they can do to help make it happen.

TIP #139: *Individual performance measures (related to inventory) should be replaced by shared, team-based performance measurements.*

This TIP will require a great deal of interaction among the supply-chain links. While some links will still require metrics unique to their area of responsibility, inventory can be a shared metric if expectations are properly communicated. For example, inventory turns are a very typical company performance metric, but so many groups have an impact on inventory turns that it is not reasonable to assign this metric to one link in your supply chain. Inventory turns are impacted by:

- Manufacturing: cycle times
- Purchasing: material lead times
- Sales and marketing: selling the product
- Process design: cycle times
- Planning: safety stock levels

I have mentioned only a few links and only one example for each. There are more. Inventory turns (or days on hand) are a metric that should be shared by the entire supply chain. The same is true for levels of inventory; this is a shared metric, also.

> **TIP #140:** *Education and training have to be an important part of your inventory rightsizing effort.*

A formal training and education are a "must do" in today's competitive world. Even if your company has only ten people, you must plan ahead and put together an education program that will allow your employees to keep their skills up to date and give your company a competitive edge in your marketplace. Don't leave this important area up to the individual links to implement. It must be companywide. The individual links will certainly have a great deal of input as to course content and who the instructor should be — but the overall program must be coordinated.

- Put together a matrix of supply-chain links by position/title/job description and then put together a list of the types of courses needed.
- Match the job position to the course program for each person.
- Meet with the individuals and discuss the educational opportunities available.
- Identify courses necessary for career advancement.
- Agree on an education strategy, individual by individual.
- Keep employee personnel records up to date.
- Recognize employee achievement with a certificate or other means of communicating their accomplishments.

The inventory type of education will vary company by company. For some people it may be a two-hour video, and for others it may be a two-week workshop off-site.

> **TIP #141:** *Human resources can take a proactive role in your inventory rightsizing effort by raising the visibility of the inventory effort through formal company communication channels.*

There are several ways this TIP can be accomplished:

1. The highest-ranking executive in the company can put out a monthly e-mail to all employees regarding the activities related to inventory.

2. For employees without access to e-mail, I have seen companies put a typed memo (from the same executive) in paycheck envelopes.
3. It can be posted on the company bulletin boards located in lunchrooms, plant floor, etc.
4. A company newsletter can be used as an effective communication vehicle, as described in this chapter.

Regardless of the media used, the important point is if you are going to make inventory rightsizing as a new way of life for the company, you must raise the visibility so that all employees are aware of what is going on.

> **TIP #142:** *Get your maintenance team involved in performing proactive maintenance. This will greatly enhance your chances to rightsize your inventory.*

You cannot manufacture or move inventory efficiently if your equipment and machines constantly break down. Your maintenance team can be a big asset in performing preventive maintenance. But if you really want to improve productivity, get your maintenance team involved in a proactive maintenance program.

- Pick a machine or work area where efficiency is not good; in all probability it will be a bottleneck work center, but it doesn't have to be.
- Assign routine maintenance to machine operators so that your maintenance team is freed up to focus on improving machine efficiency.
- Make proactive maintenance a formal program.
- Assign team members to work with maintenance.
- Benchmark current machine performance.
- Set new performance metrics.
- Have scheduled meetings with management to discuss ideas, progress, and obstacles that need to be overcome.
- If possible, ask your equipment/machine provider if he or she has another user who has improved the efficiency of the equipment, and if so, ask to visit them.

> **TIP #143:** *Maintenance personnel should be part of a cross-functional team committed to reducing machine setup times.*

Reducing setup times will be part of your proactive maintenance program, discussed in TIP #142. It is not the responsibility of maintenance alone; the operators who run the machines every day will have a lot of input into the process. After all, who knows the operation better?

■ Get the machine operator involved.
■ Form a team: machine operators, product design, process design, manufacturing, facilities management, and field service.
■ Ask your parts supplier to look at your machine setup process; maybe he or she can do something to the part to shorten or eliminate the need for the setup.
■ Have your end customers view your setup process; they might offer suggestions.
■ Make a video of the current setup.
■ Time the current setup from beginning to end.
■ Locate tools within easy access to the setup person.
■ Make as much of the new setup "external setup" (done while the machine is still running the current part).

> **TIP #144:** *Reducing machine setup times will increase capacity, reduce lead times, and decrease lot sizes, which could ultimately lead to increased sales and profits for the company.*

One of the biggest opportunities to rightsize your inventory is to reduce your machine setup times. It may also be your biggest challenge. The benefits are well worth the effort (particularly if your setup times are hours, not minutes):

■ Increased capacity: Machine is not sitting idle, it is making product.
■ Smaller lot sizes: If a setup takes minutes rather than hours, you will be inclined to make less at one time.
■ Shorter lead times: Overall manufacturing lead time will be reduced by the amount of setup time saved, and because of the shorter lead times.
■ Increased (improved) flexibility: Perhaps the greatest benefit of all is you will be able to respond to changes in customer requirements faster.

> **TIP #145:** *Get facilities management involved in your "good housekeeping" activities. It can contribute to the improved visibility of inventory, which is an important criterion in your inventory rightsizing efforts.*

Depending on the size of your company, facilities management may or may not be involved with the storage of inventory. In large companies (>500 employees) it probably has its hands full just keeping the facility running. However, in smaller companies (<100 employees) I have seen facilities management very involved with inventory storage — from keeping the aisles free and clear of debris to the erection of shelving to store inventory. It is the latter I refer to here.

Good housekeeping is everyone's responsibility, but facilities management can play a big role in making it happen:

1. Create a good housekeeping team made up of people from manufacturing, plant engineering, and maintenance.
2. Schedule facility "walks" where the team walks the facility on a predetermined schedule.
3. Write down any violation of company storage policies.
4. Make a note of any area that needs good housekeeping.
5. Document and publish findings to responsible groups.
6. Develop an action plan to correct the situation.
7. Follow up to ensure the activity has been completed; do this at least once a month.

> **TIP #146: *Don't focus your efforts on finding new space to put inventory. Focus your efforts on better utilization of the space you already have. Better yet, get rid of your inventory so you don't need the space.***

I have always found this to be an interesting phenomenon. There seems to be an unwritten rule that says "The more space you have, the more space you will use to store inventory." My suggestion here is simple. Rather than spend all that energy and time trying to figure out how to get more space or use the space you have more efficiently, spend that time and energy on figuring out how to eliminate the need for the space. You may find that the root cause of the problem is not lack of space but too much inventory.

> **TIP #147: *Facilities management can help protect inventory from being damaged during storage and internal movement through your supply chain.***

There is nothing more wasteful than to make a product, store it on a shelf, and have it become damaged just sitting there. You bought the raw material, paid for the labor to transform it into a finished product, and now it is useless. The example I used in the Woodstock story is real. I have seen goods get damaged by rain coming in through a leaky roof.

- Keep inventory off the floor; put it on a shelf or skid if possible.
- Don't keep inventory unprotected in a high traffic area where there is a lot of movement going on: forklift trucks, hand trucks, etc.
- Allow enough space in the aisles for material handling.
- Train personnel in the proper handling and storage of goods.
- When the weather is a concern, cover inventory with a protective wrapping such as a tarp or shrink wrap.

I have entitled this chapter "The Unsung Heroes of Inventory Management," because I believe they truly are. When we think of supply-chain management, we typically think of manufacturing, distribution, product design, and so forth. But a supply chain is much more than that. It is people, machines, and facilities. All links in your supply chain can have a positive effect on your inventory rightsizing efforts. Let's not forget these four important links. Table 10.1 represents the current status of the Woodstock inventory. Table 10.2 indicates Woodstock work-in-process inventory turns based on the estimated annual cost of goods sold (COGS).

Table 10.1 Inventory Balance (×1,000,000)

Month end	31 Jan	28 Feb	31 Mar	30 Apr	31 May	30 Jun	31 Jul	31 Aug	30 Sep	31 Oct
Forecast	7.2	7.9	9.7	7.1	5.9	9.0	9.3	8.7	7.0	7.4
Orders	5.8	7.4	9.6	7.7	6.8	8.8	7.7	8.8	8.0	7.5
Total starting inventory	40.0	41.0	40.9	40.3	39.0	38.1	36.7	35.7	34.1	33.1
Start FG inventory	15.5	15.7	15.8	15.3	14.9	14.5	14.2	13.7	13.0	13.1
+Production @ COGS	4.1	5.1	6.0	4.8	4.2	5.6	4.7	5.2	5.5	4.5
−Shipments @ COGS	3.9	5.0	6.5	5.2	4.6	5.9	5.2	5.9	5.4	5.1
End FG inventory	15.7	15.8	15.3	14.9	14.5	14.2	13.7	13.0	13.1	12.5
Start WIP inventory	7.5	7.6	7.7	7.4	7.1	7.1	6.5	6.2	5.9	5.5
+Material issues	3.4	4.2	4.8	3.9	3.5	4.3	3.8	4.3	4.2	3.7
+Labor and overhead	0.8	1.0	0.9	0.6	0.7	0.7	0.6	0.6	0.9	0.6
−Production @ COGS	4.1	5.1	6.0	4.8	4.2	5.6	4.7	5.2	5.5	4.5
End WIP inventory	7.6	7.7	7.4	7.1	7.1	6.5[p]	6.2	5.9	5.5	5.3
Start raw inventory	17.0	17.7	17.4	17.6	17.0	16.5	16.0	15.8	15.2	14.5
+Material purchases	4.1	3.9	5.0	3.3	3.0	3.8	3.6	3.7	3.5	3.0
−Material issues	3.4	4.2	4.8	3.9	3.5	4.3	3.8	4.3	4.2	3.7
End raw inventory	17.7	17.4	17.6	17.0	16.5	16.0	15.8	15.2	14.5	13.8
Total ending inventory	41.0	40.9	40.3	39.0	38.1	36.7	35.7	34.1	33.1	31.6

Table 10.2   Woodstock WIP Inventory Turns Improvement

Month End	31 Dec	31 Mar	30 Jun	30 Sep	31 Oct
Inventory turns	8.8	8.9	10.2	12.0	
End WIP Inventory—M	7.5	7.4	6.5	5.5	5.3
Annual COGS—M$					66.0

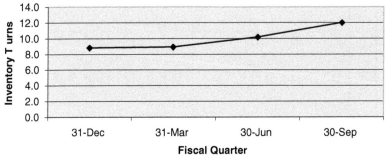

Chapter 11

Rightsizing Inventory: A New Way of Life for the Supply Chain

Harmony Team Meeting: November 30

Woodstock Inventory: $31 Million

My name is Jack and I am supply chain manager for Woodstock Lighting Group.

I've only been here 11 months but it seems like 11 years. This has been the most challenging assignment I've ever had, but in many ways it has been a satisfying year. I've met a lot of nice, bright people, and truly believe we have made great strides in our inventory rightsizing efforts. We're not quite there yet, but it is happening. I'm glad Joe is gone. He was a difficult guy to work for and we had many philosophical differences about how things should be done. I like Arnie. He is open-minded and willing to listen to new ideas and new ways of doing things.

When Joe left I thought they would put me in charge of the Harmony Team, but I'm glad they didn't. Orlando was the right choice. He has been here for 15 years and knows this place inside and out. He and Arnie work well together. In the five months since he was made the team leader, we have made far more progress than we would have with Joe challenging every step we took.

My wife thinks I'm crazy. I was offered far more money by another company, but the job didn't seem challenging enough for me. It was well on its way to becoming a world-class company, and I would have been bored within six months. Woodstock had (has) so many problems that we have nowhere to go but up. Every day there is a new surprise, offering a new challenge. I like that. I also like the idea that Adriana is involved and committed to rightsizing our inventory. People are constantly asking me: "Did Joe quit or did he get fired?" The truth is I don't know and I don't care. All I know is that I have a job to do, and I truly believe I can continue to help the company rightsize our inventory.

Rightsizing inventory isn't something you focus on for six months and then move on to something else. As the year is coming to a close, we have reduced inventory by almost $10 million. But if we pat ourselves on our backs and say "A job well done" and move on to another focus, we will only be kidding ourselves. This effort is not a project. We will never finish rightsizing our inventory. There will always be something we can do to improve our inventory position. In reality, it has to become a new way of life for us. We have to create and sustain a new company culture committed to continuous improvement. Too many companies have ineffective supply chains because they fall prey to what I call "the ten most common mistakes of rightsizing inventory." Table 11.1 lists these ten common mistakes. I will discuss each one in some detail.

TIP #148: *Avoid the ten most common mistakes of right-sizing your inventory.*

(Note: TIP = team important point.)

Table 11.1 Ten Most Common Mistakes Made in Rightsizing Inventory

Number	Mistakes Made
1	Treating inventory rightsizing as a project
2	Focusing only on inventory reduction
3	Inaccurate "BILL of Integrity"
4	Not getting all supply chain links involved
5	Not having shared performance measures
6	Assigning inventory responsibility to only one person
7	Implementing technology without having a sound inventory management foundation
8	Management not committed and involved
9	Lack of education or training
10	Not understanding the role of all your supply-chain links

Ten Most Common Mistakes of Rightsizing Inventory

1. **Treating inventory rightsizing as a project.** We have never called our inventory rightsizing effort "a project." The term *project* implies a specific unit of work or task to be accomplished with a specific start date and end date. This effort is ongoing and will never end until our inventory is rightsized perfectly — which it never will be. If we set a goal and obtain it, does that mean it's over? No, we will continuously work at reducing inventory and placing it in the right location in our supply chain. Keep in mind that the right level of inventory and the right location of inventory is not a stagnant condition. It will change over time as our business environment and strategies change. The right location of inventory today may not be the right location of inventory tomorrow.

   Too often I have seen a company set a goal for the year and achieve it, only to move on to another project. When that happens, inventory often gets out of control and the old situation repeats itself. This is also true when a key employee (often the knowledge expert or champion) leaves the company. "Business as usual" sets in and the project gets shelved. We can't let that happen here. Joe's leaving is a good example. Despite what you thought of Joe, he was our leader and was driving this effort. As soon as he left, Adriana named Orlando as our new Harmony Team leader. This was Adriana's way of telling us that this is an important part of our company strategy, and the effort would be ongoing.

2. **Focusing only on inventory reduction.** Don't get me wrong: In most cases reducing inventory is a great thing to do. But the status and location of inventory in the supply chain is also important. By status, I mean whether it is in raw material, work-in-process, or finished goods. For example, having finished goods inventory in the Beacon Lights Division is not the right inventory status for a division with an engineer-to-order or make-to-order strategy (unless, of course, we are referring to replacement parts and spare parts). By location, I mean the physical location of the inventory. At which supply chain link does the inventory reside: storeroom, manufacturing, product design, field service, or distribution center?

   There are going to be times when we will want to increase inventory rather than decrease it. The Flashlight Division is a good example of this. Until we can get our total lead time to be less than our customer delivery lead time, we have to stock flashlights in finished goods inventory (which we now do). For flashlight #030273 we have experienced far too many stockouts. In order to reduce the number of stockouts and increase customer service, sales has requested that we increase the amount of safety stock we carry, thus increasing the level of inventory stocked on this part. Although we are not pleased with the idea of increasing inventory, it is difficult to argue the point as our lead time to make the flashlight is far greater than our customer delivery lead time.

3. **Inaccurate BILL of Integrity (BOI).** It will be difficult to rightsize our inventory if the data we are working with is inaccurate. The BILL of Integrity discussed earlier focuses on the accuracy of the bill of material, perpetual inventory records, lead times, and lot size rules. If any of these four critical areas has inaccurate data, the chances of rightsizing inventory will be challenging. Data accuracy approaching 100 percent is necessary so that we can be comfortable with the data we are working with. As we all know, we have a long way to go here, but we are improving every day.

   The BILL of Integrity isn't the responsibility of any single link in our supply chain. It is the responsibility of our entire supply chain. For example, even though product design is responsible for developing the BOI, it is the responsibility of manufacturing to pick the right parts indicated in the BOI, and if any change is made in the BOI, it must be approved and changed through an engineering change notice procedure.

4. **Not getting all supply-chain links involved.** This is a very common mistake that companies make. You have heard from our "unsung heroes," and as you now know, they have a lot to contribute to our inventory rightsizing efforts. We must keep them involved. We must take the philosophy that all our employees can contribute — if only we would ask them. In order for them to help, they must understand what we are trying to accomplish. Every supply-chain manager must communicate with their team to ensure that this happens.

5. **Not having shared performance measures.** You have heard about the conflicting objectives that drive each of our supply-chain links. It is human nature that people will be motivated to attain the goals and objectives their job performance is measured by. For example, if manufacturing is measured on production output, it stands to reason it will want a steady flow of raw materials available so that it doesn't have machines sitting idle waiting for material. On long-lead-time machine setups they will want to run the largest lot (batch) possible so that they can obtain favorable production efficiencies. This may create high levels of raw material, WIP, and finished goods. Purchasing may be measured by having a favorable purchase price variance. This may lead to purchasing larger than needed lot sizes so that they can achieve their performance objec-

tives. The result will be higher levels of raw materials than is needed for the foreseeable future.

The objectives of manufacturing and purchasing may be in conflict with planning, whose performance measurement may be to decrease inventory levels. Our management team has reviewed the current performance measurements of each link in our supply chain and is in the process of moving to shared performance measurements across supply-chain links. Rightsizing our inventory is one performance measurement we are going to use for our entire supply chain.

6. **Assigning inventory responsibility to one person.** Unless you are an extremely small company, it is almost impossible to hold one person (or one supply-chain link) responsible for rightsizing inventory. There are too many functions and activities that are outside of their control. Take our company as an example. As vice president of operations, Joe was responsible for managing inventory. But when he built inventory to meet the forecast, and sales didn't make its numbers, should operations be held accountable? What happens when a key supplier doesn't deliver on time and production is late making inventory for orders? Whose fault is that? Based on my experience, it is a waste of time to try to blame some supply-chain link because inventory isn't rightsized. Inventory is everyone's responsibility and the inventory rightsizing performance metrics should be shared.

7. **Implementing technology without having a sound inventory management foundation:** We learned our lesson on this one the hard way. When MRP was initially implemented here at Woodstock, we didn't have a solid inventory management foundation in place. Our BILL of Integrity was very inaccurate. All we were doing was throwing technology at the problem in the hopes that it would solve our problems. Well, it didn't. All we did was process inaccurate information faster, so that we could make more mistakes faster than we did before. As you've heard, we had people taking materials out of the storeroom without the proper authorization. Worse than that, they were not reporting what they took. All these problems are a symptom of a poor inventory management foundation. We are in the process of developing sound operating policies and procedures so that the technology we have can be used more effectively.

8. **Management not committed and involved.** We can't say that we have that problem. I have been in many companies where the company president told me he or she was committed to rightsizing inventory. The company demonstrated its commitment by showing

me a letter it sent out to all employees, saying the company was committed to an inventory project of some sort or the other. Then I would go out on the floor and ask workers if they were aware of the company's project and the president's letter. More often than not, they were not aware of any such program or project. The word had not reached them. This was some commitment!

There is a difference between being committed and being involved. Sending out a letter to all employees and establishing inventory goals and objectives may seem like a commitment — and maybe it is. But management must follow up the commitment by becoming involved in the effort. By involved I mean attending meetings, asking questions, providing resources, and in general being very visible and available to the team.

9. **Lack of education or training:** How can you tell someone to do something, set goals, and hold them accountable without providing them with the tools to do the job right? Education is an important tool to be used in our inventory rightsizing efforts. For example, lean manufacturing is a major philosophy that we are trying to implement here that, if successful, will contribute much to our inventory rightsizing effort. It would be impossible to achieve this goal without educating the work force on what it is and how you go about achieving a lean environment. Not everyone needs the same level of education. Aimee is working with all our supply-chain managers on developing an education and training program that is right for everyone. Education on rightsizing our inventory will be available to all employees to some degree or another.

10. **Not understanding the role of all your supply-chain links:** There is an old saying, "for every action there is a reaction." This applies to decisions we made about inventory. When one link in the supply chain makes an inventory decision, that decision can also impact other links in the supply chain — and not always favorably. For example, if the company decides to move to an inventory pull system, not only does that decision impact the upstream and downstream work centers, it also has an impact on purchasing, distribution, planning, and sales.

Before an inventory decision is implemented, you need to understand what that impact is. You may find that you are just pushing your inventory problem onto another link in the supply chain and may make the problem worse. The Harmony Team is taking the right approach here. We are addressing this issue by meeting with all our supply-chain links so that we can better understand their role and responsibility related to managing inventory. Once we understand everyone's role, we will be able to see the impact of inventory decisions on our entire supply chain.

How to Avoid the Ten Most Common Mistakes

1. **Treating inventory rightsizing as a project.** I remember the time I went to my doctor and he very politely told me that I should lose weight. He said, "It took you a long time to put the weight on and it will take you a long time to take it off. It will require a change in your lifestyle (eating habits). Don't look for a quick fix or the latest fad diet." The same is true with rightsizing your inventory. There is no quick fix. It will require a change in company culture. Here are some thoughts to consider:
   - Find a champion in the company who believes in rightsizing inventory. We are lucky here; we have Arnie and Orlando who really believe we can make it happen.
   - Get the commitment and involvement of the highest executive possible. As you know, Adriana is leading this effort — you might say she is another champion.
   - Put someone in charge who understands your supply chain. First we had Arnie, and now we have Orlando. Both of them know our supply chain really well.
   - Set milestones (with dates), but don't set a final inventory goal. We have set a milestone for the year and will set a new milestone for next year. How low can we get is anybody's guess.
   - Never, ever use the word "project" when referring to your rightsizing effort. I don't believe I have ever heard anyone here at Woodstock refer to inventory rightsizing as a project.
   - When a key person on the team leaves the company or gets promoted, replace him or her immediately. We did this when Arnie got promoted to vice president of operations; Orlando replaced him on the first day.
   - Make inventory rightsizing a key company strategy every fiscal year. Adriana has made inventory rightsizing a big part of our company strategy, and she is committed to doing so every year.
   - Give the effort visibility throughout your entire supply chain. We are doing an excellent job on this point. I've been told by longtime employees that communication has never been better, and every day there is some form of communication about inventory rightsizing.

2. **Focusing only on inventory reduction.** Reduction of inventory is a benefit of rightsizing your inventory. For example, if you focus on lean manufacturing concepts, setup reduction, and an inventory pull philosophy (and do them right), the result will be a reduction in inventory. Doing all the things discussed by the Harmony Team will result in a reduction in inventory.

   ■ Make sure your inventory strategy matches your business strategy. When we started this year our inventory strategy and business strategy didn't match. They still don't — but they are a lot closer.

   ■ Make sure your inventory strategy matches your customer's inventory strategy. We have a lot to learn here. We have to keep asking our customers questions and respond to their answers by showing them we can match their strategy.

   ■ Focus your efforts on using the tools, techniques, and philosophies (as discussed in these meetings). There are so many great tools, techniques, and technologies available to us. We just have to be careful and make sure the proper business processes are in place before we do use them.

   ■ Put a sound inventory management foundation in place and follow it. As you are aware, every time you decide to implement something new, you need to make sure you have the proper procedures in place.

3. **Inaccurate BOI.** You are going to make inventory rightsizing decisions based on the data and information available to you. If it is inaccurate, you are going to make the wrong decisions. Your information must be accurate. We are addressing all four points of our BOI. It is a slow and tedious process, but we are well on our way.

   ■ Set high goals of accuracy for BOIs, lead time, lot sizes, and inventory. Our goal is 100 percent accuracy for all four elements.

   ■ Make everyone aware of the accuracy goals. We communicate the current status of all links every week and publish it.

   ■ Put procedures in place to correct errors. This is the key to improving our record accuracy. Fixing an error in a record is a good thing, but the key is to find and fix the root cause of the error so it doesn't happen again.

   ■ Implement a cycle-counting program. We are now cycle counting, and finding many mistakes that we are fixing almost every day.

   ■ Constantly review and update your purchasing and manufacturing lead times. We have a policy in place to govern how often lead times will be updated.

- Constantly review and update your lot-size rules. We are building a table of lot-size rules for varying business scenarios.
- Follow formal ECNs for BOI changes. We didn't always do this, and it caused us many problems. We now have a good handle on it and have educated everyone to follow the ECN procedures.

4. **Not getting all supply-chain links involved.** All supply-chain links can contribute to your inventory rightsizing efforts. Most companies leave inventory management up to the typical supply-chain links such as manufacturing, distribution, purchasing, and planning. As discussed in all these meetings, everyone has a role to play that can help with the team effort:

   - Don't wait for people to volunteer; ask them to get involved. We have taken an aggressive approach on this and have scheduled formal meetings with all supply-chain links.
   - Make a formal list of all supply-chain links and methodically speak with them all. We have done this even with the sublinks. By that I mean we have met with such sublinks as the shipping and receiving folks (sublinks of distribution), as well as the supply-chain manager for distribution.
   - Provide feedback on the status of the team effort and ask for ideas and suggestions. Every month we inform all supply-chain managers of the status of the inventory rightsizing effort (by e-mail) and ask that they share the results with their team. We also stress that we have an open door policy, and all questions and ideas are welcomed and encouraged. I can't tell you the number of people who have stopped by and given us some new ideas the team hadn't even thought of.
   - Recognize people for their contribution to the effort. It will be an incentive for others to get involved. We don't give out monetary rewards (we can't afford it), but we do recognize people for outstanding contributions to the effort by publishing their name in the company newsletter, and they also receive a personal note from Adriana commending them on their effort.
   - Don't forget to involve the "unsung heroes" as we discussed in our last meeting. Their contributions have been a pleasant surprise and addition to our inventory rightsizing efforts.

5. **Not having shared performance measurements.** One way of getting everyone involved (common mistake #4) is for all supply-chain links to have the same performance measures related to rightsizing inventory. All employees are evaluated on how well (or poorly) they do their job. Some companies have formal review

processes, and some do it informally. Regardless, consider the following:

- Review all job descriptions and job performance measurements to make sure there are no conflicting objectives that will harm your inventory rightsizing efforts. Aimee is working with the supply-chain managers on this; they report that they are making good progress.

- Recognize that some conflicting objectives will remain in order to have the proper "checks and balances" in place. For example, finance will continue to want inventory reduction across the board, and sales will continue to want high levels of customer service. Somewhere in between is the "right" balance of inventory for the company to maintain.

- Make some aspect of inventory management part of everyone's job description; whether it is simply an operator putting tools back at the end of the shift or human resources (HR) developing an "inventory" of education classes.

6. **Assigning inventory responsibility to only one person (or link).** No single link in your supply chain can rightsize inventory by itself. Sure, it can exert some control of the inventory it is responsible for: distribution for finished goods and manufacturing for work-in-process (WIP). But rightsizing inventory is such an integrated process that even the inventory these links control will be subject to the inventory policies controlled by the other links.

- Identify those links that control the largest portion of your inventory and make them part of your "Harmony Team." As there can only be a limited number of people on the team, these "power" links will have the greatest impact.

- Bring the "power" links together with the other links in your supply chain on an as-needed basis and as often as reasonable. There isn't a day that goes by when we are not working with one link or another. Rightsizing inventory cannot be done in a vacuum by only one or two links in the supply chain.

- Select a team leader who is most knowledgeable about your entire supply chain. First we had Arnie, and now we have Orlando, two people who know our supply chain inside and out.

- The team leader must meet the criteria of leadership discussed in Chapter 1.

- Assign shared inventory performance measures to the team.

7. **Implementing technology without having a sound inventory management foundation.** It makes no sense to implement new technology without having a solid procedure in place. Continuing to do things the "same old way" and expecting different results

just because you are using new technology to do it will be an expensive experience.

■ Develop process flow maps of the current process. We have changed many of our processes and procedures on how we handle the physical inventory and informational transactions.

■ Redesign the process flow to make it more efficient and accurate.

■ Make sure everyone understands their role in the new process. The best way to accomplish this is by open communications, which we are getting better at every day.

■ Provide education (why) and training (how) on the new technology.

■ Conduct a pilot run with the new system. Every time we change a process or procedure, we do so in a pilot environment. Only when we are satisfied that it works (and is an improvement) do we implement it into our business model.

■ Remove the bugs and fix the process as needed.

8. **Management not committed and involved.** You cannot be committed if you are not involved. Management involvement takes many forms:

■ Attendance at inventory rightsizing meetings. Adriana has attended many of our Harmony Team meetings and has been an active participant.

■ Formal communications with all employees about the status of the rightsizing effort: e-mails, newsletters, videos, bulletin board notices, etc.

■ Employee recognition for outstanding contribution to the rightsizing effort.

■ Ensuring that rightsizing inventory is part of the company strategy and business plan.

■ Communicating with customers and suppliers on inventory-related topics.

■ Ensuring that all supply-chain links are involved in the effort.

■ Providing the tools, resources, and education programs necessary to get the job done.

■ Remove barriers to success. I don't know the reason Joe is no longer with the company, but I do know there were times he was more of a hindrance than a help. It is a sad, but not uncommon, commentary when the top executive driving the inventory rightsizing effort is considered a barrier to its success.

9. **Lack of education and training.** Typically one of the first budgets cut during hard times is the education budget. This is when you probably need it the most. You cannot afford to neglect employee education; especially today with constant change taking place on

what seems like a daily basis. The supply chains that are current with the latest techniques and technologies will stand a better chance of surviving than those that are not.

- Provide some form of education and training to all employees, even if it's a 15-minute video on setup reduction or the concepts of lean manufacturing.
- Have your knowledge experts recommend classes and qualified instructors.
- Work with HR to ensure that everyone gets educated.
- Make education part of each employee's career path.
- Attend conferences on topics related to inventory management, especially if the speaker works for a competitor.
- Join professional societies and organizations.

10. **Not understanding the role of all your supply-chain links.** You cannot make intelligent inventory rightsizing decisions without understanding how that decision will impact the other links in your supply chain.

- Schedule time with the other links in your supply chain to learn what they do and how they do it, similar to the approach we are taking at Woodstock.
- Visit each area to see the operation firsthand (a picture is worth a thousand words).
- Ask them what their inventory-related problems are.
- Ask them what the team can do to make the operation more efficient.
- If practical, get formal education on the topics related to their links.
- Communicate with other links as much as possible (and reasonable).

Sustaining the Inventory Rightsizing Effort

Woodstock has made good progress in their effort to rightsize our inventory. But we can't stop at the end of this year. The effort must continue as a new way of life for the company if we want to survive and prosper. Although we still have a long way to go, we can consider the achievements thus far as the glass being half full rather than half empty. After all, we didn't have to lay off any employees (I don't like the word "downsize"), which is a good thing.

> **TIP #149:** *To successfully rightsize inventory, the effort must be sustained indefinitely on a continuous basis.*

Maintain Inventory Visibility throughout the Supply Chain

Without constant diligence our inventory rightsizing effort will lose momentum over time. To avoid this happening, we must establish an inventory awareness program. This can take many forms. The written word is a powerful reinforcement tool if used effectively. Post the numerical goals and objectives all over the facility: in offices, on bulletin boards, e-mails, etc. Update the status often using graphic forms like bar charts and line charts. Continuously recognize employees for outstanding deeds and achievements. This will improve morale and will be an incentive for others to get involved. If we have a bad month and inventory gets out of line, explain what happened without putting the blame on anybody (or any link). From the boardroom to the shipping dock, make everyone aware of the status of our inventory rightsizing efforts.

Make Rightsizing Inventory an Important Part of Your Business Plan and Strategy

Every company has a business plan, whether it is a formal written document or a plan of action in the mind of the company owner. A typical business plan is usually a high-level document that speaks in terms of dollars and percentages. As inventory is such a high cost to the company, I don't see how we can avoid having an inventory strategy as part of our business plan. Earlier we spoke of using inventory as a strategic advantage to gain a competitive advantage in the marketplace. The inventory goals for each year should be spelled out in our business plan, and the inventory goals should be carefully watched and updated to reflect the current market conditions relative to the current status of your inventory.

Look to Achieve Small Incremental Successes

It probably took us a long time to get our inventory out of balance, and it may take us a long time to get it rightsized. Look to achieve a small incremental success. I have found the best place to start is to "pick the low-hanging fruit." By that I mean, look to reduce inventory of slow-moving, obsolete items. Run an inventory aging report for all items with no activity (transactions) for 12 months or more. If we haven't used an item for a year, there is a good chance we don't need it. It is costing us money to carry in stock and taking up valuable space that can be best used for other activities.

If we do this, make sure the item can't be substituted for an active item. We will want to run a "where used" report to see if the material can be used elsewhere (in another product), assuming it is a raw material or subassembly. You will probably have to get design engineering involved, and finance needs to be aware if you are writing the item off your financial documents. This can be a tedious process but well worth the effort.

Remove Obstacles and Roadblocks

Part of management's commitment and involvement is to remove obstacles and roadblocks that get in the way of your inventory rightsizing efforts. It could be as easy as providing the right tools to do the job, or as difficult as removing someone from the supply chain who has a negative influence on the team. Management's biggest challenge will be to lead the company's culture change from one of negative thinking to positive thinking. Statements like "That won't work here," or "We can't do that because ..." should be replaced with thoughts like: "Let's try it to see if it works."

Company Culture and Inventory

> **TIP #150:** *A strong, healthy company culture will be an asset to rightsizing your inventory. A weak, sick company culture will be a liability to rightsizing your inventory.*

Top management sets the tone of the company culture by the way it acts and conducts business. New people coming into the company will adapt to the current culture as a way of survival. It is rare that a newcomer can buck "the system" and change the culture, unless he or she is coming into the company at a very high executive level. Even then it will be a challenge; people will want to test the boss. Unfortunately, it can take a company crisis, like the one of survival that Woodstock is facing, for a company to change. It is a good thing that Adriana recognizes that change is needed and has inserted herself as the change agent, leading the way. Unfortunately, Joe didn't share Adriana's sense of urgency and fought the culture change all the way.

Adriana has raised the visibility of the importance of rightsizing inventory and thus a culture change is under way. She recognizes that it won't happen overnight and has made it part of the company's annual business plan and strategy for this year and the years to come. The fragmented subcultures that existed at Woodstock are being replaced by one united culture, led by a management team that is knowledgeable and well respected by the employees. Had Joe stayed with the company, I'm not sure the culture change would have taken place as rapidly as it has. Company culture change can be driven by:

- Management's recognizing that the culture must change and setting a good example by:
- Changing company policies and procedures to support culture change
- Establishing performance metrics that support a change in culture
- Recognizing employees who contribute to the change in culture
- Hiring new managers and employees who have the cultural values to change things
- Culture change must be inherent in the company business plan and strategy
- Creating constant awareness of the new culture by communicating with all employees to reinforce the culture change
- Reinforcing the new culture by making it part of a formal company (education) orientation program
- Creating and publishing a company "value statement" or credo/motto that will become the new standard of excellence by which the company does business

Although I have spoken about culture change in generic terms, the application of the suggestions made will enhance your opportunities to rightsize your inventory. Your company president has to take the first step and recognize that change is needed.

Inventory and the Formal Versus Informal System

I have always found it fascinating how the informal system works in companies, regardless of the company size. If I didn't see this for myself, I wouldn't have believed it. Here is how it works: You have quoted a standard lead time of six weeks on all new incoming orders. The owner of the company plays golf with a customer who is also a personal friend. That customer has a problem with one of his customers and asks your president (owner) to help him out. Now, since this customer is a friend of the owner, he sells your product at cost to his friend.

The president bypasses the sales department and personally walks the handwritten order into the order entry department and says it is a rush and must be shipped as soon as possible. No one questions the edict; after all he owns the company and can do what he wants. He is also the guy who signs your paycheck. The order is shipped in less than 24 hours.

Remember, I started out by saying the lead time for this item was six weeks! That's some friend. Here is what happened:

- A production run was stopped on an existing WIP order and two new machine setups had to be done.
- Raw material purchased for another order was "borrowed" so that the rush order could be made.
- No one in purchasing was advised that the material was no longer available.
- It was found out later that the material consumed had a lead time of four weeks to replace, and it was needed next week. Subsequently, the customer cancelled the order and bought it from our competitor.
- The purchase price on the replacement inventory was increased by the supplier.
- Production had to work overtime to get the rush order finished (at time and a half).
- Because of the overtime, extra utility costs were incurred.
- The product that was in WIP (and taken off the machines) was reported as being late (to the system) and placed on an expedite list for planning to follow up.
- Shipping had to work overtime to pack up the finished product.
- Shipping had to take the shipment (drive) to the trucking firm because the last pick up of the day was missed.
- The company had to pay a freight premium to expedite the shipment.
- Capacity used to make up the rush order can never be recovered and was lost forever.
- The WIP order taken off the machines was actually late, and the customer cancelled the order. It was a very profitable order, too.
- That same customer cancelled two other orders he had with us and went to a competitor.

I figure they lost about $50,000 on this order and also lost two profitable customers in less than 24 hours. But, hey, the boss's golfing buddy was happy. I'm exaggerating a little — but not that much. This is, or can be, the informal system working at its worst. There will always be rush orders — that's the nature of supply and demand. Even then, formal procedures should be followed. I'm not saying the new order has to get at the end of the line, but I am saying that formal procedures should be followed.

The order should have been entered properly, and all links impacted by the decision should have been notified. It wouldn't have prevented all of the things that happened, but it would have prevented some of them. Right from the beginning sales could have told the president about the potential of losing two profitable customers; if he had still insisted on doing it, they all should have started looking for new jobs.

As the year comes to a close, our next meeting — and the last meeting of the year — will literally be on the last day of our fiscal and calendar year. On December 31, Adriana will address our Harmony Team and we will have an audio hookup for part of the meeting so that all employees will hear what she has to say.

Inter-Office E-Mail

To: Supply-Chain Managers   November 30
From: Harmony Team
Subject: Rightsizing Inventory
Current Inventory: $31 Million

As the year comes to an end, our inventory rightsizing effort is starting to bear fruit. Our inventory is down $9 million since the first of the year and has been repositioned in our supply chain to reflect our company strategy and plans. We have shipped over $88 million worth of product year to date with one more month to go. We will exceed last year's sales ($90 million) and come very close to our forecast for the year. Our finished goods inventory has been reduced by almost $3 million, and raw material has been reduced by $3.6 million. This has been an outstanding accomplishment, and we expect inventory to be reduced further by the end of the year. Our supply-chain manager, Jack, addressed the group this month and what follows is a summary of the meeting. As usual, you will find the latest version of our inventory rightsizing model at the end of this e-mail and the detailed minutes of the meeting will be published shortly. Please share them with your team.

1. Jack reviewed the ten most common mistakes companies make when trying to rightsize their inventory:
■ Treating inventory rightsizing as a project
■ Focusing only on inventory reduction
■ Inaccurate "BILL of Integrity"
■ Not getting all supply-chain links involved

- Not having shared performance measures
- Assigning inventory responsibility to one person
- Implementing technology without having a sound inventory management foundation
- Management not committed or involved
- Lack of education and training
- Not understanding the role of all your supply-chain links

2. Jack also gave us his thoughts on how we could avoid the ten most common mistakes. We will publish his ideas in the minutes of the meeting.

3. He stressed that we must sustain our inventory rightsizing effort and in order for us to do so we must:

- Maintain inventory (information) visibility throughout the supply chain.
- Make rightsizing inventory an important part of our business plan and strategy.
- Look to achieve small incremental successes.
- Remove obstacles and roadblocks

4. In order for us to sustain the inventory rightsizing effort, our company culture must change as we continue to focus our strategy on this. He suggested nine ideas on how we can go about this, the key of which is management becoming a role model for change and setting a good example for all employees to follow.

We have scheduled a meeting with Adriana on December 31, and you are all invited to attend. Adriana will summarize our achievements for the year and will present our inventory rightsizing model to all employees through a televised satellite hookup. Please plan on attending this important meeting. Figure 11.1 is a draft of our final inventory rightsizing model and is an attachment to this e-mail. We are in the process of finalizing it. Again, we thank you for your ongoing support and commitment.

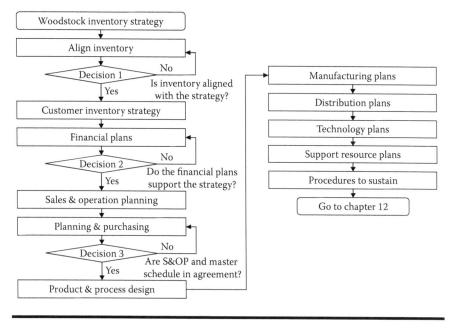

Figure 11.1   Woodstock inventory rightsizing model.

Applying the Tips, Tools, and Philosophies to Your Company

Throughout this book I have alluded to supply-chain links functioning as silos that operate as entities unto themselves. In fact, the tag line of this book is "Turning Inventory Silos into a Collaborative Supply Chain Network." By that I mean that a company has to change from a silo mentality and function as an integrated whole. Changing the boxes on an organization chart isn't going to do it. It will require a change in the company culture. A company culture is a philosophy of how business is conducted and the way things are done in the company. It has little to do with policies and procedures. Basically, it is the way people act toward their job and one another in the daily performance of their jobs. It is a set of values that define the company.

> **TIP #148:** *Avoid the ten most common mistakes of rightsizing your inventory.*

Jack has done a good job of telling how we can avoid the ten most common mistakes of rightsizing inventory. It would be redundant for me to repeat them again. I will, however, add some of my own thoughts to what Jack has suggested in this meeting.

- **Good housekeeping** is an essential part of any inventory right-sizing effort. A messy and disorganized storeroom or warehouse will contribute to the difficulty of managing inventory effectively.

- **Packing materials** are an important part of your inventory right-sizing effort. Lack of packing materials can quickly cause your inventory to get out of balance. On the other hand, too much packing material can add to the chaos of a poorly run warehouse and cause you to miss counting inventory correctly.

- **Use inventory exception reports** to take corrective action. You don't want to wade through lots of "green bar" reports or multiple computer screens to find the inventory exceptions that need to be dealt with.

- **Safety stock** should only be added to inventory to cover the uncertainty of supply and demand; it should not be used to avoid blame or make one link look good in the eyes of the other links. Remember, if each link adds safety stock to its planned level of inventory, it will grow proportionally and quickly get out of control. By having excess inventory, problems can remain hidden and not be addressed.

- **Treat A, B, and C inventory items** separately. Don't have one arbitrary percentage goal of uniformly reducing and rightsizing inventory across all items. Set different percentage/unit goals for A's, B's, and C's according to your business strategy of rightsizing your inventory.

TIP #149: *To successfully rightsize inventory the effort must be sustained indefinitely on a continuous basis.*

You have heard me mention the term "continuous improvement" throughout this book. Rightsizing inventory is not a "project-of-the-year." It has to become ingrained in the company culture. This will not happen overnight. More than likely, it will be a series of small incremental steps that will happen over many years. Some of your rightsizing improvements will be dramatic, but more often than not — after you've picked the low-hanging fruit — it will become a tedious process, taking one small step at a time. Don't be discouraged by the slow process. After all, it took you a long time to get the inventory where it is today, and it will take you a long time to get it where it should be.

While all this rightsizing is taking place you must never lose sight of customer needs. As inventory is removed from your supply chain, you must evaluate the impact on customer service. Sustaining an inventory rightsizing effort over years is a difficult task to achieve. But then again, nothing good comes easy. You have probably heard of Murphy's law: "What can go wrong will go wrong." Look at some of the obstacles to overcome:

- Money will become tight. Cash outflow will exceed cash inflow. One of the best ways of improving cash flow is to sell off your inventory and reinvest your money (not in more inventory) in technologies and techniques that will help you keep inventory "rightsized" so it doesn't happen again.
- Key people will leave the company. Contrary to what an egotist will tell you, no one person is indispensable. When a key person quits (or gets fired) replace him or her immediately (like Woodstock did). Don't let there be a time lag in your inventory rightsizing efforts.
- Your company may be bought or you may buy another company. If your company is sold, the new owners will expect you to continue your inventory rightsizing efforts, or at least it is reasonable to assume they would. If you buy another company, your inventory rightsizing efforts will just expand to include the inventory of the company you just purchased.
- An act of nature could disrupt your business. This is never a good thing, and the need to rightsize your inventory could be even greater than it was before.
- A key supplier could go out of business. You should never "put all your eggs in one basket" as they say. I never really understood that statement. I guess it means that if you drop the basket all the eggs will break, and if the eggs were in multiple baskets, then you wouldn't lose them all. You should always have alternative sources for purchased materials.
- You may lose a key customer, or you may gain a large customer. Losing a key customer or gaining a key customer will increase your sense of urgency to rightsize your inventory.

As you can see, all these obstacles aren't obstacles at all. They are actually reasons you should work with a sense of urgency to rightsize your inventory. Not having the "right" inventory could put you out of business just as fast as having too much inventory. Every year your business plan and strategy should include some element of rightsizing your inventory, whether it is reducing inventory or repositioning the inventory in your supply chain.

> **TIP #150:** *A strong, healthy company culture will be an asset to rightsizing your inventory. A weak, sick company culture will be a liability to rightsizing your inventory.*

If executive management takes a laissez faire attitude toward managing inventory, so will the rest of the supply chain. It always starts at the top. If management doesn't care, why should the employees? Why not buy and make as much inventory as possible? We'll never have stockouts, manufacturing can have long production runs, and product design can design the perfect product that does everything. Oh, finance may complain a little, and sales may complain a lot (because we have to charge so much), but our suppliers, customers, and employees will be happy. What is wrong with that?

Well, for one thing, everybody may be happy for a month or so, but then you will have to start paying for all that inventory you bought and made. It won't be long before you are out of business. Obviously nobody wants that to happen (except your competitors), so executive management does care about managing inventory. The question to be answered is, "To what degree do they care or get involved?" The only advice I can give you about this TIP is simple and to the point: **Management must establish and lead a company culture where rightsizing inventory is a way of life. It must be committed and involved for this to happen.**

Table 11.2 shows the Woodstock inventory balances at the end of November, and Table 11.3 shows the raw material inventory turns based on the estimated annual cost of goods sold (COGS).

Table 11.2 Inventory Balance (x1,000,000)

Month end	31 Jan	28 Feb	31 Mar	30 Apr	31 May	30 Jun	31 Jul	31 Aug	30 Sep	31 Oct	30 Nov
Forecast	7.2	7.9	9.7	7.1	5.9	9.0	9.3	8.7	7.0	7.4	10.6
Orders	5.8	7.4	9.6	7.7	6.8	8.8	7.7	8.8	8.0	7.5	10.0
Total starting inventory	40.0	41.0	40.9	40.3	39.0	38.1	36.7	35.7	34.1	33.1	31.6
Start FG inventory	15.5	15.7	15.8	15.3	14.9	14.5	14.2	13.7	13.0	13.1	12.5
+Production @ COGS	4.1	5.1	6.0	4.8	4.2	5.6	4.7	5.2	5.5	4.5	6.8
−Shipments @ COGS	3.9	5.0	6.5	5.2	4.6	5.9	5.2	5.9	5.4	5.1	6.7
End FG inventory	15.7	15.8	15.3	14.9	14.5	14.2	13.7	13.0	13.1	12.5	12.6
Start WIP inventory	7.5	7.6	7.7	7.4	7.1	7.1	6.5	6.2	5.9	5.5	5.3
+Material issues	3.4	4.2	4.8	3.9	3.5	4.3	3.8	4.3	4.2	3.7	5.4
+Labor and overhead	0.8	1.0	0.9	0.6	0.7	0.7	0.6	0.6	0.9	0.6	1.1
−Production @ COGS	4.1	5.1	6.0	4.8	4.2	5.6	4.7	5.2	5.5	4.5	6.8
End WIP inventory	7.6	7.7	7.4	7.1	7.1	6.5	6.2	5.9	5.5	5.3	5.0
Start raw inventory	17.0	17.7	17.4	17.6	17.0	16.5	16.0	15.8	15.2	14.5	13.8
+Material purchases	4.1	3.9	5.0	3.3	3.0	3.8	3.6	3.7	3.5	3.0	5.0
−Material issues	3.4	4.2	4.8	3.9	3.5	4.3	3.8	4.3	4.2	3.7	5.4
End raw inventory	17.7	17.4	17.6	17.0	16.5	16.0	15.8	15.2	14.5	13.8	13.4
Total ending inventory	41.0	40.9	40.3	39.0	38.1	36.7	35.7	34.1	33.1	31.6	31.0

Table 11.3   Woodstock RM Inventory Turns Improvement

Month end	31 Dec	31 Mar	30 Jun	30 Sep	31 Oct	30 Nov
Inventory turns	3.9	3.8	4.1	4.6		
End raw inventory—M$	17.0	17.6	16.0	14.5	13.8	13.4
Annual COGS—M$						66.0

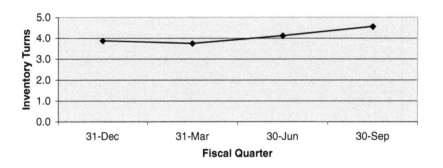

Chapter 12

Silos Can Be Turned into a Collaborative Supply-Chain Network

December 31: Supply-Chain Manager Meeting and Companywide Video Conference

Woodstock Inventory: $30.1 Million

My name is Adriana and I am the president of Woodstock Lighting Group. I'm very excited. Today is going to be a wonderful day. I get the opportunity to speak with all our employees about our accomplishments for the year and our bright outlook for the future. I'm really proud of this team and want to tell it. This will be the first time I will be using a video conference to speak with everyone in "real time," and I have spent a lot of time preparing my notes on what I want to say.

When I joined Woodstock as an accountant almost 16 years ago, little did I think that I would be president of the company one day. Well, I've been president for three years now, and I'm looking forward to many more years leading this fine group of people. To think I almost quit two years ago when the going really got tough. But my children, Austin and Marlene, convinced me to stay. It was their confidence in me that kept me going. Being president of a company isn't a "nine to five" job, and I have missed far too many soccer games and dance recitals.

I'm not a vindictive person, but Joe was wearing me out. I tried not to show it, especially when others were around. His negative attitude and his large ego alienated him from a lot of people. To this day, people are still trying to find out whether Joe quit or I fired him. But I'll never tell. Only the Board of Directors and I know what happened. Arnie was the right choice to replace Joe as vice president of operations. When I retire, I will recommend to the board that it consider Arnie for my job. That is, if he doesn't retire before I do. It's good to see how our employees have rallied around him this year. They say the sign of good leaders is that they surround themselves with good managers — and he is the best.

Today at the video conference, I will report the year-end results. I don't want to bore everyone with a lot of facts and figures so I will just hit the highlights of last year's accomplishments. But first I have a meeting with all our supply-chain managers to review our new inventory rightsizing model that was developed by the Harmony Team. This day is going to pass very quickly.

Adriana's Meeting with the Supply-Chain Managers

I personally want to thank each and every one of you for an outstanding year. We have turned the corner and have set the stage for many successful years to come. I will go into the financial results when I address all our employees at our video conference later today. But for now, I want to talk about our inventory rightsizing efforts and accomplishments for the year. As you all should be aware, I firmly believe that controlling the level and location of inventory in our supply chain will be the key to our future success. Along with the Harmony Team, you have worked hard to build a solid inventory management foundation, and you should be proud of your achievements.

The Woodstock inventory rightsizing model you have all developed together will be the model we will use to guide our business for years to come. Figure 12.1 is the current version of the inventory model. I hesitate to use the words "final version" because it will always be an ongoing, iterative process, being adjusted to fit the current business environment.

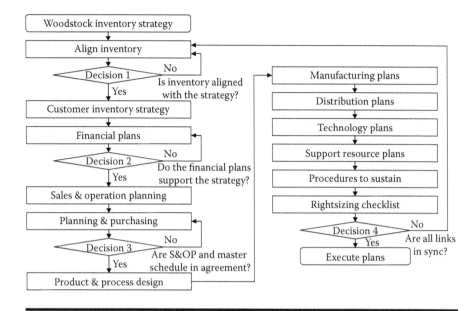

Figure 12.1 Woodstock inventory rightsizing model.

Although the flow of the model implies a "sequential process," it is in reality a "concurrent process" with all activities being worked on at the same time. I have chosen to present this model to you myself rather than have the Harmony Team present it because I strongly believe this model will be the key to our success in the future.

Woodstock Inventory Strategy

Contrary to public opinion, rightsizing inventory doesn't start with the customer. It starts with Woodstock. When we decided what business to be in and what markets to serve, we were defining our own inventory strategy. The very nature of our flashlight market dictates that we make flashlights (make-to-stock) and sell them from inventory. This is the plan until we can get our total lead time, including manufacturing, to be less than our customer delivery lead time. Since this isn't going to happen in the short term, we must make-to-stock and sell-from-stock. The spotlight market is somewhat different. The nature of that market requires that we make-to-order or assemble-to-order. Until we can reduce our purchasing and manufacturing lead time, this strategy calls for us to stock raw materials and subassemblies rather than finished goods.

The beacon light market requires a third strategy. The nature of this market is that we engineer-to-order or make-to-order (with the exception of the spare parts and service part of our business). This strategy calls for stocking a minimal amount of standard raw materials and subassemblies and no finished goods.

So you see, until we can reduce our total lead time and operate with a minimum amount of inventory, we must follow the inventory strategies dictated by the marketplace for our business. I believe it really struck home for me when the inventory got out of control last year. Around $40 million is a lot of inventory; far more inventory than we need or should have to run our business. The first place for us to start was to recognize how important inventory rightsizing is to our business. It is by far our single biggest cost of doing business, and we must pay serious attention to it.

I knew then that we had to change the way we thought about inventory and a change of company culture had to take place. After all, our entire supply chain exists to provide inventory to our customers. If we can't do it more efficiently and cost effectively than our competition, we will indeed cease to exist. The Harmony Team was established to help drive our inventory rightsizing effort. We recognized that inventory could not be managed effectively by individual silos and it would take a collaborative effort across all supply-chain links.

In order for all of our supply-chain links to collaborate on rightsizing inventory, we all needed to understand what role each link played in managing inventory. It has been an eye opener for me, as I'm sure it has been for each of you. It has taken us a year to get to know everyone's role, and even at that, we still have more to learn from each other. The Harmony Team began by benchmarking all our vital inventory statistics. We needed to understand where we are today before we could begin the inventory rightsizing effort. We did it, and it wasn't a pretty picture.

Align Inventory to Company Strategy

We compared our inventory strategies (make-to-stock, make-to-order, assemble-to-order, and engineer-to-order) with our inventory positions (raw material, work-in-process, and finished goods) and inventory locations (storeroom, manufacturing, distribution, etc.) in our supply chain. The results of this comparison were surprising. To highlight two areas, we found that beacon lights (make-to-order and engineer-to-order) had 50 percent of its inventory in finished goods, when in fact it should have no finished goods inventory. In contrast, the flashlight strategy (make-to-stock) only had 46 percent of its inventory in finished goods, and 18 percent of its inventory in work-in-process.

As you will hear later today, we are in the process of realigning our inventories to match our company inventory strategy and have made some progress. It will take us some time to get where we want to be. But as you can see from the inventory rightsizing model, we continue to go through the process of matching inventory position and location to our inventory strategy.

Customer Inventory Strategy

I started out by saying that inventory strategy is driven by our business plan, which defines the marketplaces we will service. We then need to align our inventory to match that strategy. Once under way it is important to understand the inventory needs of our customers. At this point, we are no longer talking about a "marketplace" in general terms but specific customers by name and location. Based on input from these customers (internal and external), we have developed a criterion for the perfect order and are striving to achieve that criterion. We have adopted a policy of customer literacy. We want to learn as much about the customers as possible, including learning about the needs of our customer's customer. We are also seeking to understand our customers' inventory flows and inventory planning processes.

We are exploring the possibility of allowing our customers access to our inventory information. We are in the early stages of doing this and will provide some form of inventory information to key customers next year. We also want to get access to our key customers' MRP output reports for planned orders. If we can do this it will greatly improve our planning process. This entire process of trying to get to know the customer better is called customer relationship management (CRM), and we are actually exploring the use of customer relationship management (CRM) software for next year.

We are also in the process of aligning our inventory positions, locations, and levels with the traditional inventory life-cycle phases, and have found many items to be out of alignment with the life-cycle phase they should reflect. I have visited many of our customers this year and have listened to their concerns and issues. Overall, most of them are pleased with our products, but they tell me our service needs to improve. A few of our key customers are very excited about our inventory rightsizing efforts and believe it will help improve our relationship with them.

Financial Plans

Our cash flow has improved dramatically over the year, thanks in no small part to our inventory rightsizing efforts. About halfway through the year, we started to track budgets to actual expense for each of our supply-chain links and made adjustments when they got out of line. Finance has implemented some meaningful performance metrics related to inventory valuation and has started to give feedback to each link in our supply chain. We only turned inventory 1.7 times last year and have shown some improvement this year. Our inventory accuracy last year was about 88 percent from a financial point of view and somewhere around 75 percent at the SKU level. We began cycle counting this year and have seen vast improvements. We have also sorted our inventory into ABC classifications and have established a criterion for each category.

As you will learn in other sections of our inventory rightsizing model, finance now has access to all our company planning documents, in particular our new sales and operations plan (S&OP). Rather than relying only on the forecast, the new S&OP gives finance access to information it never had before. This will greatly enhance its ability to monitor projected cash inflow and outflow. We have begun to write off certain inventory items that no longer have value in the marketplace. In order to keep these write-offs under control, any inventory write-off transaction of greater than $1,000 must be signed off by Pat and me. Inventory carrying cost last year exceeded $10 million. This year, because of the reduction in inventory and more realistic carrying cost data, that number has been reduced to $7.0 million. That is a $3.0 million savings. Not only did we achieve a cost savings, but we also freed up some much-needed space in our facilities.

Sales and Operations Planning

We have learned from sales and marketing just how competitive it is out there in the marketplace. Our competition is global, and having inventory stockouts may cause us to lose an order — and the customer as well. This past year marketing conducted a detailed analysis of the marketplace and our customer needs. Its findings are being shared with all supply-chain links. Some of the marketing programs we implemented in the past have had a negative effect on inventory. We have identified them and have stopped using them. They were doing more harm than good.

This year the sales team has a better understanding of the role forecasting plays with our inventory strategy. The forecast is now part of our S&OP process. The data is more realistic and is being shared with all supply-chain links. We have changed our sales compensation incentive programs to match our inventory strategy. Salespeople are now properly compensated to sell the large inventories of slow-moving goods that are just sitting in our warehouses. IT has found a sales forecasting package that will meet our forecasting needs, and it will be implemented early next year.

We have now formalized our S&OP process and educated all the appropriate employees who will be part of this process. All key supply-chain links are now taking an active role in developing the S&OP. The business plan is a critical input to the S&OP process. In the past, I made the mistake of not sharing the details of the business plan with all supply-chain links. I have now corrected this problem, and all supply-chain links now know the details of the business plan. The accuracy of the S&OP will be key to our successfully rightsizing inventory. The S&OP document drives all other planning processes and documents.

Planning and Purchasing

Planning and purchasing are responsible for managing the six "rights" of inventory management: the right product, at the right time, in the right quality, in the right quantity, at the right price, from the right supplier. The planning group disaggregates the S&OP plan and creates an MPS that drives the MRP process; all important steps to rightsizing our inventory. They also check for available resources to meet the MPS and MRP plans. Until recently, planning spent most of its time (about 70 percent) expediting needed materials and replanning the MPS.

That is starting to change. I met with Cyndie recently and she told me she and her team now spend less than 50 percent of their time expediting; freeing them up to fine-tune the MPS and MRP plans. This year we have implemented a new planning policy. We have divided our MPS into three separate planning zones, and different levels of authority are required to make schedule changes within those zones. Everyone now understands the impact a schedule change will make on the entire manufacturing plan. We have policies and procedures as to who should be contacted about specific changes and the time frame required to notify that group about the change.

Sales and design engineering are continuing to review our inventory for items that can be substituted, rather than going out and purchasing more inventory. This activity has helped us reduce the amount of excess and slow-moving inventory. Overall, raw material inventory has been reduced by $4 million this year, going from $17 million to $13 million. Our sales link is doing the same with the finished goods inventory. Actual sales are compared to forecasted sales every month. This information is being communicated to all of you. I am also pleased to say that purchasing has established an SRM program with several of our key suppliers, and they are working together to improve our costs and lead times. In addition to that, they have established a vendor managed inventory system with our battery supplier. This will help us reduce costs and maintain a lower level of battery inventory.

We are back on track with our MRP system, and our BILL of Integrity has become much more reliable and accurate. Our goal is to achieve 100 percent accuracy by the end of next fiscal year. We have implemented a BILL of Integrity audit procedure that I am confident will make this happen.

Product and Process Design

We now understand the importance that product design plays in the new product development process. We have found that 50 percent to 70 percent of our product cost is determined in the product design phase. Product design no longer works in a silo. It now works concurrently with all of you, and our suppliers and customers are part of the design team from the very beginning. Beyond the product itself, product design has an impact on other supply-chain costs such as packaging, storage, picking, packing, and shipping. All of these are considerations now being dealt with during the product design phase.

Manufacturing is also impacted by the product design. All new products are now designed for manufacturability and for efficient assembly.

Process design is another link that has moved from being a silo organization to being a cross-functional work team. We have reorganized the layout of the assembly areas and have turned some into U-shaped work cells. We will continue to look at other work centers to develop a more efficient layout and continuous flow of product. A rewarding by-product of this process has been the rebalancing of operation times between operators. I truly believe one of the biggest accomplishments we have made this year was the cross-training of our employees. Not only has this enhanced their personal skill sets and improved morale, but it has greatly enhanced our flexibility to respond to changing production schedules. At another level, we are balancing workloads at all work centers and work cells so that upstream and downstream workloads are in sync.

We are now using reusable standard size containers to move work-in-process (WIP) inventory through our supply chain. This will greatly improve the flow, visibility, and handling of inventory. We are developing value stream maps for every operation at every work center. All non-value-added steps will be eliminated. The next step after that is to improve the efficiency of the value-added steps that remain. We will continue to question every activity performed throughout our entire supply chain.

Manufacturing Plans

Manufacturing continues to look for ways to reduce the amount of raw materials in our supply chain. WIP inventory has been reduced by $2.7 million this year, going from $7.5 million to $4.8 million, an outstanding achievement. Manufacturing lead time has been addressed and is being diligently watched for opportunities to further reduce the total lead time. We have implemented a new load profile report that has helped us move more people to overloaded work centers. This has helped us reduce overtime expense and maintain a stable work force. I'm pleased to say that this is the first year in a very long time when we haven't had to lay off direct labor employees.

One of the biggest manufacturing undertakings this year has been the implementation of a "lean manufacturing" philosophy. Using this approach, we were able to eliminate many non-value-added steps in our manufacturing processes. Going forward into next year we will continue to aggressively pursue lean manufacturing techniques. We have identified many areas where waste can be eliminated, leaving only value-added steps in the process. As part of our lean initiative we have implemented a companywide good housekeeping program using the 5s approach. I can't tell you what a pleasure it is to walk around the plant now. It is clean and very organized. Next year we are taking the good housekeeping initiative into the offices.

As part of our effort to improve the accuracy of our BILL of Integrity, we have implemented better controls in our storeroom. No material will be moved out of the storeroom without the proper paperwork. In addition to that, storeroom personnel are now bringing materials to the work centers rather than operators leaving their machines to fetch materials.

Distribution Plans

Effective the first of the year, we will begin the process of shutting down our distribution centers in Chicago and Texas. California and New Jersey will remain. We will contract with third-party logistics providers to service specific areas of our marketplace not easily reached by our two remaining distribution centers. Unfortunately, these closures will affect 60 of our employees; all of them will be offered an opportunity to stay with the company somewhere in our supply chain. For those who choose to move on, we are putting together a financial package and will help each and every person find gainful employment in their local area.

The strain on our warehouse space has been eased by the reduction in finished goods inventory. Finished goods inventory went from $15.5 million at the beginning of the year down to $12.3 million at the end of the year. This represents a reduction of $3.2 million. I am pleased to say that we no longer have trailers full of inventory sitting in our yard. Another area that has shown some improvement this year was our order fill rate. We have gone from an average fill rate of 85 percent to 90 percent, and our goal for next year is a fill rate of 100 percent. By continuing to work together as a team I am confident that we can achieve this.

Our inventory cycle counting program is in full swing, and our inventory accuracy has improved from 88 percent overall to 95 percent. Although we didn't meet our goal of 99 percent by the end of this year, we are well on our way to achieve that goal by early first quarter of next year.

Effective the first of the year, we are going to outsource our reverse logistics function. It is not part of our core competency, and we have contracted with a 4PL who specializes in this activity and has an excellent reputation in the marketplace. I am confident that reverse logistics can be a profit center for us as we move into new markets for our products. There will be no employee layoffs because of this outsourcing of reverse logistics.

Information Technology Plans

Every single employee of Woodstock uses the services of our information technology link. Although we think of product moving through our supply chain, we also have learned that moving information through our supply chain is just as important. Information can and will replace inventory in our supply chain. IT interacts with our suppliers and customers and in some cases it interacts with our suppliers' suppliers and our customers' customers. In fact, due to the ever-growing popularity and use of the Internet, we are even communicating with the general public.

This is a good thing, and in the very near future we hope to expand the use of this service by offering an online sales catalog. You will hear more about this exciting opportunity early next year. Although IT is responsible for maintaining our BILL of Integrity once the data is in the system, we all still have the responsibility to input accurate data that can be converted into useful and meaningful information.

We have put in a no-change policy for the implementation and use of application software. This means we will no longer modify off-the-shelf software unless and until we are convinced that the modifications are necessary. The use of bar coding will be expanded next year, and somewhere in our future we will look at RFID. EDI and EDT will also continue to be part of our near future. Next year you will see an expanded use of these technologies.

IT will no longer head up end-user application implementations. Although it will continue to be a vital part of the implementation team, each of you will have end users from your team heading up application software implementations. IT is considered an asset that is important to the future of Woodstock. I expect it to keep us on the leading edge of the new technologies as they emerge.

Support Resource Plans

I wish to recognize four of our supply-chain links that are not often considered when we talk about rightsizing inventory in our supply chain. The contributions of field service, human resources, maintenance, and facilities management have been considerable.

Once again, field service has achieved its sales goals. This makes six years in a row it has done so. My sincere congratulations to all of you. A significant portion of its revenue comes from selling inventory, 25 percent of which it also installs, field service's contribution goes beyond that. This year field service staff have worked with all of you to help rightsize our inventory. They know some of our customers better than anyone, and they have firsthand knowledge about how some of our products work in the field. They have helped product design eliminate some unnecessary parts in our products. They have also identified parts that could be changed to make our products function better in operation. They are now providing important customer and product information into our CRM system, which will be automated next year. Field service is also communicating directly with our suppliers to help them improve the parts we buy from them.

We have eliminated the depot inventory that we stored close to airports, and all spare parts will be shipped out of New Jersey. We are combining field service spare parts with maintenance and facilities management inventory into one physical location in New Jersey. Rather than spending time managing inventory, field service staff can spend that time helping us in many other ways. When they are not in the field at customer sites, they are helping out maintenance and facility management, where their expertise is the most helpful. They also spent a lot of time this year on the factory floor with our industrial engineers seeking ways to improve our manufacturing processes.

Human resources (HR) has made a contribution to our inventory rightsizing efforts as well. I am pleased to announce that we now have established "Woodstock University," our own internal resource for education and training. An important part of the curriculum is the inventory management program. There are varying degrees of education and training available for all employees. Everyone will know and understand how important it is to manage inventory effectively.

HR has also been instrumental in developing the new "shared" performance measurements that we have implemented throughout the year. I know each of you supply chain managers has spent a lot of your time with Aimee and her team in accomplishing this. HR has kept up to date on the latest benefit and salary standards that apply to our industry. This has been, and will continue to be, an asset as we try to attract the very best people to join our team. The newly revised company newsletter will be rolled out in January, and I will personally write an inventory- related article every month. An employee of the month for outstanding contributions to our inventory rightsizing effort will be chosen and recognized in the newsletter. Starting early next year, HR will migrate from a legacy system over to our company ERP system.

Maintenance keeps our machines and equipment in good working order so that our supply chain can operate at the highest possible level of efficiency. Starting in the fourth quarter of this year, maintenance now publishes a schedule of preventative maintenance activities. We have never done this before and we see it as an asset to our rightsizing efforts. Maintenance has also gone beyond just performing preventative maintenance. It is now taking a proactive role in improving our machine efficiency so that we can improve efficiency without adding stress to our machine operators.

Maintenance has played a big role in helping us reduce machine setup time — and you all understand how important that is. The benefits gained thus far have been good. Maintenance personnel have reduced the setup times dramatically, going from hours to minutes. This is wonderful; it will help reduce our total lead time and have a positive impact on lot sizes. This all translates to improving our flexibility so that we can respond to customer changes faster. The new AGVS system that was approved earlier in the year will be installed by maintenance in February of next year. This will help us improve the flow and movement of inventory between our storeroom, manufacturing, order picking, and shipping.

Facilities management officials have been actively involved in our Good Housekeeping campaign. They have been instrumental in keeping our aisles safe and free of debris. The tool room, which was part of the facilities management machine shop, has been moved. All tools are now stored at point of use in the proper work center. It is no longer necessary for a machine operator to go seek out a needed tool. This will improve operator efficiency and machine productivity. Throughout the year, as we reduced inventory, facilities has been right there removing and reorganizing the shelves used to store inventory. The storeroom is looking better every day.

A new roof was installed in Building #2 this year. This will minimize the amount of damaged goods we have to deal with. I don't know if you were aware or not, but we had to scrap some inventory this year due to the leak in the roof. Facilities, too, has been working with industrial engineering to improve the plant layout so that materials can flow on a continuous basis.

Sustaining the Inventory Rightsizing Model

Thus far, I have spoken about all the positive things we have done together to rightsize our inventory. Last month Jack highlighted the ten most common mistakes companies make when trying to rightsize their inventory. I would like to see that list published and sent out to all employees with an explanation of how we can avoid falling into that category. We must install this new way of life in the minds of all our employees. We will constantly review our inventory rightsizing model and adjust it as business conditions change. We will have a supply-chain managers meeting every month, led by the Harmony Team. All supply-chain links will report on the current inventory status in their link and what they are doing to continue the rightsizing effort. Managing inventory correctly is a cross-functional effort, and the old mentality of managing inventory in silos is no longer part of our company culture. Anyone can reduce and "rightsize" inventory over a given period of time, but only a change of culture will sustain the effort on a continuous basis. That's the way it will be for Woodstock. Thank you for your time. You have done a wonderful job of changing our inventory silos into a collaborative supply-chain network.

Adriana's Video Conference with All Employees

Good morning. I wanted to share my thoughts with all of you, report the highlights of last year, and talk a little bit about our bright future together. It has been a good year, and I want to thank you all for your contributions. For the first time in a very long time our company was profitable. Although we didn't make a lot of money, we did report a profit of $5 million for the year. Our sales increased by 9 percent, going from $90 million to $98 million, and we only missed our sales target by 2 percent. All three divisions contributed to this effort.

This year we have embarked on an inventory rightsizing effort with the objectives of aligning our inventory to our business strategy and our customers' business strategy. I'm pleased to report that we have made significant progress and we are well prepared to continue our efforts into the future. As shown in Table 12.1, we started the year with $40.0 million in inventory and ended the year with $30.1 million. This represents a 25 percent inventory reduction. All three categories of inventory were reduced; raw materials were reduced by 24 percent, WIP inventory was reduced by 36 percent, and finished goods was reduced by 21 percent. Not only have you reduced inventory, but you have repositioned it in our supply chain to more closely reflect our business strategy and the inventory requirements of our customers.

Table 12.2 shows that we have gotten rid of $1.6 million of excess inventory and $2.9 million of obsolete inventory. This represents 45 percent of the total dollar amount of inventory reduction. In addition, the value of our "A" items has been reduced by $3 million.

Table 12.3 shows the greatest percentage of inventory reduction comes from the Beacon Light Division. This represents a 55 percent reduction, going from $4 million to $1.8 million. The largest dollar value reduction comes from the Flashlight Division, which represents a $6 million reduction, going from $28 million down to $22 million; a 22 percent reduction. Our Spotlight Division saw a raw material reduction of 25 percent and a total inventory reduction of 21 percent.

Based on our cost of goods this year, and our average inventory throughout the year, our inventory turns have increased from 1.7 turns ($60M/$35M = 1.7) to 1.9 turns ($66M/$34M = 1.9). Based on this formula the inventory turns didn't change much. Most of the inventory reduction came toward the latter part of the year and so this formula doesn't represent a true picture of what we have accomplished. However, based on our year-end inventory as shown in Table 12.4 the inventory turns by

Table 12.1 Twelve-Month Sales and Inventory

Month end		31 Jan	28 Feb	31 Mar	30 Apr	31 May	30 Jun	31 Jul	31 Aug	30 Sep	31 Oct	30 Nov	31 Dec
Forecast		7.2	7.9	9.7	7.1	5.9	9.0	9.3	8.7	7.0	7.4	10.6	10.2
Annual forecast	100.0			24.8			22.0			25.0			28.2
Orders		5.8	7.4	9.6	7.7	6.8	8.8	7.7	8.8	8.0	7.5	10.0	9.9
Annual orders	98.0			22.8			23.3			24.5			27.4
Total starting inventory		40.0	41.0	40.9	40.3	39.0	38.1	36.7	35.7	34.1	33.1	31.6	31.0
Start FG inventory		15.5	15.7	15.8	15.3	14.9	14.5	14.2	13.7	13.0	13.1	12.5	12.6
+Production @ COGS		4.1	5.1	6.0	4.8	4.2	5.6	4.7	5.2	5.5	4.5	6.8	6.3
−Shipments @ COGS		3.9	5.0	6.5	5.2	4.6	5.9	5.2	5.9	5.4	5.1	6.7	6.6
End FG inventory		15.7	15.8	15.3	14.9	14.5	14.2	13.7	13.0	13.1	12.5	12.6	12.3
Start WIP inventory		7.5	7.6	7.7	7.4	7.1	7.1	6.5	6.2	5.9	5.5	5.3	5.0
+Material issues		3.4	4.2	4.8	3.9	3.5	4.3	3.8	4.3	4.2	3.7	5.4	5.2
+Labor and overhead		0.8	1.0	0.9	0.6	0.7	0.7	0.6	0.6	0.9	0.6	1.1	0.9
−Production @ COGS		4.1	5.1	6.0	4.8	4.2	5.6	4.7	5.2	5.5	4.5	6.8	6.3
End WIP inventory		7.6	7.7	7.4	7.1	7.1	6.5	6.2	5.9	5.5	5.3	5.0	4.8
Start raw inventory		17.0	17.7	17.4	17.6	17.0	16.5	16.0	15.8	15.2	14.5	13.8	13.4
+Material purchases		4.1	3.9	5.0	3.3	3.0	3.8	3.6	3.7	3.5	3.0	5.0	4.8
−Material issues		3.4	4.2	4.8	3.9	3.5	4.3	3.8	4.3	4.2	3.7	5.4	5.2
End raw inventory		17.7	17.4	17.6	17.0	16.5	16.0	15.8	15.2	14.5	13.8	13.4	13.0
Total ending inventory		41.0	40.9	40.3	39.0	38.1	36.7	35.7	34.1	33.1	31.6	31.0	30.1

Table 12.2   Woodstock Excess and Obsolete Inventory

		A	B	C	Excess	Obsolete
Flashlights						
Finished goods	From	5.9	3.5	2.4	0.8	0.4
	To	5.1	3.3	2.3	0.3	0
Work-in-process	From	2.5	1.5	1.0	0	0
	To	1.5	1.0	0.5	0	0
Raw materials	From	3.3	2.7	1.5	1.0	1.5
	To	3.1	2.1	1.4	0.6	0.8
Spotlights						
Finished goods	From	0.2	0.1	0	0	0.2
	To	0.1	0.1	0		0.1
Work-in-process	From	0.6	0.5	0.3	0	0.1
	To	0.7	0.5	0.3	0	0
Raw materials	From	1.9	1.1	1.0	1.5	0.5
	To	1.5	1.1	0.7	1.0	0.2
Beacon Lights						
Finished goods	From	0	0	0.5	0.5	1.0
	To	0	0	0.5	0.3	0.2
Work-in-process	From	0.6	0	0.2	0	0.2
	To	0.2	0	0.1	0	0
Raw materials	From	0.2	0.1	0	0	0.7
	To	0.1	0	0	0	0.4

Table 12.3   Woodstock Year-End Inventory by Division

Division	Raw Material	WIP	Finished Goods	Total
Flashlight	$8,000,000	$3,000,000	$11,000,000	$22,000,000
Spotlight	$4,500,000	$1,500,000	$300,000	$6,300,000
Beacon Light	$500,000	$300,000	$1,000,000	$1,800,000
Totals	$13,000,000	$4,800,000	$12,300,000	$30,100,000

category have improved dramatically. The higher (estimated) cost of goods was due to the increase in sales.

A recent analysis shows that our overall inventory accuracy has increased from 88 percent to 98 percent by the end of this year. Equally important, we have identified the root causes of those errors and are working hard

Table 12.4   Woodstock Total Inventory Turns Improvement

Quarter Ending	31 Dec	31 Mar	30 Jun	30 Sep	31 Dec	
FG inventory turns	4.3	4.3	4.6	5.0	5.4	
WIP inventory turns	8.8	8.9	10.2	12.0	13.8	
RM inventory turns	3.9	3.8	4.1	4.6	5.1	
Total inventory turns	1.7	1.6	1.8	2.0	2.2	
FG inventory ($M)	15.5	15.3	14.2	13.1	12.3	
WIP inventory ($M)	7.5	7.4	6.5	5.5	4.8	
RM inventory ($M)	17.0	17.6	16.0	14.5	13.0	
Total inventory ($M)	40.0	40.3	36.7	33.1	30.1	
Annual COGS ($M)						66.0

to correct them. You have accomplished all this without having a negative impact on customer service. On the contrary, we have seen vast improvements in this area. Our overall customer satisfaction, based on the perfect order criteria, has increased to 97 percent, and our order fill rate is approaching 99 percent. Our customers are more involved than ever before. They are working with us on improving our existing products, helping us design new products, and are also actively involved in the manufacturing of our products.

Last but not least, I want to congratulate all of you for your team spirit and cooperation. Thanks to the efforts of the Harmony Team, we now all understand the role each of us plays in our inventory rightsizing efforts. We no longer function as independent silos. Along with our customers, we now function as a single entity. We are one cross-functional, integrated supply chain with shared goals and objectives. We have made great strides but still have a long way to go. By working together we will get there. Don't ever give up hope. You are the key to our success. By working together we have turned our inventory silos into a collaborative supply-chain network. Thank you for your time...

It has been a long but satisfying year. There will be many new and difficult challenges in the years to come. But I truly believe we have the right team and we are doing the right things to rightsize our inventory. Knowing all that, last night I slept like a baby ...

Appendix A: Bibliography

The following titles have had a significant influence on the author and this book:

Alber, K.L. and Walker, W.T., *Supply Chain Management Principles and Techniques for the Practitioner*, APICS E&R Foundation, Alexandria, VA, 1998.

Brooks, R.B. and Wilson, L.W., *Inventory Record Accuracy: Unleashing the Power of Cycle Counting*, Oliver Wight Publications, Essex Junction, VT, 1993.

Conner, G., *Six Sigma and Other Improvement Tools, for the Small Shop*, Society of Manufacturing Engineers, Dearborn, MI, 2002.

Goldratt, E.M. and Cox, J., *The Goal: A Process of Ongoing Improvement*, Revised ed., North River Press, Croton-on-Hudson, New York, 1986.

Liker, J.K., *The Toyota Way*, McGraw-Hill, New York, 2004.

Lynn, B.C., *End of the Line: The Rise and Coming Fall of the Global Corporation*, Doubleday, New York, 2005.

Orlicky, J., *Material Requirements Planning: The New Way of Life in Production and Inventory Management*, McGraw-Hill, New York, 1975.

Walker, W.T., *Supply Chain Architecture: A Blueprint for Networking the Flow of Material, Information, and Cash*, CRC Press, Boca Raton, FL, 2005.

Williams, B.R., *Manufacturing for Survival: The How-to Guide for Practitioners and Managers*, Addison-Wesley, Reading, MA, 1996.

Womack, J.P. and Jones, D.T., *Lean Thinking: Banish Waste and Create Wealth in Your Corporation*, Free Press, New York, 2003 edition.

Appendix B:
TIPS on How to
"Rightsize" Inventory

TIP #1: Communicate, communicate, communicate … with everyone.

TIP #2: Someone in the company must recognize that change is needed, become the champion, and take a leadership role to make it happen.

TIP #3: Executive management must be committed and involved for change to take place.

TIP #4: If you want to learn anything, ask questions — lots of questions.

TIP #5: When starting out on an inventory rightsizing effort, you must first benchmark where you are in terms of current inventory levels by category and location in the supply chain.

TIP #6: Rightsizing inventory is the responsibility of everyone in the supply chain, and performance metrics should be shared by all links in the supply chain.

TIP #7: Pick a team, establish goals and objectives, benchmark where you are, and identify shared performance measurements. Communicate this to everyone.

TIP #8: Delegate authority, accountability, and responsibility to those who can best accomplish the task of rightsizing inventory in the supply chain.

TIP #9: Rightsizing inventory is not "just another project" with a start date and an end date; it has to become a new way of life for the company.

TIP #10: Start rightsizing your inventory by aligning your inventory levels to match your inventory strategies by product or division classifications.

TIP #11: Gather inventory data by type, location, and business segment. Compare them to the corporate inventory strategy. Any inconsistency in inventory and strategy must be addressed and corrected.

TIP #12: Inventory is considered as an asset on the company balance sheet. Inventory is a liability if you have more than you need to satisfy immediate customer requirements.

TIP #13: The perfect order must be considered from both the viewpoints of the seller and the buyer. The perfect order criteria must be measurable so that deviations can be corrected.

TIP #14: Successful supply chains have one characteristic in common; their ability to rapidly respond to change throughout their entire supply chain, not just one or two links in the chain.

TIP #15: A supply chain is only as strong as its weakest link; being world class in one link does you little good if your other links are weak.

TIP #16: Define the perfect order criteria and measure them. Communicate this to everyone in the supply chain.

TIP #17: The customer isn't always right, but if you want to keep the customer, you should do all you can to satisfy their requirements in a professional, businesslike manner.

TIP #18: Understanding the customers' needs is a good thing, but anticipating your customers' needs is an order winner that will help you sell more inventory.

TIP #19: We must present ourselves as one united, collaborative supply-chain network to our customers and establish clearly defined lines of communication with them.

TIP #20: Know as much as possible about your customer: their needs, wants, problems, plans, and who else they buy from.

TIP #21: A successful supply chain knows its customers well and can anticipate their inventory needs. In some cases, it may be an inventory need that they don't recognize they have.

TIP #22: Don't keep inventory information a secret. Share it with your customers. Ask your customers to share their inventory information with you.

TIP #23: Lead time is defined differently for each link in your supply chain. The most important definition is related to customer order lead time: from the time they ask you to ship the inventory until they receive the inventory.

TIP #24: We need to understand not only what inventory metrics our customers are using but also how they are using (calculating) it.

TIP #25: All stages of the sales cycle are equally important and should be measured throughout the entire supply chain.

TIP #26: It's nice to know how good we are; we have to know how bad we are.

TIP #27: Get all supply-chain links involved in the product design phase. Decisions made in this phase will have a significant impact on inventory in all the other inventory life-cycle phases.

TIP #28: All categories of inventory must be aligned with the product life-cycle strategy and must be aligned well before moving out of that particular product life-cycle phase.

TIP #29: Focus on high-value inventory items first. This will have the greatest impact on aligning inventory in your supply chain.

TIP #30: High inventory levels cannot always be blamed on the need for safety stock, because of customer uncertainty. More often than not, other problems cause the high levels of inventory.

TIP #31: Inventory levels will remain unabated and uncontrolled until accountability, responsibility, and shared performance metrics are assigned, measured, and communicated to all links in the supply chain.

TIP #32: Financial documents must be prepared in accordance with all laws and regulations, regardless of how bad they may make the company look. Inventory is a major component of financial reporting and must be presented as accurately as possible.

TIP #33: Inventory moves into our financial reporting system as an asset on our balance sheet and remains there until it is shipped and billed to a customer (accounts receivable) or disposed of in some form or another.

TIP #34: Inventory also moves into our financial reporting system as a liability (if we didn't pay for it yet) as part of the accounts payable on our balance sheet and remains there until it is paid for.

TIP #35: Finance looks at inventory turns and days of supply in the aggregate, but for operations to address this issue in its inventory rightsizing efforts, inventory turns, days of supply, and COGS need to be broken down into inventory types and families at the item-level detail.

TIP #36: Analyze your inventory for activity. If there hasn't been any activity on an item in inventory for 12 months or longer, consider disposing of it. This includes raw materials and finished goods.

TIP #37: There is a direct relationship between the level of inventory carried and the cost of carrying inventory. When the inventory level increases, carrying cost increases; when the inventory level decreases, carrying cost decreases.

TIP #38: Select an inventory valuation method that best reflects the true value of your inventory and conforms to GAAP guidelines.

TIP #39: Inventory valuation must be realistic and reflect the true value of your inventory. Consider adjusting the value of your inventory downward if it falls below the current replacement cost or the current selling price of the product. Take the loss earlier rather than later.

TIP #40: Cost accounting must capture the true cost of adding value to a raw material, so that finished goods are valued correctly for sales and marketing to establish selling prices that conform to company profitability guidelines.

TIP #41: As a raw material moves through the manufacturing process, labor adds value and increases the cost of the item. If the item goes back into inventory, it goes back at a higher cost, thus increasing the total value of the inventory. If possible, delay adding value to a raw material until it can be shipped without going back into inventory.

TIP #42: Inventory inaccuracy has a negative impact on the entire supply chain, can decrease customer service and productivity levels, and can increase costs. You must improve inventory accuracy.

TIP #43: Each company must define the criteria used to measure inventory accuracy, measure accuracy against the criteria, and communicate all this to all employees in the supply chain.

TIP #44: Marketing has a direct and indirect impact on inventory levels and strategy. Typically, the higher the forecast (make-to-stock strategy), the higher the inventory level. Marketing programs and budgets should be set in proportion to inventory levels and inventory strategy.

TIP #45: Supply-chain links within a single supply chain may have conflicting inventory goals and objectives. You cannot rightsize your inventory until these conflicting objectives are resolved and balanced.

TIP #46: The purpose of establishing inventory planning zones is to recognize the degree of difficulty to make changes and to allow enough time for all supply-chain links to react to the change in an economical, efficient manner.

TIP #47: Forecasting has a direct impact on inventory levels. Overforecasting may cause inventory levels to increase if it's not sold, whereas underforecasting will decrease inventory levels but may lead to stockouts.

TIP #48: The ability to rapidly respond to forecast changes will greatly improve your ability to rightsize your inventory.

TIP #49: Selection and successful implementation of a forecasting tool will greatly improve your chances of rightsizing your inventory.

TIP #50: All sources of demand must be considered when planning for inventory supply and demand at the S&OP level.

TIP #51: The business plan is a major input to the S&OP process; a realistic, achievable production plan cannot be developed without knowing and following the guidelines that are established in the business plan.

TIP # 52: The production plan, as part of the S&OP process, is an important tool that, if used correctly, can help us rightsize our inventory.

TIP #53: Do not attempt to drastically reduce inventory levels of active items until the impact on customer service levels is understood by all links in the supply chain. Plan to reduce inventory, then measure customer service performance. If there is no negative impact on customer service, plan to reduce inventory again.

TIP #54: The S&OP process plays a major role in your inventory rightsizing efforts. All other steps in the inventory planning process are guided by the inventory planning numbers established in the S&OP.

TIP #55: The S&OP is the primary tool used to develop inventory plans for producing, purchasing, and stocking specific end products, spare parts, and subassemblies.

TIP #56: The MPS disaggregates the numbers in the S&OP, and the sum of the items in the MPS must be equal to the product family numbers in the S&OP.

TIP #57: The ability to react to change in a rapid and responsive manner will be a key to any inventory rightsizing effort.

TIP #58: Develop, document, and communicate a procedure to be followed when changes occur. Educate all employees on the importance of communicating changes to the proper links in the supply chain.

TIP #59: Changes to the MPS in zone 1 can increase costs and inventory levels. Changes in zone 1 should be kept to a minimum and analyzed for the total impact to the supply chain.

TIP #60: Every time an unplanned order (impact order) is expedited into the schedule, another order (or more) should be de-expedited.

TIP #61: The contents of the business plan related to inventory management activities should be communicated to all supply-chain employees who have an impact on achieving those goals and objectives.

TIP #62: Balancing workload (MPS) with available capacity is an important step in rightsizing inventory levels in the supply chain.

TIP #63: Reducing machine setup time will allow for producing smaller batches of inventory more frequently and will help reduce the amount of inventory carried in stock.

TIP #64: Constantly review and update your lot-size rules with a hypothetical goal of reducing all lot sizes to one.

TIP #65: The MPS must be realistic and achievable. If not, inventory will increase and customer service will decrease over time.

TIP #66: Executing the recommendations of MRP will have a significant impact on inventory rightsizing efforts.

TIP #67: Inventory accuracy must be in the 98 percent to 100 percent range for MRP to function successfully. It will be almost impossible to rightsize inventory without this level of inventory accuracy.

TIP #68: Have design engineering review the current inventory and provide a list of parts that can be used to substitute for the primary part as long as it can meet the criteria of form, fit, and function.

TIP #69: Inaccurate purchasing and manufacturing lead times have a significant impact on inventory levels and require constant review and updating. An operating policy must be in place to ensure that lead times are current and up to date.

TIP #70: Lot-size rules have a significant impact on inventory levels and should be reviewed and updated constantly. An operating policy must be in place to ensure this happens.

TIP #71: The four areas of data integrity don't just apply to MRP; these four areas are important to all links in the supply chain.

TIP #72: Because purchased material typically represents more than 50 percent of COGS, focusing on SRM with key suppliers will significantly improve inventory rightsizing efforts.

TIP #73: Implementation of a successful (and mutually beneficial) VMI program with key suppliers will benefit inventory rightsizing efforts.

TIP #74: Any drastic changes in your MRP data may cause inventory levels to rise, until inventory is rebalanced and adjusted to the new planning requirements. Over time, it will begin to correct itself and decrease accordingly.

TIP #75: Product design has a major impact on inventory costs through every link in the supply chain. The design must become a cross-functional process with inputs from all links in the supply chain, including suppliers and customers.

TIP #76: Designing products collaboratively with other links in the supply chain can benefit your inventory rightsizing effort by eliminating or reducing the total number and variety of parts that have to be planned for and stocked in inventory.

TIP #77: Use an inventory postponement strategy that shifts product differentiation as far downstream as possible, so that final inventory configuration is committed when customer requirements are known.

TIP #78: Look to substitute existing inventory into a product, rather than going out to buy a similar part, if the substituted part can perform the same form, fit, and function to meet and satisfy customer expectations.

TIP #79: A formal, structured part numbering system should be used. Item codes should be kept as short and simple as possible to eliminate the potential for translation errors, which may impede your inventory rightsizing efforts.

TIP #80: Pushing inventory to another upstream or downstream link in the supply chain will not solve your inventory rightsizing problem. It will only pass the problem on to another link in the supply chain.

TIP #81: Proper design of the manufacturing process has a significant impact on the total inventory in the supply chain, in general, and work-in-process inventory, in particular.

TIP #82: Process design must consider the impact process changes in a work center might have on the upstream and downstream work centers in its path.

TIP #83: Process design cannot take place in one inventory silo at a time. It must be a collaborative effort across all supply-chain links.

TIP #84: Operations and inventory flows must be sequenced and balanced in a work cell so that inventory flows on a continuous basis without WIP inventory increasing between operations.

TIP #85: Make use of existing space to store and move inventory more effectively, rather than looking to relocate to a new facility.

TIP #86: Use value-stream mapping as a tool to help identify non-value-added steps in the inventory flow process. This should include the process step, distance moved, and the time required for each step in the inventory flow.

TIP #87: Takt time is a tool that can be used to monitor actual customer demand against actual production, so that adjustments can be made to keep inventory supply and demand in balance.

Tip #88: In a job-shop manufacturing environment, the bottleneck operation is not stationary. It is constantly shifting from work center to work center and will create an imbalance of your WIP inventory.

TIP #89: If supply (capacity) and demand (workload) are not in balance, the change in inventory will negatively impact your inventory rightsizing efforts.

TIP #90: Calculate capacity based on your normal work week. If you normally operate five days a week, then calculate your capacity based on five days. If you always operate seven days a week, then you can calculate your capacity based on seven days.

TIP #91: Make sure your shop calendar is adjusted each year to account for nonwork days. Failure to do so will hinder your inventory rightsizing efforts.

TIP #92: Develop a load profile report by work center. Distribute it to all appropriate links in the supply chain so that each upstream and downstream link can use it as a tool to make decisions that impact inventory levels in the entire supply chain.

TIP #93: Producing defective parts will create multiple inventory problems, add to your cost, reduce profitability, and reduce capacity. Design processes to ensure perfect quality.

TIP #94: Balance workflows and production resources as much as possible so that wait time is kept to a minimum.

TIP #95: Any time the product is touched without value being added is adding cost. All non-value-added touches are candidates for elimination.

TIP #96: Inventory not needed to satisfy an immediate customer requirement is considered wasteful and reduced or eliminated when possible.

TIP #97: Company politics is a complete waste of time and energy. Change the company culture and eliminate politics.

TIP #98: To be successful in your inventory rightsizing efforts, information must be accurate and timely.

TIP #99: Working outside your job description is admirable and shows teamwork, but it can be costly and wasteful. Delegate authority, and train employees to do their job.

TIP #100: Complexity may cause problems and hinder your inventory rightsizing efforts rather than help them.

TIP #101: Begin your lean initiative in an area of your supply chain where opportunities for improvement are significant. For most manufacturing companies, this is usually the factory floor.

TIP #102: If you want to achieve success with a lean initiative, you must have a plan in place prior to starting.

TIP #103: When beginning your lean initiative, don't focus on eliminating inventory; focus on eliminating waste. A major benefit of eliminating waste will be the rightsizing of your inventory.

TIP #104: Moving from a push manufacturing philosophy to a pull manufacturing philosophy will greatly benefit your inventory right-sizing efforts.

TIP #105: If multiple locations are pulling products from the same source of production, inventory movement must be coordinated and carefully planned for.

TIP #106: When implementing a pull system, gradually reduce the lot-size quantity until you have achieved the smallest possible lot size. The ideal goal would be to produce a lot size of one.

TIP #107: The storeroom is a good place to start your inventory rightsizing efforts. Inventory accuracy begins with the receipt of inventory into the storeroom.

TIP #108: Establishing an authorized control procedure for goods moving into and out of the storeroom will greatly improve your opportunity to rightsize your inventory.

TIP #109: The more inventory locations you have in your supply chain, the higher the aggregate inventory in your supply chain.

TIP #110: Cycle counting inventory will greatly improve your inventory record (perpetual and physical accuracy) and will have a positive effect on your inventory rightsizing efforts.

TIP #111: Movement of inventory between links in the supply chain must be coordinated on a daily basis. If not, your inventory rightsizing efforts will quickly dissipate into a chaotic situation.

TIP #112: When determining the number of inventory locations (D/Cs) in your supply chain, you must look at the total cost of inventory and the impact on customer service.

TIP #113: Inventory stockouts have a negative impact on your transportation costs. Eliminating/reducing those (stockouts) will reduce transportation and handling costs.

TIP #114: Stockouts result in back-orders or customer order cancellations. Order cancellations can result in lost customers, and back-orders result in higher transportation costs.

TIP #115: JIT delivery is an effective tool to keep inventory levels low, but if your supply partner doesn't deliver quality product on schedule, it can cause a host of irrevocable problems.

TIP #116: If inventory sits in your warehouse unused for a long period of time, get rid of it. It's taking up space that can be used for active inventory or for some other activity.

TIP #117: Rather than looking to automate the movement of inventory, focus your efforts on eliminating inventory so there is no inventory to move.

TIP #118: Do not pick components for final assembly until you are assured that all components are available in inventory.

TIP #119: You cannot sell products without managing inventory to some degree, and you cannot manage inventory effectively without knowing what inventory you have and what inventory you need. Cycle counting addresses the issue of what inventory you have.

TIP #120: High levels of inventory hide many business problems you may not even be aware of. Reduce the level of inventory in your supply chain to expose your business problems.

TIP #121: In order to determine your inventory record accuracy, you must first decide on a meaningful performance metric and communicate it to all links in your supply chain.

TIP #122: Don't be lulled into a false sense of security with inventory accuracy in the mid-90s. The probability of a combination of parts being available when needed is still at risk.

TIP #123: Don't spend a great deal of time analyzing tolerances for each part number. Pick some reasonable percentage and start there. You can make adjustments as necessary.

TIP #124: Consider outsourcing your reverse logistics function if it is not part of your core competency, or you lack the resources to properly dispose of returned goods.

TIP #125: When dealing with multiple inventory systems in your supply chain, you must identify which one is the primary inventory reporting system for the entire supply chain.

TIP #126: The timing of inventory transaction reporting into the system is critical to maintaining accurate inventory records.

TIP #127: Although inventory reporting may be tracked separately for different supply-chain links, it should be aggregated into one system to monitor performance against company strategic and tactical plans.

TIP #128: Inventory must be reported by its current location in your supply chain so that you can effectively rightsize your inventory across supply-chain links.

TIP #129: Information technology is responsible for inventory data integrity once it is reported to the system. However, the actual transactions of inventory movement (physical movement) are the responsibility of the appropriate supply-chain link.

TIP #130: Do not attempt to modify or customize the inventory management applications within your ERP system until you truly identify a real need to change it.

TIP #131: Do not attempt to implement sophisticated technologies to help you rightsize your inventory until you have built a basic foundation of inventory management processes and procedures.

TIP: #132: Buying and selling inventory (products) over the Internet (through a Web site) can speed up the sales cycle, increase sales, and increase inventory turnover, but there are pitfalls to overcome.

TIP #133: Replacing inventory with information will greatly enhance the opportunity to rightsize your inventory.

TIP #134: Application software implementations should be managed by the supply-chain link most impacted by the application.

TIP #135: If you have a field service division, get it involved in your inventory rightsizing efforts; it has a lot to contribute.

TIP #136: Field service can help reduce inventory by assisting product design with the reduction of parts in your product.

TIP #137: Consolidating spare parts inventory into fewer locations can reduce the overall amount of inventory carried, without having a negative impact on customer service.

TIP #138: Field service may share resources with other links in your supply chain. By combining resources you may be able to save money and improve operating efficiency.

TIP #139: Individual performance measures (related to inventory) should be replaced by shared, team-based performance measurements.

TIP #140: Education and training has to be an important part of your inventory rightsizing effort.

TIP #141: Human resources can take a proactive role in your inventory rightsizing effort by raising the visibility of the inventory effort through formal company communication channels.

TIP #142: Get your maintenance team involved in performing proactive maintenance. This will greatly enhance your chances to rightsize your inventory.

TIP #143: Maintenance personnel should be part of a cross-functional team committed to reducing machine setup times.

TIP #144: Reducing machine setup times will increase capacity, reduce lead times, and decrease lot sizes, which could ultimately lead to increased sales and profits for the company.

TIP #145: Get facilities management involved in your "good housekeeping" activities. It can contribute to the improved visibility of inventory, which is an important criterion in your inventory rightsizing efforts.

TIP #146: Don't focus your efforts on finding new space to put inventory. Focus your efforts on better utilization of the space you already have. Better yet, get rid of your inventory so you don't need the space.

TIP #147: Facilities management can help protect inventory from being damaged during storage and internal movement through your supply chain.

TIP #148: Avoid the ten most common mistakes of rightsizing your inventory.

TIP #149: To successfully rightsize inventory the effort must be sustained indefinitely on a continuous basis.

TIP #150: A strong, healthy company culture will be an asset to rightsizing your inventory. A weak, sick company culture will be a liability to rightsizing your inventory.

Index

Y

Z

For Product Safety Concerns and Information please contact our EU
representative GPSR@taylorandfrancis.com
Taylor & Francis Verlag GmbH, Kaufingerstraße 24, 80331 München, Germany

www.ingramcontent.com/pod-product-compliance
Ingram Content Group UK Ltd.
Pitfield, Milton Keynes, MK11 3LW, UK
UKHW021836240425
457818UK00006B/214